THE
HIDDEN PLACES

of

The Heart of England

**Edited by
Mike Weil**

*Front Cover:
Bonsall Village Market, D
by Graham Lewis*

ACKNOWLEDGEMENTS

This book would not have been compiled without the dedicated help of the following:
Elaine, Hong - Administration. Les & Graham - Artists. Ron, Bob, Harvey, Jim -
Research. Chris - DTP.

Map origination by Paul and Simon at Legend DTP, Stockport, 061 419-9748

All have contributed to what we hope is an interesting, useful and enjoyable publication.

OTHER TITLES IN THIS SERIES

THE
HIDDEN PLACES
OF THE

HEART OF ENGLAND

CHAPTER ONE

North Staffordshire

Cheddleton Flint Mill

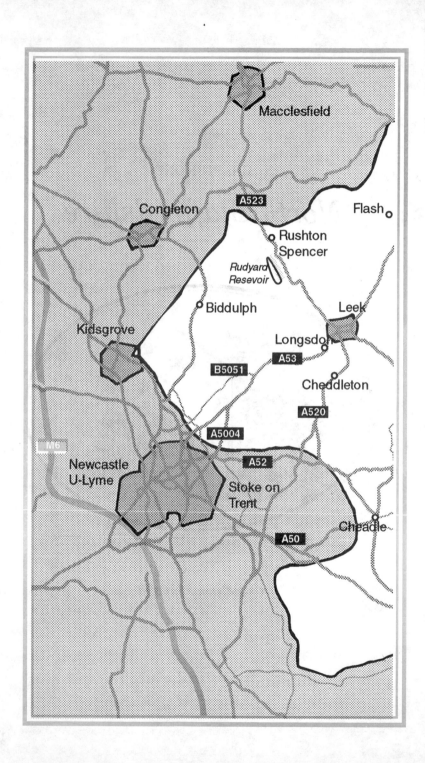

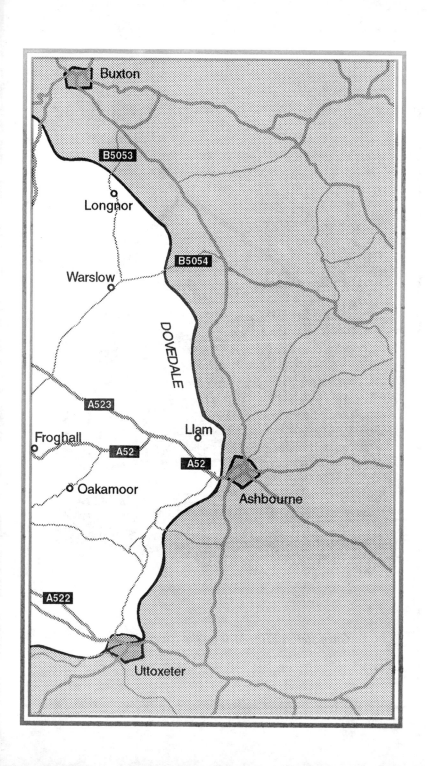

Cheddleton Flint Mill by the River Churnet.

CHAPTER ONE

North Staffordshire.

We hope that our journey through this part of England will help arouse your curiosity and interest in the landscape and architecture of the Staffordshire dales, as attractive in our eyes as many other more renowned beauty spots. **Lichfield**, for instance has a most beautiful cathedral which can hold its head amongst its peers. The villages are many and there are few without interesting tales to tell. We discovered that the county has a wealth of history which is enriched by the many famous people who were born here. Samuel Johnson, Anna Sewell and David Garrick all came from Lichfield and then there were writers such as George Eliot, Izaak Walton and Arnold Bennett whose novels of the 'Five Towns' have their own niche within English literature. As we make our journey there is more which surprises, delights and is of interest in our first area within the Heart of England, North Staffordshire.

Starting our journey in the north east of the county in **Leek,** known as the 'Capital of the Moorlands' a deserving title for this attractive textile centre. French Huguenots settled in Leek after escaping from religious oppression and helped establish the silk industry here. It was the areas abundance of soft water off the millstone grit on the moorland that made it such an ideal place for silk manufacturing. Until the 19th century it was a domestic industry, the workshops being located in the top storey of the houses, of which many examples of these 'top shops' survive today. Leek was the home of James Brindley, the 18th century engineer who built much of the early canal network. A water-powered corn mill built by him in Mill Street has been restored and now houses the **Brindley Water Museum** devoted to his life and work.

Every road coming into Leek seems to converge on the old Market Place with its cobblestones and old, slightly blackened buildings. The road west from the Market Place will take you to the parish church which seems to be largely 17th century although the original church was burnt down in 1297 and rebuilt some twenty years later. The timber roof of the nave is the church's pride and joy. It is boasted that each cross beam was hewn from a separate oak tree. In the west part of the nave, an enormous 18th century gallery rises, tier by tier, giving the impression of standing in the dress circle of a theatre rather than a parish church.

The church is very much the focal point of the town and a one time vicar, the Rev. P.D.S. Blake, wrote a guidebook about the church, in which he managed to express with biblical comparisons the approaches to Leek . '*Coming down over Ladderedge, the sight of Leek on its hill in its valley, reminds one of coming over the Mount of Olives and seeing Jerusalem standing on Mount Zion'.*

There was a lot of alteration in the church in 1865 when G.E. Street rebuilt the chancel, the reredos, sanctuary, pulpit and stalls. There is a profusion of Victorian glass including Morris glass in the Lady Chapel. Much of the embroidery work on the frontals was done by the famous Leek School of Embroidery founded by Lady Wardle in the 1870's. You can see and learn much more about this intricate and wonderful work in Leek Art Gallery.

Leeks central location makes it a good starting point for trips to the many attractions in the surrounding area. Places such as, **Alton Towers** and **Chatsworth** are nearby or you can visit pottery centres to view the wide variety of china. Close by, in the foothills of the Pennines and at the edge of the Peak National Park, lie the **Roaches**, an outcrop of rocks thought to be one of the best examples of masses of millstone in the country.

Close by Leek in **Longsdon**, you'll find comfortable accommodation and a friendly welcome at Mrs. Barbara Whites, **Micklea Farm**. Set within five acres of land, with wonderful views down the valley to Cheddleton, this charming farmhouse was built during the 17th century and still retains much of its original character. There are four lovely guest rooms and Mrs. White goes out of her way to make you feel at home during your stay. Visitors here will find themselves well fed, with a substantial breakfast setting you up for a day's exploring and on your return, by prior arrangement, a wholesome evening meal. As a touring base from which to explore the many local places of interest,

Micklea Farm is ideal. Out of consideration to others, please no smoking.

Micklea Farm, Longsdon. Tel: 0538 385006 Fax: 0538 382882

Out of Leek in a north westerly direction we eventually found ourselves on the **B5053** heading for **Longnor**. The village has some fascinating narrow flagged passages which seem to go nowhere but suddenly you emerge into the most beautiful scenery. The Longnor Market square is one of the oldest in England, dating back to medieval times and it is here in the old Market Hall that you will find the wonderful treasure trove that is **Longnor Craft Centre**. Run by the Fox family since 1991, they specialise in beautiful English hardwood furniture, with various designs of tables, chairs, dressers and other items. You can even have a piece custom made for you. In addition to the large range of quality furniture, there is also a display of locally produced arts and crafts, ranging from beautiful paintings to intricate, handmade jewellery. With a lovely tearoom to relax in after making your purchases, complete with freshly brewed tea and coffee and homemade cakes, Longnor Craft Centre is a real gem.

Longnor Craft Centre, The Market Hall, Longnor.Tel: 0298 83587

Opposite the village square and craft centre in Longnor, stands **The Crewe & Harpur Arms Hotel,** a rather grand looking brick-built establishment which gets its name from the Crewe-Harpur estate to which it once belonged. Pamela and Alan Naden are new proprietors, who came here in May 1993 having owned and run the pub opposite for over eight years. Despite its impressive exterior, when the Nadens moved in, the hotel required a considerable amount of refurbishment and through sheer hard work, Pamela and Alan have created a very special place. Ideally situated as a holiday or touring base, the hotel offers very comfortable accommodation in six well furnished guest rooms, three with en-suite facilities and Pamela's culinary talents make dining a pleasure with a varied menu to suit every taste.

The Crewe & Harpur Arms Hotel, Longnor. Tel: 0298 83205

For the curious the tomb stones in Longnor churchyard give an insight into the lifestyle of villagers in these remote areas in times gone by. One extraordinary epitaph tells of the life of William Billinge, who was born in 1679 and lived until 1791 which, according to our reckoning, made him one hundred and twelve years old! As a soldier he served under Rooke at Gibraltar, Marlborough at Ramilles and after being sent home wounded, he recovered to take part in defending the King in the rebellions of 1715 and 1745.

Only about three miles north of Longnor and through the picturesque hamlet of **Hollingsclough** is **Flash**. At fifteen hundred and eighteen feet above sea level, it is the highest village in England. Curious to know how it got its name, we were told that Flash being close to the borders of Cheshire, Derbyshire and Staffordshire became a haven to thieves and forgers. When pursued by the law they were able to make a dash for the next county thus avoiding arrest - be gone in a Flash!

Back on the **A523 Macclesfield** road lies **Rudyard Lake** from which Kipling got his unusual Christian name. His parents met here in 1863 and after their marriage they went to India where Kipling was born in 1865. Steeply wooded banks shelter this two mile long reservoir, built in 1831 to feed the **Trent and Mersey Canal**. The lake is a leisure centre in an attractive setting where there are facilities for picnicking, lakeside walks, fishing and sailing.

Four miles to the north of Leek on the A53 rise the dark-jagged grit stone outcrops of the **Roaches, Ramshaw Rocks** and **Hen Cloud**. If you like climbing and rambling this is paradise. Roaches is a corruption of the French word 'roches' or rocks, reputedly given by Napoleonic prisoners. 'Cloud' is a local word used for high hills. Just below the Roaches there is another delightful stretch of water, **Tittesworth Reservoir**, which is extremely popular with trout fishermen. It has some super trails, a visitors centre and a pretty picnic place.

About three miles south west of Leek off the A53 is **Deep Hayes Country Park** which lies in a secluded valley by the **Caldon Canal** and **Staffordshire Way**. If you walk up to the ridge here the views are breathtaking but if you do not feel that energetic, there is a very pleasant walk around two pools which has many offshoots into lovely countryside.

Rushton Spencer is a pleasant, small village, nestling under The Cloud. Its church was once known as the **'Chapel in the Wilderness'** but unfortunately we couldn't establish why. It was originally built of wood in the 14th century which has since been replaced with a fine stone building, inside though, you can still see the original timber framing.

Situated in a pretty valley in the Moorlands to the east of Leek is a village called **Onecote**, an ideal place to start exploring **The Manifold Valley**. From **Hulme End** to **Ilam** the River Manifold runs southwards through a deep twisting limestone cleft, between steep, wooded sides. For much of this dramatic course, the river disappears underground in dry weather, through swallow holes. At mid distance its tributary the Hamp joins it, having flowed northwards along a similar course from **Waterhouses**.

You'll also find in the area, **Blackbrook World of Birds** in **Winkhill**, a super wildlife haven owned by the same family that owns Hillside Ornamental Fowl in Mobberley, Cheshire. It can be found by taking the A523 from Leek and turning right after the Little Chef, following the signs for Alton Towers, and Blackbrook is the first entrance on the right. As well as a varied collection of swans, geese and ducks, there are some rare breeds of Cranes and Storks plus their longlegged counterparts, Ibis and Waders. The aviaries house a growing collection of pheasants and in the spring, you can see various chicks and ducklings taking their first wobbly steps in the bird rearing area. With various farm animals and a children's pet area and shop, you are assured of an enjoyable family day out.

Blackbrook World of Birds. Winkhill near Leek. ST13 7QR. Tel:- 0538 308293 / 0565 873282

Four miles from Leek on the A523 Ashbourne road you will find the delightfully named **Bottomhouse** and here on the top of the Staffordshire moorlands stands **The Green Man**, a family business where children as well as mum and dad are always made welcome. Your hosts, Dennis and Elaine have earned a reputation for quality and value for money with traditional ales and a wide choice of food including a big steak menu and wonderful ice creams. With an adjoining C.C. site, five caravans with electric hook ups and twenty tents can be accommodated. The pub is ideally situated for visiting Alton Towers and lies less than half a mile outside the Peak District National Park. If you're in the area pay a visit, you won't be disappointed.

The Green Man, Bottomhouse, Near Leek, Staffs. ST13 7QT 0538 304360.

10

Chinese Garden, Biddulph Grange Gardens.

Between Hulme End and Waterhouses, the **Leek and Manifold Valley Light Railway**, a picturesque narrow gauge line, used to follow the valleys of the Manifold and the Hamps, crisscrossing the latter on little bridges. Sadly trains no longer run, but its track bed has been made into the Hamps-Manifold Track, a marvellous walk which is ideal for small children and people in wheelchairs, since its surface is level and tarred throughout its eight miles. The Track can be reached from car parks at Hulme End, Waterhouses, **Weags Bridge**, near **Grindon** or **Wetton.**

At Hulme End the green railway sheds survive. Just over a mile downstream, the Track, and a public road, pass through a former railway tunnel, at **Swainsley**; look for the circular dovecote near here, now a fishing house. A copper spired folly is a reminder at **Ecton** of what was, during the 18th and 19th centuries, a great copper mine, with one shaft fourteen hundred feet deep and an underground canal network.

Wetton Mill has been sympathetically converted by the National Trust into a cafe, a very welcome sight after our travels. There are toilets here, a car park and picnic tables for those who would rather cater for themselves. Much of the hillside either side of The Track also belongs to the National Trust and is a splendid place for walks.

Nearby in the ominous sounding **Thor's Cave** on **Thor's Crag** which can be reached by a steep path up from the Track or from Wetton village. The cave is a huge aperture, carved out by water long before the valley below was formed. The view from the inside of the cave, framed by the great natural stone arch is magnificent. Listen - for the acoustics, they are very strange. Sound picks up with great clarity and you can easily carry on a conversation with someone far below. At the bottom of the crag are openings known as **Radcliffe Stables** said to have been used by a Jacobite as a hiding place after Prince Charles Edward's retreat from **Derby**.

From **Beeston Tor,** National Trust land above Weags Bridge, there are more magnificent views. Below here there is no right of way along the valley of the Manifold itself, but the Track continues up the Hamps valley to Waterhouses, where it ends at a car park and picnic area. You can also hire cycles from here just across the A523.

Grindon is a unique moorland hill village which stands at over one thousand feet above sea level overlooking the beautiful Manifold Valley. You will find it in the **Domesday Book** where it is recorded as 'an ancient manor in the twentieth year of the reign of William the Conqueror' and it is reputed to have been visited by Bonnie Prince Charlie on his way to Derby.

The splendid isolation in which the villages like Grindon,

Onecote and Butterton have always stood is confirmed when you look around their respective churchyards. The names on the epitaphs and graves reflect the close knit nature of their communities. The Salt family for instance are to be seen everywhere, followed closely by the Stubbs, Cantrells, Hambletons and to a lesser extent, the Mycocks.

It was in Grindon church that we saw a memorial that again made us realise how bleak winter can be in these isolated spots. This particular memorial records the death of six R.A.F. men in 1947 who were killed when their Halifax aircraft crashed in a blizzard on Grindon Moor when trying to parachute food packages down to the villages who were totally cut off.

Fortunately the weather was much kinder during our visit to this beautiful area of Staffordshire. **Ilam,** being a model village of great charm was a place in the area where we were happy to linger. The village was bought by a wealthy manufacturer, Jesse Watts Russell in the early 19th century and he spent much of his wealth refurbishing the houses and building a fine mansion, Ilam Hall for himself. Seemingly very much in love with his wife he had this house built in a romantic Gothic battlemented style. In the centre of the village there is more evidence of his devotion to his wife; he had an 'Eleanor Cross' erected there in her memory. The church has a saddleback tower and is of ancient origins although it was largely rebuilt by Gilbert Scott in 1855. The visitor is not allowed to forget the village's benefactor here. There is an enormous Watts Russell mausoleum which dominates the north side. On the south side there is a little chapel which was rebuilt in 1618 and contains the shrine of that much loved Staffordshire saint, Bertelin. Otherwise it seems that if it is not some member of the Watts Russell family in evidence then it will be of the Meverell family of Throwley. Robert Meverell and his daughter who married the 4th Lord Cromwell are both buried there. Ilam Hall is no longer there but the park and woodland are in the hands of the National Trust and have been since 1934.

The River Dove runs nearby Ilam and on the Staffordshire side stands the Izaak Walton Hotel. Its correct postal address is Dovedale, Nr Ashbourne, Derbyshire DE6 2AY but we speak in truth when we say the hotel is on the Staffordshire side of the river. Before we tell you about the hotel it is probably a good moment to tell you something about this very different Englishman.

Eastgate Street, Stafford, - more of Stafford in the next chapter - is the birthplace of the famous author Izaak Walton, now renowned worldwide for his literary talent in the world of angling because of his book, ' The Compleat Angler ' which is considered to be the ideal handbook. Although little is recorded of his upbringing or education, we know that he was the son of an innkeeper named

Jervis Walton. By the time he was twenty, Izaak had gone to seek fame and fortune in the City of London, serving as an apprentice draper to his kinsman, Thomas Grinsell. It did not take Izaak long to become a well respected member of the community and he was invited to become a freeman of the Ironmakers Company. The year 1637 was to be a memorable year for Izaak when the distinguished regard in which he was held by the City Livery Company caused him to be elected warden of their yeomanry.

Then, as now, membership of a City Livery Company did not necessarily imply that members were actively engaged within that given trade. To become a member was a social distinction rather than having to qualify as an occupational employee of the trade. At this time Izaak was in fact engaged as a Mercer in Fleet Street. He retired from this business in about 1644. The business had now moved to Chancery Lane and he was fortunate enough to retire with a modest fortune.

Being a staunch Royalist, Izaak was later to return to his native home town of Stafford. It was considered to offer greater safety during the upheaval of the Civil War, which was then raging. Izaak was known to have performed a considerable service to the Crown when, in 1651, after the Royalist defeat at the Battle of Worcester, he retrieved one of Prince Charles' Garter Jewels and conveyed it safely to its custodian, a Royalist officer, then imprisoned in The Tower of London.

Later, he was appointed Steward to Doctor George Morley, the Bishop of Winchester, an appointment which recognised his loyalty to the Church and Crown. The Church figured greatly in the lives of the Waltons; his son, Izaac, became a canon of Salisbury Cathedral and his daughter, Anne, the wife of a prebendary of Winchester Cathedral. Izaak remained within the bishop's household until his death at the substantial age of ninety. Izaak's wife, Anne, had died some forty years earlier. He was buried in Winchester Cathedral where there is to be found to this day a superb memorial to this great man.

Although responsible for many biographies, his most famous book of all is considered to be 'The Compleat Angler', renowned as an anthology. The book was intended to serve the purpose of being humorous and digressive, a style well suited to the contemplative man's recreation. Izaak incorporated recipes, legends and poems into his text.

His love of angling often took him to Dovedale, situated between Leek and Ashbourne. It was whilst en route to Ashbourne that we discovered The Izaak Walton Hotel, a magnificent 17th century farmhouse where he regularly stayed, enabling him to indulge his love of fishing in the nearby Dove. It was this area which inspired and encouraged him to collect his material for The Compleat Angler.

Just five miles away from this beauty spot and hardly a ' Hidden Place ' but all the same equally difficult to ignore is **Alton Towers,** the vast leisure park boasting the latest in gravity defying rides and other attractions, including attractive gardens surrounding a 19th century mansion which was partly built by Pugin. Though the nature of Alton is somewhat against the ethos of this book and ' Hidden Places ' should you be in the area and particularly with children it will be hard to avoid a day there. Not wanting to give the impression of being old 'stick in the muds' we have to admit to having paid a visit and quite enjoying it although some of the rides were not quite to our liking - being the type that don't enjoy hearts in mouths whilst upside down. The Rapids and Logs were more to our liking but there are over one hundred and twenty five rides to choose from for those with more daring tastes.

In contrast the village of Alton is one of great beauty. The remains of a castle perch high on sandstone rock above the river. It faces Alton Towers Flag Tower and as a result the place has been given the nickname of Staffordshire's Rhineland. The steep climb up to Toot Hill Rock is rewarded with magnificent views. The castle is now a school but substantial remains of the medieval castle have recently been found. The castle in its present form was mainly built by Pugin. Two miles south of Alton lies **Croxden Abbey**, founded by Cistercians around 1176, the attractive ruins are now overseen by the English Heritage Society

A short drive away situated on the **A522** at **Lower Tean, The Dog & Partridge** is an excellent freehouse pub and restaurant owned by Ron and Iris Chandler. Divided into a series of cosy little 'rooms',

The Dog & Partridge, Uttoxeter Road, Lower Tean, Stoke-on-Trent
ST10 4LN 0538 722468

seating between two and eighteen the main restaurant area has a warm, intimate ambience, while by contrast there is an airy conservatory restaurant, which enjoys lovely views. Here the tasteful decor and luxurious furnishings blend perfectly with the beautiful Masons Regency Staffordshire china upon which your meal is so attractively presented. The menu is both extensive and varied and in addition to a fine complementary wine list, there is a special selection of wines for the discerning palate. This a lovely place for a family meal out, with a play area to the rear for the children, but popularity makes weekend bookings advisable.

In the little market town of **Cheadle** which lies to the west of Alton the Roman Catholic church catches the eye, Pugin was responsible for its tall spire that dominates the town. In the High Street stand some pleasant 18th and 19th century houses and even one old three-gabled timbered Tudor house.

To the north east of Cheadle the **Hawksmoor Nature Reserve** overlooks the Churnet. The **Churnet Valley** has remained unchanged for hundreds of years and escaping development. The river runs freely, and the countryside around is beautiful. Much of the valley is inaccessible by car but **The Caldon Canal** runs through it and narrow boats ply their way on a route that has to be one of England's most scenic waterways. You can just gently follow the woodland trails stopping at the old-fashioned canal pubs and riverside restaurants or simply go picnicking. Not so many years ago this wonderful stretch of water from **Etruria**, near to Josiah Wedgwoods original factory, to **Froghall** was overgrown and unnavigable. Staffordshire County Council with the British Waterways Board have overseen the areas regeneration with great consideration.

From here we visited the pretty village of **Oakamoor** whose industrial links have now almost gone. It was once the home of the factory that produced some twenty thousand miles of copper wire for the first Atlantic Cable but industrial decline has seen the area cleared and transformed into an attractive picnic area astride the river. You get marvellous views of Alton Castle from here.

Awarded a Two Crowns Highly Commended grading by the English Tourist Board and 5Q Premier Select grading by the AA, **Bank House** is the charming home of Muriel and John Egerton Orme. A 'hidden' gem, it can be found tucked down Farley Lane in the village of Oakamoor about two and a half miles from Alton. Elegantly furnished throughout, this delightful house provides superior accommodation in three fully equipped en-suite guest rooms each with the added touch of a welcome tray for your arrival. The aroma of freshly baked bread entices you down to breakfast and you can enjoy the 'house party' atmosphere of an optional four course dinner each evening. The residential licence means you can complement Muriel's fine home cooking with a choice bottle of wine. There is ample private parking and the beautifully laid out garden provides the perfect setting for a pre-dinner drink on a balmy summer's evening.

Bank House, Farley Lane, Oakamoor, Staffs. ST10 3BD 0538 702810

At the **Star Crossroads** on the Oakamoor to **Cotton** road you will find a delightful pub, **Ye Olde Star Inn.** There has been an inn on this site for over 400 years and the present building, believed to be the oldest licensed house in Staffordshire, was at one time a courtroom and gaol. The attractive stone exterior with white shutters at the windows is matched by the beautiful interior where oak furniture is complemented with rich red carpeting, brass ornaments and stucco walls. Here in a warm, friendly atmosphere you can enjoy a delicious menu of bar food and a selection of fine ale, which on fine summer days can be taken into the lovely beer garden.

Ye Olde Star Inn, Star Bank, Cotton, Near Oakamoor, Staffs. ST10 3DW 0538 702489

Cheddleton seems to perch dangerously on the side of a hill which is why it has such spectacular views. You can look down on the Caldon Canal and the river in all its beauty. The church stands in open country and has some wonderful Morris windows and a lot of interesting Victorian decoration as the result of the restoration by George Gilbert Scott junior in the 1860's. The restored **Cheddleton Flint Mill**, houses a small Museum whose collection includes a rare 18th century 'haystack' boiler and a Robey steam engine. You can visit here at any time of the year. The water powered mill drove machinery which crushed flint. The material was brought in and taken away by narrow boat on the Caldon Canal to be used in hardening pottery at Stoke. You can also take trips along the canal on narrow boats.

The station is home to the **North Staffordshire Steam Railway Centre and Museum** which will give great delight to railway enthusiasts. There is a small collection of beautifully preserved locomotives and other railway mobilia bringing back many memories. It is open to the public at weekends in the summer with trains in steam summer Sundays and Bank Holidays.

We nearly missed **Consall Forge** which is a beautiful spot hidden in the deep valley downstream from Cheddleton. The little cottages keep in close company with the little bridges over the river and the canal. There is a boatman's pub, **The Black Lion** which is only accessible via **Consall** village or down the Devil's Staircase in Consall Nature Park.

Froghall is on the floor of the valley and here after passing through a short tunnel, the Caldon Canal ends its journey at Froghall Wharf. The old buildings and a fine battery of lime kilns around the wharf have been restored and an excellent picnic site has been created. You can walk if you wish some way along the remains of the gravity-operated incline, down which loaded tramway wagons brought the limestone from Caldon quarries, three miles away.

Situated on the **B5053** just outside the village of Froghall, you will find a lovely holiday base at **The Hermitage**, home of Wilma and Frank Barlow. Set in 73 acres of rolling farmland, this charming late 16th century farmhouse enjoys a lovely setting high above the Churnet Valley and is an ideal base for touring the many attractions in the area, such as Alton Towers, The Potteries and Dovedale. The farmhouse is beautifully furnished throughout and the splendid oak panelling, exposed beams and lovely spiral staircase all enhance its character and charm. The cosy bedrooms are all tastefully decorated and provide very comfortable accommodation, whilst outside, excellent self-catering accommodation is provided in The Hermitage Lodge which sleeps up to seven and has facilities for the disabled.

The Hermitage, Froghall, Staffs. ST10 2HR Tel: 0538 266515

At **Endon** we wandered slightly to the west and found that we had taken the **B5051** and turned left into **Hough Hill** heading north to **Lask Edge**. With such an intriguing name we felt we had to visit **Mow Cop** whilst in the area. As you drive you'll notice the land rising to Biddulph Moor from which the little village can be seen perched on the escarpment. The castle at the top of the hill, Mow Cop Castle, is in fact a folly. In 1807, the place gave birth to Primitive Methodism when Hugh Bourne, a Stoke-on-Trent man and William Clowes, a champion dancer from Burslem, called a meeting at the prehistoric camp which lasted almost fourteen hours. When Mow Cop Castle was given to the National Trust in 1937, ten thousand Methodists marked the occasion with a meeting on the hill. A small museum of Primitive Methodism can be viewed on Sunday only, from April to September in the afternoon between 2pm-4pm, in the school room of Englesea Brook Chapel just north of Balterley. The Chapel is one of the oldest Primitive Methodist Chapels to survive.

John Wesley was a frequent visitor to **Biddulph** which has a history that goes way back before it found itself becoming enveloped in the upsurge of Methodism. After the Norman Conquest the manor was granted by William to Robert the Forester, an overlord of what was then the extensively forested area of Lyme. Biddulph Grange belonged to the Cistercian monks of the Abbey Hulton until the dissolution. The Biddulphs, a staunchly Catholic family took control of the area. John Biddulph fought under the royal flag and was killed at the Battle of Hopton Heath. His son entrusted the defence of Biddulph Hall to Lord Brereton, who withstood a determined siege until 1644 when he was finally subjected to heavy artillery. The hall was then demolished to prevent its re-garrisoning.

You don't have to be a horticultural enthusiast to appreciate the sheer natural beauty of **Biddulph Grange Garden,** a superb example of traditional Victorian gardening. Situated on Grange Road in Biddulph, this is a National Trust owned property which has preserved all the gardening traditions of the Victorian era with plants brought from all over the world. Ranging from the exotic influence of a Chinese 'willow-pattern' to a damp Scottish glen. With such diversity of landscape there is something to inspire and appeal to everyone, from the weekend amateur to the professional gardener. Originally the creation of three people, James and Maria Bateman who owned Biddulph Grange, and their friend marine painter, Edward Cooke the garden was acquired by the National Trust in 1988 and has been carefully tended and preserved ever since as a natural monument for all to enjoy.

Biddulph Grange Garden, Grange Road, Biddulph, Staffordshire
ST8 7SD 0782 517999

It felt like a fitting visit to end our journey in this part of Staffordshire that had thus far given us many pleasant moments. It was only a matter of miles further along the road to our next area and its ' Hidden Places. ' The next chapter shall uncover our discoveries which we hope you'll share with us as we journey around the ' Potteries ' in this journey through the ' Heart of England'.

20

CHAPTER TWO

The Potteries

Izaak Walton's Cottage, Stafford

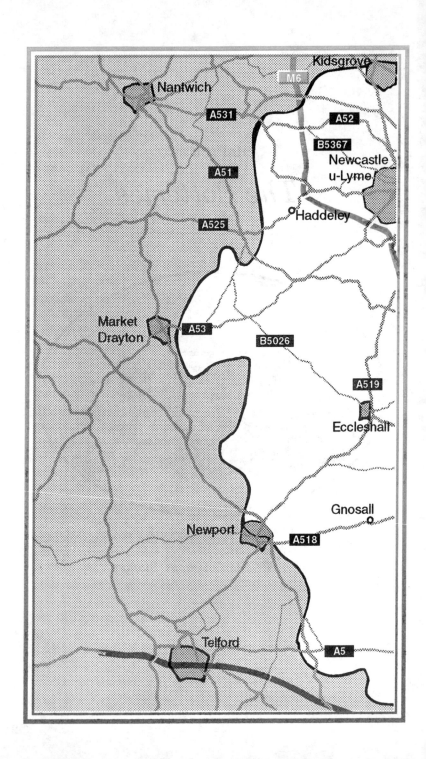

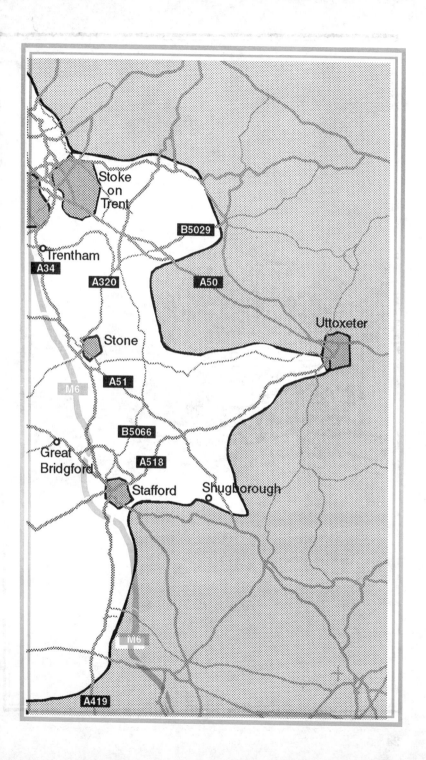

Harecastle Tunnel.

CHAPTER TWO

The Potteries

One of the main reasons to visit **Kidsgrove** is its connection with canals. The two **Harecastle Tunnels**, major engineering feats, carry the Trent and Mersey Canal from Cheshire into the Potteries. It might not be unfair to say that the canal created the town as Josiah Wedgwood dreamt of building a canal and became one of the pioneers of canal construction. He fought hard and long to get a Bill through Parliament for a canal linking the Potteries with the Trent and Mersey, undaunted by the fact that a tunnel nearly three thousand yards long would be needed to go through Harecastle Hill.

The Bill having been passed, many still scoffed at Wedgwoods conviction, but despite all, construction began and took eleven years to complete. Certainly some years later there was almost catastrophe when the hill started subsiding but fortunately Thomas Telford was on hand to design and build another alongside the first, thus averting disaster. The two tunnels which are still there today are an impressive sight and although Josiah's original tunnel is not in use, the Telford tunnel has been restored.

We then moved on towards the ' Five Towns' of Arnold Bennett which, before they amalgamated to form **Stoke-on-Trent**, became six with the addition of Fenton. The Cities crest, of an ancient Egyptian potter at his wheel, in one quarter, sums up the fortune which has come to this area as **'The Potteries'**. The joint motto translated means 'Strength is stronger for unity ' and that has to be true when you consider all the marvellous things that have been created from the wealth of talent amassed here. Each one of the old towns is represented in the crest.

Basford, which has become part of Stoke-on-Trent was a rural location in the mid-nineteenth century between **Newcastle-under-Lyme** and **Etruria**. It consisted of Basford Hall and estate,the Queen's Inn and a farm with outlying cottages. It was during the years following 1861 that the Burslem and Tunstall Freehold Land

Society offered for sale plots of land, totalling nine acres, which subsequently were built upon to create the most northerly part of Basford as it is today. Basford immediately became a very desirable place of residence for the affluent pottery owners and the properties reflected this wealth.

The five pottery towns immortalised by Arnold Bennett are well known to be **Burslem, Hanley, Longton, Stoke** and **Tunstall. Fenton** should have been included but it was forgotten then and many believe it still is but we found much of the area to be very much alive. **The Potteries** is a Shopping Centre situated in the heart of Hanley and is every shopper's dream with a fantastic range of famous shops all brought together in a beautiful environment. Natural daylight cascades through the Centre's many glazed roofs and plants, trees and water features, create an outdoor feel.

There are sixty five shops spread over three spacious malls and linked by glass lifts, escalators and feature stairways. The Centre forms one side of the pedestrianised Market Square in the heart of the prime shopping area. Lewis's and Littlewoods department stores are fully integrated in the same way as one hundred and twenty market stalls, so it is full of life. Street theatre adds more colour to this busy area and should you need sustenance after you have looked round you'll find a five hundred seat food court with an amazing variety of foods and refreshments. From the rather elegant conservatory area to ten different food kiosks all providing a wide choice of meals and snacks to suit every taste. Car parking for twelve hundred cars is linked to the Centre by an enclosed walkway and there are bus stops just outside, as well as a special coach park for long distance visitors. The Centre provides a professionally staffed play-centre from 9.30am - 4pm for children from 2 - 5 years.

Our next stop was **Trentham Gardens,** just two minutes from junction 15 off the **M6.** The earliest reference to Trentham relates to a nunnery which was established by St Werburgh, daughter of the Anglo-Saxon king of Mercia in 680 AD, later by the daughter of Alfred the Great around 907. Ownership passed via Edward the Confessor and William the Conqueror to William Rufus. As a result of the Dissolution of the Monasteries by Henry VIII, the estate was bought by James Leveson, a wealthy wool merchant who founded the dynasty of the Dukes of Sutherland, owners of the estate for over three hundred years.

The gardens were landscaped by Capability Brown and given a more formal style by Sir Charles Barry, whose work can be observed in the lovely Italian gardens. Although the hall was sadly demolished in 1911, this style can still be recognised in such buildings as the orangery and sculpture gallery which remain today, to form a framework for the outstanding conference, exhibition and banqueting centre that is Trentham.

You can enjoy Trentham to the full in many ways. There is normally unrestricted access to eight hundred acres of woodland, lake and gardens, with opportunities for woodland walks, boating and jet skiing. There are first class facilities for trout and coarse fishing and clay pigeon shooting. Tuition in fishing and shooting is available for the individual or for parties.

The main complex houses a superb restaurant and bars, a ballroom, conference and exhibition centre and is the frequent venue for fairs, banquets and special events that take place throughout the year. The vast grounds and lake create a huge natural amphitheatre in which many sporting and other outdoor events take place in idyllic setting under a backdrop which is breathtakingly beautiful in all seasons.

We'd recommend anyone coming to Stoke-on-Trent visiting The Wedgwood Museum and Visitor Centre at **Barlaston.**(Tel :- 0782 204141/204218) It is like an Aladdin's Cave with all manner of wonderful exhibits of the products of Josiah Wedgwood, the pottery manufacturers, from 1750 to the present day. You might remember our earlier references to the Caldon Canal and mention of Etruria where Josiah had his first factory. Here at Barlaston Wedgwood have re-created those 18th century workshops, complete with a reconstructed bottle kiln and an original engine turning lathe, which is still in use today.

The display vividly brings to mind the working conditions of those days and we were able to look at more than two centuries of the company's history. In rooms designed to recapture the style of specific periods there are hundreds of Wedgwood pieces from those eras. George Stubbs and Joshua Reynolds both painted portraits of the Wedgwood family and they are hanging in the art gallery. In the craft centre we were able to watch potters and decorators at work using traditional skills to create today's Wedgwood products. There is a cinema at the centre and a comfortable refreshment lounge. Never far away on these occasions is the souvenir shop where the temptation to spend money on acquiring some of the beautiful pieces is strong.

As one would expect there are a vast number of extremely good museums and galleries in Stoke-on-Trent. One of the finest and largest collection of pottery and ceramics in the world is to be found at **The Stoke-on-Trent City Museum and Art Gallery** (Tel :- 0782 202173). Apart from the sheer joy of seeing so much that is beautiful and priceless, the museum also tells the story of pots and potters in chronological sequence, showing the importance and expansion of the city.

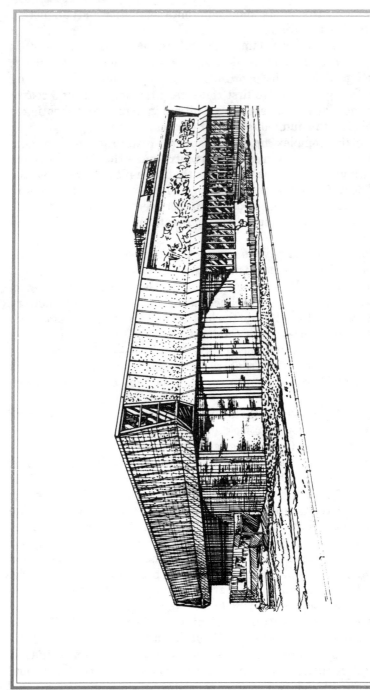

City Museum & Art Gallery. Stoke on Trent.

Housed in three separate galleries are constantly changing exhibitions. Two of them have been designed to be totally flexible and you would be amazed at the variations of art forms that you can see. Anything from the traditional to the avant-garde can greet you. The third gallery surprised us too, for here is an unusual indoor Sculpture Court visible from all levels in the museum.

There is a Decorative Arts Gallery, a Natural History Gallery, a Social History Gallery and last, but by no means least, a fascinating Archaeology Gallery, in which there are displays of Staffordshire sites of all periods from the mesolithic to the 18th century and range from a cave shelter to a Cistercian abbey. The bias is towards the understanding of the origins and growth of the local ceramics industry but that is a blessing and makes it simpler to get the best out of the many museums in Stoke devoted to that craft.

We hope that we will not offend if we do not go into greater detail about these well known places but we feel that Stoke not only has a wealth of the finest ceramics in the world but also has one or two different kinds of talents. One such place that demonstrated this was The Lowen Gallery, which displays a select range of crafts by leading national and local craftsmen and women, including innovative and exciting work by talented newcomers. The **Gladstone Pottery Museum** (Tel :- 0782 319232) in Uttoxeter Road, **Longton** also appealed to us. It is a working museum of British pottery. Housed in a Victorian pot bank, it tells the story of ceramics with a variety of pottery wares and demonstrations.

Our last visit was to **Chatterley Whitfield Mining Museum** in **Tunstall**. (Tel :- 0782 813337) We were taken to an underground gallery where we could see local mining techniques old and new and all explained to us by knowledgeable former miners. This was not all, because on display are steam winding engines, locomotives and the delightful, courageous pit ponies.

From the Potteries we went west along the **A525** until we came to **Madeley**. Sited on a packhorse route from Newcastle-under-Lyme, the name comes from the Anglo-Saxon 'maden lieg', which means 'clearing in the woods'. The centre of this enchanting place has been designated as a conservation area, the focal point of which is The Pool, which was formed by damming the river Lea to provide water power for the corn mill built at its northern end. Madeley's grandest building is **The Old Hall** an excellent example of a 15th century squire's timber framed residence. This beautifully preserved building, with its magnificent brick chimney, is now a two star listed building, standing in the centre of the village close to the pool.

Although it still possesses many of the original motifs, its most striking feature must be the inscription carved into the main beam on the west front facing the road; "*Walke knave what lookest at 47 I.S.B.*" The statement is thought to have been directed at local Roundheads so they would not suspect the owners of being sympathetic to the Royalist cause.

Newcastle-under-Lyme itself, received its first Charter from Henry 11 in 1173 and for several centuries it was the largest town in north Staffordshire. The town gave us several hours of enjoyment as we wandered round the centre stopping to look at the many listed buildings. The town centre is designated a conservation area and many of the buildings carry an identification plaque.

The Borough Council have established two town trails which take in these buildings. Both of these walks begin in Nelson Place. The first follows Queen Street, visiting St George's church which was built in the early 19th century and Mayer House which was the former home of a famous veterinary family. There are two museums for you to see and in King Street, we fell in love with the fine Georgian houses. In Marsh Parade is a vast, imposing 19th century building which once housed the town's first silk mill. Holy Trinity Church for Roman Catholics was built of local stone in 1834 and finally on this walk is an old barracks which is now a centre for craft industries.

Borough Museum & Art Gallery, Brampton Park. 0782-619705

The second walk takes in the eye catching, Merrial Street from which there are marvellous views and then moves on to St Giles's church where the base of the tower dates from the 13th century. The medieval church was replaced by a brick church in 1720 but the prodigious talent of George Gilbert Scott shows in the second rebuilding in the 1870's. He managed to recapture all the beauty of the medieval times. High Street which has some fascinating buildings like the Pork Shop which was once the Golden Bell Inn, a timbered framed building of about 1600. This wide street and market area emphasise its medieval origins being surrounded by entrancing narrow lanes and alleys.

On this route you will see The Guildhall which was built in 1713 to replace an earlier timber building and beside it is the base of a medieval cross. From there to Cheapside which is very narrow and was the Ironmarket, so called because of the flourishing local iron trade. Finally back to the starting point, Nelson Place, which was reclaimed from marshland in 1782 and laid out as a central open space with several short streets radiating from it.

The village of **Betley**, north west of Newcastle under Lyme receives mention in the Domesday Book and, as you might expect with such an ancient village, the influence of the centuries is etched in the variety of architecture. One particularly interesting building is **Betley Court** where the facade and elaborate wrought iron gateway carry the arms of John Craddock, an attorney at law, who built it in 1716. Originally a simple rectangular building, later additions have created a property of character with red and blue chequered brickwork and a slate hipped roof. The well laid out garden was designed by William Eames, an associate of Capability Brown and to the rear of the house there is a very attractive later 17th century dovecote.

Inside there is an ornately carved 18th century staircase and a drawing room which was remodelled by the celebrated John Nash in 1809. Adjacent to the house is the Gallery where you can see the '"Madeley Head", the oldest stone in the building. There is also an exact copy of the famous Betley Window (now in the Victoria and Albert Museum). There is much of interest here and history and art lovers will find a visit most rewarding.

Betley Court. Main Road, Betley, Newcastle -u- Lyme, Staffs. Tel : 0270 820652

Situated in North-West Staffordshire, close to the border with Cheshire and Shropshire, **Madeley Village,** originally a small agricultural community, has been extended to form a substantial residential area. The centre of the village merits a visit, with its village street bordering the mill pool, and narrow lanes around the church retain much of the village's original character and charm. Madeley Pool is the essential feature which distinguishes Madeley from other villages , and is bordered by former turnpike properties.

At one end of the pool is the former mill,while at the other, you can glimpse All Saints Parish Church through the trees. The Church standing in a raised churchyard with yew trees, is cruciform in plan, extensively enlarged during the 15th Century and the Chapel was rebuilt in 1872. A handsome building, it has interesting window glass and a pulpit with ornamented panels, but more notable are the early 16th Century alabaster tombs of Ralph Egerton and his wife, and the Egerton family memorial brasses. Madeley village has many buildings of historical interest that make it well worth a visit.

Madeley Village & Church.   Nr. Newcastle -u- Lyme, Staffs.

For anyone visiting the area there is an interesting day out to be had just over the border in Cheshire, in **Nantwich** at **Stapeley Water Gardens**, the complete gardening experience that's a must. The world's largest water garden centre,Stapeley really is a whole day out for all.Set in 65 acres of green belt,with ample parking and easy access for the disabled to the whole site,there is a truly surprising variety of things to see and do.

For the gardener the main centre offers over two acres undercover where, in addition to a wide selection of shrubs,roses,trees,heather and border plants, every conceivable sundry item can be found, including gifts,furniture,houseplants and outdoor clothing. Stapeley are, naturally also well known for their extensive range of water gardening supplies and aquatic plants.

The Gardens also boast the most complete angling shop in the area as well as a large range of tropical,cold water and marine fish and equipment,and an extensive pet section ranging from birds and hamsters to chinchillas.

Stapeley also have a most reassuring policy on environmental issues. Glass, paper, metal and garden waste generated on site are recycled. Only captive bred pets are sold. Environmental education packs are available to school parties. And Stapeley sponsors conservation days,with the likes of wildlife painter David Shepherd,alongside its craft fairs,antique shows and falconry displays.

The Palms Tropical Oasis is a vast one and a third acre glass pavilion open all year round, housing exotic plants ranging from 30ft palm trees to giant Amazonian water lilies, displays from the National Rex Begonia Collection and National Water Lily Collection. Here you can see rare and protected species of birds and animals breeding,stingray lagoon,even piranhas,or have a try at the nature quiz, available to children during most school holidays.

Afterwards visitors can relax in the licensed Terrace Restaurant,with piano accompaniment at weekends or the Italian Garden Restaurant, both set amongst exotic flowering plants and pools, or alternatively rest in Palm court next to the Koi pool, with its avenue of palms and a beautiful sequencing display fountain at its head.

And that isn't all; the Yesteryear Museum is a fascinating display and includes a Churchill tank,toys, agricultural antiques and fashions. Inspired by over an acre of display gardens and water gardens? Why not buy a copy of the Stapeley Book of Water Gardens, from the garden centre and learn how to have a go yourself?

Stapeley Water Gardens. London Road. Stapeley. Nantwich.
0270 628628. The Palms 0270-623868

Keele, which is just two miles west of Newcastle is famous as the first of the post-war universities. It is now one of the largest and one of the most attractive of Britain's campuses. Some eighty five percent

Keele Hall

of students and staff actually live in residence which is extremely unusual but has made it so successful. The small village only has one shop, a post office, a parish church, village hall and a pub, The Sneyd Arms.

The A53 from Newcastle will lead you all the way to **Market Drayton** and on the way there is some beautiful countryside and pleasant villages. **Whitmore** is the first and it lies protected from the sight and sound of Newcastle and the Potteries by the plantations of **Old Swynnerton Park.** It is a neat place with a fine medieval church with timbered bell turret and west gable.

Situated in a pleasant rural setting only four miles from Newcastle -under- Lyme, **Whitmore Hall** is a splendid country mansion built in rich red brickwork with stone dressings and a stone balustrade at the top. It is not immediately obvious, but the Hall is actually of four stories, constructed around an older timber-framed house. Whitmore has been the home of the Mainwaring family since Norman times. As you stroll through the vast and ornately furnished rooms, you can trace the family history from paintings. Close by, to the west, there is a sandstone stable block, dating from the late 16th Century.

The Hall is set in an elegantly landscaped park, and the original drive forms an avenue taking you to the nearby medieval Church of St.Mary and All Saints. This Church, largely 12th Century, was extensively restored in the 1880's. It is worth a visit just to see its timber-framed clock tower which is the only example in North Staffordshire of this form of construction. The Hall is open Tuesdays and Wednesdays from 2.00pm - 5.30pm from May to August.

Whitmore Hall & Church. Whitmore. Necastle -u- Lyme. Staffs.
Tel: 0782 680235

The first turning on the right after you leave Whitmore will take you to **Willoughbridge,** a remote sort of place that laid claim to fame when Lady Gerard, of Gerard's Bromley, discovered warm springs here, and built a bath house. It almost became as fashionable as Tunbridge Wells but settled back into the quiet spot it is today.

The Borough of Newcastle -under- Lyme has many places of interest to discover, and one such place is the **Dorothy Clive Garden.** This beautiful garden extends over eight acres and was created by Colonel Harry Clive for his wife Dorothy. Today it is open to the public and you don't have to be a keen gardener to appreciate its sheer natural beauty. There are various walks through the garden and at every corner you are rewarded with a myriad of brightly coloured flowers, herbaceous borders and beautiful trees - some of the species being quite rare.

On the hillside, not far from the car park, is a lovely wisteria covered gazebo; whilst on the loose-gravelled scree, alpine plants and dwarf shrubs cling perilously, adding their own particular charm. The azaleas provide a lovely burst of colour and the pool with its water-based plants has a different appeal, and is home to a variety of insects. With eight acres to wander round, you will be amazed at how quickly time seems to pass, and you can easily spend a few hours at this beautiful oasis tucked away in the rolling countryside of North Staffordshire.

The Dorothy Clive Garden. Willoughbridge,nr. Market Drayton.
Tel: 0630 647237.

Almost into Market Drayton and still on the A53 there is one thing we are certain and that is the delightful surprise we experienced in **Ashley**, a stones throw from Loggerheads. Here the church from the outside looks very ordinary and typical of the latter part of the 19th century but inside it is a feast for the eye. There is a very short nave with only two bays, a fairly long chancel protected by a beautiful rood screen, which allows you to catch a glimpse of the glory to come - the brilliant, lavish, gilded reredos screen. There are marble floors, a marvellous organ gallery and some excellent furnishings. The church must also be blessed by an excellent and devoted team of cleaners whose labour of love includes cleaning the brass candelabra which are everywhere.

Meandering via **Loggerheads** we then took the **5026** and wandered in and out of the turnings to the many small villages, eventually arriving at Eccleshall. The very best way to see and enjoy **Eccleshall** is to take a guided tour with one of the professionally trained Village Guides. You meet your guide outside the Kings Arms Hotel and you will be taken all round this charming small town with its distinctive High Street and much that will remind you of its earlier days when it was on the busy coaching route between London and Chester and many of the buildings date from that period. The Parish church is impressive and stands at the end of the High Street beckoning you on towards the beauty of the miles of wooded countryside around, which we had already experienced as we drove along the road to this appealing town.

Just by the crossroads in the centre of Eccleshall stands **The Old Smithy** pub which houses a superb restaurant called **Fletchers Forge**. This is one of those rare 'hidden' gems which offers the connoisseur the finest cuisine imaginatively prepared and beautifully presented. Everything on the extensive and mouthwatering menu is homemade, from the bread to the delicious chocolates and petit fours which complete your meal. Granité is served between courses to refresh the palate and each main course comes with a choice of six different vegetables and two types of potato dishes. The small garden to the rear, complete with patio provides the perfect setting for an intimate dinner on those warm summer evenings and Julian Ankers is a welcoming host who goes out of his way to give his many customers complete satisfaction.

Fletchers Forge at The Old Smithy, 8-12 Castle Street, Eccleshall
ST21 6DF 0785 851220

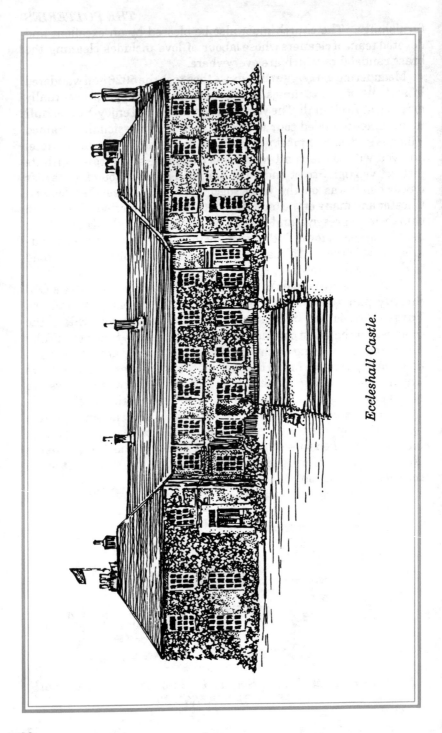

Eccleshall Castle.

For over a thousand years **Eccleshall Castle** was the palace of the Bishops of Lichfield but at the beginning of this century it became a family home when the Carter family moved from Yorkshire. The present simple sandstone house is typical of the best architecture of the William and Mary period, and incorporates part of the earlier 14th century castle. The interior of the house has been augmented by successive members of the family, one of whom added a magnificent Victorian staircase and dome.

Perhaps to remind them of the county from which they came, the Carters have collected a very interesting number of 19th century paintings by Yorkshire artists which gave us great pleasure. The Library is full of superb books, amongst them many first additions, including a complete set of the works of Charles Dickens. All over this very nice house you can find delightful pieces of porcelain, on display from all over the world, especially good are the Oriental displays and some fine 18th century European pieces.

There are fine examples of craftsmanship with furniture ranging from the 17th century to Victorian times. Charles 1 visited Eccleshall in 1640 and you can almost imagine him sitting in one of the splendid chairs. Sir Walter Scott was another visitor here and would probably have found much to inspire him.

The gardens have been created around the ruins of the old Castle and have a great deal of romanticism. The old walls give wonderful support to the espaliered pear trees and all the busy climbing plants and shrubs. The rose garden stands serenely sheltered by the walls too. We had a thoroughly pleasant time wandering along the moat which was drained in 1820 and looking at the magnificent trees. Because the grounds are so sheltered unusual birds are frequently to be seen and apparently kestrels nest every year in the old Castle tower. Eccleshall Castle is a place to be savoured and this you can do from Easter Sunday until the second Sunday in October. The open days are Mondays, Tuesdays and Sundays from 2pm -5.30pm.

Situated five miles south of Newcastle-under-Lyme and junction 15 of the M6 or three miles north of Eccleshall, **Mill Meece Pumping Station** provides a fascinating day out for the whole family. This is the home of the Gentle Giants, vast working steam engines which were once used to pump drinking water to Stoke-on-Trent. Today you can view the coal fired boilers which used to keep going all day, producing the steam necessary to power the steam pumping engines. There are various water processing displays and a selection of short videos, whilst outside children will particularly enjoy the hands-on exhibits and landscaped area for them to 'let off steam'. During the summer, additional events include steam weekends, Morris Dancing and craft fairs.

Mill Meece Pumping Station, Near Eccleshall Tel: 0785 813087

From Eccleshall we decided to move again along the A5026 but now in an eastwards direction towards **Stone,** where once thirty eight coaches a day pulled up at the bow-windowed Crown Hotel, the best building in the High Street. Today it is an attractive shopping and residential town. In the early days when Henry 11 granted the monks a market in 1251 it was a mecca for all the little hamlets around. The Augustinians founded a priory here in the 12th century but only one arch and some cloisters remain today.   The present parish church dates from 1750 and contains several   interesting monuments, including a bust of Admiral Earl St Vincent, the hero of the great naval victory off Cape St Vincent in   1797.It also contains the magnificent stained glass windows depicting the martyrs Wulfid and Rufin.

The Trent and Mersey Canal played a large part in the town's early economic development and even today it still brings work to Stone through the building of holiday canal cruisers and a growing tourist trade. Situated on the High Street in Stone, you will find **Country Lady,** a superb boutique which specialises in elegant wedding outfits and accessories for mother of the bride and guests. This high class boutique was established over fourteen years ago by the friendly and very professional proprietor Elizabeth Ball and the first Saturday of every month holds an in-store fashion show. Following major expansion just over two years ago, it now houses Stages Coffee Shop and Bistro. As with the boutique, everything within this delightful licensed bistro is of the highest quality, all the food freshly prepared and offering much more than standard café fare. With a choice of teas, coffees, homemade cakes and light lunches available, it is the perfect place to relax and consider your fashion purchases.

40

Country Lady / Stages Bistro. Stone, Staffs Tel: 0785 813214

Along the **B5027** from Stone is **Uttoxeter**, a town perhaps best known for racing. In the market place there is a little memorial to Dr. Samuel Johnson who when he was quite an old man, stood, bare-headed, on a pouring wet day, as a penance for having, in his youth, refused to help his father with his bookstall in the market. Wednesday is the busy day here when the traditional livestock and street market is held. There are several nice timbered buildings here but disastrous fires in 1596 and 1672 destroyed the majority of the town's architectural heritage.

From Uttoxeter along the **A518** and passing by **Amerton Working Farm**, visitors to the County Town of **Stafford**. A place well worth visiting during your stay in Stafford is The **Ancient High House,** a

The Ancient High House. Stafford Borough Council,
Riverside, Stafford. Tel: 0785 223181

beautiful Elizabethan house built in 1595 that is in fact the largest timber framed town house in England. Through painstaking efforts

41

Colleigate Church of St. Mary. Stafford.

over several years, Stafford Borough Council have restored this amazing piece of architecture to its former glory and today the building houses the Museum of the Staffordshire Yeomanry and the Tourist Information Centre. You can follow The Ancient High House's varied history through the permanent displays in period room settings taking you through the 17th, 18th and 19th centuries and telling the life stories of people who came to know this house so intimately. Not surprisingly, the house has Royal connections, with both King Charles 1 and Prince Rupert having stayed here in 1642. The house also has a small heritage shop selling a variety of interesting and locally crafted gifts for those seeking a memento of their visit.

Close to the High House is the Collegiate Church of St. Mary. This is an unusual building which dates in part from the late lath century, but has received additions in the early English, Gothic and Victorian styles. The huge tower arches in the nave seem to divide the building into two, which is in fact exactly what they were intended to do, as St. Mary's is two churches under one roof. The nave was the parish church of Stafford with its own altar, whilst the chancel beyond was used by the Deans of the College of St. Mary, whose duty it was to pray for deceased members of the royal family. Although the 'college' was abolished in 1548, the screens which divided the church remained until 1841 and the church today is still referred to as the 'Collegiate'. It is easily spotted in the the town by its unusual octagonal tower dating from the Perpendicular period (14th - 15th century). Also worth noting is the splendid north transept and its beautiful doorway with carved leaf capitals, flowers and fleurons in the arch. St. Mary's looks across from its memorial gardens to the picturesque Church Lane, with its black and white cottages and 16th century coffee house.

Stafford Castle, Stafford Borough Council, Council Offices, Riverside, Stafford. Tel: 0785 223181.

Situated high up above the town, one Stafford landmark that is

Church Lane. Stafford.

viewed by countless travellers along the M6 are the impressive earthworks of the **Norman Castle** which can be reached via the **A518** Newport Road, about a mile and a half from the town centre. Set within 20 acres, the remains of this splendid fortress are open to the public and visitors can follow an illustrated trail which leads from the outer bailey, and onto the site of a borough settlement. There is also a modern Visitor Centre where a video and detailed model reconstructions bring the past vividly to life. The Castle grounds are often used for historical re-enactments by such groups as the Napoleonic Society and are often the site for Sealed Knot battles as well as other outdoor entertainment which provide an added attraction if you happen to visit at the right time. A call to the local Tourist Information Centre should provide you with details of such events.

Shugborough Hall, Shugborough. Tel: 0889 881 388

South east from Stafford and probably one of the most impressive attractions within Staffordshire is **Shugborough,** the 17th century country seat of the Earls of Lichfield. This magnificent 900 acre estate includes Shugborough Park Farm, a Georgian farmstead built in 1805 for Thomas, Viscount Anson, where you can see rare breed animals and traditional farming methods, including hand milking, butter and cheese making and shire horses at work. In the former servants' quarters you find yourself taking a step back in time to the 19th century as you get a taste of life 'below stairs' wandering through the restored brewhouse, kitchens, laundry and coach houses. The mansion itself is a splendid piece of architecture, altered several times over 300 years, but always retaining its distinct grandeur. Passing through the vast rooms with their ornate plasterwork and cornicing, you can't help but be impressed and the collection of paintings, ceramics and silver plus a wealth of elegant French furniture is simply breathtaking. Outside as you explore the beautiful parkland you will spot an outstanding collection of neoclassical monuments dotted around and

45

St Mary the Virgin. Ingestre.

the Lady Walk leads you along the banks of the River Sow to the delightful terraced lawns and rose garden. Before leaving this splendid country estate, a visit to the walled kitchen garden provides you with the ideal opportunity to buy a living memento in the form of cottage garden plants.

Close to the main **A51** is the old village of **Great Haywood** which has the longest packhorse bridge in England. The 16th century Essex Bridge still has fourteen of its original forty arches spanning the River Trent. From here it is a good opportunity for a visit to the beautiful church of St Mary the Virgin at **Ingestre**, just two miles east of Stafford off the A51. It sits quite close to the Jacobean, Ingestre Hall and was probably built to Wren's design in 1676. One of the few churches that he designed outside London. Inside the church is totally elegant with a rich stucco nave ceiling and some of the earliest electrical installations in any church. In the chancel, which is barrel vaulted, there is a delightful garlanded reredos. There are many monuments to the Chetwynds and Talbots who were the Earls of Shrewsbury from 1856 and whose seat was Ingestre. The church is only open in daylight hours during the summer but we were told that in the winter months a key is available.

Izaak Walton Cottage, Stafford Borough Council. Riverside, Stafford. Tel: 0785 223181

Set in beautiful grounds in the tiny hamlet of **Shallowford**, near **Norton Bridge**, **Izaak Walton Cottage** is a pretty 17th century half timbered cottage which was once owned by Izaak Walton, famous biographer and author of 'The Compleat Angler'. Walton bequeathed the cottage to Stafford Borough Council and it was subsequently transformed into the museum you find today. Within the grounds there is an authentic 17th century herb garden, a lovely picnic area and orchard. Keen fishermen may also be able to fish the River Meece only yards from the cottage, where Walton himself fished for trout

47

some 350 years ago. The cottage is open daily Tues - Sun from 11.00am - 4.30pm and Bank Holiday Mondays from April to October.

Enjoying a lovely riverside location on the **A5013** Eccleshall Road, just outside Stafford, **The Mill at Worston** is a delightful stopping-off point in any journey. Originally built in 1814 by J. Milner, there are records of a mill on this site dating back as far as 1279, possibly before and there are records of a court battle of ownership of the present mill between Henry Le Whyte and Elena De Wynerston. Later, the mill came under the ownership of Ranton Abbey, after whose dissolution it passed through the hands of various local landed gentry until J. Milner bought and rebuilt it in 1814. Today, much of the machinery used during the mill's working life is retained and can be viewed by the many visitors here. In these characterful surroundings you can enjoy a pint of fine ale and a tasty bar meal, or alternatively choose from an extensive menu in the pleasant surroundings of the restaurant. There is a delightful nature trail to follow and on warm summer days, the beer garden and adventure playground provide the perfect setting for the whole family to enjoy a meal 'al fresco'. With a large function room seating up to 150, it is no surprise that this is a popular venue for wedding receptions and family celebrations.

The Mill at Worston. Great Bridgeford, Stafford. Tele: 0785 282710.

Back along the main **A518** in an easterly direction we came to **Gnosall.** There are some beautiful ash and sycamore trees here which form a delightful shaded arch over the road. It also has a ghost! On the night of January 21st 1879 a man was attacked at Gnosall canal bridge by an alarming black monster with enormous white eyes. The police were quite sure it was the ghost of a 'man-monkey' who had haunted the bridge for years after a man was drowned in the canal.

Wandering south from Gnosall we saw a sign for **Weston-under-Lizard** and discovered that it was uncertain whether it belonged in Staffordshire or Shropshire. We took the opportunity to visit **Weston Park,** home of the Earls of Bradford for three hundred years. The house is situated on the site of the original medieval Manor House. This was successively the property of the de Westons and the Myttons. The last of the Myttons, Elizabeth married Sir Thomas Wilbraham who disliked the gabled building and pulled it down, replacing it with another of his own design.

The lack of male heirs in the 18th century meant two more changes in Westons ownership, both through the female line, first to the Newports, Earls of Bradford and then in 1762 to the Bridgemans, an old family whose origins went back to Devon. Disraeli was a frequent visitor here and at one time presented the house with a grotesque stuffed parrot. The parrot became famous when the present earl after leaving Cambridge published a book entitled 'My Private Parts and the Stuffed Parrot'. The stuffed parrot still enjoys the hospitality of Weston.

The present earl has achieved such great things here. Lord Bradford's mother undertook all sorts of improvements in the house and Lord Bradford was determined to revitalise Weston Park.

At one time Lord Bradford had a restaurant in London's Covent Garden, Porters, which was very successful and it is this knowledge of catering that has enabled him to radically and enthusiastically improve the standard of catering at Weston Park. Gourmet dinners are quite regularly held in the magnificent dining room as well as private banquets and wedding receptions.

The Park at Weston has matured over several hundred years into a masterpiece of unspoilt landscape. Many have left their mark, yet each successive generation has taken note of its predecessors. Disraeli loved the Park and in one of his letters to Selina, 3rd Countess of Bradford, refers to the 'stately woods of Weston' There are some wonderful architectural features in the park including the Roman Bridge and Temple of Diana, both designed and built by James Paine for Sir Henry Bridgeman in about 1760. There are Fallow deer and rare breeds of sheep roaming the vast parklands, you can follow an architectural trail or the many nature trails. We can list for you so many things to see and do, like the Miniature Railway, the Aquarium, the Butterfly farm, a Museum of Country Bygones and by no means least, the Adventure playground and pets corner.

As we meandered towards the next chapter in search of ' Hidden Places in East Staffordshire we made our final visit in this intriguing part of the county where rustic scenes were within easy reach of the urban centres. **Moseley Old Hall** once stood in a remote part of Staffordshire, surrounded by its own agricultural estate. Today that remoteness no longer exists for the outskirts of Wolverhampton reach

Weston Park.

to within a mile of the house and motorway access is clearly signposted from Junction 1 of the M54. We wanted to take a look at it because The Hall once sheltered King Charles II for two days after the Battle of Worcester in 1651. There have been innumerable accounts of the King's concealment there which have given the house its place in history. You would be forgiven for thinking the house belonged to the 19th century at first sight, but look more closely and you see the two groups of Elizabethan windows were replaced by casements. Much of the original panelling and timber framing inside the house are still visible. In 1962, by the generosity of the Wiggin family, who had acquired the house in 1940, the Hall and one acre of land were transferred to the National Trust. The house was virtually empty then and almost all the furniture and pictures now shown have been lent or given to the Trust. Although not of great architectural merit, the part played by Moseley Old Hall in the preservation of King Charles and thus in the restoration of the Monarchy make it a very interesting place to visit.

Moseley Old Hall.   *Telephone 0902 782808.*

Dorothy Clive Gardens, Willoughbridge

CHAPTER THREE

East Staffordshire

Fallow Deer

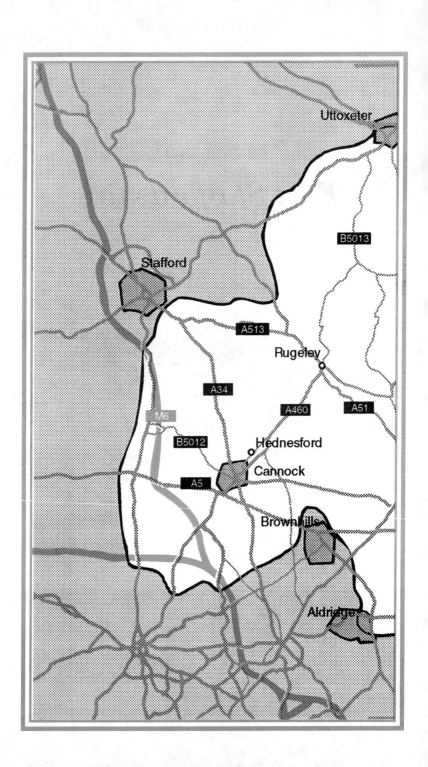

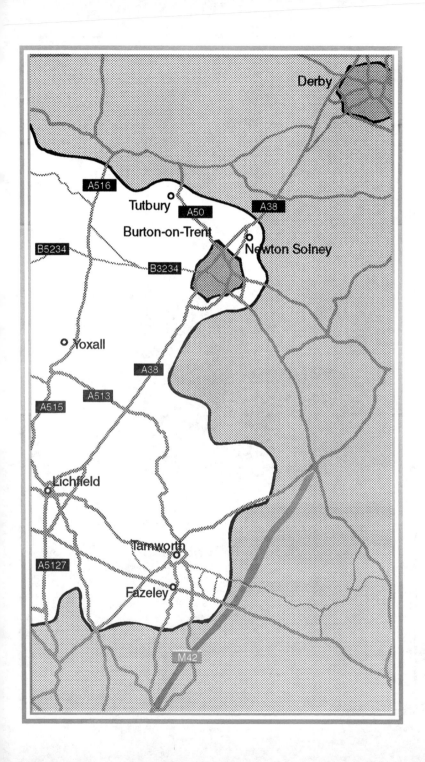

Butterfly. Hednesford Hills.

CHAPTER THREE

East Staffordshire.

Penkridge, the starting point for a journey through East Staffordshire continued to confirm our impressions with its many delights for visitors. The whole of the centre of the village has been designated a conservation area, so rich in character and history. From churches, cottages and houses to tombstones and even trees, nothing is allowed to be tampered with or altered in any way. A market can be traced to the granting of a market charter by King Henry 111 in 1244. Queen Elizabeth 1 is reported to have visited The White Hart Inn and other ancient features include the church of St Michael and All Angels, the stocks and gaol at the constables house, Cruck Cottage, Bellbrook - the Old Deanery Farm House and Church Cottage.

Without a doubt the most dominant feature in the centre of Penkridge is the parish church which was one of the six collegiate churches in Staffordshire before the Reformation. **Hednesford** lies by **Cannock Chase,** its oldest building is The Cross Keys Inn which is a splendid hostelry built somewhere about 1746. The Anglesey Hotel was built in 1831 by Edmund Peel of Fazeley as a form of summerhouse which stands proudly at the end of the main square, designed in a Tudor style with stepped gables.

Opened in May 1989, **The Valley Heritage Centre** is a new concept in the world of museums, arts and crafts. Once a former mining site, the Valley Heritage Centre took three years to convert and now is reporting far greater popularity and numbers than anticipated. Galleries provide different exhibitions, rooms are dedicated to The Natural History of the Hednesford Hills, the Shops Of Old Hednesford as they used to be and Castle Ring Hillfort, an exhibition which takes you back to the days before the Roman conquerors. Subjects covered in these galleries change every six months to deal with as many aspects of the area's history as possible.

The Valley Heritage Centre is only one of the many wonderful parts of Cannock Chase. The Council have encouraged visitors by helping in the conservation areas of beauty. **Brindley Heath** for example, is four hundred and twenty acres of beautiful mixed wood and heath and the nearest part to Hednesford. Its name reminds us that the Brindley family worked on the Chase for over three hundred years. **Brindley** village is of a much more recent origin. During the Great War a Military Hospital was built here, and later the Coal Board workers lived in the buildings.

We learnt that for thousands of men killed in France during World War 1, Cannock Chase was their last billet in England and so in some ways the surrounding beauty serves as a lasting memorial to them.

Hazel Slade Reserve very near to Hednesford which is just to the west, is a site where people are as important as nature, where it is possible to live next to nature and with care and effort conserve it for its own sake and for the interest and enjoyment it can give. People have always used this site. Thirty five years ago the old broadleaved wood that grew here was felled for timber. Hedges were planted and fields grazed. A small area of the wood managed to recover and grow from the stumps and seeds remaining in the ground. Thirty years ago the pool and marsh started to form as the land sunk through the mining subsidence and it became a popular fishing spot. More by luck than judgment, man's activities in the past have produced an old fashioned countryside of small fields, hedges, streams and pools, marshes and woods.

Rising over seven hundred feet above sea level, **Hednesford Hills** are a prominent local landmark, bringing the countryside of Cannock Chase into the heart of Hednesford. Originally covered in oak and birch these three hundred acres of heathland have been the scene of varied activities over the years. They have been quarried for sand and gravel, mined for coal and used for sport and military training. The land is now a registered common. It is wonderful; the Hills are a tract of wild landscape with a plethora of heathland plants, abundant wildlife and the opportunity for recreation for the people who live nearby.

The Hills have other sporting connections too. Cock fighting once took place at **Cockpit Hill,** but we didn't find the exact location of the old cock pit. In the last century prize fighters prepared themselves at the nearby Cross Keys Inn for boxing bouts on the Hills. Horse racing was another important part of life in those days. The area was well known for the stabling of horses in the 18th and 19th centuries. Meetings were held regularly until 1840 when the racetrack at **Etching Hill,** near **Rugeley** became more popular. Grand National winners were stabled and trained here. Jealousy won the race in 1861, Eremon in 1907 and Jenkinstown in 1910.

The Military also liked these hills for their mock battles. In 1873 there were extensive manoeuvres on Cannock Chase with one army based at Etching Hill and the other army at Hednesford Hills where the battle took place.

Cannock is still a colliery town but do not dismiss it because of this, there is much to see. It lies on the southern edge of Cannock Chase and goes back to the Conquest. In the Domesday book you will see it called 'Chenet'. It has an attractive market place with three busy market days, Tuesday, Friday and Saturday. The ancient bowling green has been there since time immemorial.

Overlooking the green is an imposing Georgian house that once housed the council and nearby is the former conduit head building of **Cannock Conduit Trust,** founded in 1736 to bring a water supply to the town. Known as the Tank House, it supplied water for the area until 1942.

There are some nice shops around the Market Place and in the attractive precinct on Market Hall Street. Henry 111 granted Cannock a market charter in 1259. On the far side of the Market Place is the parish church of St Luke. According to the records, the church had a chantry and a grammar school linked to it as early as 1143. The battlemented church tower dates from the 14th century and together with the west end of the nave are the oldest surviving parts of the building. The arms of Humphrey de Stafford who was killed at the Battle of Northampton in 1460 are on display.

During the 18th century **Lichfield** was a prominent city, but it failed to compete with other towns in extensive rebuilding programmes and consequently still retains medieval grid pattern streets with elegant Georgian houses and mixed in amongst them, black and white Tudor cottages. Little alleyways, such as Tudor Row, invite shoppers to visit specialist boutiques and a 16th century cafe - so different from the usual high streets found in today's cities and towns.

The Lichfield Heritage Exhibition & Treasury is part of **St. Mary's Centre** in the Market Place at the very heart of the city. A church has stood on this site since the 12th century, with the present building being the third one, dating from 1868. Due to the declining population in the city centre over the last thirty years, drastic action was needed to save St. Mary's from redundancy, or even worse,

The Nave. Lichfield Cathedral.

demolition. In 1977/78, with the co-operation of local civic and church authorities, together with many private individuals, The St. Mary's Project Committee was formed. From this evolved the ambitious and imaginative plan to convert St. Mary's into the unique Community Centre which we have today.

The Guild of St. Mary's Centre.Lichfield. Tel: 0543 256611

It opened in 1981 and comprises: The original Dyott Chapel & Chancel which were retained as the Parish Church and thereby ensured the continuance of worship here for the future; a day centre for senior citizens; a gift shop; a coffee shop; the Heritage Exhibition & Treasury.

The Lichfield Heritage Exhibition & Treasury, being on a new mezzanine floor, has additional access by lift for the elderly and disabled and is based on the history of Lichfield through its people. Together with many other exhibits, it has two A.V. presentations, one entitled 'Lichfield - A Walk Through History' and the other 'The 1643 Siege of Lichfield Cathedral during the Civil War'. The beautiful Treasury houses many fine examples of the silversmith's art with collections of civic, church and regimental silver. The Muniment Room displays ancient city archives and charters. The latest attraction for visitors is a viewing platform 40m high in the Spire of St. Mary's which provides unique and spectacular panoramic views over the city and nearby countryside. This is proving to be a photographer's delight. Open daily 10.00am - 5.00pm except for Christmas Day, Boxing Day, New Year's Day and Spring Bank Holiday Monday.

Apart from the historic pleasure that Lichfield gives there is also large amounts of open water and green parkland to enjoy within the city. Beacon Park and Museum Gardens for instance where some seventy five acres of park encloses playing fields, a small boating lake and a playground. As we wandered we came to a statue in the museum gardens to Commander John Smith, the captain of the ill-fated Titanic. It was sculpted by Lady Katherine Scott, widow of 'Scott of the Antarctic'.

There are two wonderful pools, Stowe and Minster, the former is a large area of water used for fishing and sailing and is the site of the Festival fireworks display each July. The Minster Pool is beautiful, it was landscaped in the late 18th century by Anna Seward and is now a haven for wildfowl.

Anna Seward is one of Lichfield's famous sons and daughters. She lived in the Bishop's Palace and was a poet, letter writer, and centre of a literary circle in the late 18th century. There are many well known names to add to hers. Samuel Johnson, of course, but also Elias Ashmole the Antiquarian and herald whose collection became the basis of Oxford's Ashmolean Museum. He was born, like Samuel Johnson, in Breadmarket Street. Then there is Erasmus Darwin, the doctor, inventor, botanist and poet who lived in a house in Beacon Street on the corner of The Close. David Garrick probably the greatest actor-manager of the 18th century theatre, had a home which stands opposite the west gate of the cathedral.

Just behind the industrial units at Lichfield, out in the countryside you will find a rural gem at **Curborough Hall Farm**. The land here has been farmed by the Hollinshead family for many years and since 1989 the family have been steadily converting the farm outbuildings to create a variety of small craft workshops which will keep browsers fascinated for hours. Within one of these workshops you will find Frank Daysh, a highly skilled man who originally trained as a scientific glassblower, a job requiring highly precise skills. Since 1985, he has used these skills to develop his profession and visitors are welcome to watch him at work in his upstairs workshop. Frank is a lamp glassblower which means that rather than working from molten glass he reheats glass tubing and rod, modifying it to produce some simply exquisite pieces such as decorated perfume bottles and chess sets. The showroom also has an interesting range of glass by other workers including animal sculptures, paper weights, jewellery, glass domes and even a glass grand-daughter clock. The only dilemma for visitors is deciding which piece to choose as a memento! There is also a lovely tearoom and having enjoyed a look around you can relax in the tearoom garden, weather permitting, with a refreshing cuppa and a tasty homemade cake. For self-catering enthusiasts, the Hollinshead family provide excellent accommodation in four self-contained cottages at nearby Elmhurst Dairy Farm. All the cottages are equipped to a very high standard and graded Commended with a Three or Four Key rating by the English Tourist Board, a sure sign of the quality of accommodation you can expect. Opening times Wednesday to Sunday 10.30am - 5.00pm.

Curborough Hall Farm Craft Centre, Curborough Hall Farm, Watery Lane, Lichfield. 0543 262595

Situated on the **A461**, 100 yards from the **Muckley Corner** roundabout on the A5, **Copper's End** is an ideal touring base for this lovely part of Staffordshire. Lying just three miles outside historic Lichfield with its Cathedral and Heritage and Treasury Centre, not to mention Cannock Chase Country Park and Shugborough, the Earl of Lichfield's family home, there are numerous attractions within easy driving distance tempting you to prolong your stay. Copper's End was built during the 1930's as a police station, today it offers far more comfortable accommodation than the former cell which is now the lounge. The bedrooms are all very well equipped and tastefully furnished with guest comfort always a prime consideration and breakfast is a substantial treat that sets you up ideally for a day's exploring. All major cards taken.

Copper's End. Muckley Corner, Lichfield. Tel: 0543 372910

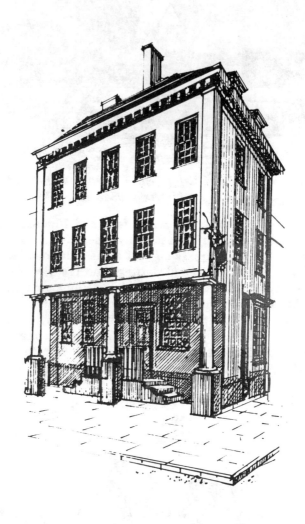

Dr. Johnson's Birthplace Lichfield..

On our way to **Tamworth** we stopped to take a look at **The Museum of the Staffordshire Regiment (The Prince of Wales's)**, which incorporates the former South and North Staffordshire Regiments which were amalgamated in 1959. Its origins go back to 1705 when the 38th Foot, (later the 1st Battalion of the South Staffordshire Regiment), was raised at Lichfield. The museum exhibits a good range of uniforms, shako and helmet plates, belt plates and clasps, badges and buttons,and weapons from pistols to machine guns. There are relics from the Sikh Wars, the Crimea, Indian Mutiny, Zulu War, Egypt, Sudan, South Africa and both World Wars. You realise the bravery of the Regiment when you see amongst the medals no less than thirteen Victoria Crosses awarded to the men.

The Old Stables Farm Shop and Bakery, Packington Moor Farm, Near Whittington, Lichfield. 0543 481223

Close by one 'hidden' place well worth seeking out is **The Old Stables Farm Shop and Bakery** at **Packington Moor Farm** near **Whittington**. To find your way here, take the Whittington turn off the A5 and the farm shop is situated midway between the **A5** and **A51**. The shop sells a wide selection of homegrown produce including meat, vegetables and dairy products such as cheese and ice cream and while you browse, children can play on the swings and make friends with the small farm animals. There is a bakery on the premises which produces delicious bread and cakes and in the tearoom and courtyard you can relax with a cup of tea and a tasty homemade snack. There are 'pick your own' fruits available in the summer months and you can book a 'childrens party in the Barn' should you wish.

Just south of Tamworth lies **Drayton Manor Park and Zoo,** another popular theme park in 60 acres. It has over fifty different rides,a Zoo and farm which combine to promise an action packed day out,especially for families.We entered **Tamworth** unsure of what to expect. We found a young town with an ancient history. It straddles the famous Roman Watling Street (A5) and has had a fascinating and turbulent past. The earliest reference is the 8th century when it was the capital of the Kingdom of Mercia and its king, Offa, built his palace here. The Danes managed to destroy the town twice and it was invaded later by the Scandinavians. You can see evidence of this in the names of streets such as Gungate. Alfred's daughter Ethelfleda was busy here too and there have been excavations in the town centre which produced Saxon fortifications.

Dominating the town is the fine Norman motte and bailey castle set in the Pleasure Grounds which have truly magnificent floral terraces. The sandstone castle and superb herringbone wall dates originally from the 1180's, having replaced a wooden tower on the present artificial mound constructed shortly after the Norman Conquest.

Daniel Defoe called Tamworth, 'A small but very handsome market town'. Much has gone but something of this can still be seen in the 18th century buildings of Market Street and Lady Bank. The Town Hall is charming with open arches and Tuscan columns below. It was built in 1701 and paid for by Thomas Guy, the local MP, who is famous for founding the London hospital which bears his name. He also gave the town its fourteen almshouses in Lower Gungate, which were rebuilt in 1913.

Tamworth's most famous son was Sir Robert Peel, who was Prime Minister under both William 1V and Victoria. In front of the Town Hall is a fine bronze statue of this great man. The parish church is vast, founded in 963, it was rebuilt after the Norman Conquest and again after the Great Fire of Tamworth in 1345. The splendid 15th century tower at the west end contains a most remarkable double staircase. The mixture of Victorian and modern stained glass is remarkably harmonious.

The bustling town centre's modern shopping facilities include a street market every Tuesday and Saturday and the attractive Ankerside Shopping Centre is a covered precinct opened by the Queen in 1980. There is a fascinating glass mural by John Lawson here which depicts Tamworth's past.

On a warm summer's day there can be few nicer modes of transport than by boat, travelling at a leisurely 4mph and watching the world go by. At Canal Wharf in Fazeley, **Debbie's Day Boats** give visitors the opportunity to experience this pleasure with a small fleet of 15 foot, luxury, all-weather cruisers which can be hired by the hour, half day, or full day. Run by Debbie and Tom Hayes, the business was set up in April 1993 following Debbie's prize-winning business plan. Seating up to five adults, the boats, all of which are named after members of Debbie's family, are easy and safe to drive, with full tuition provided before you set off. As a picnic venue they are ideal and the trip takes you past many canalside pubs.

Debbie's Day Boats, Canal Wharf, Fazeley, Tamworth.

We were enchanted as we drove through the village of **Alrewas** on the A38. Lining the main street are delightful black and white thatched cottages, some of which have stood since the fifteenth century. The village is surrounded by countryside and this had made our drive, very pleasant. The River Trent and The Trent and Mersey canal run through the village adding to its beauty. This canal links the River Trent near Derby with the Mersey at Runcorn, a substantial part of it being in Staffordshire.

We wrote earlier about Josiah Wedgwood and the Harecastle Tunnel but whilst the towpath has gone from Telford's tunnel, it is still used by pleasure boats, as is the whole of the canal. South of the Potteries, the Trent and Mersey runs close to the River Trent, passing the wild expanse of Cannock Chase and the busy **Fradley Junction** where there is a connection to the **Coventry Canal** before leaving Staffordshire by way of **Burton-on-Trent.**

The church of All Saints in Alrewas is as beautiful as the village. Doorways remain from a Norman church to which the beautiful chancel was added in the 13th century. The church is open every day from 9am -5pm.

King's Bromley is a little to the west of Alrewas and is one of Staffordshire's oldest villages. Lady Godiva lived here with her husband Leofric. It was also the scene of Leofric's death. King's Bromley was a crown property for many years after the Norman Conquest and it had other royal connections in the 12th century. Henry 1 loved hunting and stayed here, close to the forests. When Charles 11 needed to escape he was sheltered by the Lane family who were locals and it is they who engineered his route to freedom.

Yoxall is one of those villages which is designated a

67

Tamworth Castle

conservation area. It is a romantic sort of place and we were not surprised to learn that, according to legend, Robin Hood was lord of the manor and married Maid Marion at nearby **Tutbury.** There are some very nice buildings and the parish church is worth a visit. Visitors to this tranquil village will discover an excellent touring base at **The Moat,** the charming home of Pam Hopkins. The original manor house on this site was blown up during the battle of Burton Bridge during the Civil War and the present house was built about 100 years ago using bricks from the mill which stood next door. Standing in two and a half acres of beautiful landscaped gardens the house is surrounded by a dry moat dating back to the 13th century and believed to be the deepest of its kind in the Midlands. Pam is a welcoming hostess who provides very comfortable accommodation in three en-suite guest rooms. Awarded a Two Crown Highly Commended rating by the English Tourist Board, there are full facilities for the disabled including a chair lift and guests can be provided with an evening meal by prior arrangement.

The Moat, Town Hill, Yoxall, Staffs. Tel: 0543 472210

Ridware Arts Centre just outside Rugeley is within the Tudor walls of the ancient manorial site of Hamstall Hall and there we found a fascinating group of shops, studios and a restaurant. Everywhere there was activity. Demonstrations of the various skills of the occupants hold the visitors interest. There are always changing exhibitions at Ridware so it does not matter how often you come back as there is always something new to see. The Malt House Craft Shop shows an enormous variety of

British craftwork including unusual porcelain, fascinating wood boxes, toys and turned bowls as well as some delightful domestic pottery which are collectors' items. In the Gate Barn there is a collection of plant containers from every corner of the world. All sorts, shapes and sizes to take plants small and large and designed to fit into odd corners of your home.

Rugeley gained an unhappy notoriety in Victorian times as the home of the poisoner, Dr William Palmer, who murdered his victims after insuring them. We decided to take a walk through the town along a designated route. As we left Market Square we were told to look along Anson Street to our left and note the interesting three-storey Victorian buildings and varied roof line. Opposite was the old 'Penny Bank' building. We wonder how many people remember this great institution.

Market Street has long been the main street of the town. In it is 'The Shrewsbury Arms', a former coaching inn dating from about 1810 although parts may be even older. It has changed its name once or twice. Between 1860 and 1967 there was a cattle market at the rear and a market bell was rung from the steps of the inn summoning the farmers back from lunch.

The Tudor House that you can see is one that was rented by the evil Doctor Palmer. He got his just desserts though and was publicly hanged in Stafford in 1856. A bit further down the street we came to The Red Lion, an attractive timbered building of about 1600. Inside one wall has linenfold panelling. At the junction of Bryans Lane we were reminded how small the town once was. 'The Sycamores' is a much altered farmhouse built about 1600 and parts of the timber frame are still visible.

The Old Chancel across Station Road is Rugeley's original parish church, founded in the 12th century. The tower, chancel and north chapel which remain, date mainly from the 13th and 14th centuries. The nave of the church was demolished in 1823 to help pay for the new church. Next to the Old Chancel is Church Croft, a Georgian house where William Palmer was born.

Brook Square saw us back in the old town centre where we took a short detour up the narrow Upper Brook Street to Horse Fair. Until 1932 there was an annual horse fair here with dealers coming from all parts of the country, France and Ireland. A thousand and forty horses were recorded at the 1867 fair. On the far side of Horse Fair are a pair of 16th century timber houses and a restored 18th century stone wall. Lower Brook Street took us back to Market Square.

Out of the town, travelling on the A51 Lichfield to Rugeley road, if you turn left opposite Longdon village and continue up to the junction, turn left and continue round a right hand bend past a cottage, you will see an entrance on your left leading to **Longdon Old Hall,** an impressive 300 year old Grade II listed farmhouse. This is the lovely home of Charles and Rosemary Cliffe, welcoming hosts who provide very comfortable accommodation in seven guest rooms, all attractively furnished and some with en-suite facilities. The atmosphere is very relaxed and you are welcome to breakfast with Charles and Rosemary. Breakfast is a substantial affair, cooked on the Aga and offering a choice of duck or hen eggs, coddled for those who prefer! This is an ideal touring base, lying within easy reach of many local attractions and sporting activities.

Longdon Old Hall, Longdon, Rugeley, Staffs. Tel: 0543 682267

A few miles north of Rugeley is **Hoar Cross**. The church of the Holy Angels which delighted Sir John Betjeman who said; 'The church of the Holy Angels, Hoar Cross, is the masterpiece of its late Victorian architect, G.F. Bodley'. Much of its beauty, indeed its very being is down to one remarkable lady, Emily Charlotte, eldest daughter of Sir Charles Wood, 1st Viscount Halifax and widow of Hugo Francis Meynell Ingram.

To write about Hoar Cross without mentioning the **Meynell Hounds** is like thinking about **Stratford** without Shakespeare. Meynell is perhaps, the most famous of all names in the world of Fox Hunting and for many years the hounds were kennelled at Hoar Cross. In those far off days anyone who could beg, borrow or steal a horse was welcome to follow Meynell's hounds and share in the days sport. As well as this, such a large establishment of horses and hounds provided occupation for most of the people in this small community.

We were recommended by colleagues to visit **Abbots Bromley**, a delightful 13th century village, on the first Monday after the 4th of September. On this special day the villagers celebrate the annual Horn Dance. This ancient fertility dance is performed by many men wearing reindeer antlers, amongst other things!

After all this excitement you may need a drink and whilst in

Burton-on-Trent we visited the **Bass Museum of Brewing** in Horninglow Street. Take a few thousand gallons of good Burton brewing water and combine it together with best English Malt in a traditional Mash Tun, then run the resultant sweet malt liquor into huge boiling coppers and add to the brew good old English hops. When it has cooled, run the wort (Malt liquor) into wooden fermenting vats and pitch in the breweries own strain of yeast. Seven days later under the watchful eye of the Head Brewer, traditional Beer is ready to be racked off into casks. This is the traditional way that beer has been brewed for centuries, and here at the museum we were offered the opportunity of seeing, sniffing and sampling!

They have restored the original Buxton-Thornley steam engine, scrapped in 1970 and are proud to have it back home and in steam again. They also have one of the largest 'bottled beers' collection in the United Kingdom. They are open all the year telephone 0283 42031 for more information.

On the edge of **Newton Solney** on the **B5008** from Burton -on-Trent you will find an excellent place to stay at **Newton Park Hotel.**

Newton Park Hotel, Newton Solney. Tel: 0283 703568

Built in Italianate style in 1798 by a wealthy local gentleman, this delightful country house hotel enjoys a lovely setting, with wonderful countryside views and yet lies only three miles outside Burton-on-Trent. Traditionally furnished throughout, in keeping with its age and character, this impressive establishment boasts 51 en-suite guest rooms, all of which are equipped to the highest standards. The elegant restaurant with its ornate ceiling and oak panelling provides a relaxing setting in which to savour a fine menu of traditional English cuisine. Stained glass is a major feature, with glass panels on the main staircase depicting the seasons and months of the year, and in the Derbyshire Bar, further glass panels depicting attractive countryside scenes, enhancing Newton Park's distinctive charm.

On the main **A50** road three miles from Burton upon Trent we stopped at **Tutbury**, a small market village, lying in the lush **Dove Valley** on the Staffordshire/Derbyshire border. In 1989, the village held a 'Tutbury 900' festival. This was a special year as St Mary's Priory Church was founded exactly nine hundred years ago by Henry de Ferrers. Its splendid Norman architecture makes the priory one of the most impressive relics of the Conqueror's England. Tutbury owes its existence and its name to the naturally defensive outcrop of rock on which the ruins of the 14th century castle now stands.

It came somewhat as a surprise to us that Tutbury is still seemingly undiscovered as a tourist attraction. A beautiful village with many Georgian fronted shops, it has held onto the historical charm and character from this period in time. We visited **Tutbury Mill Mews** a shopping complex, originally an ironmongery and wheelwrights to Lord Burton, the Mews now houses many extensive antique showrooms.

A guided tour is a revelation in itself and we were told of its history. The town of Tutbury had been renowned for glass making for as long as five centuries, as far back as Mary Queen of Scots time. In 1980 when the old glass factory, then under the control of a major national company, was forced to close, due to the economic recession, sadly one hundred and fifty employees were to find themselves out of work. However, just two years later, the factory was to rise like a phoenix from the ashes, all due to five past employees, who took up the challenge of reopening the factory. Through hard work and determination, this age old tradition synonymous with the ancient town of Tutbury has been brought back to life and its all due to five enterprising and ambitious people. A visit to **Tutbury Crystal Glass** (Tel:- 0283 813281) will enlighten you to the process of glass making.

R.A.James M.B.H.I., 14 High Street, Tutbury. Tel: 0283 814596

Church of Holy Angels. Hoar's Cross.

On the High Street in the centre of Tutbury you will find a fascinating place with the impressive title **R.A.James M.B.H.I.** above the door. The James family have been horologists since 1918 and Robert James, the current owner, specialises in repairs and renovations of antique clocks, watches and barometers. He makes regular trips abroad where he is able to buy more unusual and interesting pieces with which to fill the shop, tempting the passer-by and habitual browser to call in. With pieces of every style you can imagine, there is something here to appeal to every taste and if your own clock or barometer is broken or has seen better days, Rob's skill as a craftsman can bring it back to its former glory.

At the end of the High Street in Tutbury, you will discover a first class restaurant called **Mulberry House.** This delightful 200 year old listed building boasts a mulberry tree in the centre of the rear patio which is also over 200 years old and has a conservation order to protect it. Inside, the restaurant has a cosiness and warmth which is enhanced by attractively laid tables, beamed ceilings and lovely dried flowers. Open for everything from morning coffee and cream teas to lunchtime snacks and a full à la carte dinner, Mulberry House offers an excellent menu of traditional homecooked fare throughout the day. You can enjoy a game of croquet on the lawn or purchase one of the gifts on sale, and for those wishing to stay, there are also four lovely guest rooms to choose from.

Mulberry House. 19 High Street, Tutbury. Tel: 0283 815170

Almost next door to Mulberry House is the fabulous **Crystal Studio** glass works, run by Geoff Press and Mike Underwood.

This is a real treasure trove and, as its name suggests, the studio specialises in glassware and crystal, which is handcut and finished on the premises. Mike and Geoff also produce crystal sports trophies and can make repairs and renovations to any glassware. The vast array of goods on show are of the highest quality, with something to suite every taste and pocket. Beautiful vases, glasses, decanters and trinkets are all attractively laid out, leaving you spoilt for choice when it comes to choosing a memento or gift.

The Crystal Studio, 22 High Street, Tutbury. 0283-520917

CHAPTER FOUR

The Black Country

Dudley Castle

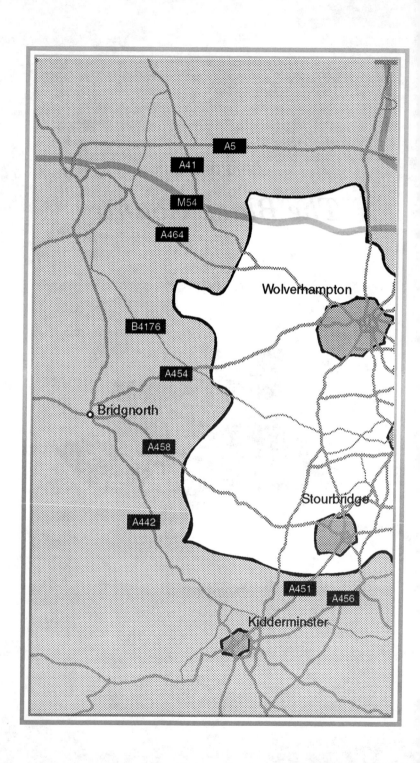

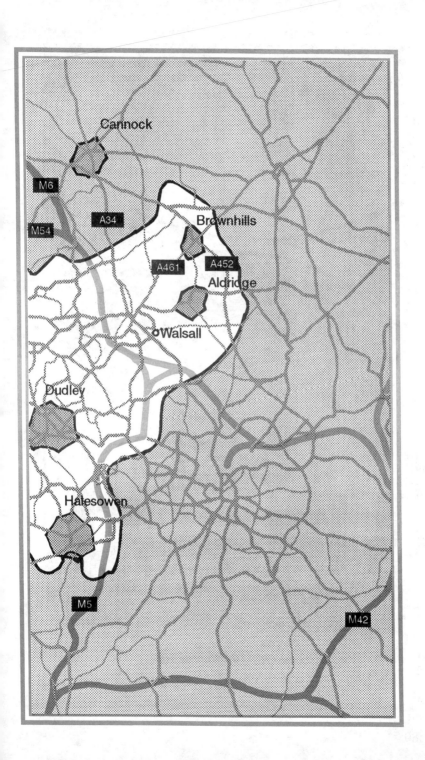

Interior.Chillington Hall.

CHAPTER FOUR

The Black Country

Our starting point in this chapter was something very different from what the term ' Black Country' conjures up in the mind. The name itself originates from the 19th century expansion of previously small iron and coal industries into more or less a continual conurbation. The pollution generated by the industrial expansion helped coin the name we still call this part of the country although it is now, without doubt cleaner. Dickens called the area a modern hell, *"....as far as the eye could see....tall chimneys,crowding on each other.....poured out their plague of smoke,obscured the light and made foul the melancholy air...........strange engines spun and writhed like tortured creatures; clanking their iron chains,shrieking in their rapid whirl from time to time.....and making the ground tremble with their agonies."*

We went from Cannock along the A5 going westwards and then took a turning to the left at **Horsebrook** which brought us into **Brewood,** a village mentioned in the Domesday book. It was once the centre of the nail making industry. It is hard to believe that this peaceful place is only three miles from the M54 and just eight miles from **Wolverhampton.**

This small, but busy market town is a delight. It is of medieval origins and has the **Shropshire Union Canal** running through it. The Shropshire Union Canal is Telford's masterpiece. He was intensely proud of it and with reason. It leaves the Staffordshire and Worcestershire Canal at **Autherley Junction**, near Wolverhampton,and in Telford's inimitable fashion, runs north west to Nantwich in Cheshire often through deep cuttings, the most spectacular of which are at **Norbury** in Staffordshire, with its famous high bridge, and at **Tyrley**, with its sheer rock sides.

At Brewood, which is pronounced Brood, are two interesting works; the aqueduct over which Telford's canal crosses the same engineer's Holyhead Road (now the A5), and the ornamental bridge - or short tunnel - which he was obliged to construct to take the canal beneath the avenue to **Chillington Hall.** You'll find this Tudor

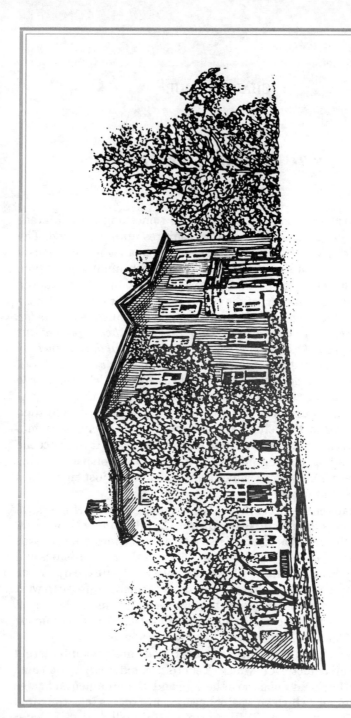

Bantock House Museum.

house on an unclassified road just before the M54. It was rebuilt by Francis Smith of Warwick and later Sir John Sloane in the 18th century,its garden laid out by Capability Brown. Tourist Information will have details of its limited opening times.

There are some beautiful buildings including the Tudor Brewood Hall and Blackladies, an old monastery. If you like Queen Anne and early Georgian houses you will love Brewood. The parish church of St Mary the Virgin and St Chad date back to the 13th century and has a wonderful sense of peace about it as well as being extremely beautiful.

When we left Brewood, we drove along crossing the busy M54 until we came to the bustling village of **Codsall** which is only a few miles north west of Wolverhampton and is famous for its lupins. We were told that they are a result of the medicinal springs in the Codsall Wood area.

Just north of the village is **Pendrell Hall**, built in the 19th century. It is a weird architectural mixture, some Gothic and some Tudor style. The house sits on top of a slope and has the most superb views of the Welsh Marches, Cannock Chase, Wolverhampton and the Black Country. It belongs to Staffordshire County Council and is used as a residential college. The parish church of St Nicholas is well worth looking at. It has an impressive Norman archway and an Early English square tower.

It was during the Saxon times that the town was first recorded as a community. Ethelred the Unready gave a charter to a local lady, Lady Wulfruna. In 994 she gave a plot of land at the highest point of High Town for the construction of a monastery. It is on this site that St Peter's church now stands. Outside the church is the town's most ancient relic. It is a Saxon preaching cross which is believed to have stood there since the mid-9th century. It stands fourteen feet high, and isn't really a cross but rather a circular pillar with a decorated shaft that is worn almost smooth with age.

In Bantock Park, the **Bantock Museum** has some wonderful 18th century enamels for which neighbouring Bilston was famous, and First Period Worcester porcelain.

There are perfectly preserved examples of houses with the Civil War Connection. One such house is **Moseley Old Hall** which once stood in a remote part of Staffordshire, surrounded by its own agricultural estate. Today that remoteness no longer exists for the outskirts of Wolverhampton reach to within a mile of the house. The Hall once sheltered King Charles ll for two days after the Battle of Worcester in 1651. There have been innumerable accounts of the King's concealment there which have given the house its place in history.

Dudley Castle

You would be forgiven for thinking that the house belonged to the 19th century at first sight, but look more closely and you will see the two groups of Elizabethan chimneys, star-shaped in section,towering over the roofs. Little in the way of structural alteration appears to have been done to the house until about 1870, when the outer walls were covered in brick, and the Elizabethan windows were replaced by casements. Much of the original panelling and timber framing inside the house is still visible. In 1962, by the generosity of the Wiggin family, who had acquired the house in 1940, the Hall and one acre of land were transferred to the National Trust. The house was virtually empty then and almost all the furniture and pictures now shown have been lent or given to the Trust.

Further west **Boscobel House** has royal connections as it is where King Charles is said to have hidden in an Oak Tree while Cromwell's troops searched the house and grounds for him. Legend has it that the Royal Oak outside the house is a descendant of that original tree which sheltered the King.

Three miles west of Wolverhampton stands **Wightwick Manor,** pronounced Witick, this National Trust property is a half timbered and half bricked building built in the late 19th century by paint manufacturer Theodore Mander. Inside you'll see 19th century decor with Morris wallpaper and fabric, stained glass and examples of pre -Raphaelite paintings.

On the outskirts of the town, a long defunct Great Western Railway track bed now forms the Valley Park footpath along which we walked with great pleasure enjoying the excercise.

Dudley can justly claim to be the showpiece of what canals can offer visitors. **The Dudley Canal Trust** and its boat trip company carry over a hundred thousand visitors a year, deep underground beneath Dudley Castle, through canal tunnels into the caverns which supplied the Black Country iron foundries with limestone. A spectacular audio visual presentation with dramatic floodlighting brings back the days when the miners worked by candlelight in dangerous conditions to mine the limestone.

Adjoining the canal is the **Black Country Museum**. Apart from a wide variety of buildings which have been rebuilt to form a Black Country 'village' scene, including a Methodist Chapel and a canal pub, there is a faithful reconstruction of a narrowboat building yard and a restored wharf where limestone was loaded into boats from kilns.

Dudley Castle, perched on a limestone ridge dominates the town. It was first mentioned in the Domesday book in 1086. The first stone castle was built in the 12th century but was destroyed less than a hundred years later following the rebellion against King Henry ll.

Black Country Museum, Dudley

From the 13th century, rebuilding and extension work continued up to the 16th century. In 1554 the Duke of Northumberland lost the castle, and his head, for treason. And in 1575 Queen Elizabeth stayed here whilst travelling through the Midlands.

During the Civil War, the castle paid the ultimate price for being a Royalist stronghold, the Parliament ordered it to be 'sleighted' in 1647. This destroyed much of the keep, gatehouse, barbican and curtain wall, ensuring that the castle was useless for military purposes.

The Black Country Museum is already ranked as one of the nation's best 'living' museums. From the moment you enter the site your senses are kept busy. A vintage single deck tram ride takes you past a recreated Black Country Colliery, where you see the conditions of the early days of mining. The display has easy access. A series of concrete tunnels sunk into the ground with a walk in facility providing a series of galleries featuring miners and their equipment.

In the village is a priceless collection of cottages and Victorian terraced houses which were carefully removed, brick by brick, from clearance sites all over the Black Country and rebuilt to their original design to create a typical Black Country street scene. All the houses are furnished and equipped in the original style with outhouses and small chain shops where the outworkers made chain for the bigger companies. Shops, too, form another fascinating feature in this time capsule of Black Country life as it was. Amongst the shops are a chemist, haberdashers, bakery and hardware merchants.

The Bottle and Glass Public House with its traditional furniture and real ales is exactly what you would expect to find in a pub of this age. The building was removed from its canal side site near Brierley Hill and rebuilt alongside the canal leading to the Dudley tunnel and the trip boats. Close by is the disapproving Methodist Chapel originally from Darby Hand at Netherton, complete with its original furniture and some time special services are still held here.

One of the museum's most prized possessions is a replica of the world's first **Newcomen Beam Engine** which was installed in **Tipton** to pump water from mine workings. The engine is not always in steam but for more information telephone: 021-557-9643.

Did you know that **Willenhall** produces ninety per cent of all the locks we use in this country? We didn't but once here we were made very much aware that during the reign of Queen Elizabeth 1, the town was granted the exclusive right to manufacture locks for the state and has done so ever since.

Willenhall also has a very nice market place which is the centrepiece of a splendid conservation area resurfaced with blue brick pavements and cast iron kerbing, restoring it to its 19th century splendour.

If you love snuff boxes and little enamelled trinkets you will enjoy spending time in **Bilston.** Somehow in the midst of the Industrial Revolution and backstreet workshops, 18th century enamellers carried on their craft. They called themselves toymakers but they were not talking about children's toys. They provided society with such items as patch boxes, snuff and sweetmeat boxes, scent boxes, bonbonnieres following the fashion set by the French at Versailles. Their product was infinitely cheaper than the French because they worked on copper rather than gold or silver.

The museum at Mount Pleasant holds the world famous collection of Bilston enamels and it is a delight to see.

Glassmaking has been carried out in the Stourbridge area for nearly four hundred years. During that time the towns of **Amblecote, Wordsley, Brierley Hill** and **Stourbridge** have produced some of the world's most memorable glass. Stourbridge glassware has been supplied to stately homes and palaces throughout the world and is as much in demand today as it ever was. Modern technology has not replaced the actual skills of centuries ago which still apply in the final stages.

The glass industry dates back to the beginning of the 17th century when 'gentlemen glassmakers' originating from Normandy and Lorraine, in eastern France, settled in the area, attracted by the plentiful supplies of coal to fire their furnaces and fire-clay from which to make their melting pots.

We had noticed in our journeying from Wolverhampton, the **Red House Glass Cone.** In fact you cannot fail to see it. It is the sole survivor of dozens in continual use in the glass industry. The cone housed the circular furnaces which the glass makers worked around. Today, it is one of only four surviving in the country. It is imposing, almost 100 ft tall and was built about 1790.

A priceless collection of glass from Roman times up to the present day can be seen at the Stourbridge glass industry's museum at **Broadfield House,** Compton Drive, **Kingswinford**. The exhibits come from donations from individuals, private collections and glass manufacturers with particular emphasis on the dazzling range of coloured glass and crystal for which the name of Stourbridge became internationally famous.

To the west lies some attractive country for walking or simply a pleasant day picnicing. Kinver Edge is National Trust Property consisting of moorland and you'll find the remains of a hill fort there.Alternatively south of Stourbridge lie the Clent Hills, also

National Trust property and rising to a height of 1036 feet. Close by is **Hagley Hall,** built in the middle 18th century by a Sanderson Miller for the first Lord Lyttelton. The interior is rich with ornate plastering by Frncesco Vassali. In the gounds there is a sham ruin and a classic temple.

When we went to **West Bromwich,** we could be forgiven for thinking of it as just a thriving town created by the industrial revolution. Such thoughts are entirely incorrect. It has been in existence for well over eight hundred years and All Saints' parish church has been the site of religious worship for more than a thousand years. The Domesday Book lists the Manor of West Bromwich under the possessions of William Fitz-Ansculph, Baron of Dudley. The Manor House was rescued from dereliction in the late 1950's and is now a restaurant. The Great Hall of the house was built in the closing years of the 13th century. It is possibly the most complete example of such early construction.

In Oak Road is **The Oak House,** a magnificent Tudor house built in the reign of Henry Vlll which has survived intact. It was once the centre of a considerable estate owned by the Turtons. During the Civil War, the Turtons sympathised with the Parliamentary forces and legend has it that many Roundheads sheltered here. This lovely house is furnished throughout in the Tudor style as if the Turtons were still in residence.

Methodism played a large part in the history of the Black Country. **Sandwell** can claim a part in the growth of Methodism in the U.S.A. It was at **Asbury Cottage**, Newton Road, **Great Barr,** where America's first Methodist bishop, Francis Asbury, spent much of his childhood. He was apprenticed to a blacksmith named Foxhall at the Old Forge, at what is now Forge Mill Farm in the Sandwell Valley. He became active in Methodism and began attending West Bromwich Church. Eventually, he became a Methodist preacher and a friend of John Wesley. Meanwhile, Mr Foxhall's son had gone to America to become a wealthy iron merchant and eventually built the Foundry Methodist Church at Washington DC.

Sandwell Valley is a tribute to a foresighted Council, who prevented the urban sprawl engulfing it with factories and housing. It is wonderful countryside with a long history. One thousand years ago, an isolated hermitage stood in the valley close to pure spring water flowing from the sandstone rocks. It is from this ancient spring that the area - and eventually the Metropolitan Borough, gained its name, Sandwell. Today it is the home of sailing, fishing, horseback riding, playing fields, golf courses, working farms, forming Sandwell's major open space leisure area.

Around 1189, William Fitz-Wido, Lord of the Manor of Bromwich, founded a Benedictine Priory on the site of the old hermitage. The Priory was dissolved in 1525 and given to Cardinal Wolsey who, in turn, passed it on to what is now Christ Church College, Oxford. When Wolsey fell from grace in 1539, the King reclaimed the estate which the Crown passed to the Clifford family. They were succeeded by the Whorewood family who built Sandwell Hall in 1609 on the Priory site.

Walsall, dates back to the 11th century, it is an important place today at the centre of a large metropolitan borough but it is still dominated by the past in the beautiful shape of its 14th century parish church. Like most of the towns round the Black Country its open air market was established by Royal Charter. Walsall's came in 1219 and it was an important trading centre even then long before the industrial revolution arrived with its collieries, blast furnaces and ironworks.

Jerome K. Jerome was born in Walsall at Belsize House in Bradford Street. You might recall that he wrote 'Three Men in a Boat'. The house is now a museum and is quite fascinating. He was not the only famous son. General Booth, founder of the Salvation Army. was also born in Walsall.

The Museum and Art Gallery is one of the finest in the Black Country, and has a Garman-Ryan collection of art treasures, comprising some three hundred and sixty drawings, paintings and sculptures chiefly of the late 19th and early 20th centuries. Like other towns, Walsall's industry benefited from the canals but they were allowed to fall by the wayside and it is only recently that restoration work has brought them back to regular use and the pleasure of visitors and townsfolk alike. The towpaths are popular as walking routes.

We took a walk along the **Hay Head Nature Trail** at Longwood Lane, two miles from the town centre. The trail follows the final stretch of the old Hay Head branch of the Wyrley and Essington Canal through an area rich in wildlife.

Walsall Leather Centre Museum was is a different experience. You realise how important leather has been to life in Britain. From jugs and bottles, bridles and saddles to forge bellows, musical instruments, luggage and clothing, leather has always been a vital material. We had no idea that today over a hundred and twenty five Walsall companies are still involved in the manufacture of leather products. In this museum you'll see how leather is prepared and worked. Original workshops re-create the conditions, the atmosphere and even the distinctive smell of Walsall's traditional

90

trade. Every day there are live demonstrations, special displays and frequently trade exhibitions are held here as well. It is a vibrant place and what is more there is no charge to go in!

We had such an enlightening and interesting time in the Black Country that we hope we have whetted your appetite as we did our own. There is far more to this area than its label 'The Black Country' conjures up in the minds eye and its easy access via many major road networks make it an ideal area to visit for both daytrippers and the hardened tourist.

St. Peter's Church, Wolverhampton

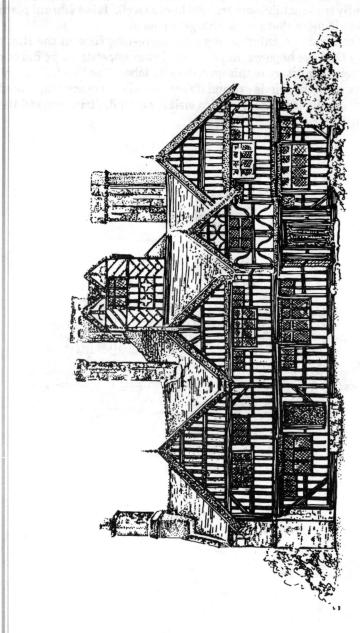

The Oak House, West Bromwich

Birmingham To Coventry

Blakesley Hall

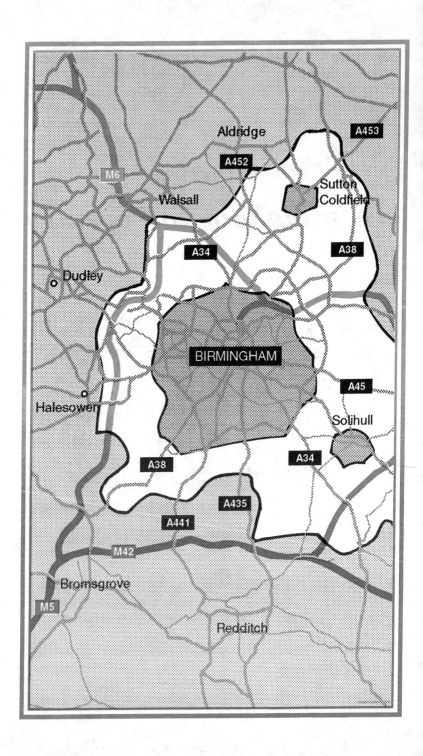

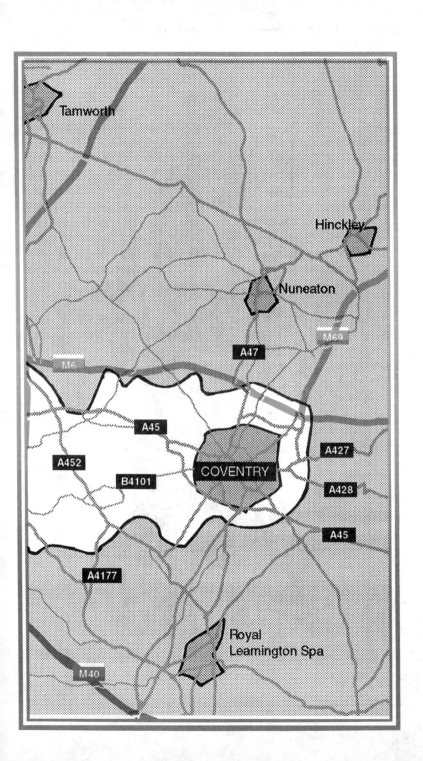

Narrowboats in Gas Street Basin, Birmingham.

CHAPTER FIVE

Birmingham To Coventry

A city a large as **Birmingham** would justify a book in itself but for obvious reasons we can only give you a 'taster' of this interesting city and its surrounding area which as the chapter titles indicates, includes Coventry.

The Domesday book tells us that in the survey of 1086, the hamlet of Birmingham was among the least prosperous manors in the area. As is often the case, geography played a large part in its later rise to prosperity, it was a dry site with a good supply of water and routes converged at Deritendford across the little River Rea. We know from our recently culled knowledge of the Black Country that there was easy access to coal, iron and timber.

Peter de Bermingham obtained rights of trading in a Market Charter granted by Henry ll in 1166 and in 1250 William de Bermingham was given permission to hold a four day fair at Whitsun.

By 1538 there were some fifteen hundred people in two hundred houses, one main street with a number of side streets, grain and livestock markets and mills for tanning. Already, the smiths were selling their knives and all manner of tools all over England. Lorimers and Nailers had joined the growing industry. This growth was helped by the demands of the Parliamentarians during the Civil War for pikes, swords and armour so Birmingham emerged with a strong reputation as a metal centre.

Less than two hundred years later the population had become twenty three thousand and by the 18th century during the Industrial Revolution, Birmingham had become the industrial, commercial and cultural Capital of the Midlands. This was largely due to the industrious

'Brummie' people and not much has changed in that direction today. Many more people of course, more nationalities and more industry make up the core of this humming city.

There have been many famous people over the centuries who have been able to call themselves Brummies. In the 14th century church at **Aston** there is an effigy to Ralph Arden, an early ancestor of Shakespeare, and a black marble and alabaster of the 17th century knight, Sir Edward Devereux plus two unidentified armoured knights. In Birmingham's parish church of St Martins there are memorials to the two Lords of the Manor, the de Berminghams.

Whilst we are talking about churches do take a look at St Alphege in the Square at **Solihull**. This church was a favourite of John Constables who used to come here regularly to draw the enchanting window tracery, foliage and corbels in the 13th century chancel. The beautiful Chantry Chapel of St Alphege was built in 1277 by Sir William de Odingsells, who employed a priest to do nothing but pray for the souls of his parents. The priest lived on the job as it were, his home was the crypt below in which there was a fireplace installed to keep him warm. It must have been a daunting home. The church is open from 8am - 6pm Monday, Wednesday and Thursday and from 7am on Tuesday, Saturday and Sunday.

Just three miles to the north-east of Solihull is a lovely village in the heart of the ancient Forest of Arden. **Hampton -in- Arden** is said to have been the setting for Shakespeares 'As You Like It', something we could well believe as we wandered along the delightful streets taking in the pretty ornamented cottages and reaching our destination, the church of St Mary and St Bartholomew which graces the village. It has a perpendicular tower which until 1643 was topped by a spire. There is a Norman and 13th century nave and a Norman chancel. The chancel which is entered through an arch adorned with crockets and carved heads and has some medieval blue and white tiles in the floor. The icing on the cake here is the fine **Hampton Manor House** which has a most interesting pyramid clock tower.

You will find **Sarehole Mill**, inspiration for J.R.R.Tolkeins 'The Hobbit' and 'Lord of the Rings' about five miles south-east of the city centre and to get there we followed the Stratford Road (A34) to its junction with Cole Bank Road. We turned right into Cole Bank Road and continued over Sarehole Road. The Mill is on the right hand side and we found easy parking in the neighbouring recreation ground. The present buildings are mainly Georgian, having been rebuilt in the 1760's, and were in use, commercially, right up to 1919. The mill then fell into disrepair but was carefully restored to working order in the 1960's.

98

We had the opportunity to see the interior with some of the machinery in action; one of the two waterwheels is regularly operated, subject to the availability of water in the millpond. The process of corn grinding can be followed on all three floors of the mill, whilst in the adjoining building a reconstruction of a blade-grinding workshop showed us how the mill was partially converted to industrial use in the 18th century. The granary contains displays on local agriculture and rural life, illustrated by farm and craft tools, machinery and horse drawn vehicles. The engine house was added in the 1850's and contained a steam engine that supplemented the water power from the River Cole. The original engine was removed many years ago, but one of similar type was installed in the 1970's when the building was restored. A 19th century bakehouse faces the mill building across the yard and reminded us that some of the flour produced at Sarehole was used by the miller.

For classical music lovers the **Birmingham Symphony Orchestra**, recognised as one of the front runners in the music world, often hold concerts in the classical Roman style **Town Hall** built by Joseph Hansom of the hansom cab and an E. Welch. Mendelssohn gave several organ recitals in here.

Sporting facilities are extremely good in Birmingham. The famous Belfry Golf Course is open to the public in Lichfield Road, Wishaw, near Sutton Coldfield attached to the Belfry Hotel which is a marvellous place to stay even if you are not a golfer. There are public squash courts at the Birmingham Squash Rackets Centre in Rotton Park, Edgbaston and at Wyndley Leisure Centre, Clifton Road, Sutton Coldfield to name but two. At Wyndley Leisure Centre there is swimming as well as many other sports activities. To get full details of these facilities do pick up one of the many guides that are available at the Tourist Centres. If you enjoy soccer then in the area Aston Villa, Birmingham City and of course not very far away Wolverhampton Wanderers, West Bromwich Albion and Walsall all provide opportunities to find a good match in the season.

There are no less than six thousand acres of parkland and open space in Birmingham and we are reliably informed that there are six million trees. The highlights are **Cannon Hill Park,** Edgbaston with eighty acres of flowers and ornamental gardens which are a joy to explore and the **Botanical Gardens** and glasshouses with an Aviary and tropical species thrown in for good measure. **The Nature Centre** with all its wildlife was a place of great interest for us and at Edgbaston Reservoir there is every kind of water recreation you could wish for. County and Test Cricket is played at Edgbaston too, of course.

We haven't broached the question of shopping yet - the focus for

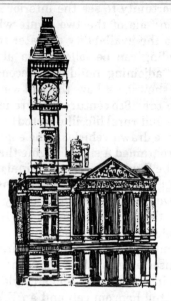

Birmingham Museum & Art Gallery

Botanical Gardens & Glasshouses.

the department stores is New Street, Corporation Street, The Bull Ring Shopping Centre and coming away from these areas are some very attractive Victorian arcades which house the smaller speciality shops. Birmingham traditionally is the centre of jewellery, indeed there is an 18th century church in St Paul's Square, from which it takes its name, known simply as The Jewellers Church. You will find jewellers still abound especially in the Hockley area. Gunsmiths are also to be found here, another craft for which Birmingham is renowned.

Poking around in indoor markets has long been a great pleasure to us and Birmingham is outstanding for this. It is a tradition that stems back to the first Market Charter some eight hundred years ago. You will find them close to St Martins church. The Rag Market is the place to spot a bargain whereas The Bull Ring Open Air Market and the Bull Ring Centre Market Hall deal in anything from food to household goods and the more specialised precious goods. Monday is the day to go looking for antiques in the Rag Market.

One would expect a city as flourishing as Birmingham to be a natural centre for Theatre and it is. **The Hippodrome** was once a music hall but it has become one of the leading opera houses in the country as well as a centre for musicals, international ballet and some wonderful pantomimes. The theatre has been restyled quite recently and without losing the magic of an old theatre it has become one of the best equipped anywhere.

More restyling and rebuilding has gone on to produce the **Birmingham Repertory Theatre** which has become celebrated for major musical shows, comedies, classics, Shakespearian and stage productions being tried out before their London runs. There is a smaller 'Studio Theatre' attached to it which pioneers new ideas in the theatre and encourages new writers. Touring companies bring classics and comedies and sometimes there are premieres of shows booked for the West End at the **Alexandra,** which is another great venue.

Once a year Birmingham has a **Jazz Festival** which attracts big name stars from the world of Jazz and there are never less than forty bands taking part. The weeks activities include over a hundred performances, many of them free, in pubs, clubs and hotels as well as open air concerts and street corner Jazz sessions.

It would be surprising if a city like Birmingham was not able to indulge anyone's interest in Art and Architecture. We found the 17th, 18th and 19th centuries represented in some super displays in the **Museum and Art Gallery** in Chamberlain Square, with one of the best collections outside London, including the world's finest examples of works by the Pre-Raphaelites. The contemporary art of sculpture has one of the best displays you can see. In fact there is costume,

101

silver, textiles and ceramics as well as works of Ethnography from around the world among which is a rare and very large copper Buddha from Sultangani.

In the City Centre your eyes will be drawn to the many murals on all sorts of subjects. In Colmore Circus the mural depicts a Civil War Battle,and another one of the Industrial Revolution. Holloway Circus has an enormous mural of 85'x 14' showing The Horse Fair of 1908.

When we looked up the facts we discovered that in spite of what seems a sparcity of old buildings there are some two thousand listed buildings, Elizabethan, Jacobean, Georgian, Victorian and more that have been beautifully restored. The 1879 built neo - Renaissance **Council House,** magnificently represents the achievements and successes of the city. Another colonnaded building is the **Curzon Street Goods Station** built in 1838 by Phillip Hardwick. Its Ionic portico seems to celebrate the wonder of the railways as they were then regarded then and which doesn't really say much about contemporary attitudes when you compare the building with the modern **New Street Station**.

It has been said that Birmingham has as many canals as Venice. some of the waterways have been neglected but if you ever want to get away from the bustle of the city, the **Gas Street Basin** is as good a place as any to start your escape. If you prefer a quiet stroll or even an energetic ramble, the towpaths are ideal. The Worcester and Birmingham Canal stretches to the south west from here and passes through the Norton Tunnel. You can also follow the path to the Worcester Bar, the centre of the English canal system. The canal heads north to Wolverhampton. The Birmingham and Fazeley Canal has thirteen locks that narrowboats have to pass through. There are many old buildings, locks, factories and cottages to see, as well as the plants and animals that live there. We watched several people just sitting behind an easel and either sketching or painting the very pleasant scenery.

The Cadbury World located in the heart of the famous **Bournville** factory, follows the story of chocolate, taking you through tropical rain forests to 16th century Spain and onto Georgian London before arriving at the beginning of the Cadbury story in Victorian Birmingham. When we enquired about it we were told that if we wanted to find out about the Milk Tray hero who is always taking incredible risks to please his love, or how Cream Eggs were made, then all the answers will be revealed at Cadbury World. Even the chance to sample the real thing from their own production line! Cadbury World is on the outskirts of Birmingham, close to the M5 and M42 and it is just as easy to get to by rail or bus. It is open every day except Christmas Day. If you want more details about visits then ring 021-433-4334.

Blakesley Hall is about five miles from the city centre. You follow the Coventry road (A45) to the Swan roundabout at South Yardley and then take the A4040 Church Road northwards into Stoney Lane to Blakesley Road. Turn left into Blakesley Road and the Hall is on the right hand side. Birmingham Museum and Art Gallery own Blakesley Hall which is Birmingham's finest Elizabethan building. Built in 1590, the hall is an extremely attractive timber-framed farmhouse which has been carefully restored. Its rich decorative framing and jettied first and second floors reflect the wealth of its Elizabethan owner and builder, Richard Smallbroke, one of the leading merchants of the 16th century. A diminutive Long Gallery which is rare survives whilst in his bedroom the original wall paintings were uncovered in 1950. A more recent discovery is the original lavatory shaft beside the hall chimney!

You are able to imagine how the family lived there three hundred years ago. Some twelve of the rooms are furnished as they were in 1684 when an inventory of the house's contents was drawn up.

One special attraction is 'The Bailiff's Pots' from Temple Balsall, which represents probably the most important collection of early country pottery ever found. Excavated at Temple Balsall Old Hall, near Knowle, in 1981, the pots represent the discarded contents of the bailiff's household pottery and glassware, deposited in the cellar when his family moved house in 1741.

Having got to Blakesley Hall the next step was to explore the delightful **Old Yardley Village**, one of the city's outstanding conservation areas. It is within walking distance of Blakesley Hall and is truly remarkable with its medieval church and Trust School. We particularly liked the pretty Georgian cottages.

Aston Hall, just three miles from the centre of Birmingham, was one of the last great Jacobean country houses to be built in England. Like Hatfield House and Blickling Hall, it has a highly intricate plan and a dramatic skyline of turrets, gables and chimneys. It is also administered by Birmingham Museums and Art Gallery who have done much to make it such a memorable place to visit. The house was built between 1618 and 1635 by Sir Thomas Holte and remained the seat of the Holte family until it was sold in 1817. King Charles 1 came to Aston Hall in 1642 at the beginning of the Civil War, and it was later besieged and sacked by Parliamentarian soldiers. Much Jacobean decorative work of high quality, still survives, especially the moulded plasterwork. The house has the most wonderful staircase and long gallery.

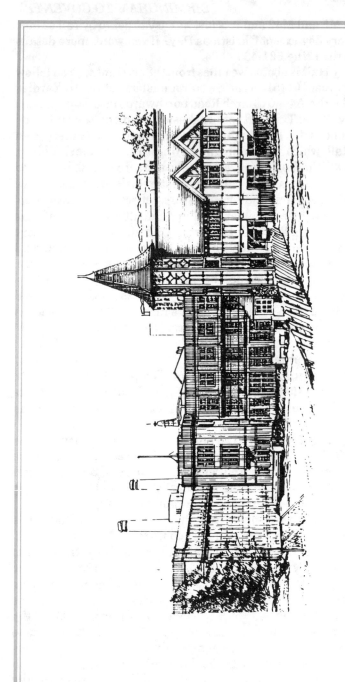

Cadbury's Bourneville.

Something totally different was our visit to **The National Motorcycle Museum** at **Bickenhill** which is opposite the National Exhibition Centre. It is a breathtaking collection of British motorcycles displayed in this purpose built complex. The purpose was to ensure that the sixty years of British motorcycle design and construction should not be lost to future generations. There are over seven hundred machines to see, each of which has been painstakingly restored to its original specification. Alongside the machines are a wealth of historic documentation and photographs. These certainly helped us to get the flavour of historic motorcycling. We got a great deal of fun out of this visit, not least from some of the odd names the motorcycles were given, like 'Slippery Sam', the winner of five production TT's on the Isle of Man. The complex has also been designed to provide seminar and conference facilities with the versatility to meet all types of business needs. Along with these facilities is some pretty high standard catering, you can dine sumptuously or merely have a snack.

Just while we are dealing with various forms of transport we thought we would tell you about the entertaining time we had at **The Railway Museum** at **Tyseley.** You step back in time here to an era of fire-breathing steam locomotives, tiny tank engines, opulent Royal carriages and much more besides. On steam days, visitors can actually ride behind a steam engine. A special gallery allowed us to see the workshops where restoration and repair projects are taking place all the time. You really feel you are back in the old days and watching a traditional locomotive works. If you want further details write to the Museum at 670 Warwick Road, Tyseley, Birmingham, B11 2HL.

Going further south on the A41, **Solihull** is worth visiting. It began to grow in importance during the 1930's having been until then, a sparsely populated part of the country, today it is a Metropolitan Borough. Somehow the Industrial Revolution passed it by. Its motto 'Urbs in Rure' - Town in Country - is well deserved. The cottages and houses built in medieval times were characteristically attractive and blended well with the green vegetation which covers a large part of the region. As the number of buildings grew it still remained orderly and today the 17th and 18th century houses clearly demonstrate the good planning which has continued today.

Many historic buildings have been carefully restored. Elizabethan **Grimshaw Hall** in **Knowle** is a fine example. **Chester House** is not far away and originally built in the mid-14th century it has been successfully refurbished and converted into a library offering a practical service to today's community. Another fine old house **Baddesley Clinton,** has been highly recommended for its excellent home-cooked food. This sounds as though it is just a good

Blakesley Hall.

restaurant but that is not the case. It is another of the hidden gems of the West Midlands. This romantic, medieval moated manor house is little changed since the 17th century. Set against the backdrop of the Forest of Arden, Baddesley has strong Catholic connections, shown in the house with a tiny chapel and secret priests' holes. Modern needs have not been neglected we took great pleasure in visiting the super ice rink which is the second largest in the country.

Heading north you'll find by the M42 and A45,**The National Exhibition Centre**, now world famous so we do not intend to write about it but, what we would like to say is that Birmingham wants you to enjoy a visit to the full and to do so they have placed The Birmingham Convention and Visitor Bureau, which has a ticket shop and tourist information, right in the city centre and another one at the National Exhibition Centre. You will find, as we did, that the staff are friendly, helpful and knowledgeable. They will answer any questions and encourage you to visit the many wonderful places in the Big Heart of England. Stratford-upon-Avon, the Severn Valley, Warwick Castle and the Cotswold Hills are all within easy reach of the city. The Bureau will also book theatre and concert tickets for you and make hotel reservations.

Coventry is only thirty minutes away from Birmingham but it is a different world. Although on the fringe of the West Midlands conurbation, it is surrounded by some of the finest scenery and heritage in the country. It claims amongst many of its famous residents, George Eliot, who attended boarding school in Warwick Row and lived with her father between 1841 - 49 in Floeshill Road; more recently the controversial poet Philip Larkin was born in the city in 1922. Coventry is almost in the centre of England and lies at the heart of the national motorway network and on the main Inter-City rail route from the Midlands to London. It is only minutes away from **Birmingham International Airport** and also possesses its own local airport which caters for executive jet traffic. A busy place you may well say, this is true, but in amongst all the commerce are places and things of great beauty.

Standing in the ruins of the old 14th century **Coventry Cathedral**, destroyed by fire in the savage bombing of the city in World War II, can be a strange and moving experience. The altar is made of broken stones gathered from the night of horror on the 15th November 1940. It is surmounted by a cross of charred roof beams and a cross of medieval nails, behind which are inscribed the words from Calvary 'Father Forgive'.

The new Cathedral stands by its side and together they symbolise 'sacrifice and resurrection'. It is not only in the two cathedrals that Coventry has shown its indomitable spirit. It is hard to imagine that

National Motor Cycle Museum, Nr Birmingham

Museum of British Road Transport, Coventry

in the space of one night in November 1940 the city centre was gutted, forty six thousand homes severely damaged and nearly seventy five per cent of the industrial area was almost destroyed. The Cathedral Visitor Centre situated in the Undercroft is where you can see and hear 'The Spirit of Coventry', which tells the story of the historical events which took place in Coventry, including The Blitz and its aftermath and the cathedral's role in reconciliation world wide through the Community of the Cross of Nails. The Treasury in St Michael's Hall has many important exhibits and the Walkway of Holograms.

Whereas the magnificent Gothic tower of the old cathedral dominates, standing over three hundred feet, the new cathedral is dominated by Graham Sutherland's tapestry of Christ in Glory and John Piper's magnificent Bapistry window which beams a kaleidoscope of colours onto the nave as the sun passes over. Whatever one may think of the new, it works. The small chapels each have a dedicated purpose. The Chapel of Unity is where groups of different faiths meet, the Chapel of Gethsemane is an area for private prayer. The Chapel of Christ the Servant has become the Industrial Chapel.

The city's most famous legend tells of the story of **Lady Godiva** who rode the streets naked to reduce taxation on the 11th century town dwellers. A bronze statue in Broadgate has been erected to her memory. There are authorities however, who say that the famous ride never took place or that perhaps, she rode minus her jewels and was in that sense naked. Leofric should instead be praised, for it is he who started commerce and industry in Coventry as early as 1043, when he chose the small Saxon township as the site for a Benedictine monastery. He gave the monks land on which to raise sheep, laying the basis for the wool trade which made Coventry prosperous for over five hundred years. The story has it though, that this hard hearted man taxed the people too heavily and Godiva begged him to lessen the burden. She apparently took the precaution of sending her messengers to ask everyone to stay indoors behind closed shutters before she rode forth. Peeping Tom disregarded the request and was struck blind - or so legend would have you believe. The Earl, duly chastened, relented, the taxes were cut and no doubt Leofric and Godiva were reconciled. If you look at the clock in the arch over Hertford Street you will see the figures of Godiva and Tom re-enacting the legend hourly.

There are still many old buildings in this very new city; **Bond's Hospital** and **Ford's Hospital** are delightful half-timbered Tudor almshouses, still very much in use, while Bayley Lane and Hay Lane are places of peace and tranquillity reminding us of the illustrious past. A medieval cul-de-sac has been created in Spon Street, some

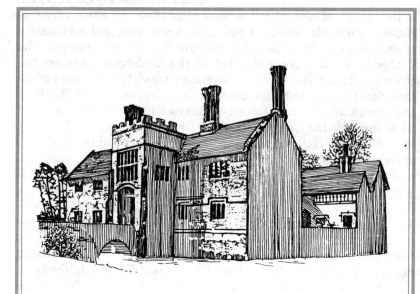

Baddesley Clinton.

Coventry Cathedral

of the buildings have been re-sited from other parts of the city. Medieval shops, taverns and dwellings abound in this living heritage of Coventry.

Across in New Union Street you'll find **Cheylesmore Manor House,** a half timbered building that was once owned by the Black Prince. Close by at Whitefriars Gate, the **Toy Museum,** has a collection of toys dating from the mid 18th century. Nearby on London Road stands **Whitefriars,** a renovated Carmelite friary dating from the 1342. Exhibitions of art, theatre and concerts are put on in this attractive building. Back in towards the centre and close to the cathedral is the **Herbert Art Gallery and Museum,** in Jordan Well. The ground floor has natural history displays, social history,which includes the story of Coventry and reconstructed rooms showing weaving or other skills that became associated with the city. Upstairs the galleries have 18th century furniture,silver and art that includes a collection of Graham Sutherlands sketches for the tapestry in the cathedral.

In Bayley Lane is **St Mary's Guildhall** where Kings and Queens have been entertained and Mayors appointed to their office since the 14th century. The medieval Guildhall contains a splendour of old glass, a wealth of carving and a delightful minstrels' gallery with the additional bonus of a unique tapestry. This is one of England's finest guildhalls dating back to 1342. Here we saw the Arras tapestry, the breathtaking Great North Window, the oak ceiling and many suits of medieval armour. It really is a stunning place and open daily from Easter to October with guided tours available.

Over the next two hundred years, clockmaking and silk weaving became Coventry's main industries but in the 19th century the French started exporting silks and the Swiss, clocks, which brought about a rapid slump. Faced with unemployment many families emigrated to America leaving behind those who were not adventurous enough or who had the wit to see that other industries could make them prosper once again.

Cycle making and engineering started the new wave of prosperity and by 1896 Daimler and Humber had opened the city's first car factories. It was not long before they were joined by other companies and Coventry became a magnet for labour from all over Britain. It was the city's skills in engineering that brought it to the attention of the German bombers during World War 11. Today the city is one of the most up to date of our industrial cities and now boasts the fastest growing Science Park in the U.K., based at Warwick University and potentially the finest Business Park in the country.

The Museum of British Road Transport is in Hales Street just a few minutes walk from the Cathedral and Shopping Precinct. It is

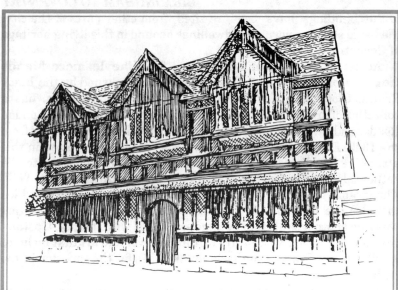

Fords Hospital. Coventry.

Coombe Abbey.

one of the finest in the country with a collection of transport which portrays the enormous contribution made by Coventry to the transport industry. There are more than four hundred exhibits on show including bicycles, motor cycles, commercial vehicles and numerous makes of cars.

'Memory Lanes' is an exhibition concept which recreates the atmosphere of the formative years of motoring history. The 'Street Scene' presentation brings together the pioneering 'horseless carriages', the elegant Edwardians and those cars from the Golden Age of Motoring, the 1920's. Just by passing through doors and archways we found the whole development of the motor car unfolded before us.

The museum's collection of cycles now numbers over two hundred machines and includes all of the important machines from the original Hobby Horses right through to the B.M.X. of today. We would think it is the finest technical collection of cycles in Western Europe, the newly created display includes photographs, costume and period artefacts presenting the atmosphere of cycling as it has progressed through the ages.

We thought the exhibition of 'Royalty on the Road' was super. Queen Mary's 1935 Limousine and the King George V1 1947 State Landaulette form the centre-pieces of a special exhibition which depicts the Royal family's contribution to the British motor car industry. The extensive photographic gallery includes copies of pictures from the Royal Archives, all in situations connected with road transport. The museum also contains Monty's Humber Car which he used when entering Berlin and an interesting display of the Coventry Blitz.

Coventry has places for the theatre lovers; **The Belgrade Theatre** (0203 225834), in Corporation Street was the first Civic theatre opened after the war and has a busy programme of plays and concerts to meet the needs of theatre lovers. Alternatively, the **University Arts Theatre** (0203 524524), four miles out of town in the University of Warwick has constantly changing attractions that also includes a film theatre. Tourist Information will, naturally, have details of the programmes on offer during your visit.

If you enjoy the fun of a medieval banquet or have never experienced one then do go to **Coombe Abbey** which stands in magnificent grounds which are part of a country park landscaped by Capability Brown. It is a wonderfully romantic spot. Only a few parts of the original monastery remain but its history goes back to 1150 when the land was given to the Cistercian Monks by Roger de Mowbray. Over the years the Abbey has been associated with the Wars of the Roses, Lady Jane Grey, the Gunpowder Plot and the

English Civil War. The monastery was dissolved in 1539 and was eventually sold to the Craven family who owned it until 1922.

So it is in this historic setting that the Baron and Baroness invite you to join them in the romantic candlelit splendour of the ancient Abbey. You will be welcomed and attended by the gracious and talented ladies of the Court in their colourful medieval gowns, and served with Lindisfarne mead, wine and succulent dishes. Once replete you will then be regaled with the food of love - music, traditional medieval entertainment is part of the evening too, presented by accomplished performers. To take part just ring Coventry (0203) 452406. To get there is not difficult either. The entrance to Coombe Abbey is through Coombe Country Park on the A427 Coventry to Lutterworth road or from the M6 (Exit 2) take the A46 Coventry road and turn on to the A4082 (signposted Coombe Abbey).

If you want to take a trip to Coombe Park in the daytime you will find it is delightful with three hundred acres of formal gardens, woodland nature trails, angling and paddle-boating for the children. There is also Birdland with its innumerable highly coloured birds of all sorts and sizes.

Coventry provided moments of sheer delight which was contrary to what we had expected. Being city dwellers sometimes makes you blind to the beauty and attraction of other large urban areas. Besides all that, Coventry and Birmingham are excellent bases for the very many wonderful places around them, more of which we shall reveal in the forthcoming chapters.

CHAPTER SIX

Shakespeare Country

Anne Hathaway's Cottage

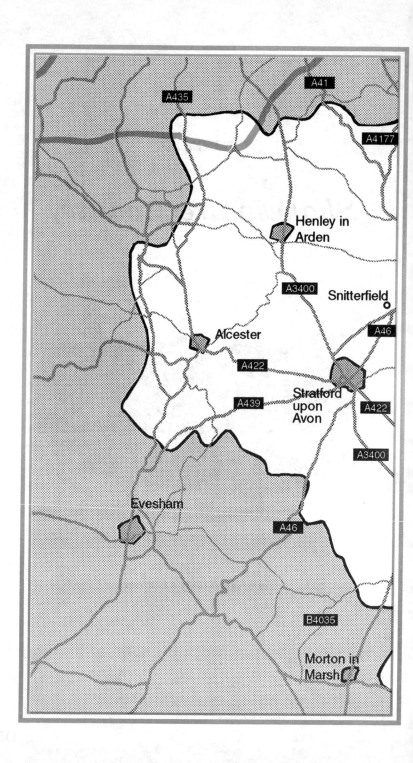

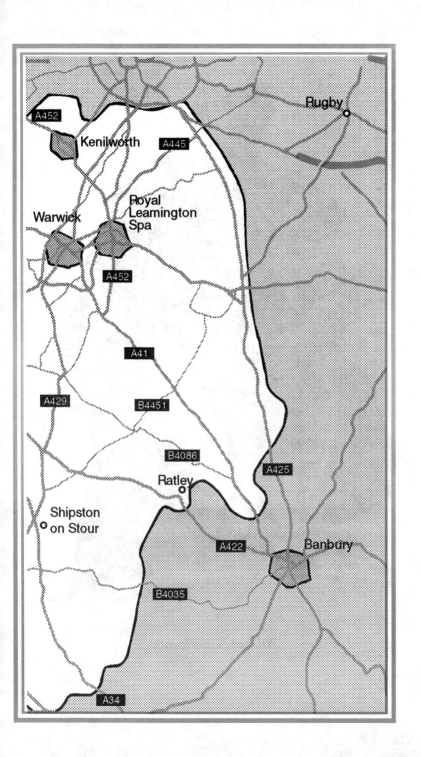

William Shakespeare.

CHAPTER SIX

Shakespeare Country.

When you think of England, and the very best of England, you might well be thinking about leafy Warwickshire, Shakespeare's country. The areas attractions draws an influx of tourists from all over the world. The county has much to offer with delightful contrasts from the rich vein of Tudor history at the heart of Warwickshire to **Royal Leamington Spa,** an elegant 18th century Regency town with wide tree-lined streets, imposing terraces and beautiful gardens. To the North, **Nuneaton** offers fascinating historical associations with George Eliot, one of England's greatest novelists. **Rugby** home of the famous public school which introduced the game Rugby is also close-by. As if this were not enough, there is a great Palladian stately home at **Ragley,** the romantic ruins of **Kenilworth Castle, Warwick Castle** and a wealth of beautiful National Trust properties. Set in the geographical Heart of England there is easy access by the motorway network. Once off the high speed roads, experience a change of pace and explore the timeless qualities of the real England.

The Warwickshire heritage spans many generations and the Bronze Age King Stone standing on the high ground above Long Compton is one of the few surviving features of pre-history in the county, but when we come to Roman times remains are more plentiful. The final battle between the Roman Army and British troops led by Queen Boadicea in AD 60 took place at **Mancetter** and there are other Roman settlements at **Alcester, Chesterton** and **Tiddington**. There is little on these sites for visitors to see but at **Baginton,** a substantial part of the first century AD fort, known as **The Lunt** has been dramatically reconstructed. The Norman Conquest saw the establishment of Warwick Castle as a royal stronghold. In order to keep the local population under control, a number of smaller castles were also erected and a fine example can still be seen at **Brinklow.** The county has seen the hatching and subsequent discovery of the

Gunpowder Plot of 1605 and the first major battle of the Civil War was at **Edgehill** in 1645.

After the Commonwealth, when Oliver Cromwell ruled England as Lord Protector, there was a period of relative prosperity. Country houses such as **Ragley, Farnborough, Upton** and **Compton Verney** were built or extended, symbols of good taste, power and wealth. The 18th century saw the re-design of country estates, including Capability Brown's work at Warwick Castle, Charlecote, Ragley and elsewhere. At the close of the century Leamington Priors began to develop as a spa. At the other end of the social scale, Joseph Arch was born in 1826 at **Barford**. A pioneer of the farm workers union movement and later an MP, the Joseph Arch Inn at Barford must be one of the few pubs in England to be named after a trade union leader.

Even people living in Warwickshire may not be aware of the history they drive over; the hump back bridge can hide an altogether different world when seen from below. Waterways form an important and extensive part of the two thousand miles of Britains inland network. The Oxford and Grand Union Canals pass through the county as do restored lengths of the Stratford canal and the upper Avon.

We decided to start our tour of Warwickshire at the most obvious place, namely **Stratford-upon-Avon.** We found it difficult to know where to begin when attempting to describe all the many attractions on offer and although this is Britain's biggest tourist centre after London, they arrive because of one man, **William Shakespeare**. He was born here, found fame in London and retired here to die in 1616, some 500,000 visit Shakespeares birthplace alone. There has been interest in him ever since, and this ancient, prosperous town has been a backcloth to his genius and his life.

A short walk along Meer Street brought us to the very centre of the Shakespeare cult - his **Birthplace** in Henley Street. The two timber framed buildings consist a museum in the east half and the west half is furnished in the style of a 16th century home.

On High Street you'll find **Harvard House**, dating from 1596, this is where John Harvard's mother, Katherine Rogers, spent her childhood. The building was restored and presented to Harvard University in 1909. Further along on Chapel Street stands, New Place and **Nash's House.** This half-timbered building was inherited by Shakespeare's granddaughter, Elizabeth Hall, from her first husband, Thomas Nash. It now contains a museum of local history. By it you'll find the gardens on the foundations of New Place, the house that Shakespeare bought and retired to in 1611. The house was torn down by Reverend Francis Gatrell in 1759 after a dispute over rates with the Corporation. On the corner opposite is the **Guild Chapel** and

120

Harvard House.

Nash House & New Place Museum

beyond is the **Grammar School** where it is believed that Shakespeare was educated.

In fact you will not regret a visit to any of the fascinating old buildings in Stratford. The old market site in Rother Street has a history dating from 1196, when a weekly market was granted by King John. In the square is an ornate fountain-cum-clock tower, a gift from one G.W. Childs from Philadelphia in the jubilee year of Queen Victoria. It was unveiled by the famous actor Henry Irving who, when knighted in 1895, became the first ever "Sir of the Stage".

An excellent and luxurious base from which to explore the mysteries and delights of the surrounds is the **Melita Hotel,** situated close to the centre of town. The impressive Victorian house was built in 1888 and is an RAC acclaimed Private Hotel. The walled garden is lovingly tended and has any awards over the years. Hanging baskets and miniature fir trees adorn the front of the hotel, along with the royal blue canopies over the entrance and windows.

Melita Hotel.   Stratford upon Avon.

All attractively furnished rooms have tea and coffee making facilities, TV and telephone and are ensuite. The breakfast menu is extensive and caters for all tastes and although no evenings meals are available the Melita is licensed with a residents only bar to relax in and enjoy the warm welcome of their hosts.

Stratford has become the mecca of the theatre lover and they flock to enjoy an evening at one of the three theatres. On the walls of a pub called "The Dirty Duck" is a gallery of glossy signed photographs of familiar faces. These are of some of the actors and actresses who have appeared at the Royal Shakespeare Theatre just across the road, and popped in for a drink there. This attractive pub with its famous customers sums up Stratford, it manages to go about its busy life with thousands of visitors arriving from all over the world each year. The first celebration was organised by the actor David Garrick (of Garrick Theatre fame) one hundred and fifty years after his death, and people have been celebrating ever since. When the first Shakespeare theatre was burned down, George Bernard Shaw sent a one word telegram - Congratulations! Apparently the building was very ugly, but there are few such buildings in Stratford. Even the Marks and Spencers has the facade of a coaching inn with colonnaded entrances that once belonged to the Washington Irving Hotel.

The Royal Shakespeare Company has a marvellous reputation both in the UK and abroad. To see Shakespeare performed at the Royal Shakespeare Theatre is quite possibly every theatre lovers dream. Perhaps Stratford has something just little more special in atmosphere than say ,the Barbican in London. However, wherever you see the RSC perform you are certain of witnessing performances of a high standard.

The company has operated in its present manner since 1961, but the history of Stratford and theatres goes beyond that. The first permanent theatre was built as a result of local brewer, Charles Edward Flower, who gave a two acre site on which to build a theatre in Shakespeares birthplace in 1875 and then launched an appeal for funds.

This theatre opened in 1879 with a performance of ' Much Ado about Nothing'. starring Ellen Terry and Beerbohm Tree. The season was limited to one week as part of the summer festival. It was so successful that under the direction of F.R. Benson it grew to spring and summer seasons and toured Britain in between. In 1925,because of the excellence of the performances and direction, the company was granted a Royal Charter. Sadly, a year later the theatre perished in a fire. The company, not deterred, continued by giving performances in cinemas whilst a worldwide campaign was launched to build a new theatre, which was opened on April 23rd, 1932, traditionally thought of as the Bards birthday.

A theatre tour gives you the opportunity to discover what's goes on behind the curtains. The itinerary for the tours vary according to rehearsal schedules and the incidence of technical work on stage but they are great value and usually include the RSC collection as well as both the Royal Shakespeare and Swan Theatre. Weekdays the tour times are 1.30pm and 5.30pm excluding matinee days and on Sundays at 12.30pm. 2.15pm, 3.15pm, and 4.15pm with just a slight variation from November to March when first tours start at 11.30am. The tours takes around 45 minutes. You can book by calling 0789 296655 or writing to the RSC.

The RSC collection has over a thousand items on view. The costumes, props, pictures and sound recording which illustrate changes

Guild Chapel.

Anne Hathaway's Cottage

in staging from medieval times to the present and compares past productions with the current season's plays. You can spend fascinating time browsing, reading reviews and in the souvenir shop.

Disabled people have also been included in the lay out with front row seats for the disabled and those in wheelchairs. There is also an audio frequency induction loop system in the theatres for the hard of hearing. Special parking spots are reserved for disabled drivers but it is advisable to inform the Booking Office as early as possible about your intended visit. For more information you can join the Company's mailing list by writing or phone for more information on 0789 295623.

Royal Shakespeare Company.   Stratford upon Avon.

One of the best places to stay must be **The Stratford House Hotel,** which also has **Shepherds Restaurant.** It has the virtue of only being 100 yards away from the Royal Shakespeare Theatre; and as would expect in such a position, the hotel is very attractive both inside and out. There are 10 guest rooms, furnished with a tasteful mixture of antiques and modern furniture, and all ensuite, with TV and telephone.

Once upon a time the Stratford was owned by a Stonemason, Mr. Shepherd, who decorated the pathways and walls and you can see his work in the courtyard garden which is ablaze with colour during the summer months. The flowering shrubs, hanging baskets and water feature make the courtyard a delightful place to sit on warm summer evenings.

The Stratford has acquired many recommendations, Egon Ronay, AA, Tourist Board 4 Crowns and mention in American and French guides. In 1981 the hotel was voted one of the best six in Europe. The additional pleasure here is the food in Shepherds Restaurant. It is a stylish, modern restaurant with a charming conservatory that leads into a walled garden. You can have your meal here if you wish or dine in the restaurant. The menu changes regularly and you can rest assured that whatever the choice,it will be extremely palatable and made from freshest of produce.

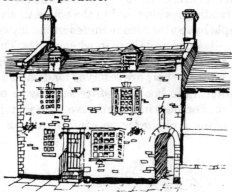

Stratford House Hotel & Shepherds Restaurant. Stratford ..

Holy Trinity Church, an inspiration for many poets because of its beautiful setting beside the Avon, is where Shakespeare is buried. Dating partly from the 13th century it is approached down an avenue of limes and the north door has a sanctuary knocker that, in the past,allowed any fugitive who reached it, thirty seven days grace. Anne Hathaway, their daughter Susanna and her husband are also buried here. The tomb of the great man himself carries a warning inscription:

> *Good friend for Jesus sake, forbeare*
> To digg the dust enclosed heare;
> Blese be ye man yt spares these stones
> *And curst be he yt moves my bones.*

Bancroft Gardens near to the fourteen arch Clopton Bridge is but a short walk from the centre of Stratford. This delightful leisure area contains the great Shakespeare Memorial which was designed by Lord Ronald Gower and built in Paris. The work took twelve years to complete and was finally presented to.the town in 1888.

Only a few yards away is a preserved industrial tram, employed on the horse-drawn tramway connecting wharfs in Stratford with those in Shipston-on-Stour and Moreton-in-the-Marsh in Gloucestershire. The canal was completed in 1816 but fell into disuse with the advance of the railways.

In Bishopton Lane, you'll find a very elegant and comfortable Victorian house overlooking the canal called, **Victoria Spa Lodge.** This attractive house, owned by friendly hosts Paul and Dreen Tozer, was built in 1837 as a spa; later the hotel and pump rooms were later divided into three separate residences.

Victoria Spa Lodge.   Stratford upon Avon.

There are seven beautifully decorated and comfortable bedrooms, mostly ensuite. They all have drink making facilities and television. Breakfast is sumptuous meal with choices which include a continental breakfast. The essence of Victoria Spa lodge is service and comfort in amiable surroundings. With the surrounding attractions constantly drawing thousands of visitors all the time, you'll find the Lodge open and a comfortable place to stay whatever the time of year you decide to visit.

On Birmingham Road, Stratford upon Avon, there is one of those pleasant bungalows that is in fact a nursery. **Bishopton Hill Nursery,** is run by Muriel Hardwicke and has two comfortable ensuite bedrooms to let. Muriel provides a substantial breakfast but she is happy to provide an evening meal if that is what you want. Bishopton Hill is open all year round and Mrs Hardwicke accepts mid week bookings but unfortunately dogs aren't permitted with guests.

Bishopton Hill Nursery.   Stratford upon Avon.

About a mile from Stratford in the village of **Shottery**, the birthplace of Shakespeare's wife and you'll find the Elizabethan farmhouse, **Anne Hathaway's Cottage**. Incidentally Anne and William were married in 1582. We found it a delightful, though a popular spot and is everyone's imagined perfect thatched cottage. Hathaways have lived here since the 15th century until less than seventy years ago when the Shakespeare Trust decided it was time to allow public access.

The other notable house connected with the poet is his mother, **Mary Arden's House** in **Wilmcote,** about three miles from Stratford. This Tudor farmhouse is most impressive, but this maybe because it is slightly off the beaten track and doesn't attract the thousands of visitors which flock to some of the other attractions. There are guided tours available and a museum of farming and rural life. Notice particularly the bread oven doors, made of bog oak, which never burn and are only seen very rarely now in England. Perhaps, best of all though is the dovecote. Robert Arden, being lord of the manor, was the only man in the village allowed to have one. It has over six hundred pigeon holes and at nesting time would house about three thousand birds.

Wilmcote itself is a very pretty village and in the 19th century fifty five per cent of the population worked at the local quarries producing high quality floor stone and marble, some of which was used at the Palace of Westminster. It is one of the few small villages left to retain its Victorian Gothic railway station. Alongside the railway runs the Stratford Canal. After years of neglect it has been taken over by the British Waterways and now carries many holiday boats on their way to join the Avon. You'll also found the parish church of St. Andrew in Wilmcote. It is an almost unique Gothic revival church built in 1841 to a design by William Butterfield.

Across the A3400 in the village of **Snitterfield**, you'll find some self catering accommodation off the beaten track at **Luscombe Farm Cottage.** Recently modernised, the red brick cottage is quite luxurious. Three bedrooms, with bed linen provided, accommodate two in each, the master bedroom is ensuite whilst downstairs the oaked beamed lounge is comfortably furnished. The kitchen has all requirements including a dishwasher whilst a second ground floor bathroom eases the demands of a full house. Double glazed and centrally heated, the cost of which is included in the rent, combine to make this a superb base for touring central England.

Please Don't Forget...

To tell people that you read about them in

The Hidden Places

From Stratford we decided to head towards **Alcester**, an ancient Roman town. On the way we stopped in **Exhall**, recorded in the Domesday Book but its history probably goes back to Roman times as

Roman coins have been found in a garden in the village. The architecture is varied, reflecting the history and development from Elizabethan to modern times. There are some interesting black and white half-timbered buildings and a farmhouse dating back to the 16th century. Most of the houses stand on steep banks on each side of the road and this adds much to the picturesque quality of the village. The parish church of St. Giles is fairly unremarkable, having been heavily restored in Victorian times, but it has a fine Norman door and the views from the churchyard are beautiful.

Standing in the middle of Exhall are **Glebe Farm Holiday Cottages** a working farm, parts of which date back to Tudor times. For several centuries it was home of the local clergymen who preached in the tiny church next door and cultivated the land.

William Shakespeare is alleged to have referred in a poem to 'dodging Exhall' and the tag has remained ever since. Quite what he thought Exhall was dodging has never been established, but it is true to say that if you wish to dodge the hustle and bustle of the 20th century you could do no better than to visit Glebe Farm. Peace and quiet you will have in plenty, although it is only a ten minute drive to Stratford and twenty minutes to the National Exhibition Centre. Broadway in the Cotswolds is not much further, so you'll realise soon what lovely country you are in.

Glebe Farm Cottages.   *Exhall.*

Glebe Farm Holiday Cottages, originally farm building are now compact, comfortable, single story cottages surrounding the old collection yard close to the farm. Inside, all are furnished to a good standard with fitted kitchens, pine furnishing, bathrooms with shower, bed linen and towels. Ragnill and the thatched Long Blechmoor cottages sleep three, Lower Sandhill four whilst Mill Meer is suitable for the disabled with a ramped entry and sleeps three.

Patios are laid out pleasantly and there are a number of footpaths from which you can enjoy this lovely countryside. Pets are welcome and there is a pay phone, shared laundry and small shop to make you stay as pleasant as possible.

Whilst in the Alcester area we suggest a visit to **Ragley Hall**, a 17th century house with a magnificent great hall by James Gibbs. This is one of England's great Palladian country houses. The perfect symmetry of its architecture remains unchanged except for the massive portico added in 1780. The present owner, the eighth Marquis of Hertford inherited Ragley in 1940 when he was only nine. During the second world war the house was used as a hospital, and thereafter became almost completely derelict. In 1956 the Marquis married and he and his new wife set about making the Hall their home. All the main rooms have been redecorated in colours similar to the original ones and the process of restoring and improving seems to be forever ongoing.

The main formal garden, to the west of the hall, descends in a series of wide terraces, now entirely occupied by roses. The rest of the garden, covering twenty four acres, consists of shrubs and trees interspersed with spacious lawns providing vistas across the four hundred acre park. The lake, created in 1625, is now used for fishing, sailing, swimming and water skiing and the cricket pitch is in regular use. There is also a country trail of about two miles through the park and the woods ending at the very popular Adventure Playground.

The Golden Cross.   Ardens Grafton.

The Golden Cross, on Wixford Road, **Ardens Grafton** is somewhat difficult to find but if you take the B439 out of Bidford -on-Avon turning left at Cranhill and then the left fork you'll arrive at the pub. This 200 year old place is well worth seeking out standing on high ground with splendid views over towards the Malvern Hills and Worcestershire. Fine ales and good food on the menu at reasonable prices are available whilst a wonderful collection of antique dolls,

130

belonging to landlady Pat Vardy Smith, are on permanent display. Numbering over 350 and dating from 1845 the collection is for your enjoyment and curiosity whilst enjoying the hospitality at the Golden Cross.

Cutting across country we came to **Welford -on- Avon,** an attractive half timbered village with some outstanding houses and a maypole standing on the village green. Further on we came to the straddling village of **Long Marston.** Charles II stayed at a house here after his flight from the Battle of Worcester. The 14th century church has a half timbered turret and porch. Across the B4632 and you'll pass **Meon Hill,** where are Iron Age Fort stood dominating the valley. Further along the road you'll come to **Ilmington,** at the foot of the Ilmington Downs; the north eastern Cotswolds. This village is eye catching with its old houses and church which inside has oak furnishings by Robert Thompson from Yorkshire which you pass through a 16th Norman arch to view. This is truly a 'hidden place', and certainly one of the most picturesque one could ever wish to find. Lying in the valley between the Campden and Foxcote hills, it is surrounded by green fields and Cotswold countryside. We saw many fine old stone cottages with roses around the doors, and gardens full of colour .

Ilmington, its name means "the elm grown hill", has only six hundred inhabitants. It was made famous on Christmas Day 1934, when the first radio broadcast by George V was introduced by Walton Handy, the village shepherd and relayed to the world from **Ilmington Manor,** a fine Elizabethan house once owned by the De Montfort family. The remains of a tramway, once the main form of transport to the village, can still be seen. The nearby Ilmington Downs are at 850 feet, the highest point in the county and command fine views of the surrounding country.

The Bird in Hand.   Newbould -on- Stour.

Back on the A34 you'll find **Newbold-on-Stour,** and in the heart

131

Ragley Hall, Nr Alcester

of the village a friendly pub, **The Bird in Hand,** run by Katie and Peter Fenwick. Dating back to the mid 19th century, it is a traditional pub serving fine ales. The main bar is as you might expect in a village pub, with skittles, dominoes, darts but the lounge is quieter and here you can choose, if you wish, from daily blackboard specials or a set menu with a wide range of choices. Childrens meals are also available.

Further south along the A34 in the direction of **Shipston -on- Stour** stands **Honington Hall,** an interesting building reflecting the tastes of the late 17th and 18th century. There is limited opening for the house but you might be pleasantly surprised should you visit this delightful house.

The Black Horse Inn.   Shipston -on- Stour.

You'll find the historically interesting, **The Black Horse Inn** in Station Road, Shipston -on- Stour. It dates back eleven hundred years, originally a row of cottages for sheep farmers. Ale was brewed illegally on the premises until a full licence was granted in 1540. Earlier this century the inn was known for its home brewed wine. Inside is fascinating with pieces of Cromwellian armour, horse brasses, collars and traces decorating the walls whilst copper glints by the inglenook fire. The pub is run in a traditional manner, the beer is well kept and the food simple, but well cooked, is very palatable to both mouth and pocket. The beer large garden and a room for children to play in when the weather is bad make this a ideal place to stop for rest and replenishment during your tour.

Shipston -on- Stour has many 17th and 18th century houses and one such was the 300 year old building containing **The Old Red Lion** in Church Street. This licensed restaurant has been selling beer since 1703 but nowadays under the guidance of Peter and Elaine Roberts you're more likely to get substantial portions from their small but delicious menu. There are also three comfortable letting rooms and considering the feast like breakfasts that are served by the Roberts, who are masters of their craft, you might be wise to consider an overnight stay.

The Old Red Lion.   Shipston -on-Stour.

Several miles east of Shipston stands **Upton House,** a late 17th century National Trust property built of a mellow local stone. The house was remodelled in 1927-29 for the 2nd Viscount Bearsted, this was done to house the growing collections, and also to modernise the premises. The collections in the house are the chief attraction; they include paintings by English and Continental Old Masters, such as El Greco, Brueghel, Bosch, Hogarth and Stubbs. Brussels tapestries, Sevres porcelain, Chelsea figures and 18th century furniture are also on show. In the fine gardens there is a typically English scene of white clad cricketers in summer and in winter, the Warwickshire hunt hold their meet.

A mile or so beyond is **Edge Hill,** where in 1642 the first and indecisive battle of the Civil War took place. Initially the Royalist cavalry routed the opposition but a lack of discipline saw their advantage lost. The Castle Inn pub stands above the battlefield and is reputedly the point where Charles I's standard was raised. The pub itself is a sham, built in 1749 by Sanderson Miller the squire of Radway.

In a 11th century building that was constructed for the builders of Ratley church you'll now find **The Rose and Crown Inn.** This lovely inn still has stone floors, mullion windows, vast beams, original fireplaces and inglenooks. Close to the battlefield at Edgehill, local belief is that a Roundhead was found hiding in the chimney of the pub by the Cavaliers. The inn serves real ale and an excellent brew, Hook Norton Best Bitter. A 22 seat restaurant offer a menu of seasonal food, well presented and cooked at reasonable prices. The beer garden is popular where children can play whilst adults enjoy a drink or meal in pleasant surroundings.

There are two very comfortable letting rooms for those wishing to take advantage of the pretty village of Ratley or its closeness to Stratford, Warwick, Royal Leamington Spa, Banbury and Oxford.

Did You Know...

The Hidden Places Series

Covers most of Britain?

For our full list see back of book

Only one road leads into Ratley, and none lead out of it. It lies in the folds and valleys over the crest of the Edge Hills on the border of Oxfordshire. The inhabitants will tell you that it is both the oldest and the highest village in Warwickshire and that during the war, from the hill that leads up behind the inn, they saw the fires of both London and Birmingham as they burned after the German bombings. The cottages here are built of the yellow-ochre ironstone indigenous to all these border villages and which looks so lovely when the sun throws shafts of light down on them.

Whilst at the Rose and Crown and seeking first class accommodation they will no doubt direct you to **Lockhill Farm,** only a hundred yards or so from the inn.

Lockhill Farm.   *Ratley.*

It is a traditional style farmhouse, complete with beamed rooms, natural wood doors, fully centrally heated and double glazed. Mr and Mrs Thompstone, the owners of this charming house, go all out to provide their guest with every comfort. Children are welcome and Mrs Thompstone will provide a baby sitting service and day minding should it be required. On this working farm you can also book horse riding lessons. The traditional full English breakfast served will set you up for a days riding or touring in this lovely part of the world.

Up from Ratley on the B4086 you'll come to **Kineton**, a market town that is now a quiet backwater. The village has an old Court house and several 17th and 18th century houses. The church tower is from the 14th century but the rest was rebuilt around 1755. Before crossing the Fosse Way, the Roman road that runs from Exeter to Lincoln you'll pass by **Compton Verney**. Although not open to the public, this delightful 18th mansion standing in a wooded valley is worth stopping to catch a glimpse.

Ettington used to have another public house called The Saracen's Head. It took its name from a legend which states that a knight and his squire returning from the Crusades stopped to drink by a spring, but their gory trophy, namely the Saracen's head, fell into the water and fossilised. The spring is said never to stop flowing even in times of drought, but it doesn't say what the water tastes like.

A couple of miles further along the A429 from here is **Charlecote House,** the great house associated with the Lucy family. The house belonged to them from the 12th century until 1948, but only the gatehouse survives intact from the Elizabethan building. Inside there is no hint of the house Elizabeth I would have seen; the rooms are all 19th century, but no less impressive for this. The hall contains an interesting collection of family portraits including some by Gainsborough. It also houses a huge table bought from the Fonthill Abbey in 1823. More of the Fonthill furniture can be seen in the tapestry bedroom.

We then visited Charlecote Mill which is situated on the site of an earlier mill originally mentioned in the Domesday Book and valued at 6s 8d. In 1978 this 18th century building was restored with the help of numerous volunteers from Birmingham and the west water wheel was repaired at the expense of the BBC for their film "The Mill on the Floss".

A short drive north along the A429 will take you to **Hampton Lucy,** and here we found **Sandbarn Farm**, an enormous 17th century timbered, farmhouse. The accommodation is luxurious and theatre lovers - Stratford is only three miles away - will find the owner, Helen

Waterworth very helpful. She will book tickets in advance, or you can enjoy horse riding whilst staying at this friendly farmhouse in its beautiful setting.

Sandbarn Farm.   Hampton Lucy.

On a riverside just a mile from Stratford is **The Elms Camp** at **Tiddington**, one of the oldest established camp sites in the Midlands. It has fifteen acres of secluded ground for touring caravans, campers and permanent caravans. On site there is a shower block, laundry room and a general shop. There is a play area for children and Stratford Bowls Club at the camp site entrance welcomes visitors. Mr Reading and his staff are helpful and will tell you about all the nearby sporting and leisure facilities which include golf, fishing, riding and boating.

Did You Know...

There is a full list of
Tourist Information Centres
at the back of the book?

Warwick was our next destination and although separated from **Royal Leamington Spa** by two miles, the two places have very different atmospheres. The castle which dominates Warwick is surely everyone's ideal of a medieval building. It is one of the few that still

Gatehouse at Charlecote.

serves as a home and retains the greater part of its original masonry. Standing as it does by the River Avon, Warwick is in a good defensive position and became part of Crown lands as recorded in the Domesday Book in 1086.

Much of the castle was destroyed during the baron's revolt in 1264 by troops led by Simon de Montfort. The majority of the present castle dates from the 14th century. The towers at each end are very impressive, one known as Caesar's Tower is shaped rather like a clover leaf. The armoury houses one of the best private collections in the country and in the state apartments are some superb art treasures including work by Holbein, Rubens and Velasquez. The sixty acres of landscaped gardens were by Capability Brown with a famous display of peacocks.

A strong link with the castle is found in the Collegiate Church of St Mary, a fine landmark towering over the town. Of pre- conquest origin, the church contains the Beauchamp Chapel, built in the 18th century to house the monuments of Richard Beauchamp, Earl of Warwick and his family.

History of a different kind can be seen at Oken's House, an ancient building owned by Thomas Oken, a self made businessman who died childless in 1573 and left his fortune to found almshouses for the poor. Today his home houses the **Warwick Dolls Museum,** literally a hundred yards from the Castle. There are many displays and the thing that strikes you is the attention to detail in the dolls costumes.

You will find among the displays the Joy Robinson Doll and Toy Collection, which has been at the museum since the 1950's and contains an incredible number of pieces. In addition are dolls,toys and games from Warwickshire Museum's own collection. Downstairs, the main collection of dolls is arranged according to material,age and maker which helps give an insight into costume history. The museum is open from Easter to the end of September, Monday to Saturday 10.00am - 5.00pm and on Sundays 2.00pm - 5.00pm.

At the top of High Street is the **Lord Leycester Hospital**, a beautiful collection of 15th century half timbered buildings; galleried courtyard, Great Hall and Guildhall was established as a home for retired ex-servicemen. The candlelit chapel dates from 1123 and the Regimental Museum of the Queen's Own Hussars are some of the things of interest in this medieval treasure.

Italian sunshine is reflected in the food at Sicilian brothers, **Giovanni and Guiseppe Restaurant** also found in Smith Street. From the outside the neat building does not give you any idea of what you will find inside. Italian style dominates the decor whilst chef Giovanni puts the authentic touches to the menu. All the pasta dishes are delicious, the meat and fish choices as well as English dishes available make sumptuous meals. Washed down with wine from their list, you will enjoy a memorable evening or lunch in this attractive and friendly restaurant.

Giovanni & Guiseppe Restaurant.   Warwick.

We quote from Alan Burgess writing in 1950," *They come to Leamington to die. Like Cheltenham, Bath and Eastbourne, it is one of those sleepy, graceful backwaters for the retired, the weary and the infirm.*

Like ageing elephants, in clubs, hotels,in bars and baths, the silver grey and the gay Edwardian ears foregather to dream and exchange reminiscences. It is a town of memories. A quiet,graceful, tree shaded place, where memory sits on every branch and years that rolled away before we were born again in every scarlet rose."

It is not quite like that nowadays but **Royal Leamington Spa** is a very attractive town with its mixture of smart shops and Regency buildings. The Parade is undoubtedly the handsomest street in Warwickshire. It starts at the railway bridge, dives between a double row of shops and comes up with a rather startled air but a small stone temple announcing, ' The Original Spring Recorded by Camden in 1586'.

In 1801 very few people knew of the existence of Leamington but by 1838, the famous waters were cascading expensively over the dozens of patients and the increasingly fashionable spa was given the title 'Royal' by permission of Queen Victoria. The Pump Rooms were opened in 1814 by Henry Jephson, a local doctor who was largely responsible for promoting the Spa's medicinal properties. Immediately opposite are Jephson's Gardens containing a Corinthian temple which houses his statue. The town's supply of saline waters is inexhaustible and a wide range of 'cures' are available under supervision.

140

We travelled on to **Henley-in-Arden**, possibly the finest old market town in Warwickshire. Its mile long High Street is lined with almost every kind of English architecture from the 15th century onwards. Little remains today of the Forest of Arden, setting for Shakespeare's ' As You Like It '. The town, once a commercial centre for the forest, still has many old timber framed houses built from Arden oak. The forest was diminished during the 18th century when providing timber for navy but nothing could diminish from the beauty of Henley. The town emerged initially,under the protection of Thurston de Montfort, Lord of the Manor in 1140. Beaudesert Castle, the home of the de Montfort family lies behind the churches of St John's and St Nicholas where remains of the castle mound can still be seen.

In the centre of Henley-in-Arden you'll find **The White Swan,** an inn that has been looking after travellers since 1350. Doctor Samuel Johnson regularly stayed here, there is a four poster bed named after him. His friend Boswell stayed as did the poet Shenstone. Whether you decide just to drop in for a drink or dine at the excellent restaurant you will find a high standard along with a warm welcome. The White Swan is encompassed by a cheery presence, almost as if Doctor Johnson was still around. He might wonder at the modernisation since his day but he'd certainly recognise and appreciate the comforts and hospitality at this remarkable inn.

The White Swan.   Henley-in-Arden.

The 15th century church of St John the Baptist has a tower that dominates the High Street where it narrows near the ancient Guildhall. The Guildhalls roof is supported by oak beams which were growing at the time of the Norman invasion and a wooden candelabra hangs from the ceiling. At one end of the hall is a huge dresser,displaying a set of pewter plates from 1677. The charter granted to the town has a royal seal embossed in green wax and is kept in a glass case.

The Court Leet still meets yearly with the Lord of the Manor at

Warwick Castle.

Lord Leycester Hospital

their head. Other members are the High Bailiff, the Low Bailiff, the Ale-Taster, the Butter-Weigher, the Mace bearer, the Town Crier, the Town constable, the Two Affearers and the Two Brook Lockers. In 1655 they noted, *"that usually heretofore there have been at Henley-in-Arden several unlawful meetings of idle and vaine persons about this time of yeare for erectings of May Poles and May bushes and for using of Morris Dances and other heathenish and inlawful customes, the observacon whereof tendeth to draw together a greate concourse of loose people."* The next parish Beaudesert, 'a beautiful waste land' is older than Henley and contains a few timber framed cottages and the beautifully restored Norman Church of St Nicholas.

Just one mile from Henley on the A34 Birmingham Road stands the late 1800's, **The Bird in Hand.** Used by many businessmen and travellers or the years, the pub has developed a good reputation for its well kept beers and fine food. Decorated pleasantly, with a good dining area where you can choose between either a good home cooked meal or first class dinner all with ingredients freshly prepared after you order.

The Bird in Hand.   Henley -in- Arden.

Whichever way you approach **Wootton Wawen**, a couple of miles south of Henley, its situation in a hollow is dominated by its church. In every hamlet in Warwickshire you'll hear that their church is the oldest in the county but Wootton Wawen does have a strong claim to this distinction. The name is part Saxon and the suffix Wawen was added to distinguish it from other Woottons and comes from the Saxon thane who held the land prior to the arrival of the Normans.

The village church of St Peter's retains its Saxon tower and is stands within a picturesque churchyard which has won the Diocesan ' Best Kept' award several times. The main building is actually three churches in one; there are three completely separate chapels tacked onto each other with total disregard for architectural design. It does

143

not however, detract from its charm. Next to the church stands Wootton Hall, dating from 1637. Maria Fitzherbert, the wife of George IV, spent her childhood here and is thought now to return in the form of a ghost, the 'Grey Lady', that apparently wanders around the Hall.

The main road through **Studley** is the Roman Rykneild Street, now the A435. Recorded in the Domesday Book in 1086 as the Saxon ' clearing for horses', it takes its name from the original farmstead hacked to form the edge of the ancient Forest of Arden. Before Henry VIII disagreed with the Pope, there was a Priory here but now the place of worship is the church dedicated to the Nativity of the Virgin.

It has Norman foundations and some original features survive the rebuilding that occurred in the 15th century and later. There is an early 18th century manor house with stone pilasters and columns, protected by striking iron gates. A castle once stood here but the massive Gothic building dates from 1834 and was home for Studley College.

The Griffin, in Green Lane, Studley dates back to the early 1800's and was once a Needle Mill. It is only a small pub with one room that has been divided into four small rooms which combine to make a pleasant and intimate atmosphere. There is a wide range of bar snacks, available daily and at reasonable prices and a good selection of Traditional and Keg beers, wines and spirits. Occasionally a guitarist entertains in the background whilst you replenish yourselves in this pleasant pub which was recently fighting to obtain a preservation order to save it from town planners.

The Griffin.   *Studley.*

We made our way to the village of **Coughton**, two miles north of Alcester and just a stones throw away from Studley. The parish church was built by Sir Robert Throckmorton between 1486 and 1518. It has six bells which were restored in 1976 but are still carried in their original wooden frame. Inside there are some interesting oddments;

a faceless clock, fish weather vanes and dole cupboard from which wheaten loaves were distributed.

The crowning glory of this pretty village is the superb manor house, **Coughton Court**, which came into the possession of the Throckmorton family around 1409 and remained there for five and a half centuries until given to the nation in 1945.

About six miles north west of Warwick on the A4177, at the unusually named **Hasely Knob**, you'll find **The Croft Guest House.** This large, friendly house makes an ideal holiday centre in the midst of Warwickshire, where the owners Pat and David Clapp will know just how to care for you. All their rooms are centrally heated and furnished to a high standard which include colour TV and tea/coffee facilities. There is a separate, comfortable residents lounge and dining roomed, well stocked with tourist information. A full English breakfast or other choices is served and evening meals are available when you'll be able to sample the delights from Pats kitchen where she uses home grown produce for many of her appetising dishes.

The Croft Guest House.   Haseley Knob.

Haseley Knob was once a much larger place, the remains of the medieval village are in the grounds of the present Victorian manor. The Church of St Mary's, which is part Saxon and part Norman has some of the best brasses in the county; during recent renovations a section of the wall revealed medieval religious paintings.

In Hatton you'll find the award winning **Hatton Craft Centre**, situated at George's Farm and described as 'a family trip in the Warwickshire countryside'. The farm was built by descendants of Sir Richard Arkwright of Spinning Jenny fame. It became known as George's Farm after a cowman with the same name in the 1920's.

As farming methods changed the small cow stalls, granary and carthorse stables became impractical so a new use was found. The old 19th century buildings were converted into craft workshops. Now in this flourishing centre you'll find workshops with jewellery, knitwear, ceramics, hand made furniture, toys, an art gallery, candlemakers, house signs, concrete ornaments and engraving. In addition to the workshops, there are farm trails, a Cafe, Farm shop, Garden Centre, One Stop Animal Shop as well as a farm park which features rare breeds of animals and poultry, a collection of agricultural machinery and childrens playground,all with access for the disabled.

Hatton Craft Centre.   Hatton.

Nearby **Shrewley** boasts a marina on the Grand Union Canal and its well known landmark, the Hatton flight of twenty one locks that stretches for two and a half miles up Hatton Hill. Just before the village you'll find **Shrewley House**, a delightful 17th century farmhouse.

Shrewley House.   Shrewley.

Here you'll find traditional comfort and hospitality given by owners Mr and Mrs Green. In addition to bed and breakfast in the house where each room has a four poster bed, they have two superbly furnished, centrally heated holiday cottages with all requirements for those preferring self catering. The kitchens are equipped with every modern convenience, the lounges have televisions,phones and dining facilities for up to six people. Upstairs, amidst a wealth of beams the luxury double and twin bedded rooms all have ensuite bathrooms. The Greens are very knowledgeable and will gladly help with suggestions of things to do in this area of Warwickshire. In the village you'll find a comprehensive general store and locally there is a riding school and a country club with a sports complex and restaurant.

From Shrewley it is only a matter of miles to **Lapworth** where the Grand Union and Stratford canals meet. You'll also find the large and imposing Georgian, **Lapworth Lodge**, formerly a farmhouse set in two acres of garden and surrounded by lovely countryside.

Lapworth Lodge.   Lapworth.

The Lodge is in a quiet lane about two miles from the village and you can also reach it via Henley -in- Arden and the A3400, when after passing a 'Little Chef' you turn right and a quarter of a mile further on stands this lovely place. Peter and Dawn Staite own Lapworth Lodge and will share their knowledge of the house and its surroundings. It was part of the demesne of the lords of Lapworth, including Robert Caseby, instigator of the Gunpowder Plot. Established in medieval times, the demesne included a hunting park. In the 1480's William Catesby, nicknamed 'The Cat', a great favourite of Richard III was granted a further six hundred trees to enlarge the park. Around 1650 the park was divided into two farms, Lapworth Park and Lapworth Lodge. The present house was built in the 1780's and in recent years fell into a state of disrepair until the Staite's hard work and determination turned the Lodge around. Now, it has gained a reputation as one of the finest country houses in the area. The house is decorated beautifully in keeping with the period character and all rooms have remote control TV, tea/coffee facilities as well as magnificent views. Two guest rooms are on the ground floor are suitable for disable

147

access. Lapworth was the one time home of the Edwardian artist Edith Holden of 'Country Diary' fame and you'll find the dining room decorated with 'Country Diary' plates. Being a mere 15 minutes away from the NEC and the major attractions of Stratford and Warwick only a half hour away Lapworth Lodge is a delightful place to stay whilst visiting the area.

Just a short distance from Lapworth Lodge is **Packwood House**, lying in the Forest of Arden. The House is famous for its topiary gardens but less well known for the immense care in repairing, restoring and addition of new buildings by Graham Baron Ash, the donor of the property to the National Trust in 1941. The house has a collection of furniture,tapestries and works of art.

Just east of Henley is **Claverdon** which is spread over a wide area now but there is evidence of a medieval village enclosed in a deer park during the 14th century. All that now remains to mark the site is Park Farm,which is near the church with its 15th century 'embattled' tower. In the church there are some fine monuments to the Spencer family.

Woodside Country Guest House, is a friendly, pleasant house owned by Doreen Bromilow who makes you feel immediately at home. The spacious, comfortable rooms are individually furnished in cottage style with wash basins and adjacent bathroom. Each room has a hospitality tray for tea/coffee making which you can enjoy whilst looking out onto lovely views. Breakfast and dinner are served in an attractive dining room where you will be well fed with superb home cooked food, including home produce. Woodside is not licensed but Mrs Bromilow does not object to you bringing your own drink to enhance her delicious meals.

Did You Know...

There is a full

Town and Village Index

at the back of the book?

Further east in **Harbury,** history goes back almost as far as possible. Mid-distance between Warwick and Stratford, the skeletons

Packwood House.

of Plesiosaurus and Marine Dinosaurs have been found in the quarries by the village, a giant Ichthyosaurus is on exhibit at the Natural History Museum. By 500 BC, the Iron Age chief Hereburgh ruled her tribe from here and it is she who gave the village its name. The Roman Fosse Way marks one of the village boundaries and behind the Norman church stands the Old Wagstaff School founded in 1611.

Back in the southern part of the county and further south of Harbury on the border between Warwickshire and Oxon is the impressive **Farnborough Hall.** This particularly lovely house was the home of the Raleigh family of Devon, in 1684 they sold it to the Holbech family for £8700. Around the entrance hall are busts of Roman Emperors and the plasterwork is a feature in the old dining room where it forms permanent frames for copies of paintings by Canaletto and Pannini. The parish church of St Botolph was begun in the 12th century and has since been added to. On the first Saturday in July, the church fete is held. Known as the Farnborough Wake during which a Wakes pudding, a rich form of bread pudding, is eaten.

In the village stands **The Butchers Arms**, parts of which date back to the 15th and 16th century. Specialising in trout from the local trout farm the pub also serves a variety of meals that also caters for vegetarians. With its friendly, warm atmosphere, the pub is adorned with old farm implements and water colours, you'll find this an ideal place to take a break from your travels where you and your children can relax and replenish yourselves before continuing your tour of Warwickshire.

Please don't forget...
To tell people that you read about them in

The Hidden Places

The Butchers Arms.   Farnborough.

We moved on and passed once again through **Kineton** or Kington as it was once known during the royal residence of Edward the Confessor. The village is mentioned in official records from as early as 969 AD and in feudal times people depended up the gentry for their living.

Just a half mile outside Kineton is **Willowbrook House**, a peaceful, comfortable house set in four acres in lovely countryside. Guest accommodation consists of two twin bedded rooms, one single room and one double ensuite with tea/coffee facilities in them. Guest have their own large sitting room with TV and log fires for chilly evenings. A full English breakfast is 'served in the dining room and nearby is the Country Club which guests from Willowbrook can use for a nominal fee. The Howards, who own the house also run a small holding - some of their produce will be served to you - are charming and hospitable hosts who will help make your stay a memorable one at their home where they make reductions on their reasonable rates for stays of five days or longer.

Willowbrook House.   Kineton.

We ended this part of our meandering tour in **Kenilworth**, made famous by its Castle and also, in some part, by Sir Walter Scott's romantic novel ' Kenilworth'. Although the town was there before Domesday, Kenilworth's name is invariably linked with its castle. The keep, the oldest part of the ruins,was built in 1150 -75. After Simon de Montfort's death at the battle of Evesham in 1265, Kenilworth was held by his son. At that time the castle was surrounded by the Kenilworth Great Pool; a lake covering about 120 acres. Henry VIII's army failed in its attempt to storm the castle by using barges to cross the lake . Eventually the castle fell after six months siege when starvation forced de Montfort to surrender.

About three hundred years later Elizabeth I visited Kenilworth, then held by her favourite the Earl of Leicester. He laid on celebrations that cost around £60,000, in which the Queen was welcomed by the ' Lady of the Lake' floating on the lake.

The remains of the abbey can be seen in the churchyard of the parish church St Nicholas in the High Street. Much of interest was discovered during excavations, and there are many relics on display in the church, including a pig made of lead. It is said that this formed

Kenilworth Castle.

part of the roof at the time of Dissolution, but was then melted down and stamped by the Commissioners of Henry VIII.

To the East of Kenilworth, by the village of **Stoneleigh** stands **Stoneleigh Abbey**, a baroque mansion by Francis smith of Warwick. The 14th century gatehouse and Norman doorways survive from the Cistercian Abbey. The Royal Agricultural Show is held in July every year in the park.

CHAPTER SEVEN

North Warwickshire

Rugby School

Guildhall, Aston Cantlow

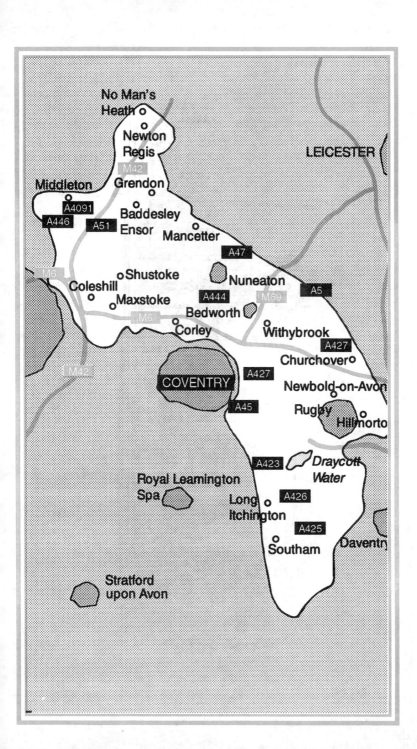

Rugby School.

CHAPTER SEVEN.

North Warwickshire.

Rugby is the only town of any great size in north eastern Warwickshire. Its market place is a reminder of the towns origins during the reign of Henry III, surrounded as it is by old buildings Standing majestically in the centre of the market place is a clocktower that was erected to commemorate the jubilee of Queen Victoria The parish church of St Andrew in Church Street has an unusual tower which looks like a fortress with battlements and wall over three feet thick. It was built by the Rokeby family after their castle was destroyed by Henry II. The towns Roman Catholic church of St Mary's is attractive ,with its slender tower and spire reaching two hundred feet into the air.

The Three Horseshoes.   Rugby.

We heard that Rugby has more pubs per square mile of town centre than anywhere else, so we thought we'd at least try to check the truth of this statement. Coaching Inn are almost always full of character with a wealth of history attached to them and **The Three Horseshoes** in Sheep Street is no exception. It is a gracious three storey building in an excellent state of preservation and today it is a hotel that maintains a high standard of hospitality. Its thirty two bedrooms are ensuite with radio, TV, trouser press, hairdryer and drink making facilities. In the restaurant you will find well prepared and presented food and an extensive,reasonably priced wine list. Right in the heart of Rugby and close to other attractions, The Three Horseshoes, offers all that a visitor could require whilst visiting the 'Heart Of England.

Rugby is probably most famous for its public school, founded in 1567. There are many fine buildings, largely by Butterfield housing such treasure as stained glass,believed to be the work of Albrecht Durer, the 15th century German artist and engraver. The game of Rugby originated here when William Webb Ellis broke the rules during a football match in 1823 by picking up and running with the ball. His commemoration stone states that, *"with fine disregard for the rule of football as played in his time, first took the ball and ran with it, thus originating the distinctive feature of the rugby game."* Then of course the town is the setting for Thomas Hughes's 'Tom Brown's School Days'. Some of the schools illustrious pupils include Rupert Brooke, the First World War poet, Charles Lutwidge Dodgson better known as Lewis Carroll and the writer Matthew Arnold.

The school has not always been the calm and peaceful seat of learning that it is today. In November 1797 the Riot Act was read to a group of rebellious pupils who made a bonfire of books, pictures and other school property before retreating to the moated island in the school grounds. They were eventually captured by a large force of soldiers, school masters and volunteer civilians who waded through the water to the island.

The James Gilbert Rugby Museum.   *Rugby.*

If you are a rugby follower, then you will probably know about **The James Gilbert Rugby Museum** in St Matthew Street. The museum is in the building which, since 1842, the Gilberts made their world famous footballs. You cannot miss it as you walk down St Matthew Street because of the distinctive thirty five pane shop front in black and gold; its the original shop window. Inside, there is a treasure trove of fascinating photographs, documents and artefacts all relating to the game of rugby football and its origins here in the town of Rugby.

Rugby is as far inland as one can get in the British Isles, yet it is an excellent centre for all kinds of water based activities. **The Oxford Canal** winds its way through the borough, providing many miles of scope for 'messing about on the river'. There are many places where you can hire a boat and enjoy the waterways. The Rivers Avon, Leam and Swift also pass through the borough and provide good angling, pleasant walks and places to picnic. Ryton Pool offer a picnic area and lakeside walks whilst Draycote Water Reservoir is a square mile of water in the midst of a Country Park.

Another pleasant park is **Caldecott Park** which has an Organic Herb Garden. At Lawford Hill Farm, children aged five to twelve can spend a day during holidays on the farm tending animals in the 'childrens farmyard'. Unique in Britain and possibly the world, claims **Ryton Gardens** of their twenty two acres devoted to chemical free gardening. After strolling around this interesting garden you can enjoy a snack at their award winning cafe which uses only additive free produce for the food they have on offer.

In the mid 1700's many men were set to work digging the canals that would eventually link the many parts of England. At **Hillmorton** near Rugby the Oxford Canal was under construction and the men needed to be housed, hence the building you will recognise today as **The Old Royal Oak.** This one time hostel for navvies fell into decline long after the canals were abandoned for faster modes of transport.

The Old Royal Oak.   Hillmorton.

In the mid seventies the pub was bought by Elaine Chapman who

161

lovingly and sympathetically restored it to its former glory. The low beamed ceilings, open fires and canal outside add much to the ambience of the pub which is helped when on warm days you can sit in the lawned gardens and watch as boats pass by. The food here is excellent and imaginative with a varied menu that caters for all tastes. A three course Sunday Lunch is available but popular during the summer months when booking is advisable.

Tucked in between the railway and the canal, and standing apart from the village is the 13th century church of St John the Baptist; worth seeking out for the fine memorials to the Astley family who built it. The canal was built by James Brindley in 1769 but not completed until 1790. It skirts Rugby before arriving at **Newbold -on- Avon,** providing pleasant mooring for boats behind the Boat Inn just outside the village. Slightly isolated in a loop of the Avon is the parish church of St Botolph which like so many churches was improved during Victorian times.

Churchover, close to the Warwickshire/Leicestershire border has less than one hundred dwellings. It sits on a hill, overlooking the Swift Valley and its church dedicated to the Holy Trinity, was mostly restored in the 19th century but still has a Norman front with a cover dating to 1673 as well as two interesting 16th century monuments. One of these commemorates the Dixwell family, who lived at the Coton House, about a mile outside the village. John Dixwell (1607-1689) was one of the signatories on the death warrant of Charles I. At the restoration of the monarchy, he was forced to flee the country and became one of the founding fathers of Newhaven, Connecticut. The church also has a 15th century tower and beautiful oak screen at the entrance to the chancel. It was erected by Queen Elizabeth, the Queen Mother, to the memory of her late godmother Mrs Arthur James, who, with her husband were tenants of the Manor House which now stands on the site of Coton House.

On the village green near the church stands **The Haywaggon,** a pub run in the best traditions by Beck and Ian Bedford. It has been a pub since 1756 and retains much of its olde worlde charm with oak beams and large inglenooks. The pub serves real ales and guest beers which change weekly and can be enjoyed, weather permitting, in the large beer garden. There are two eating areas seating 22 and 20 people and the choices on their extensive menu include some eleven starters, casseroles, fish and char grilled meals. All this can be followed by sweets of the day and washed down by a fine wine from their cost conscious list. Vegetarians are catered for and those not wishing a meal can choose from a large variety of bar snacks which include daily specials. On Sundays, a three course traditional lunch is served between noon and 1.45pm.

The Haywaggon.   *Churchover.*

Not far from Churchover, and near Dow Bridge - known as Doves Bridge 300 years ago - is the site of Tripontium. Excavations started in 1964 have revealed extensive evidence of Roman occupation. Adjacent to the site is Caves Inn, now a farm but the birthplace in 1691 of Edward Cave, founder in 1731 of 'The Gentleman's Magazine'. The son of a cobbler, he was educated at the original public school in Rugby market place. He later became a printer and journalist; his magazine achieved a circulation of fifteen thousand copies during his lifetime. In 1732, Cave started publishing regular Parliamentary reports compiled by Dr Samuel Johnson, who was then sub editor of the magazine. Then, journalists were not allowed into the House so information was gained by sending in ordinary people who would report back. After the death of Edward Cave in 1754, the magazine continued to survive until the early years of this century.

Skirting close to Coventry we headed for **Withybrook.**

Originally called Willowbrook because of the vast number of willow trees that grew alongside the brook. Withes were produced here and used for thatching the local homes and buildings. In the village you'll find **The Pheasant,** originally built in the 17th century but since been extended. In bygone days when it was called The Half Moon, coal, pigs and petrol were sold from it. The name was changed in 1976 but you might still here the pub being called by its old name. The interior is very traditional, york stone floors, beams and brasses, old farm tools and pictures. As well as a variety of beers,lagers and spirits there is a fine selection of non alcoholic drinks. The Pheasant serves food from a choice off the blackboard specials or the bar menu or alternatively from its restaurant menu. You'll be confronted with something like 27 starters, 16 fish and seafood dishes and 22 house

163

specialities or 10 vegetarian meals. After this you'll realise why the pub has built a reputation that has seen it mentioned in the Egon Ronay Good Pub Guide, The Good Pub Guide and the Sunday Mercury Pub Food Award.

The Pheasant.   Withybrook.

We journeyed south to **Long Itchington,** the Anglo Saxon, 'Farm by the River Itchen'. Its population at the time of Domesday was larger than that of Coventry. The Church of Holy Trinity is a great interest here, its earliest part dating from 1190. The tower has only the remains of its original spire which collapsed when struck by lightening during a Sunday morning service in 1762. The carvings on the chancel arm of worth looking at, with a monkey and her young and the head and shoulders of what is commonly believed to be a jester.

The Green Man, in Church Road Long Itchington is a four hundred year old pub which still retains its feel of a village inn with low ceilings, beams and tap room.

The Green Man   Long Itchington.

The beer is well kept and a menu is available for the hungry with all meals at reasonable prices, including a cow pie described as a monster! You can camp or caravan on a field at the back of the pub which runs down to the River Itchen where you can get permission to fish. The Green Man is the ideal place to unwind after a hard day by the rivers edge.

South of the church is the 15th century timber framed manor, now called Devon House,with its alternating diagonal and herringbone strutting. In 1572, Queen Elizabeth I was entertained in Long Itchington by the Earl of Leycester whilst on her way to Warwick Castle. She dined in the Tudor House facing the green, latterly owned but seldom used by the Sitwell family.

Southam was our next destination to see where Charles I spent the night before the Battle of Edgehill. The Roundheads also came into the town and Cromwell himself arrived with seven thousand troops in 1645. In the main street is the surprisingly named Old Mint Inn, a 14th century stone building that is said to take its name from an occurrence following the Battle of Edgehill. Charles I commanded his local noblemen to bring him their silver treasure, which was then melted down and minted into coins with which he paid his army.

Nuneaton, is where we continued our tour. Originally an Anglo - Saxon settlement called Etone, Nuneaton is mentioned in the Domesday Book in 1086,and the prefix 'Nun' was added when a wealthy Benedictine Priory was founded here in 1290. The remaining ruins of the Priory adjoin the Victorian church of St Nicholas which stands on a Norman site which has a beautiful carved ceiling dating from 1485.

Coal mining began in Nuneaton as early as 1300, bricks and tiles were manufactured and label hand looms produced ribbons. Later, as communications improved, so did the prosperity of the textile and hatting industries. Today Nuneaton is still an industrial town with trades ranging from precision engineering to printing, car components to double glazing.

In **Riversley Park** there is a large recreation and adventure playground for children, a sports centre and boating facilities as well as conservatories and aviaries. You'll also find the **Nuneaton Museum and Art Gallery** here, where archaeological specimens from prehistoric to medieval and items from the local earthenware industry are on display. There is also a permanent exhibition of George Eliot's personal mementoes.

The daughter of a prosperous land agent she was born at Arbury Hall in 1819 and named Mary Ann Evans. She grew up to be a plain but serious and intellectual woman by the time she left Warwickshire for London. There she met George Henry Lewes, a 'bohemian type' who occasionally wrote and acted but also had a wife and three

Arbury Hall.

children. Eventually they set up house together, which in those days was quite a courageous act. As we know she became an extremely successful novelist during her lifetime, some of her better known works include Adam Bede, The Mill on the Floss, Silas Marner and Middlemarch, recently serialised for television.

We visited **Arbury Hall** to fit another piece of the jigsaw of George Eliots life into place. It is only ten minutes from Nuneaton and is the ancestral seat of Viscount and Viscountess Daventry and the home of the Newdigate family for four hundred years. This once Elizabethan house was built out of the ruins of an Augustinian monastery and is now one of the best examples of 18th century Gothic architecture in the country. This was largely the creation of Sir Roger Newdigate who began the work in 1748. Prior to that, in the 1670's, Sir Richard Newdigate had built an impressive stable block - partly designed by Christopher Wren. However the character of the house originates from the 18th century. The opening times are limited so check with Tourist Information before making a visit to this lovely place.

A few miles to the north towards the Northampton border you'll find **Hartshill Hayes Country Park.** This is an ideal centre for exploring the developing rural tourism of the Midlands despite the fact that you are surrounded by a network of roads that soon take you into the major conurbations and attractions in the area. Woodland trails and walks, which give you the opportunity to appreciate the country and magnificent views. Hartshill itself was the birthplace of the poet Michael Drayton (1563-1631).

Manor Farm   Upton.

Although the postal address is Warwickshire and it is only five miles from Nuneaton, **Manor Farm** in **Upton** is in fact in Leicestershire. The White family has farmed here for three generations which accounts for the delightful lived in feeling you get when you arrive here. There are two double bedrooms, one family room and a

Bedworth Parish Church.

twin bedded room to let,all comfortably furnished. A full English breakfast which will set you up for the day, is served in the dining room. The farm has the luxury of a heated swimming pool which guests are welcome to use. Manor Farm is a perfect base for a holiday where you a close to Hinckley, golf at Atherstone and slightly away from the Midlands the Derbyshire hill wait those who enjoy hill walking.

We travelled on to **Bedworth,** a small town that was part of the North Warwickshire coalfield that was established at the end of the 17th century. It was local people who were largely responsible for the construction of the Coventry Canal which was built in 1769 to connect the fast growing town with the great new trade route, the Grand Trunk - now known as the Trent and Mersey Canal and to provide Coventry with cheap coal from the Bedworth coalfield.

It is also here that French Protestant families, fleeing from persecution sought refuge, bringing with them their skills for silk and ribbon weaving. The shopping precinct and open air market share the central area with the splendid Chamberlain almshouses in All Saints Square,founded in 1663. The Parish church, completed in 1890, is a good example of Gothic revival and outside there is a Scented Garden, designed for the blind. The **Bedworth Sports Complex** provides for more energetic pastimes and the Civic Hall has regular shows and concerts.

Mancetter now almost joins Atherstone due to sprawling urban development. This former Roman camp is situated on a rocky outcrop overlooking the valley of the River Anker and was one of a line of forts built as the Romans advanced northwards.

The village is chiefly associated with the Mancetter Martyrs, Robert Glover and Joyce Lewis, both of whom were burnt at the stake for their religious beliefs.

The martyrs are commemorated on wooden tablets in the fine church of St Peter, which is of early 13th century origin. The glory of the building is the rich glass in the east window of the chancel, most of which is 14th century and thought to have been made by John Thornton, builder of the great east window of York Minster. Between the manor and the church are two noteworthy rows of almshouses dating from 1728 and 1822.

Close by in the village of **Grendon** you'll find **The Boot Inn**, an 18th century coaching inn and the second oldest building in the village. Traditionally furnished throughout, the inn has two comfortable bars, adorned with pictures of stage coaches and horses; scenes synonymous with the life of this village. As well as good beer there is a wonderful selection of mixed grills, steaks and more, all prepared with local produce and a special childrens menu all of which has proved to be very popular. This friendly village pub is a place you won't regret calling into whilst on your travels when in need of refreshment.

Did You Know...

There is a full

Town and Village Index

at the back of the book?

Grendon once boasted its own mint owned by Sir George Chetwynd of Grendon Hall. It was this same Sir George who was enamoured with Lillie Lantry and who fought Lord Lonsdale in a fist fight to win her favours. He had a very extravagant lifestyle, spending a lot of time at race meetings and entertaining the Prince of Wales with the result that Grendon Hall had to be sold and was unfortunately pulled down in 1933.

Across from Grendon, divided by the old turnpike road which until recently still had toll houses standing, is **Baddesley Ensor.** In 1848 Baddesley's ancient church was pulled down and its old pulpit bought by the Wesleyan Methodists and installed in their chapel. This five sided black pulpit is claimed to be one from which the Protestant Bishop Latimer preached nearly four hundred years ago; the Bishop was burned at the stake during Mary Tudors reign. In 1772, when they were given the freedom to worship, Baddesley Quakers built a meeting house and up until 1931 Quakers from many parts of the Midlands made a yearly pilgrimage there.

Across to the east you'll find **Kingsbury Water Park** near to the M42, six hundred acres of landscaped park with over twenty lakes. It is by the River Tame and linked by miles of footpaths and nature trails through woodland, pasture and the waters edge. All sorts of water sports are pursued on the lakes and for those that own canoes and such this is an ideal place to practice their leisure pursuits. The Visitor Centre provides information about the nature trails, footpaths, bird hides and nature reserves as well as audio visual shows. Alongside

170

it you'll find a gift shop and cafe which all together make this Park,that is open all year round, an ideal day out.

A couple of miles further and you'll arrive at **Middleton** where you'll find the working farm, **Ash End House Farm.** Here is the unique opportunity to see a huge variety of animals at close quarters which since the opening ten or so years ago, has proved popular with families and school outings. Children are encouraged to make friends with the animals such as goats, sheep, pigs, hens,ducks, shire horses, donkeys and calves. Joan and Bob Rawlins, the owners, include a small bucket of food with the admission which helps children establish a 'friendship' with the animals. Most facilities are undercover so the weather shouldn't deter a visit. Guided tours can be arranged and the guides will keep you fully informed about the animals and their roles within the farm. It is worth remembering that old clothes or wellington boots are recommended when you visit this interesting and entertaining farm.

Ash End House Farm.   Middleton.

To the west of the village lies **Middleton Hall** which was, until recently, the oldest inhabited building in Warwickshire. The oldest part of the house is Norman, and until the 15th century the property of the Marmions of Tamworth Castle. It was later acquired by the Willoughby family around 1528. It was a moated residence but in 1868 the moat was drained to reveal the skeleton of a rider in armour and a horse. It was believed that he was a courier in the Royalist Army, who when leaving the Hall in dense fog lost his bearings and ended up in the moat. The remains are buried in the churchyard and the gauntlet glove and helmet are on display in the chancel of the church.

A place to hear more tales is **The Four Counties Inn**, so called because it is situated at the meeting of the borders of Warwickshire, Staffordshire, Leicestershire and Derbyshire. The Inn has stood for

171

nearly 200 years and in days gone by was a haven for people of 'doubtful character'. It was law that no person could be arrested by an officer of the law outside of his jurisdiction and as the Inns rooms are in different counties one can imagine the rapid movement of people from one room to another as the law arrived! Today there are no such problems in this warm and friendly inn that has been run by the same family for over thirty years. You can enjoy their fine ales and good food by the fireside or on warm days outside with views of the surrounding open countryside.

The Four Counties Inn.   No Mans Heath.

We moved on along the A453 to **Newton Regis**, one of the least spoilt villages in North Warwickshire; it has been voted the ' Best Kept Small Village' several times and built around a duck pond which was once a quarry pit makes you understand why. The name Newton Regis probably derives from its former royal ownership by Henry II who reigned from 1154 to 1189. It has also been known as King's Newton and Newton -in-the- Thistles. The latter might have referred to the abundance of thistles or specially grown teasels which is used in the carding of flax fibre. Linen looms were worked in the house which is now The Queens Head Inn.

Alvecote Priory, just on the border with Staffordshire is an ideal picnic spot, where there is a distinctly religious atmosphere that emanates from the Benedictine Priory that was formed here in 1159. The 14th century remains include a fine moulded doorway and dovecote. The priory was founded by a William Burnett who built it as a penance after believing that his wife had been unfaithful during his pilgrimage to the Holy Lands. Alvecote Pools are formed by the River Anker in flood and are now nature reserves with specimens of many plants, insects and bird-life.

Back in a southerly direction we came to **Coleshill**, which derives its name from the River Cole, a clear and shallow waterway that passes under the lower part of High Street. It is a town of great antiquity, once being a royal manor during Norman times. It gained in importance when it became a staging post in coaching days along the main London to Holyhead route, boasting more than twenty inns.

Near the church are Coleshill's most known treasures, a combined post, stocks and pillory, the stocks were last used in 1859. One infamous inhabitant was John Wynn, owner of a cinema, who during the Second World War operated a transmitter from the roof of the building and was caught giving information to the Germans.

Maxstoke, some two miles to the east, is a privately owned castle but **Maxstoke Priory** is an early 14th century building which has two letting rooms. One is the old priors lodging and you'll take breakfast in the oak panelled dining room with its amazing armorial painted ceiling. The priory was nearly demolished during Dissolution but was rebuilt in the 1600's as a farmhouse without losing its sense of history.

Shustoke, a peaceful place close to Coleshill makes it hard to believe that you are only seven minutes or so away from the NEC and Airport. Here you'll find the old railway station has been turned into **Ye Olde Station Guest House.** Some hundred and ten years ago you would have arrived here to celebrate the opening of the railway station but now you'll be welcomed by present owner, Ann Thompson, who has turned the building into a comfortable, friendly establishment. The Guest House has six letting rooms, three of which are ensuite and for those with children, a baby sitting service can be provided. You can, if you wish, dine at this licensed house, as well as bed and breakfast where the food is both delicious and substantial.

Ye Olde Station Guest House.   Shustoke.

Not far from the village centre is Shustoke Reservoir which supplies some of the water for Coventry and where you'll find a sailing club and a place for enthusiastic anglers to enjoy the surroundings.

173

Maxstoke Priory.

Furnace End, so named in 1700, takes its names from the furnaces of the Jennens family in the Bourne Valley. The present village is a group of older houses at a crossroads in an area of wooded countryside dotted with small mixed farms. The village boasts a post office, butchers and a pub plus guest house.

Did You Know...

The Hidden Places Series

Covers most of Britain?

For our full list see back of book

The pub is **Ye Olde Bulls Head,** a 16th century inn with a large bar and restaurant and ample car parking facilities. Three large open fires provide warmth throughout the winter and its low ceilings and exposed beams add to it warm, cosy atmosphere. The bar is tastefully decorated and recently been refurbished with polished oak panelling that was originally the altar together with pew seats from the local church. Real ales along with a fine selection of wines, spirits and liqueurs are available. A large selection of bar snacks are served and in the restaurant there is a variety of choices from a simple but delicious menu prepared by the chef Richard who is renowned for his soups, sauces and pastries. Vegetarian dishes and a childrens menu is available whilst live entertainment is on offer six nights a week. A private garden to the rear is full of flowers and shrubs and an ideal, safe place to enjoy a drink. Be sure to get here early, especially if you want to eat as the Inn is a popular place for many from miles around.

Close by is **Corley**, where disaster struck in the 1920's with foot and mouth disease which was fortunately confined to the area. On a happier note you'll find here the friendly and welcoming, **Red Lion Inn**, parts of which are over three hundred years old. The lounge side of the restaurant was once a morgue and once was the local carpenters cottage during which time it was shared with the blacksmith. Now, the Inn serves well kept Ruddles Best and Websters traditional ales as well as lager. The restaurant side specialises in steaks, home made dishes and sweets. Children are welcome in the snug, which still has its original inglenook fireplace, though not in the lounge or main bar.

However, there is a large garden outside with climbing frames and swings whilst perhaps best of all, an animal farm which has goats, sheep, rabbits, ducks and a large aviary.

Did You Know...

There is a full list of
Tourist Information Centres
at the back of the book?

So we finally took our leave of Warwickshire and headed into the next chapter, Northamptonshire. We had found many places of interest both 'hidden' and not but we hope that our tour has helped give you an insight into an attractive and often surprising county in the Heart Of England.

CHAPTER EIGHT

South Northhamptonshire

Cannon's Ashby house

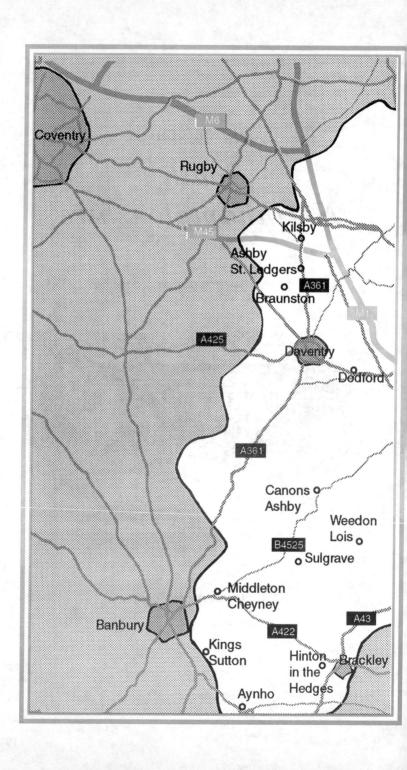

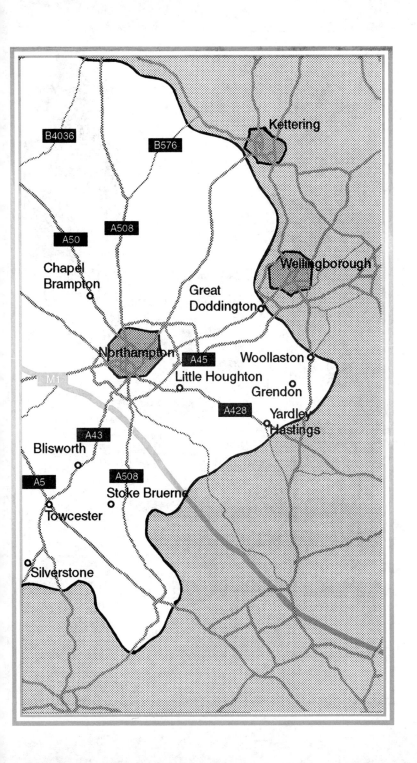

Entrance to Castle Ashby.

CHAPTER EIGHT

South Northamptonshire.

Northamptonshire is shaped like a laurel leaf and the **River Nene** is its most distinctive feature. Wherever you journey across the county you are never far from its banks and the reflection of the trees in high summer on its shimmering waters can be quite breathtaking. The alluvial soils and gravel terraces of the Nene Valley have been continuously farmed since Neolithic times and there are remains of many Anglo-Saxon settlements. Bones of horses, woolly rhinoceroses and mammoths have been unearthed giving some hint as to the kind of animal life Paleolithic man used to contend with. Polished stone axes indicate that their basic way of life was mixed farming.

During the Roman occupation, the Nene Valley lay within the most densely populated region of Britain, but we're only thinking in dozens here. Forts were built a days march apart round the Fens and towards the Trent and Humber. One such fortress, some thirty acres in size was discovered at Lonthorpe near Peterborough and as the legionaires advanced towards the north and west they built their famous straight roads.

The most impressive sections are those of Watling Street (A5), which enters the county at Old Stratford and runs in a rigid straight line for eight and a half miles to Towcester. The line of communication continues north through Watford Gap - now thought of only as a motorway service area. This route was followed by the Grand Union Canal in the 18th century, by the London to Birmingham railway in the early Victorian period; and by the M1 motorway in contemporary times. There can be few places that have played such an integral role in communications for over two thousand years.

The county abounds in steeples and it is unusual to see less than three at any one time. So graceful and abundant are these different styles of towers and spires that even the pylons and telegraph poles of todays landscape can hardly extinguish the effect. The Saxon church at **Brixworth** which is the most impressive and has been described and we quote the Tourist Information as *"probably the most imposing architectural memorial of the 7th century north of the Alps"*.

Whatever your taste in scenery there is something for everyone from rolling meadows to a spectacular view over seven counties. The main centres of population all have their own delightful corners, but the county is perhaps even better known for the many picturesque villages which dot the landscape. From **Harringworth** in the north to the equally lovely **Chipping Warden** in the south, Northamptonshire abounds with charm complete with true country hospitality in welcoming local pubs and cosy tea shops.

Both the **Grand Union** and the **Oxford Canals** run through Northamptonshire, meeting at **Braunston** where there is a large marina and a choice of canal-side inns.

If your interest is spectator sports, there is plenty to enjoy. The county town is host to a first-class county cricket team, a professional football club and a redoubtable rugby fifteen. Elsewhere in the county **Silverstone** hosts not only the best in Formula one motor racing, but also motor cycle racing and many club meetings. For the more ambitious, Silverstone also has a racing school with special race meetings for pupils, as well as providing instruction in advanced driving skills and skid correction techniques.

Brafield, near Northampton, caters for stock car and hot rod racing enthusiasts. For those whose interests lie on the race track, **Towcester Racecourse** is famous for its National Hunt meeting and horse trials are held at several venues around the county. If you prefer less nerve racking sports, the World Conker Championships are held at **Ashton** every year. Coarse, fly fishing and rough shooting are also available within the county. Add to these superb golf facilities and a wide selection of cultural activities, and it is easy to understand why Northamptonshire proves such a popular county for the young of all ages.

We decided to start our tour of Northamptonshire at the southern-most tip and our first port of call was **King's Sutton,** which boasts its own Anglo-Saxon saint called Rumbold, an extremely un-saintlike name we thought. The River Cherwell rises at **Charwelton** and its willow-lined course forms the boundary of the shire in its extreme southwest corner as it goes south into Oxfordshire on its way to the Thames. The King's Sutton church of St. Peter and St. Paul has a 14th century spire rising from the handsome tower and a band of pinnacles is linked to it by dainty flying buttresses.

At **Studleigh Farm** you will not find the usual accommodation offered as bed and breakfast at the farmhouse. The accommodation is of an extremely high standard and definitely upmarket. There are two guest rooms, both furnished very tastefully and thoughtfully with their own bathrooms. The farmhouse was built around 1700 as a dairy and bakery, you can still see the old ovens where the bread was baked. Surrounded by eight acres of pasture land the scenery is wonderful with a vista of rolling countryside. The River Cherwell forms a boundary on one side as it winds its way towards Banbury and the farm is a good base from which to vist the many historic sites in the area.

Studleigh Farm.   Kings Sutton.

We next travelled to the pretty village of **Aynho**, six miles south west of Brackley. The parish church of St. Michael and All Angels has a wonderfully detailed 15th century tower which is rather startlingly attached to the church whose shape and symmetry give it the air of a villa. The body of the church was transformed in 1723 by a local carpenter-cum-architect called Edward Wing. It is furnished with a pulpit, box pews and a distinguished west gallery classically of the period. Aynho is picturesque with steep leafy lanes and apricot trees trained into fan shapes are a lovely feature, leaning against limestone cottage walls. The former manor house is called **Aynho Park** which gives a delightful character to this sleepy place.

Hinton-in-the-Hedges, is a village of thatched rooves and clipped yew hedges. The village green is triangular in shape and is still the centre of this tight settlement which has never grown beyond hamlet proportions. Here the Normans built a low tower, and from under its narrow parapet with a pyramid cap of the 13th century, eight heads peer down on each side. Three of the bells in the tower are older than the Reformation. We are, of course, talking about the church and

183

inside there is a charming Jacobean pulpit supported on a finely carved pedestal.

The origin of **Brackley** is to be found in a cluster of farms two and a half miles to the north. Here was the centre of the old Saxon parish of Halse with a church mentioned in Domesday Book. This medieval seignorial borough grew to be quite prosperous in the early Middle Ages and then rather faded away.

The Saxon old town is distinguished by its huddle of houses round a tangle of streets. The prosperity brought by the marketing of wool in the broad High Street in the 13th century enabled the church of St Peter's to be rebuilt with its fine early English west tower and south aisle. Magdalen College School founded in 1548 by William of Waynflete incorporates the chapel of a Hospital of St John and St James, and the Town Hall, with its fine clock tower built in 1706 stands in High Street. The Duke of Bridgewater was responsible for the latter and its open arched windows on the ground floor used to be an open market place. The outsize station built in the 19th century is called Brackley Central whilst in fact it is on the northern edge of town.

Two miles west of Brackley off the A43 in the tiny village of **Steane**, is the little chapel of St Peter, built by Sir Thomas Crewe in his park in 1620. It has the appearance of being genuinely medieval although it isn't. The south doorway may have been added in the mid 17th century but it does contain good furnishings and fine monuments to his family and includes work by the Christmas brothers.

Moving north, and still on the religious theme at **Middleton Cheney,** about five miles beyond Brackley on the A422, you'll find the Church of All Saints. This 14th century church has a beautiful tower and perpendicular spire, its steeply roofed porch is built entirely of interlocking stones. Above all though, it has splendid stained glass by a galaxy of pre- Raphaelites - Morris, Webb, Rosetti - and includes the original Burke -Jones's ' Six Days of Creation'.

There would seem to be little connection between an Elizabethan manor house and the USA as we know it today. Yet it was from **Sulgrave** along the B4525 that George Washington's ancestors emigrated to a new life in the New World. **Sulgrave Manor** today is faithfully preserved and open to the public as a Washington Museum. The house was sold to Laurence Washington, George's great grandfather, in 1539, a distingiuished wool merchant and twice Mayor of Northampton.

The walls and ceilings have been stripped of their plaster and the panels of their coats of paint. The massive oak beams and the planks of the floors now gleam with a deep golden lustre as they must have done when Elizabeth I paid a visit. The seven feet wide fireplaces are
184

fitted with medieval implements and there is a captivating miniature dresser with a child's play set of cups, plates and pots all made of shining pewter. George's black coat has pride of place and there is a fragment of Martha Washingtons wedding dress on display.

Outside the porch bears the family coat of arms, sometimes regarded (doubtfully) as the origin of the 'stars and stripes'. The village church, St James the Less contains a memorial brass to Laurence Washington and his wife and the 17th century Washington family pew. It has also been enriched over the years by gifts from American pilgrims, one of which is a light oak tower screen with tracery picked out in scarlet and blue where the flags of England and the US hang side by side. Another gift is the organ donated by the colonial Dames of America. On the village green are the old stocks which actually pre-date the United States.

Due north of Sulgrave is another interesting stopover in the village of **Canons Ashby.** This pretty village contains the church of St Mary, which was once part of the Black Canons' Monastery church, although it is much smaller since the Dissolution by Henry VIII. Excavations in 1828 established foundations more than one hundred feet east of the present building. Recently the south west corner of the cloisters was uncovered. The population of Canons Ashby was recorded in Domesday Book in 1086 as sixteen and by 1377 had risen to eighty two.

Canons Ashby House was built from part of the priory after Dissolution. Home of the Dryden family since 1551, it is largely unaltered with Elizabethan wall paintings and outstanding Jacobean plasterwork. The terraced garden with yews, cedars and mulberry trees are delightful. The park has five pairs of gates and is stocked with a pure breed of spotted deer said to be unique in the country.

Heading towards Towcester we discovered the burial place of Edith Sitwell (1887 - 1965) in the hamlet of **Weedon Lois** then further east at **Slapton** the church's interesting 14th century wall painting. It is only a matter of miles before you reach **Silverstone,** its facilities we have already mentioned.

Britons, Romans, Saxons and Normans have all had a hand in shaping **Towcester** although little remains to testify to this. It does however, lie on Watling Street, and was during Romans times a walled town called Lactodorum. During the Civil War, it was the only Royalist stronghold in the area and later during the heyday of coaches it was an important staging post between Holyhead and London.

The Towcester church of St Lawrence contains the work of many centuries; the crypt, reached by a doorway from the sanctuary is 13th century, and the arcades with their lofty piers originate from the 13th and 14th centuries. On the arch of the south chapel is a carved jesters

Sulgrave Manor.

Cannon's Ashby house

head, probably six hundred years old. The massive ninety foot tower with carved angels and font are about five hundred years old.

To the east you'll come to the Grand Union Canal, constructed between 1793 and 1805, winding its way and taking its place in tranquil scenes until its waters are raised by seven locks and vanish into the Blisworth Tunnel, which is nearly two miles long.

At **Stoke Bruerne**, old canal buildings have been converted into a fascinating Waterways Museum. Nostalgia for those times are aroused as replicas of the gaily painted boats makes visits here. Among the exhibits are an enormous padlock and key used to secure lock gates, used around 1770 but failed to shackle the famous escapologist Houdini one hundred and sixty years later.

The Canal Museum at the heart of Stoke Bruerne, is housed in a restored canalside cornmill. Children can learn why canals were built, about the pioneering engineers who put so much research into the construction of the canals and the boats that worked on them. Canal families have always had a lifestyle of their own and the museum gives an insight into the engines and range of colourful traditions. The exhibits include working engines, original photographs, waterway wildlife, workmen's and boatmen's tools and full size models of a boat horse and a traditional narrow boat cabin.

The Canal Museum.   Stoke Bruerne.

The most important thing about Stoke Bruerne is that it offers so much more than just a museum. You can explore both the flight of seven locks and Blisworth Tunnel, through which 'leggers' propelled narrow boats laden with twenty five tons of goods. In fact you will gain a fascinating insight into two hundred years of canal life on the Grand Union. The museum brings alive the vital part that the canal network played in the industrialisation of Great Britain. There is always plenty of activity on the canal. Boat trips are available and passing modern holiday craft contrast with the original working narrow boats moored outside the museum. Stoke Bruerne provides the perfect location for a family day out or for organised groups and school parties, who incidentally should book the time and the date of their visit with the Canal Museum Office (0604) 862229. An attractive tearoom serves morning coffee, lunches and afternoon teas whilst at the shop you will find a selection of souvenirs. In the summer the museum is open daily from 10.00am - 6.00pm including bank holidays. In winter, from October to Easter, it is open daily from 10.00am - 4.00pm except Mondays, Christmas Day and Boxing Day when it is closed.

Close by you'll find a super restaurant, **Bruerne's Lock Restaurant,** in a Georgian building that has mellowed with age and has a welcoming interior. Fine black and white prints on the walls tell of the old days of canal life. The building started life as the private house of the Amos family who were rope and twine makers and has changed hands several times since before becoming a restaurant. That happened in August 1989 and since then restaurant has been carving its own gastronomic history. The accent is on personal service to complement the excellence of the 'Modern English 'cuisine. The delicious food is well presented using fresh ingredients supplied locally and everything is cooked to order. Complimented by an extensive wine list this canal side restaurant is a place well worth seeking out.

Bruerne's Lock Restaurant.   Stoke Bruerne.

Stoke Park, a the great house standing in four hundred acres, built in 1630's and attributed to Inigo Jones, was the first in England to be built along the Italian lines. Only the two pavilions and a colonnade remain, but they are well worth seeing with the stately pool and its elaborate centre piece of statuary. Check before visiting as opening times are limited.

At the north end of the longest canal tunnel in England by which

188

the Grand Union penetrates the hill from Stoke Bruerne is the pretty village of **Blisworth**. There are roses everywhere in summer, in the cottage gardens, in the Tudor and Jacobean houses and forming a fragment and colourful garland round the old grey 13th century church. It's most precious possession is a high screen of the 15th century complete with doors. The newel rood stairs which led to the top of it are still in perfect condition. There is an interesting tablet near the altar which tells the story of the wife of a sergeant-at-arms to Elizabeth I. She lived a maid for eighteen years, was a wife for twenty years and a widow for sixty one years, dying in her ninety nineth year.

It is hard to imagine anything as well appointed as **The Blisworth Hotel**, in Station Road Blisworth. Converted from what was a British Rail station, it is now a frindly hotel run by extremely efficient staff under the guidance of owners Mr and Mrs Dewfall. There are fourteen comfortable and tastefully furnished bedrooms with TV, telephone and tea/coffee making facilties. Ten of the rooms are ensuite. Three bars downstairs provide a relaxing atmosphere where as well as the drinks you can order bar meals from an extensive menu, available daily. Alternatively, you can eat in the elegant Hunters Moon restaurant where you'll find an interesting and extensive menu and wine list. Being so near to Northampton, The Blisworth attracts many people who uses its facilities which include a banqueting suite with its own bar or who come to one of the speciality evenings that are often put on at this delightful hotel.

Please Don't Forget...

To tell people that you read about them in

The Hidden Places

We followed as best we could the Grand Union canal via **Upper Stowe,** and arrived at **Weedon**, which stands close to Watling Street. Approached along an avenue of limes, the church here was built thirteen hundred years ago by the King of Mercia, whose daughter St

Weburgh - buried in Chester - founded a nunnery among the swamps of the River Nene.

The church at nearby **Dodford,** contains some interesting brasses medieval monuments worth looking at whilst on your way to **Daventry.** Its streets of dignified Georgian houses follow the lines of the medieval thoroughfare and there is still a twice weekly market, held on Tuesdays and Fridays. In the High Street you'll see many fine old buildings and in the Market Place stands Moot Hall, built in 1769 of ironstone.

A hill fort lies on **Brough Hill,** six hundred and fifty feet above sea level and is the third largest fort of its kind in the country. Oval in shape, it is more than two miles round and covers an area of 150 acres. The hill is part of a range forming the great water divide of the Midlands and from this point you can see into seven counties.

Weltonfield Narrowboats.   *Braunston.*

Shakespeare mentions Daventry in his plays; once when Falstaff tells the tale of a shirt stolen from an innkeeper. It is said that Charles I spent his last six nights in the Wheatsheaf Inn before losing the Battle of Naseby and hence his kingdom. During the coaching era whip making was the chief industry of Daventry. About seven miles further along the **A45** lies **Braunston** an important junction on the Grand Union Canal. The canal links Braunston with the Thames, the Trent and the Midlands. Here you'll find **Weltonfield Narrowboats,** run by Judi and Hugh Mayes. This highly succesful company hires out narrowboats which allow you to explore the canals and the many pubs that lie along them. The boats are fully equipped with spacious berths, ample storage and galleys with fridge and cookers. They also run a narrowboat for the Spinal Injuries Association which caters for all the needs of the disabled and where they can take part in the activites. It is a superb way to spend a holiday whilst at the same time seeing the lovely countryside around and evoke visions of when the canals were in their heyday.

Nearby **Ashby St Ledgers** has a church with 14th century paintings and the manor house belonged to Robert Catesby and was used by the Gunpowder Plot conspirators as a meeting place. On November 5th 1605 he rode the eighty miles from London in seven hours bringing the news that the Plot had failed. Afterwards fleeing to Holbeach in Staffordshire he was tracked down on November 8th and shot dead after refusing to surrender.

The church, standing near the lovely three gabled Tudor Manor house was refashioned by John Catesby in the 15th century. Inside, there is much to see including Jacobean pews and a canopied chancel screen painted red and green with exquisite tracery and a frieze of foliage. There are many brasses of the Catesby's, a Norman font and on various walls the traces of medieval paintings among which you can make out the Last Supper, women at Christs tomb and the crucifixion.

The Hunt House Restaurant.   Kilsby.

Further north along the B361 you'll arrive at **Kilsby** where you'll find **The Hunt House Restaurant**, a former hunting lodge built in 1656. This restored and historically listed building is now run by Ian and Jan Geggie where you'll find superbly prepared food using fresh produce and where quality is the watchword.

Using modern communication to further our quest for ' Hidden Places ' and knowledge of the past we used the **M1** to cut back across Northamptonshire and continued our journey from junction 15 by skirting Northampton and arrived by way of the A428 at the little village of **Yardley Hastings,** which used to belong to a Saxon earl and then to William the Conqueror's niece, Judith. It can be reached through the great beech avenue of Castle Ashby Park, remnants of the forest that once covered the whole of this countryside.

The building of **Castle Ashby** was started in 1574 in the area of a 13th century castle that had been previously demolished. The original plan of the building was in the shape of an 'E' in honour of Queen Elizabeth I, and is typical of many Elizabethan houses. About sixty years later the courtyard was enclosed by a screen designed by Inigo Jones. One of the features of Castle Ashby is the lettering around the house and terraces. The inscriptions, which are in Latin, read when translated *'The Lord guard your coming in'* and *'The Lord guard your going out'*.

Inside there is some wonderful restoration furniture and paintings of the English and Renaissance schools. The building of these great dwellings was one of the extravagance of the time and the hospitality offered continued to act as a magnet to royal company and the court in the age of Elizabeth I.

On a much smaller scale the old manor house makes a delightful picture by the church; it has a dungeon and there is a 13th century window with exquisite tracery set in the oldest part of the house near a blocked Norman arch. The poet Cowper loved to wander amongst the trees, some of which are said to have been planted by the Countess Judith herself. The tree that attracts the most visitors is called Cowper's Oak, the branches of which spread twice as far across as the tree is high. There is a tradition that it will never die because Cowper stood beneath it one day during a heavy thunderstorm and was inspired to write his famous hymn: *'God moves in Mysterious Ways'*.

The church is as old as William the Conqueror and still has in its walls stones laid at the same time as he gave this piece of England to Judith. A couple of miles north east of Yardley Hastings we drove past the old stone cottage and houses that line **Grendon's** long and twisting main street. The village is built on a slope, and the brown and grey tower of the 12th century church is one of the best known landmarks in the River Nene valley. It pokes up from between thatched and slated roofs, and overlooks an orderly patchwork of outlying fields. The church has been added to every century and the latest addition is a striking, black and white marble floor put in by a rector in 1914 in memory of his three children.

Grendon Hall is a Queen Anne mansion, once the home of earls and marquises of Northampton. The hall, now owned by the County Council, still has rooms with early 18th century panelling. Two other notable houses in Grendon are the Grange built in 1850, with a lantern cupola on its roof and the gabled 17th century Manor Farm House.

Nearby **Wollaston** is separated from its neighbour **Great Doddington** by the gently flowing Nene and there is a local industry making mats from the rushes of the river. Beacon Hill gives us a wide and lovely view, in which it is said, some twenty seven towers and spires can be seen on a bright sunny day. There are many 17th century houses built of the local brown ironstone and the spire of the church has eight sides of rich 14th century tracery in its openings. In 1737 most of the medieval church fell to the ground but part of the transept and the beautiful central tower still remain.

We decided to follow the path of the river for a few miles as it meanders through this lovely part of the world on its way to the county capital, Northampton. The most remarkable thing about the Nene is its valley, which is two miles wide in places. We arrived at **Cogenhoe** which overlooks the Nene Valley, where, set high on the hillside are delightful Tudor and Jacobean farmhouses. One gabled house bears the date 1684 and the initials of the builder.

We next came to **Little Houghton** where the poet, John Clare would often come on the walks he was allowed to take from his asylum in Northampton. There are traces of the moat of the old manor house near the 13th century church, and nearby are the village stocks.

There are many 17th century houses built of the local brown ironstone and the spire of the church has eight sides of rich 14th century tracery in its openings. In 1737 most of the medieval church fell to the ground but part of the transept and the beautiful central tower still remain.

In the square you can admire Sir Thomas Tresham's House, one of the trinity of buildings associated with his name; the others are the Lyvedon New Building at Brigstock and the Triangular Lodge at Rushton.

Just over the river at **Ecton** lived the ancestors of another famous American, Benjamin Franklin. Traditionally, for three hundred years, the eldest Franklin son was always the village blacksmith. During his visits to England Benjamin searched the Ecton registers and found a Franklin there from 1558, when records were started, and discovered that he was the youngest son of the youngest son for five generations. His father, Josiah, took his wife and three children across the Atlantic in 1685. There he had four more children and, on the death of his wife, he remarried and had another ten. Benjamin said that he remembered thirteen siblings sitting at the table at one time.

Today, unfortunately, the smithy and the Franklin home have disappeared and until 1910 there was nothing in the church to commemorate this world famous citizen, when a group of pilgrims provided a bronze tablet and bust. The inscription is from one of his speeches; ' *The longer I live, the more convincing proof I see of this truth, that God governs in the affairs of men.*' Opposite the church is

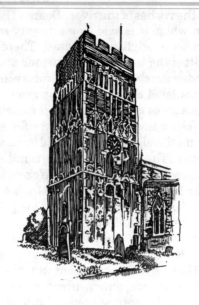

Earls Barton Church.

All Saints Church. Northampton.

Ecton House built in 1778. **Ecton Hall,** not to be confused with Ecton House, takes the place of the old nunnery and was rebuilt in 1756 and extended about 1880 all in the Tudor Gothic style. In the wooded grounds is an avenue still known as the Nun's Walk, and a summerhouse which has been there for several generations.

If you enjoy riding or if you are complete beginner, pay a visit to **East Lodge Farm Riding Centre.** novice or experienced riders are welcomed with equal enthusiasm. Children from the age of three are eligible for tuition and the Whites pride themselves on their standards of safety and professional knowledge. The centre is open from 9.00am -7.00pm Tuesday to Sunday and offers gropu or private tuition.

East Lodge Farm.   Ecton.

A few miles north and you'll find the **Sywell Country Park** which has a delightful waterside walks and a picnic meadow where you are able to observe a multitude of wildlife. There is a visitors centre; free admission and free parking. A stone's throw from Ecton in the village of **Earls Barton** is the most impressive Saxon church tower in the country, not just Northamptonshire, and there are some pretty impressive churches here. It looks today as it did a thousand years ago with its mass of decorations by medieval craftsmen.

In 1934 workmen found, embedded in the wall fifty feet from the ground, a horse's tooth. There was a pagan belief that the burial of horses' skulls improved the sound acoustics and that the skulls of forty horses were once laid in rows between the joists with the idea of improving the tone of an organ which stood over them. That wasn't here though - so maybe the tooth was meant to improve the sound a little bit, or more likely a horse belonging to one of the workmen had eaten too many lumps of medieval sugar.

The remarkably well preserved Norman doorway is one of the treasures of this lovely old church and is dated 1180. But it is inside that a profusion of colour can be seen where the chancel screen gleams as if encrusted with jewels. Set into this 15th century gem are hundreds of dazzling butterflies on the wing and beside the screen stands a wonderful heavily carved, black oak Jacobean pulpit. In West Street the **Earls Barton Museum** of local life is well worth a visit to see the exhibits of local industries including shoe and lace making.

We decided to spend a the day in the county town of **Northampton** and it's just as well for there is much to see. Most of the town was destroyed by the Great Fire of 1675, but is was rebuilt in such a spacious and well-planned way that Daniel Defoe (1661-1731) called it, *'the handsomest and best built town in all this part of England'*. This thriving market town offers a fascinating mix of historic and modern attractions. Fine Norman churches, Victorian architecture, museums, an art gallery, modern shops and entertainments will spoil you for choice. Northampton's history goes back beyond the Romans, certainly to the Iron Age as settlements have been found in and around the town. In the town centre almost all the medieval buildings were destroyed by the Great Fire. The Market Square is reputedly the second largest in England. The most distinguished building is **Welsh House**, rebuilt in 1975 to its original 16th century form. It is a relic of the days when Welsh drovers brought their cattle to the market. The focal point is the Victorian Gothic Guildhall, with its intricate carved statues outside depicting scenes of Northampton history.

There is a fine **Central Museum and Art Gallery** in Guildhall Road, with a collection which includes Italian art of the 15th to 18th centuries,ceramics and sculptures, some of the work is by local artists. There is also what is believed to be the finest collection of footwear in Europe. A room has been fitted out as an old home cobbler's shop before the days of factories. On display there is a wide variety of footwear including some Roman sandals, Queen Victoria's wedding slippers and Margot Fonteyn's ballet pumps. The strangest item is a huge boot worn by an elephant which was taken across the Alps in 1959 in a re-enactment of Hannibal's crossing. The smell of leather is very pleasant and there is an old saying that you know when you are within a mile of Northampton by the smell of the leather and the sound of the lapstones.

Further down Guildhall street is the **Royal Theatre,** home of the Northampton Repertory Company. The modest exterior belies the gorgeously decorated auditorium which was designed in 1884 and was then known as the Opera House. A short walk away is the oldest building in Northampton, the **Church of the Holy Sepulchre** in Sheep Street. One of the four surviving round churches in England, it owes its character to the inspiration of the Crusaders and is a replica of the original in Jerusalem. The Nave was built in 1100 and is

The Round Church of the Holy Sepulchre, Northampton

completely round. The choir section was built half a century later and the result is a disjointed exterior, but the interior has all the fascination of rarity.

All Saints, in the very heart of the town, is also most striking. Rebuilt after a fire, its entrance is reminiscent of St. Paul's Cathedral in London. The architect, Henry Bell used Christopher Wren's chief plasterer during the reconstruction. The great Portico is crowned by a statue of the dissolute Charles II who gave one thousand tons of timber for rebuilding. He stands above the open parapet wearing the bizarre mixture of Roman toga and an English wig! We were reminded sadly of another figure who used to sit in the shadow of the huge round columns, the poet John Clare. He would wander down from the asylum and sit here for hours watching the throng go by. Born in 1793 in a cottage in Helpston (then in this county) he lived for forty years within the countryside and county that was to inspire him.

It was after his wife Patty gave birth to their seventh child that a friend took him to a mental home. He escaped, so his long term friend Lord Fitzwilliam paid eleven shillings a week to keep him in Northampton Asylum, where he lived for a staggering twenty two years. Patty could not bear to visit him and never saw him again. She died and was buried in a unmarked grave. He died in 1864 after seventy one years of melancholic existence and extreme poverty.

Ever since King John bought a pair of shoes here for ninepence in the early 13th century, the boot and shoe trade has flourished mightily and Northampton has become famous throughout the world for its footwear. Names like Barrett and Mansfield are just two of the huge chain shoe shops that started life here in a small way. It is said that two thousand shoe shops in England belong to Northampton firms. Cromwell's Parliamentarians, with whom the town sided during the Civil War, were sent one thousand five hundred pairs and many other famous armies up until today have been supplied with footwear made here.

The other great Northampton industry is lace-making and no-one is quite sure how far back the tradition goes. The influx of lace-makers from the Continent in the 17th century exerted a great influence. They were Protestants seeking sanctuary from religious persecution and this transfer of skill enhanced the industry considerably. For three hundred years nearly every village in the county had its lace-makers. As agricultural wages were low, the skilled wife could often earn more than her husband.

Wherever you look in Northampton we saw lawns and trees, a meadow or park. It has four hundred acres of open spaces and playing fields and there is a disused racecourse on the highest ground from

Althorp House

here to the North Sea. There is also a delightful children's lake, one of the most spacious open-air pleasure centres in the county and no less than three excellent golf courses.

From Northampton we travelled on north to **Chapel Brampton** and wondered what the distinction was between it and **Church Brampton,** its neighbour. Domesday mentions only one Brampton and when the parish was carved into two, the senior village retained the name of the church and also held onto a strip of land only one field width reaching to the Nene in the south. The nearby Althorp Estate erected substantial gabled neo-Tudor housing in 1848 at both Bramptons and these are still evidence.

From here the next stopover, especially for those interested in our Royal Family, is the family seat of the Princess of Wales, **Althorp House**. It is popular for visitors, especially those who are after a glimpse of the Princess's earlier life but the house itself originates from the 16th century with alterations added the 18th century. Inside you'll find an interesting collection of paintings, ceramics and furniture.

The estate was bought in 1508 by John Spencer a sheep farmer and the house begun in 1573. The entrance hall os lofty and impressive, with a magnificent ceiling of hundreds of flowers set in six sided panels. In 1786 the red brick house was refaced with grey-white brick tiles and the moat filled in as the gardens were remodelled by Samule Lapridge, Capability Brown's assistant.

Just west of Althorp lies **Great Brington** where the tombs of the Spencers and Laurence - ancestors of George Washington - can be found. Also close by you'll find **Holdenby House,** a Tudor building that was used to hold Charles 1 as prisoner in 1647. Sir Christopher Hatton, Elizabeth I 'Dancing Chancellor' was born here but the original house built by him has given way has given way to a 19th century house of great diginity and beauty with something of its stately past in the ground in the form of the Elizabethan gateways dated 1583.

Cotton Manor Gardens is near at hand should you be interested to visit an attractively laid out garden. Please note that the opening times for the two attractions mentioned above are limited and should be checked before making a visit.

To the west you'll find **Moulton** lying on high ground which has a church at one end and a chapel at the other. The medieval church, built of ironstone had buried in its foundation of the nave. The chapel is where William Carey first started preaching in 1875 combining it with his other tasks as schoolmaster and cobbler.

Here you'll also find the **Artichoke Inn** built in 1608 on the site of a meeting place for knights about to go off on the Crusade. Now you
200

won't have to face any knights only warm hospitality, fine ales and a most comprehensive menu of meals that caters for all tastes including vegetarian.

The Artichoke Inn.   Moulton.

Further north is **Pitsford**, the church here has a remarkable Norman doorway showing a strange animal struggling with an armed man. The door itself has fine ironwork and the 14th century font is notable for its great variety of carving. **Pitsford Water** is an eight hundred acre reservoir with trout fishing, boats for hire and attractive picnic areas.

Brixworth, is just beyond and famous for its already mentioned church. Most original 7th century work with much re-used Roman material. This sophisticated building was a monastery that survived Danish raids in the 8th century although added to in medieval times an ancient atmosphere still prevails.

Roughly three miles beyond lies **Lamport Hall.** Again opening is limited for this 16th century building that was the seat of the Isham Family but you'll see examples of the work of John Webb from the 1650's. Inside there is splendid decoration and fine furniture, including two large 17th century cabinets and some excellent 17th and 18th century Chinese porcelain. An outstanding collection of paintings charts the history of the Ishams for four hundred years. In the wooded gardens are cedars, box trees and an alpine garden.

Just a few miles west of Lamport is another old house, **Coton Manor,** built in 1662 from the ruins of nearby Holdenby Hall which was destroyed by Cromwell after the Civil War. The Coton Manor Gardens cover ten acres on different levels where clever use has been made of a stream which is a habitat for a variety of water fowl.

There is an air of dignity and prosperity about the wide streets of **Guilsborough,** flanked by 18th century houses of brivk and ironstone. The vicarage here used to be Guilsborough Hall, where Wordsworth cam e to stay and it is said that he bought with him from the Lake District the yellow Cumberland poopy that grows profusely here. The church has lovely windows by Morris and Burne-Jones. The nearby Guilsborough Grange has a wildlife park and a pets corner for children. Its acres of grassland, pond and streams make the Grange an ideal picnic spot.

Naseby played a significant part in the course of English history as this was where on June 14th 1645 the battle was fought that decided the outcome of the Civil War with Cromwell's defeat of Charles I. Here, Cromwell and Fairfax with fourteen thousand Roundheads faced the Royalists forces who advanced outnumbered two to one. Charles's right hand man, Prince Rupert, positioned his army first on Dust Hill; Cromwell drew in his army on the opposite side of the valley, on Red Hill and the first attack came at 10.00am. After heavy fighting, Fairfax won a resounding victory, capturing all the King's baggage, including about £100,000 in gold and silver. Eleven months later Charles surrendered in Newark ending the Civil War.

Today Naseby is one of the least spoilt of English battlefields and in it a large obelisk, erected in 1823, states that the battle had been,' *a useful lesson to British Kings never to exceedthe bounds of their perogative'.* A more modest memorial records the position of Cromwells cavalry before their decisive charge. **Naseby Battle and Farm Museum** (0604 740241) contains a minature layout of the battlefield with commentary as well as relics from the battle. It also has on display a collection of bygone agricultural tools and machinery. The actual site of the battle is marked by a column erected in 1936.

Nearby **Kelmarsh Hall** was built in 1728 by James Gibb, a follower of Sir Christopher Wren. The church is colourful with polished granite piers in the nave and in the chancel, the walls, floor, reredos and latar rails are of many coloured marbles and mosiacs bought from Rome.

To the west of Naseby lies **Cold Ashby,** the highest village in Northamptonshire at seven hundred feet above sea level. From **Honey Hill** a mile away you get fine views across into Warwickshire and Leicestershire. **Sibberfort,** lies at the northern end of the tableland where the Battle of Naseby was fought. The River Welland, rising nearby, flows a little to the west before beginning its eastward journey, forming the northern boundary of Northamptonshire. In a wood to the north east are extensive earthworks though to be a Norman motte and bailey castle. The medieval church is restored and the vicar here for twenty one years was the botanist, Miles Joseph Berkeley.

Briwworth Church.

Naseby Memorial

Finally, we cane to **Marston Trussell** on the Leicestershire border. After the Battle of Naseby many fleeing Royalists were surrounded and cut down here, their remains are in the churchyard. Four cedars have cast a shadow over the church for many centuries and both doorways into this 13th century place of worship are medieval. Inside there is a statue of Mark Brewster who made a fortune in Russia from piracy. He donated four shillings to the poor and forty pounds to the church for a new bell. He returned to England to retire on his ill gotten gains but the long finger of the Tsar tapped him on the shoulder. He was taken back to Moscow where he was tried and executed in 1612. The 17th century hall refashioned in the last century stands in beautiful grounds with a island studded lake.

CHAPTER NINE

North Northamptonshire

Memorial Chapel, Oundle School

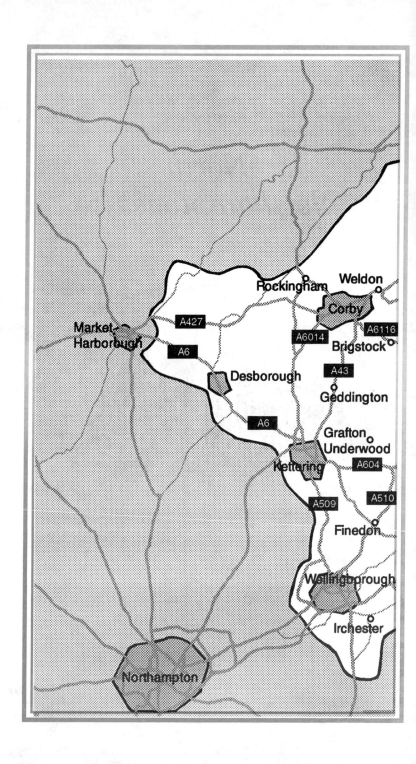

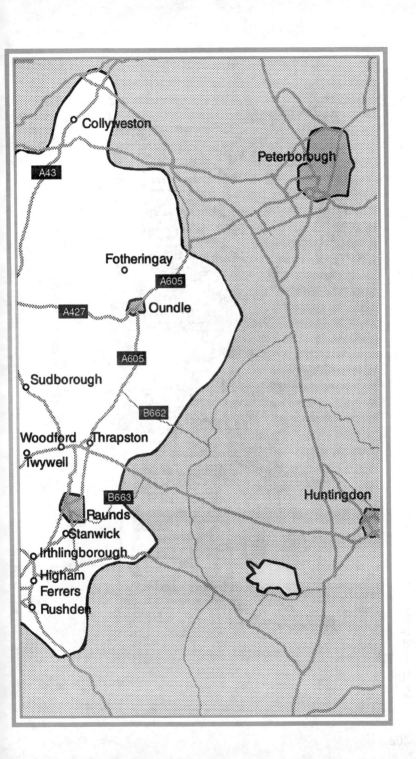

Market Square Higham Ferrers.

North Northamptonshire.

We started our tour of North Northamptonshire in **Irchester** originally a Roman settlement; a walled Roman town was uncovered last century and known as The Burrows. It is eighteen acres in area and part of the eight feet thick walls can be seen. Saxon England has also been discovered here, an extensive cemetery was found with four hundred graves all facing east. Many of the coffins were stone and in one eight bronze vessels were found packed into a bucket. Norman England is evident in the church where there are some columns and piers resting on Norman plinths. The six arched bridge, which crosses the River Nene, is 14th century and bears the crossed keys of Peterborough Abbey and the wheel of St Catherine.

There is a country park just outside Irchester which is on the way to **Wellingborough.** The town sits near the point where the River Ise joins the Nene and the medieval church spire can be seen for many miles. There are fine avenues of trees leading to the town which has, over the years, swallowed up the smaller villages surrounding it. Wellingborough is noted for its industry of iron mills, flour mills and tanneries.

In and around the Market Square there are several interesting old buildings. The Hind Hotel with its gabled roof and handsome windows looks out on the square. It has a 17th century oak staircase, a fine stone fireplace and a room furnished inn oak and called the Cromwell Room because it was being constructed whilst the Battle of Naseby was being fought. There is another fine old house called Croyland Abbey, with dormer windows in the five hundred year old roof. Near to it, in public grounds, stands an old tithe barn, stone walled and thatched, seventy feet long and twenty two feet wide. It was built in the 15th century and has two great doorways at either side, one of which is thirteen feet high. All these buildings escaped a great fire which razed most of the town in fours hours in 1738. The handsome 13th century tower and spire of the parish church of All Hallows rises amongst the trees in the centre of town. The great tower seen from across the Nene is that of St Mary's, a modern church built between 1906 and 1930.

To the east is the delightful old town of **Higham Ferrers** on the outskirts of the footwear manufacturing town of **Rushden.** Its long main street widens into a market place where there is a medieval cross. Just off the market place is a narrow lane leading to the church and a group of medieval buildings.

One striking house has a great stone panel along its front, with fiery dragons linked to each other. Henry Chichele was born here in 1362; he progressed from bakers boy to Archbishop of Canterbury, a post he held for thirty years until his death in 1443. He never forgot his birthplace and his statue looks down from the church tower, and the house of charity he built, called Bede House is in the churchyard.

Irthlingborough is a small town thriving on leather and iron industries. It has two fine bridges across the Nene, one built in the 14th century and the other in the 20th. The medieval bridge has ten ribbed arches and the arms of an ancient monastery carved on one of its stones suggests that the bridge was built by monks from Peterborough. The modern bridge running parallel to the old is a landmark with great arches stretching for half a mile over the low land by the river. Across the wide valley the handsome tower of the medieval church can be seen with its double rows of battlements, turrets and many windows.

Stanwick, just east Irthlingborough, is set high on a hill, its glorious 13th century church and spire soars high above the Nene Valley. On each side of the belfry are window arches which allow the sound of the bells, one of which is dated 1360, to be heard for miles.

Raunds is known chiefly for the manufacture of army boots and its dolls. In May 1905, Raunds came into the national consciousness when two hundred men marched to London in protest at the low rates of pay for bootmakers. They arrived in the capital to find a crowd of ten thousand supporters waiting. After ten days, concessions were finally made and the strikers victorious.

To the east **Finedon** has a character of its own. It has a well known inn called The Bell, which, by tradition occupies the site on which there has been an inn since 1042. The much restored old Hall with some Elizabethan rooms, a handsome rectory, a charity school built in the reign of Queen Anne and some ironstone houses of the 17th century are well worth noting. The school has a fine doorway and the inn, built in 1872 is a good example of the Gothic revival. Hereabouts, there is an odd tower which stirs the curiosity of the traveller, called the Wellington Tower. It is said that the Duke of Wellington used to stand on this spot when visiting a friend and point out where the countryside around resembled the field of Waterloo.

Finedon Hall, the near neighbour of the church, has a courtyard with embattled walls and an ancient covered walk like a cloister, but the house, with its fine ornamental gables, is mostly 19th century. This is the handiwork of the former squire who rejoiced in the name of William Harcout Isham Mackworth-Dolben.

Following the river north we came to **Woodford**, where within the Norman church a human heart was found in one of the columns during restoration work in the 19th century. It was presumed to be the heart of one of the Traillys, Lords of the Manor seven hundred years earlier. It's though to be the heart of one of the family who died during the Crusades and brought back by his followers so that he may rest with his ancestors. It is now enclosed in a cloth and in a glazed recess in the pillar in which it was found. There is also some medieval brass and over one hundred carved oak figures in the church.

Woodford's most unusual and possibly fittest inhabitants was a Josiah Eaton, who was born towards the end of the 18th century. He was only 5 feet 2 inches tall, but he accomplished feats of incredible endurance. In 1815 he started a marathon walk around Blackheath, completing a mile every hour. Apparently he did this without stopping for six weeks! Eventually he covered an astonishing eleven hundred miles.

Thrapston by the A604 and A605, stands on one of the loveliest reaches of the River Nene which flows under the towns medieval bridge. It is surrounded by fine pastureland, created when the flood waters and rich mud subsided following the two ice ages. Since the days of King John, the quiet of Thrapston has been disturbed on market days with farmers coming to sell their cattle and produce.

The castle has vanished and much of the church has been modernised, its main attraction is the stone tablet on the west wall which bears the stars and stripes. It is thought that the American flag was designed with this tablet in mind, it being the coat of arms of Sir John Washington who died in 1624. Thrapston and more specifically the church have become part of the George Washington pilgrimage made by many Americans. Not far from the church is Montagu House, believed to have been the home of Sir John Washington.

The Mill Marina and Caravan Park, in Midland Road, Thrapston is a self sufficient park run by the Phillips family. It is a unique place where the caravan park, boat moorings and angling facilities all blend together to make this a wonderful place to stay. The four and a half acres is bounded by a disused railway viaduct on one side, the River Nene on another whilst a mill stream runs through the middle. There are five static sites, thirty pitches for touring caravans and twelve pitches for campers. At the moorings there is room for twenty five boats.

The Mill Marina and Caravan Park.   Thrapston.

Twywell is perhaps the last place you'd expect to find with links to Africa. Yet two Africans, who helped carry explorer David Livingstone's embalmed body eight hundred miles to the sea on its way to Westminster Abbey, lived here whilst the Livingstone Journals were being prepared for publication. In the church there are three stones from Calvary in the window by the altar. These were sent by the rectors friend, General Gordon who wrote a letter saying that he hoped to visit the Pope on his way back from Palestine. The letter can be seen in the vestry and the choir stalls are carved with animals including a lion, a hippo, an elephant and other carvings depicting chained and yoked African slaves being driven towards the Cross.

It seems appropriate to find a pub called **The Old Friar**, in the village. Named after a nearby monastery this pub is steeped in history and was once popular with American servicemen flying out from Grafton Underwood on bombing raids during the Second World War.

The Old Friar.   Twywell.

This family run pub welcomes children and has a large selection of non alcoholic drinks along with its fine ales, wines and spirits. The Carvery Restaurant seats seventy and you can also choose from an a la carte menu. The oak beamed ceilings, stone walls and open fireplace give the pub a rustic feel that enhances its informal friendliness where you will be made to feel welcome when youarrive.

At **Grafton Underwood**, three miles away, you'll find a memorial to the crews of the B17 flying fortresses who were based here and just a mile or so beyond is **Sudborough.** Here you'll find **The Vane Arms**, the main hostelry in the village which has accommodation. The letting rooms are in a renovated barn which are furnished in Victorian pine and include TV and tea/coffee facilities. The traditional food served is prepared with the freshest of ingredients and are of a size that would satisfy the largest of appetites. A fine selection of reals ales is available which makes the Vane Arms, named after Sir Henry Vane, a popular place with both locals and visitors.

The Vane Arms.   *Sudborough.*

We travelled west and came to the second biggest town in the north of the county, **Kettering.** It stands above the River Ise and the name is familiar far and wide, for its produces clothing and shoes. It is here that the missionary William Carey and the famous preacher Andrew Fuller founded the Baptist Missionary Society, which gave a new impetus to the cause of foreign missions all over the world.

Kettering's great parish church, built of Barnack stone is one of the most impressive in the country. The tower and spire, rising one hundred and seventy eight feet, are a landmark for miles around. Much of the old town has disappeared in its rapid growth, but a few old houses linger in narrow lanes. There are delightful gardens by the Art Gallery and across the road is a group of almshouses built in 1688.

A couple of miles north of **Rothwell** which stands by the A6, at the **Rushton Triangular Lodge**, you'll find a fascinating piece of pious

Rushton Triangular Lodge

eccentricity built by Sir Thomas Tresham. He owned Rushton Hall, and he built a folly in 1593 to symbolise the Holy Trinity, and everything about it related to the number three or multiples thereof - it has three sides, three stories and is twenty seven feet high. Each side has three windows and three gables and the theme is continued in the triangular decoration. It even has a three-sided chimney. It is difficult to understand the full meaning of Sir Thomas's personal philosophy, but the building is nevertheless quite beautiful. In a way it still partly fulfils his original idea, for it certainly provokes the visitor to think about this strange embodiment of religious fervour. Nearby **Rushton Hall** was Treshams home but is now school of the Royal Institute for the Blind.

Desborough is a small town with old ironstone houses ; it used to be a Saxon settlement and many treasures have come to light in recent years. Three massive stones have been unearthed in the Rectory gardens, the biggest carved on two sides with Saxon scrollwork and a crude picture thought to represent Daniel in the lion's den. Also found here was found the grave of a Saxon lady still wearing a beautiful necklace of thirty seven gold beads with a pendant cross of gold. It is one of the earliest Christian crosses in the country and is now in the British Museum. In another grave a Celtic bronze mirror exquisitely engraved with a spiral design, and an elaborate handle six inches long was found. The church has been here for seven hundred years, though its pinnacled tower with a fine spire is early 16th century. The church house dates from about 1700 and the Market Cross, at the north end of the High Street, was built in the 18th century.

The fields outside **Geddington** bear the remains of more than seventy miles of trees. They were laid out in the 18th century by the 2nd Duke of Montagu, nicknamed John the Planter. He had an idea to plant an avenue from Boughton House all the way to his London home, but when his neighbour, the Duke of Bedford, refused to let the trees cross his estate he planted avenues of equivalent length on his own estate. Unfortunately, Dutch Elm disease destroyed much of his work but the present owners, Boughton Estates, are gradually replacing the old trees with limes and beeches.

Just north of here is evidence of one of the most poignant of love stories, namely that of King Edward I and his wife Eleanor. They enjoyed thirty happy years of marriage during which time Eleanor's devotion was exhibited in her risking her life for her Lord by sucking the poison out of the wound he received from a poisoned arrow. Many years later, the King was on his way to see her after she became dangerously ill but he arrived too late and, heartbroken, he embarked on the one hundred and fifty mile funeral procession to London. At every place her coffin came to rest each night, an **Eleanor Cross** was

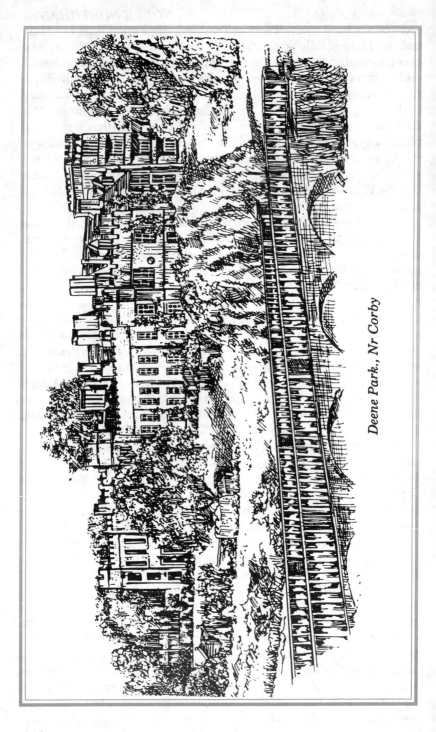

Deene Park., Nr Corby

later erected. Out of twelve built, only three are still remaining; at Geddington, at **Hardingstone** near Northampton and at **Waltham Cross** in Hertfordshire. The Cross, now overseen by English Heritage, stands in a triangle near the church where three roads meet, rising from seven steps to a height of nearly forty feet. It is elaborately carved with statues of Eleanor gazing down upon the passer by.

Still further north on the banks of a tributary of the Nene called Harpers Brook is the Saxon village of **Brigstock** in the Rockingham Forest. The church of St Andrew has a substantial Saxon tower built and its bell used to be tolled three times a day as a guide for travellers through the forest. The forest itself was once the hunting grounds of Norman aristocracy but evidence has been unearthed to show that Brigstock had been settled during the Iron Age and during Roman occupation. The village has delightful old stone cottages, and a 16th century manor house. By the little tree-covered green a quaint Elizabethan cross stands on four steps and is carved on four sides. On the top stands a ball weather-vane.

About a mile away is **Fermyn Woods Hall**, a house which has grown through the centuries from the 14th to the 19th. It was a forest hunting lodge six hundred years ago, its gateway was brought from the house known as the Old Building (or Bield) at Lyveden and bears the coat of arms of Sir Lewis Tresham, second son of Sir Thomas the Builder.

His New and Old Buildings at **Lyveden** are about two miles from Brigstock; one a farmhouse, the other a ruin, bearing witness to the erratic devotion and architectural interest of their creator.

A good time to go to **Corby** is during the colourful 'Pole Fair', but as this only happens every twenty years, you will have plenty of time to plan your holiday. But beware, for on the day of the Fair any stranger may be carried off astride a pole and placed in the stocks where he must stay until a toll is paid - apparently its a Danish custom. Even as a tiny village, Corby has been in contact with the mainstream of British history. It has been recorded very briefly since the time of King Edgar in the 10th century and there is evidence of pre-Roman and Roman occupation. The actual town itself is rich in open woodland, a surviving reminder of the once great Rockingham Forest. Kingswood, a nature reserve, Hazel Woods and the East Carlton Country Park offer natural habitat on the doorstep. The latter contains the **Steel Making Heritage Centre** and tells of Corby's connection with that industry. There is also an attractive boating lake with small boats and canoes available for hire and fishing facilities in season. Alongside the Civic Centre, the Festival Hall and Theatre and the indoor swimming complex is the Lodge Park Sports Centre, offering exactly what you would imagine. The Corby Festival takes place over a week in July every year; events include drama, puppets, art exhibitions, folk and jazz 'happenings', concerts and poetry readings and programmes of popular music.

Weldon is an attractive village situated near to Corby and surrounded by marvellous places to visit. We found the village had a whole host of nice restaurants and pubs as well as good shop and post office. The history of Weldon is interesting because it has its own industry, quarrying the stone which bears its name. This stone was used to build **Rockingham Castle**, **Old St Paul's** and **Great St Mary's** in Cambridge. The village has a variety of good stone houses dating from the seventeenth century to today, some with date stones. Haunt Hill House for example was built at the time of Charles I. On the green adjacent to the school is the windowless 'Round House' which was used as the Parish lock-up. St Mary's Church, with its backcloth of tall trees, is reached from the village by a raised walk over the bridges across Willow Brook.

In the midst of the village you'll find **Weldon Holiday Cottages** - four cottages, Brandy, Nags Head, Stable Croner and Cobblers Flat for rent. Tom and Ann Nunnerley run the cottages from their estate office on the village green and you'll find each place fully equipped with washing machine, fridge, television,bed linen, towels, toiletries and such. There are facilities for the disabled. Electricity and heating are included in the rent whilst in the village you'll find pubs, restaurant, a shop and post office.

Weldon Holiday Cottages.   Weldon.

North East of Corby, we came across **Deene Park** standing amid gardens filled with old-fashioned roses and rare trees and shrubs. Originally a medieval manor, it has been transformed over the last four hundred years into a Tudor and Georgian mansion by successive members of the Brudenell family. Today Deene Park contains fine examples of period furniture and beautiful paintings. The oldest visible part is an arch circa 1300 in the east of the house which comprises a Hall of about 1450. The Great Hall was completed at the end of the 16th century and has a magnificent sweet chestnut hammerbeam roof. The most famous member of the Brudenells was James, 7th Earl of Cardigan, who led the charge of the Light Brigade at Balaclava and interesting records and relics are on display.

Kirby Hall, now an English Heritage property, dates from 1570 was given by Elizabeth I to her favourite courtier, Sir Christopher Hatton. 17th century alterations have been attributed to Inigo Jones and despite the house being abandoned during the following century it is still a fine example of Tudor and Renaissance influenced design and construction.

Three miles north west of Corby is **Rockingham** which, according to Domesday Book, was wasteland when William the Conqueror ordered a castle to be built there. Today, as in Norman times, the castle stands sentinel-like on the tree clad slopes of Rockingham Hill with the thatched and slated cottage of the village's wide main street spread out below. At Rockingham it is possible to trace the development of English domestic life and cultural taste over nine hundred years. Entering between the Norman towers it is not difficult to image the royal cavalcades thundering in the Middle Ages. The armour in the Tudor Great Hall reminiscent of the Civil War, when Rockingham was captured by the Roundheads. Indeed the castle was used by the BBC during filming of the series 'By the Sword Divided' where it was renamed Arnescote Castle. Situated in the wide Welland Valley between Rockingham Castle and Stamford is the picturesque **Harringworth.** A very pretty conservation village of mainly stone and thatch, it still remains unspoilt.

The White Swan.   Harringworth.

The White Swan in the village is a 15th century coaching inn which has been refurbished but still retains its character. Here you can choose between self catering or bed and breakfast. In the pub you'll find a wealth of old beams, stone walls, traditional furniture, which enhance the atmosphere. A selection of traditional English and international dishes are served in the bars and main dining room. Daily specials are on the blackboard as well as set dishes from their menu.

Oundle is famous far and wide for its public school, its fine stone houses, its noble church and its old inns. It has been described as the most delightful town in Northampton and you might be inclined to agree, with its pleasant pastoral setting near the Fenlands and the River Nene flowing on three sides. We entered the town across the North Bridge which used to have thirty arches until it was destroyed by a tempest in 1570. There are four old inns in Oundle and the best of them is the Talbot built in 1626. The materials were brought from nearby **Fotheringhay Castle** and the Jacobean staircase inside the Talbot Inn is supposed to be where Mary Stuart took her last steps before her execution.

The other three inns are the White Lion built in 1641, The Old Ship with its low beams and winding stairs, and The Anchor. The town has three sets of old almshouses, and some charming private houses. The two churches, one medieval, one relatively modern, and the old school buildings make a fine spectacle. The school was founded by Sir William Laxton in 1556 and an inscription to his memory is written above the 17th century doorway in Greek, Latin and Hebrew. The medieval church has a magnificent tower with a spire two hundred feet high. All the walls are about eight hundred years old and it is certainly one of the most impressive churches in the country.

Just outside Oundle there is a country park, a marina and a golf course and then Fotheringhay which used to have three castles. The first was probably built around 1100 by the husband of William the Conqueror's daughter Judith. The famous castle was built in the 14th century by Edmund of Langley, 5th son of Edward III. Henry VIII gave Fotheringhay to Catherine of Aragon in their happier days and later it became the prison of Mary, Queen of Scots. She was brought here in bands of steel and executed in 1587 in the Banqueting Hall .

The castle was pulled down in 1627 and two hundred years later a gold ring was found with a lovers' knot entwined around the initials of Mary and Darnley; it is thought that it fell from her finger as she was executed. It is now a peaceful scene that surrounds the site of the vanished castle with the river winding through the meadows. Thistles still grow in the grounds where they were planted by the tragic queen and they thrive every year reaching a height of eight feet or more.

Nearby **Elton Hall** dates back to 1474 and is a fascinating mixture

Memorial Chapel. Oundle School.

Fotheringhay Church.

of styles reflecting the tastes and interests of succeeding generations. It has some wonderful furniture, fine paintings and books and lovely gardens.

We headed towards are final part of Northamptonshire past another fine building some three miles north west of Oundle, **Southwick Hall.** It has examples of 14th century, Tudor and later building work but again be aware of its limited opening times.

Our final stop was in the delightful village of **Collyweston**. Its houses are a picturesque mixture of 17th and 18th century stone-walled buildings roofed with stone slates, bounded for some distance on the west by the lovely winding River Welland. The village changed counties in the re-organisation of 1974 and is now in the north eastern sector of Northamptonshire. There are many 17th century houses built of the local brown ironstone and the spire of the church has eight sides of rich 14th century tracery in its openings. In 1737 most of the medieval church fell to the ground but part of the transept and the beautiful central tower still remain.

The Cavalier Inn in the village has six bedrooms all ensuite and beautifully decorated should you wish to stay and explore the area. The inn was built in 1856 and its open plan interior has an open fireplace and log fires in both the lounge and cocktail bars. The decor is soft and the well appointed tables all have interior views of the pub. A 76 seat restaurant is available for you to enjoy the good food on offer or alternatively you can choose from their large range of bar snacks.

The Cavalier Inn.   Collyweston.

We now move on to the neighbouring county of Leicester and hope we have given an insight into a much underrated county prompting you to explore it for yourself.

Elton Hall, Nr Oundle

Garden at Deane Park

CHAPTER TEN

Leicestershire

Old Grammer School, Market Harborough

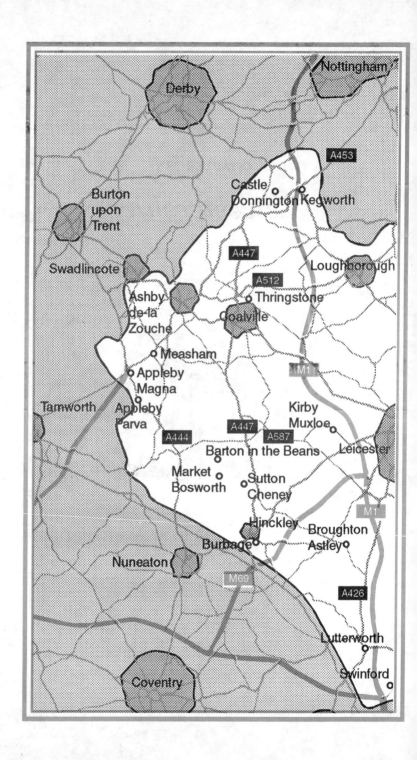

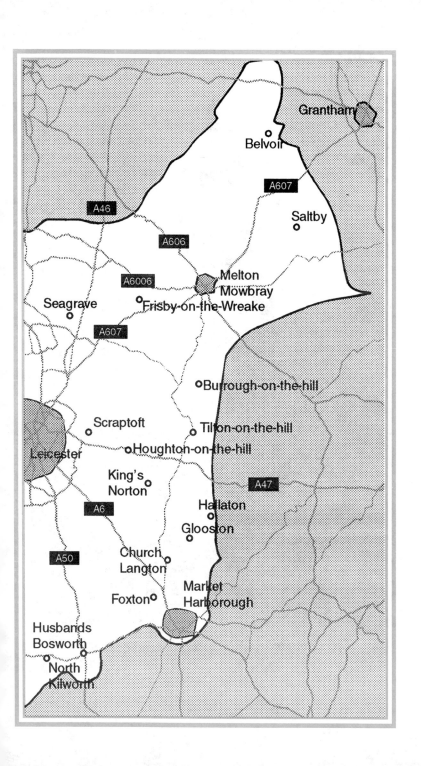

The Campanile, Queens Park. Loughborough.

CHAPTER TEN

Leicestershire.

Leicestershire, in the very heart of England covers eight hundred and twenty square miles of pleasant countryside. Most counties suffer from popular myths and Leicestershire is generally dismissed by those who have merely driven through it as flat, pretty well covered with red brick towns and villages, and somewhere in the background a lot of fox hunting goes on.

Its most attractive features are shy and quiet and have to be sought out but they amply reward the explorer. The county is divided into two almost equal parts by the River Soar which flows northward into the Trent. It separates the east and west by a broad valley, flowing like a silver ribbon through historic **Leicester** in the very heart of the county. This capital town was thriving in Roman days and is one of the oldest towns in England. It has managed to retain outstanding monuments of almost every age of English history.

Nearly half of the county live in Leicester, the rest are in over two hundred villages. Agriculture and industry grew hand in hand; the long hair of the sheep is famous for producing fine woollens, and the end of the 17th century saw the beginning of the now world-wide hosiery trade. **Loughborough** has been famous for making bells for more than one hundred years, their product pealing from many of England's church towers.

Leicestershire has, amongst other things created, three magnificent foods in its time - gastronomic creations that have a national reputation; they are Stilton, Red Leicester cheese and pork pies. At Melton Mowbray, these wondrous pies have been made on a commercial scale since 1830 and if you have only ever had a factory pork pie you have not lived. Stilton was named after a village on the old Great

North Road (which is in Huntingdonshire), but despite the name attached to it, it remains a wholly Leicestershire creation. It was widely eaten for years before the landlord of The Bell Inn at Stilton got to hear of it, obtained supplies and made it famous to all who stopped at his inn on their coaching journeys. Red Leicester cheese was made in the southern part of the county in the 1700's but now the only genuine product is made at Melton Mowbray, which also makes Stilton and of course the superlative pork pies. There can be few towns in Britain that immediately make the mouth water just to think of the gastronomic perfection it produces.

Every schoolchild knows the name of **Bosworth Field**, one of the momentous battles which changed the course of English history. Henry Tudor defeated Richard 111 in the battle in 1485 to become Henry V11. Fought on an August morning in the west of the county, the countryside around Bosworth has changed little in five hundred years. For followers of English history it is a necessary part of a pilgrimage and a comprehensive museum reveals the details of this event.

All who know Leicestershire know **Swithland Wood** and the experience of walking through the dense carpet of bluebells in early summer is without parallel. **Charnwood Forest** has an area of sixty square miles, but the little mountain region has lost much of its woodland. Even so it remains an area of outstanding natural beauty, rich in flora and fauna of all kinds.

We do not wonder that Leicestershire has long been famous for its churches in towns and villages, and many have a rare beauty which time has not changed, indoors many are rich in historical treasure. About forty of them still have some ancient glass and thirty have kept their medieval screens. All in all, there is much to see and so we will arbitrarily embark on our journey around Leicestershire in **Market Harborough.**

One of the most attractive features of the picturesque small town is its wide main square. Its most notable building is the former grammar school, built in 1614. It stands above the street on carved wooden pillars; pedestrians can walk underneath it. The space below the school used to be a butter market but sadly no more. The parish church of St Dionysius, built circa 1200, is topped by a steeple which is a landmark for miles around. The interior of the church has galleries added since 1683 to accommodate an overflow in the congregation. The town was a trading centre as early as 1203, and markets are still held every Tuesday and Saturday. Industrial development has not destroyed the town's wealth of fine Georgian buildings. The inn sign that swings outside The Three Swans is a worthy example of 18th century ironwork.

230

Charles I made his headquarters in the town before the Battle of Naseby, and when he was defeated Cromwell occupied Market Harborough and from here wrote to Parliament telling them of his victory.

North of Market Harborough lies the historic village of **Foxton**. It is such a picturesque place, close to the Grand Union Canal and the famous **Foxton Locks.** Travelling a couple of miles west from Market Harborough we came to **Husbands Bosworth** and could not help but comment on such an intriguing name, indeed Leicestershire is full of places with unusual names. The name was chosen to distinguish it from Market Bosworth, some miles away. It was the 'farmers Bosworth' while the other was a market town. It stands high on the south border and an amble round can make an enjoyable break in a journey with its attractive old brick houses, including a Baptist Chapel of 1807.

There is a chilling story of nine local women who were tried and convicted of witchcraft in 1616. A boy of twelve, was thought to be bewitched as he would suddenly have violent fits, striking himself repeatedly and making animal noises. He accused the women of making the spirits of animals enter his body and they were all burned at the stake. The boy's fits continued, and a few months later six more women were accused. It was only the intervention of King James himself who recognised the boy's epilepsy that saved the women from the same fate as their unfortunate sisters.

The Fernie Lodge in Berridges Lane, Husbands Bosworth, is a lovely Georgian building that is a delight to the eye.

Fernie Lodge Hotel & Restaurant.   Husbands Bosworth.
Tel: 0858 880551

As you drive up to this hotel and restaurant with its pillared porch, you will see cascading hanging baskets full of colour in the summer and in winter when this myriad display has gone the house is

231

Old Grammar School. Market Harborough.

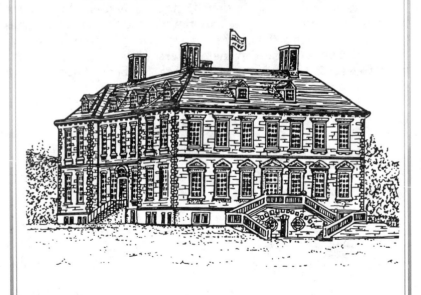

Stanford Hall

complimented by the trees and shrubs which surround the drive and house. Inside, it is elegant and the bedrooms will be found on the ground floor, which is ideal for the disabled. Every bedroom is ensuite with furnishings to suit the age and grace of the building and include tea/coffee making facilities, TV and direct dial telephones. The highly reputed restaurant is a gourmets delight, and whether you have breakfast, lunch or dinner you will not be disappointed. There is something for everyone on the menus and a comprehensive wine list is available to compliment the food.

Between Husbands Bosworth and **Lutterworth** is **North Kilworth** and just beyond the village is the tranquil and picturesque Leicester arm of the Grand Union Canal. Lutterworth is notable for the fact that Wycliffe was rector here, under the protection of John of Gaunt. His widespread opposition to papal abuses was bad enough but when he instigated the translation of the Bible into English he became totally persona non grata. He died in 1384 and was buried in the Lutterworth church, but when he was excommunicated in 1428 his body was exhumed, burned and his ashes scattered on the River Swift.

For many a favourite pastimes when travelling around the various counties is to visit stately homes. The more interesting ones are almost always those where a family is still in residence. This is so at **Stanford Hall**, just one and a half miles from **Swinford**. Mentioned in the Domesday book, the parish of Stanford is an ancient one. Some years after it was given to the Benedictine Abbey of Selby by a Norman companion of the Conqueror in 1069, another grant of Stanford land was made in 1140 to the Abbey by King Stephen. When the dissolution of the monasteries took place, Sir Thomas Cave purchased the original manor from Henry VIII in 1540.

The present building dates from the reign of William and Mary, around 1690, and has a majestic facade that adds to the its pleasing design. Inside, the rooms contain interesting collections of Stuart and Jacobite paintings, costumes and furniture. The stables house a motor museum.

Hinckley has been done scant justice by many writers on Leicestershire. Shakespeare touched the old market town with immortality when he referred to Hinckley Fair in Henry IV. He may have wandered along Church Walk where the old timbered houses still lean forward under the bent brows of their thatch. In 1834, Joseph Hansom made the first hansom cab and drove it along Regent Street at full gallop to demonstrate that it could not be overturned. He received only three hundred pounds for his invention, and it did not become popular for another twenty years. In those days the assizes for the whole county were held here having been moved from Leicester in

1610 because an epidemic of the plague was raging there (over one hundred and forty people died in Hinckley alone in 1626).

The name **Burbage** was originally Burbach and evidently came from the bur thistle which grew abundantly in its fields. It was a stylish and prosperous village at one time and one of its earliest incumbents was the 9th Earl of Kent who was rector here for fifty years. Burbage has a fine large common and a wood which attract people from far and wide. The River Soar rises here to begin its winding journey to the Trent and the church of St Catherine has a spire which can be seen for miles.

From Burbage it is easy to get to **Broughton Astley** along the B581, one of those thriving, expanding villages which has managed to retain a character of its own in spite of incorporating two other villages, **Sutton Elms** and **Princethorpe**. The reason is that the area has become a commuter base for London, Coventry and Rugby.

Ye Olde Bulls Head stands in the Main Street of Broughton Astley and is run by Geoff and Linda Stokes. The first thing you notice is the extraordinary central copper chimney in the lounge. It is a good place to take children as the family room is well equipped and the large, spacious garden has frames and swings to keep youngsters happy. The food here is simple but plentiful and all reasonably priced with every meal cooked to order. There is also a full selection of bar snacks if you do not want a full meal. With plenty of good walks such as the old Leicester - Rugby railway line now a splendid Nature Trail tempting you after a meal or drink, Ye Olde Bulls Head make an ideal stop whilst on your travels.

Ye Olde Bulls Head.   Broughton Astley.

To the east, **Sutton Cheney,** is traditionally where Richard III took communion on the morning of August 22nd, 1485, just before he went to battle a mile away on Bosworth field. The battle was actually fought mostly along the ridge of high ground running south west from the village and known as Ambion Hill. The Wars of the Roses came to an end when Richard was killed and Henry Tudor became Henry VII. There is a permanent exhibition at Ambion Hill where visitors can follow the battle and gain an insight into medieval life. There is a film theatre, book exhibitions and models, illustrated battle trails and a series of medieval attractions. The village is an interesting place with a stone framed farmhouse which, in Elizabethan times could call itself a manor, and some 17th century almshouses with an end gable curiously holed in rows from top to bottom as if to shelter pigeons.

Market Bosworth is just a couple of miles north of Sutton Cheney and it is from this small seven hundred year old market town that the Battle of Bosworth took its name. It is a village of no great size but its former grammar school had a high reputation in the Midlands. Originally founded in early Tudor times, in 1601, it was given a new lease of life by Sir Wolstan Dixie. It was to this school that Samuel Johnson came to teach after leaving university. He hated it so much that even Boswell failed to induce him to talk about his time here. Across the market place from the school is a fine house with its portico and cornice and handsome Georgian windows. It was built by the Dixies about 1700. The prettiest of streets leads to the church rising among the trees, the pinnacled tower crowned by a spire.

Just north of here is the wonderfully named **Barton-in-the-Beans**. Apparently the county used to be called 'bean-belly Leicestershire', on account of the crops of beans which formed part of its staple diet in more poverty-stricken times. The beans grown were supposed to be sweeter and more tender than anywhere and consequently were considered food fit for men, whereas in other counties they were fed only to swine. A writer in 1720 said they are 'so luxuriant that they appear like a forest towards harvest time'. Barton-in-the-Beans has never had a church but the Baptist Chapel, founded in 1745, was later rebuilt in 1841, and is said to be the earliest of the General Baptists in this part of the Midlands.

Twycross is the home of an interesting church and an interesting zoo. Amongst the yew trees the church stands on hillock and in its east window glows stained glass seven hundred years old. When the French Revolution threatened the lovely Sainte Chapelle in Paris, much precious glass was taken for safety from the Gothic shrine and bought by a rich Englishman, some of it eventually finding its way to Twycross and is a rich and rare treasure. A term which could be applied to the zoo if you like animals a lot. There are gorillas, lions and elephants, a pets' corner, children's adventure playground, a miniature railway and in the summer you can have a go at riding on a donkey.

There is also a shop, a cafe and a bar and the zoo is open daily from February to November.

Appleby Magna further along the **A444** has a 14th century church and a moated manor house which unfortunately is not open to the public. In the adjacent village **Appleby Parva** the grammar school building dates from the 17th century.

Measham is a place of brickmaking and coalmining, with the Ashby Canal flowing darkly past and the River Mease meandering nearby. A number of stone hammer-heads have been excavated here and solid wooden wheels and wedges of flint bound in hazel and have survived for thousands of years preserved in peat. Measham Hall lies about a mile east of the village off the road to Swepstone and is a fine example of Georgian architecture.

Sir Walter Scott's romantic novel 'Ivanhoe' sets the scene well for the North West region of Leicestershire whose history, natural beauty and charm combine to offer a warm welcome to visitors and tourists alike. The superbly named **Ashby-de-la-Zouch** was noted for the noble sport of jousting where no doubt many a maiden's honour was won or lost by knights in shining armour. Such tournaments took place near **Ashby Castle,** which was later attacked by Cromwell's Roundheads and consequently ruined.

Much of the region's attraction and beauty dates back still further; to the east is the edge of the Charnwood Forest, whose exposed volcanic rocks and granites are over two thousand million years old.

Although the Leicestershire coalfield is not far away, Ashby remains a pleasant little town and there is much to see. Market Street takes its name from the weekly market granted in 1219, and there were also no fewer than four annual fairs. Visually the most rewarding part of the town is the west end of Market Street where the Spa quarter is situated. Old, half-timbered buildings blend with modern architecture to make an attractive town with good shopping facilities, a number of impressive churches, parks and an imposing castle ruin. The Bull's Head is thought to be the oldest building. Cromwell reputedly had a drink here when the 15th century castellated manor was taken by Parliament after a years siege in the Civil War.

In the former upper courtyard of the castle stands the 19th century Manor House, now a school. Also of interest is the elegant seventy feet high monument to the Countess of Loudoun erected in 1874 and inscribed with a tribute to her from Disraeli. The castle ruin has a massive keep and many of the rooms are easily identifiable.

By the B447 on the way to Coalville you'll arrive at **Donington-le-Heath** where you'll discover **The Manor House.** Originally built in the 16th - 17th centuries it had considerable alterations around 1820. The house has now been restored to its original splendour and charm
236

where you can spend a pleasant few hours inside or in the beautiful gardens. After admiring this splendid place you can end your visit by enjoying light snacks and drinks in the cafe which is found in an adjacent stone barn.

The Manor House.   Donington-le-Heath.

By contrast, **Coalville** could hardly sound less romantic. Originally called Long Lane, this town sprang up on a bleak common when Whitwick Colliery was opened in 1824. George Stephenson was responsible for establishing the early railway here in 1832 as well as erecting the churches. By the colliery village of **Thringstone** we came across the remains of **Grace Dieu**, a 13th century Augustinian nunnery.

Further north is **Castle Donington,** was originally called just Donnington, but adopted the prefix when the Norman castle was built to command the River Trent crossing. It was demolished by King John to punish the owner for supporting Magna Carta and rebuilt in 1278 when no less than four of its subsequent owners were executed. The high-spired 13th/14th century church displays a pleasing blend of Early English, decorated and perpendicular architecture with interesting features. As well as timber-framed houses and shops, sports fields and clubs, there are facilities for angling and boating from the nearby marina on the River Trent. Beautifully set by the river at Kings Mills, an old castellated stone house once used as a priests house, is now a hotel and restaurant. The Mills are recorded in Domesday Book (1086) and have had a continuous history almost to the present day, not only for corn-milling but also for various industrial purposes. The Mills stand on the edge of **Donnington Park** where the vast Hall was built in 1793 in the 'Strawberry Hill' Gothic style with castellated turrets. It is now famous for its motor racing circuits and racing car collection.

Kegworth is a large village with several interesting examples of

Ashby Castle.

what is now called 'vernacular architecture', ie. native building including much dating from the days when it was a manufacturing village full of framework-knitters. Reckoned to be an 'almost faultless' late decorated church, is largely 14th century with some stained glass and a splendid Royal Arms dated 1684.

On the A6 between Kegworth and Hathern by the A6 is **Whatton Gardens,** twenty five acres of formal and wild gardens, with trees, shrubs, rock pools with fish and plants, and a very nice picnic area.

We travelled south and came to **Loughborough**, known for its bells, which have rung around the world since 1858 when the bell foundry of John Taylor moved to the town from Oxford. They made the 'Great Paul' for St Paul's Cathedral in London and their craft is an interesting one. We felt that a great deal of mystique surrounds this ancient craft so decided to visit the museum and factory in Freehold Street. It is a unique experience. The museum certainly provides an insight into the mysteries of moulding, casting and tuning bells from the 13th century onwards and is the only museum of bells and bell-founders in Britain.

The tower of the parish church of All Saints has a peal of ten bells, and contains a memorial to the bell-founding Taylor family. Much of the building dates from the 14th century despite its 19th century appearance, and the aisles have windows dating from about 1300. The oak roof of the nave is carried on beams which spring from carved musician angels resting one stone supports and the west wall is decorated with 15th century brasses.

The old 13th century rectory is gable fronted and in 1962, after extensive renovations it was opened as a museum. The striking Italianate town hall in the Market Place - there has been a market here since 1221 - was built in 1855 and on the second Thursday in November, the ancient November fair is held dating from 1228. For those interested in steam trains, go to the Central Station and there you will see Loughborough's links with the steam age preserved. The Main Line Steam Trust runs locomotives from here to Quorn and Birstall, a distance of about ten miles and includes the Swithland Reservoir viaduct.

In the little village of **Seagrave** just four miles from Loughborought, the Roman Gartree Road runs just south of here. The church of John the Baptist was founded in the 12th century, but has now been rebuilt retaining only the piscina and font that are medieval. At the west end of the village is the moated site of the medieval manor house which was brought by the Brudenells of Deene in 1632 and still belongs to them.

The White Horse Inn.   Seagrave.

The White Horse Inn sits almost next to the village church and its landlord is dedicated to the resurrection of Real Ales. Not an inn where you'll get meals but it does serve some excellent home made bar snacks which will fill a hungry corner. In the summer barbecues are held at weekends so if you are in the area look out for this inn that is a delightful watering hole where you can replenish yourselves before continuing on your journey.

One of **Rothley's** two greens - Town Green - incorporates some of the finest timber framed houses in the county. One or two are cruck-built, in which curved tree trunks are joined to form the framework of the house. Slightly more 'modern' are the Tudor box-frame houses also in evidence here. Town Green lies on the edge of Rothley Park, site of Rothley Temple which was built in the 13th century by the Knights Templars. The temple was later incorporated into an Elizabethan house which was added to over the succeeding centuries and finally converted in 1960 into the Rothley Court Hotel. From about 1550 it was the seat of the Babington family. William Wilberforce, a family friend, drafted his bill for the abolition of slavery at the house while on a visit in 1791. A small monument records the occasion. In 1800, the historian Thomas Babington Macaulay, later Lord Macaulay of Rothley, was born here, and the hotel maintains the room as it was on the day he was born.

The original Templar chapel is still used for occasional services and the parish church of St Mary the Virgin has some fine memorials and a carved Norman font. In the churchyard is a Saxon cross of the 8th or 9th century. Rothley Station, which was built for the Central Railway in the 1890's, is restored to its original condition, complete with nostalgic advertising where you can catch the restored steam train from Loughborough.

Our next leg of the journey was in the ancient city of **Leicester**. The historic centre of this ancient city still retains much of interest from Roman times to the 20th century. We began in the great open air market held in the square near **Gallow Tree Gate.** It has been here on the same site since at least 1200 and probably long before. There is something going on here every weekday; but the most interesting days are Wednesday, Friday and Saturday, and there are many bargains to be had or you can just soak up a wonderful atmosphere. Leicester was founded just before the Roman conquest and they called it Ratae Coritanorum (capital or Coritani); it is also mentioned in Domesday Book under the name of Ledecestre.

If you enjoy ancient ruins, **The Jewry Wall Museum and Site** in St Nicholas Circle is to be recommended being devoted to Archaeology to 1500 AD. It is a modern building adjacent to the Roman bath site and houses some extremely important exhibits. We found the Bronze Age Welby Hoard, and the Roman Milestone from Thurmaston here. There are several important Romano-British mosaics, Roman wall plaster and Anglo-Saxon burial. The displays and the information on them in this museum make a visit extremely interesting. At some time, late Medieval painted glass was removed from Wygston's House and brought to Jewry Wall and the second century Roman wall and bath site are open to the public.

Did You Know...

There is a full

Town and Village Index

at the back of the book?

St Nicholas Church, close to the Jewry Wall, is one of the best known Anglo-Saxon churches in England. It stands on the site of the Roman basilica and was built with materials from the Roman ruins. In the walls we could see stones from four different periods namely Roman, Saxon, Norman and Medieval English. Courses of herringbone masonry formed by Roman tiles are round the massive central tower

241

Steam on the Great Central Railway

built by the Normans and enriched with arcading. There is Saxon masonry in the west wall and two deeply splayed windows, their round heads formed by double rows of Roman tiles.

Our next stop was the **Guildhall** in Guildhall Lane and you can certainly understood why it is described as one of the most remarkable civic buildings in England. The Great Hall was built of timber in 1390 as a meeting place for members of the Corpus Christi Guild and later used by the Mayor and his brethren. The hall was used as the town hall until the new municipal building 1876 was erected. The Mayor's Parlour, adjoining the Great Hall, was built early in the reign of Henry VII, and has a wonderful oak panelled chimney-piece. Set in the leaded panes of the windows is black and gold painted glass showing the Tudor Rose, the Prince of Wales feathers, a chalice and some of the seasons.

Did You Know...

The Hidden Places Series

Covers most of Britain?

For our full list see back of book

We left the Guildhall and entered Wygston's House. This important medieval building at 12, Applegate, St Nicholas Circle, houses a fantastic display of 18th-20th century costume.

Wygston's House.   Leicester.

The materials and colours are superb and when you look at some of the fantastic gowns you can almost hear the swish of silk skirts as the ladies moved round a room. In addition to the costumes there is also a reconstruction of a draper's and shoe shop of the 1920's.

From here it is just a short walk to the Castle. The 12th century Great Hall is now concealed within 18th century brickwork as it is used as the Crown Court. It has a charming setting, however, with the riverside gardens on one side and the spacious green on the other. The remains of the original Norman motte (or central mound) can still be seen.

In a wonderful setting on the edge of the castle green above the River Soar is the **Church of St Mary de Castro**. It was founded in 1107 by the first Earl Leicester as a collegiate chapel, and was extended several times during the next three hundred years. Near the altar are five stone sedilia, or seats for the clergy, which date from 1180 and are regarded as the finest of their kind in England. Its spire rebuilt in 1783, makes a dramatic impact and acrobats were once wont to slide down a rope from the top to the castle green below.

If you want to get a clear understanding of the past history of Leicestershire then a visit to **Newarke Houses Museum** will delight you. It is a social history collection from 1500 to the present day. There are displays showing 17th century panelled rooms and a 19th century street scene amongst others. An amazing array of clocks is laid out in one room, musical instruments in another and sports and pastimes have not been forgotten either. Even the garden has been kept in period with the right flowers and a marvellous herb garden.

The Newarke Houses Museum.   Leicester.

The 16th century Chantry House forms part of the Newarke Houses Museum. If you enjoy things military then it is well worth while popping into **The Museum of the Royal Leicestershire Regiment**, its address is The Magazine, Oxford Street just by

244

Newarke. You will get a complete picture of the history of the Royal Leicestershire Regiment (17th Foot) including momentous battle trophies and relics all housed in this early 15th century Newark Gateway.

The city is a good transport centre with seven great roads radiating from it. There are also three railway stations and the Grand Union Canal linking it with the Trent and the Thames. It was from Leicester that Thomas Cook organised his first excursion, to Loughborough of all places, and of course, never looked back.

Leicester only gained city status in 1919 and the **Church of St Martin** became a cathedral in 1926. It stands dignified and quite impressive close to the Guildhall, although it is a little swamped by modern buildings which surround it. The noble tower and spire are fairly distinctive and we enjoyed ambling around this relatively modern but none the less interesting place of worship.

Close to the St Martins shopping complex you'll find **The Farmhouse Kitchen**, which during the summer months has tables and chairs outside and inside the style is a mixture of reproduction pine, flower arrangements and prints adorning the walls. You can enjoy first class, good quality traditional food from an extensive menu. With its central location The Farmhouse Kitchen is a perfect place to stop in between the visits to the many historical attractions that surround it.

The Farmhouse Kitchen.   Leicester.

Leicestershire Museum and Art Gallery, in New Walk is considered to be the major regional Art Gallery, which, when you have seen what they have in their collection, you are sure to agree. The European art collection from the 15th century includes German Expressionists and French Impressionists.

The Art Collection is by no means the only treasure in this fine building. There are displays of natural history including the Rutland

Dinosaur. There is glass and silver and a particularly impressive collection of English drinking glasses and French art glass. There is English silverware from Elizabethan times to the present day. If you interested in Egyptology, then there is the Ancient Egypt Gallery, full of fascinating items and if you happen to be in the Museum on a Thursday between October and March, you can enjoy one of the super lunchtime concerts.

Leicestershire Museum & Art Gallery.   Leicester.

Several 18th century buildings survive in Leicester, among them is Belgrave Hall in Church Road, built during the Queen Anne period in 1709 and two miles north of the city centre. Very carefully **Belgrave Hall,** has been kept in its original state. Everything about it retains the atmosphere of an 18th and 19th century house. The rooms are all delightfully furnished with items of the era. In the stable block there are well preserved coaches, the harness room has tack still hanging on the walls and there are agricultural implements that would have been in use at that time. The gardens are a sheer pleasure, some period, some botanical including a rock and water garden and green houses with over six and a half thousand species of plants.

The chief interest in **Kirby Muxloe** is its castle which is unusually built of brick and not stone. It was the first medieval brick building in Leicestershire and the bricks were all made on site. Dated 1480 but only the great gatehouse and one of the four angle towers remain intact. Surrounded by a moat fitted with gun ports and with its flotillas of moorhens and ducks, it is a very picturesque place to visit.

Scraptoft just north east of Leicester is much less spoilt than many of the peripheral villages in this part of the country. The church of All Saints is of ironstone fabric with limestone dressings, all built around 1300. Nether Hall is dated 1709 and is built of brick with Swithland slate roof and guarded by noble iron gates. We felt as though the houses, church and hall seemed to peer over a cliff onto the pasture below and although there seems to be little that is spectacular, it is pleasant to amble through these little villages .

We travelled next to **Glooston**, a village in a hollow, which was occupied during Roman times. The site of a villa was discovered in 1946 on the east bank of the stream and the Roman Gartree Road runs just south of here.

For the more energetic holidaymaker a walk to **Hallaton** is a very pleasant way to spend an afternoon. Mentioned in Domesday Book as Alctone, the village lies in rich grazing lands of the Welland Valley. Every Easter Monday the villagers of Hallaton turn out in force to challenge neighbouring Medbourne in a boisterous 'bottle kicking' contest, steeped in pagan ritual. First a huge hare pie is cut into portions and distributed by the rector. Some is left over to be scattered on Hare Pie Bank.

The T-shaped house at the eastern end of the village reveals, behind its 17th century facade, a remarkable 13th century house. The old hall, south east of the church is an H-plan house built in 1650. Near the church is a medieval bridge of three arches and the church itself is surrounded by sycamore, oak and beech trees. It is notable for the great beauty of an aisle in the south transept which has a twenty feet window flooding it with light. In the tower arch the huge clock pendulum can be seen swinging.

All these villages surround the Langtons chief of which is **Church Langton** which is famous for one of the finest churches in the county. It is a lovely place beautified by a famous rector in the 18th century, William Hanbury whose passion in life was music and flowers. His great ambition was to found a music festival here but that was not to be.

We travelled north to **Kings Norton,** on the edge of the east Leicestershire hill country. It has one of the most appealing village churches in the Midlands. We felt it was almost cathedral like, as we first saw it across the fields. Built in 1757 by a Leicester architect called John Wing, the church has been called 'L' perfect expression of 18th century Anglicanism'. Inside all is clear light and serenity and it retains all its original fittings and the beautiful three decker pulpit, box pews and west gallery are a joy. Close to the church is the old manor house and nearby is a brick dove-cote of the late 17th century.

A little further just north and you will come to **Houghton on the Hill** which has a matchless situation of the great escarpment of the county, above the Plain of England. Not far from the village of **Tilton-on-the-Hill**, the delectable rolling park of **Launde Abbey** lies close to the Rutland frontier. We felt it was nestling in its own world of lonely lanes and ancient woodlands being so far from the main road.

From all directions the drives lead to the house, an H-Shaped Elizabethan and 17th century manor with gabled wings and dormers. Unexpectedly, we came upon the chancel of the Augustinian priory church standing behind the north wing, still in use for worship.

Burrough-on-the-Hill stands nearly six hundred feet above sea level on the marlstone escarpment and the great earthwork of Burrough Hill is the grandest Iron Age hill fort in the county. Some of the ancient mounds are still twenty feet high and the countryside is seen in a vast panorama all around from this eighty two acre site.

The Stag and Hounds.   Burrough on-the-Hill.

Edward VIII and Mrs Simpson used to secretly meet in the village and rumour has it that he was asked to leave **The Stag and Hounds** after having ordered drinks without the cash to pay for them - the landlord refused to believe who he was! A more jovial air surrounds this four hundred year building today and you'll find beer from Britain's smallest brewery actually in the car park - Parish Special Beer, Poachers Ale and Baz's Bonce Blower served, all which have won several awards. Good home cooking is served in the restaurant with house specialities. The Stag and Hounds is a place you'll enjoy to visit and want to return to again.

All the more surprising, therefore, that **Frisby-on-the-Wreake** became front page news when an 18th century rector here, Rev. William Wragge, suddenly startled the village by announcing that he would marry any couple who came before him without banns or license. He did a roaring trade until the law caught up with him and he was sentenced to fourteen years transportation. Far too old for the sentence to be carried out, he faded into obscurity and the Leicestershire Gretna Green once more became the quiet farming village we see today.

We crossed the elegant bridge built in 1832 across the Eye (a tributary of the Wreake) and the canal, and found ourselves in the ancient market town of **Melton Mowbray.** The Tuesday market - there is also one on a Saturday - was recorded as a profitable concern in 1077 and certainly dates from Saxon times. For those of us who enjoy browsing it is a gem. The Old English settled here as early as the 5th century, one of their pagan cemeteries has been discovered on the outskirts of the town. Melton takes the second part of its name from the great Norman family of Mowbray who owned the manor by 1125.

We found this town bright and cheerful with many decent 18th and 19th century houses. There are several notable buildings. The so called Anne of Cleves house, though now used as a restaurant, is basically 15th century and was either a Chantry House belonging to the church or perhaps the dwelling house of one of the rich woolmerchants, who must have subscribed to the magnificent enlargement of the once Norman church of St Mary in the late 15th century. Opposite the church is the Masion Dieu founded as an almshouse in 1640 and in the market place the former Swan Inn retains a fine porch over the pavement. Melton became the hunting metropolis of England; the meeting place of the Quorn, Cottesmore and Belvoir hunts and was frequented by the nobility and gentry from all parts of the country. As late as 1939 it was said that, at the beginning of the season, a thousand fine hunters were stabled in the town. Many of the stables have now been converted into flats, but a number of the larger houses belonging to the wealthy, are still to be seen.

Today only one Pork Pie Bakery remains in the town, that of Dickinson & Morrison, **Ye Olde Pork Pie Shoppe** on Nottingham Street. Here skilled bakers proudly uphold the towns heritage by following a time honoured recipe and baking style to produce a truly authentic Melton Mowbray Pork Pie, crafted in the traditional way.

Ye Olde Pork Pie Shoppe.   Melton Mowbray.Leics LE12 1NW.
Tel: 0664 62341

Hallaton Village Green.

Nottingham Street. Melton Mowbray.

Its deliciously rich crunchy pastry and seasoned meat filling have recently received much acclaim from respected food critics and connoisseurs alike. If visitors are interested in seeing the traditional craft of hand raising Pork Pies, then demonstrations can be arranged. The attractive period style Shoppe also offers an interesting range of speciality bread and confectionery lines. However, they also have another house speciality, The Original Melton Hunt Cake. This superbly rich fruit cake was first made by John Dickinson in 1854 and its recipe remains a company secret today. It has a fascinating history and shouldn't be missed.

Only a few minutes walk from the town centre is **Kirmel Guest House**, where guests will find five comfortable furnished bedrooms.

Did You Know...

There is a full list of

Tourist Information Centres

at the back of the book?

One is a family room which accommodates two adults and two children. There is also a ground floor twin room with toilet which is suitable for the disabled. The lounge doubles as a dining room where tea/coffee facilities are always available. Breakfast is served between 7.00am - 9.00am and you'll find the Guest house an ideal place to stay during your visit to Melton Mowbray.

A very pleasant way to walk off pies or cakes as well as for the enjoyment is to follow the Jubilee Way - a fifteen and a half mile waymarked walk mostly on field and woodland path between Melton Mowbray and Woolsthorpe, just across the Lincolnshire border. It will take you through the Vale of Belvoir, via Scalford, Belvoir Woods and Castle and eventually, if you really have overindulged, you can link up with the Viking Way at Woolsthorpe!

A gentler meander for us was the **Egerton Park Riverside Walk** in Melton and we then ended up in the **Melton Carnegie Museum** at Thorpe End. It has good coverage of the history and the environment of the Borough of Melton. Here we saw local exhibitions, hunting pictures, and displays on Stilton cheese and pork pies. It frequently has special exhibitions of other prints and paintings as well.

Please Don't Forget...

To tell people that you read about them in

The Hidden Places

An Agricultural college is perhaps on the face of it not the most likely place the general public would wish to visit, however there are always exceptions and at Melton Mowbray Brooksby Agricultural College is that exception. **Brooksby Agricultural College** is a bustling place where whilst staying in one of the simple but comfortable student rooms you can learn about rural pursuits.

Brooksby Agricultural College.   *Melton Mowbray.*

There are some marvellous farm walks with a track going around the estate connecting each farm. Bird watchers will love the busy wild life and at the end of the day there is simple wholesome food and good company in which to enjoy your meal.The Villiers family feature prominently at Brooksby and if you look back at their history you will see that not only did they produce Sir George Villiers, the infamous first Duke of Buckingham, the favourite of King James I but the line included Barbara, the famous Lady Castlemaine, the most greedy of all of Charles II's mistresses. Apart from the infamous, the Villiers connection also gave the country the two William Pitts, the Great Duke of Marlborough, the two Earls Spencer, Winston Churchill and many more.

Saltby was our next port of call, high up towards the Lincolnshire border. It has a little seven hundred year old church, one of its farms has a windmill and under its surface a Roman pavement has been found. Not far away on Saltby Heath are the mysterious earthworks known as King Lud's Entrenchments, a long mound of earth with a tumulus at each end. Lud was the sky god worshipped by the ancient Britons and tradition has it that King Lud was buried at one end during the Dark Ages. There was certainly a King of Mercia call Ludeca, who was killed in battle in 827, but it is more likely that the mounds were the boundary between two ancient Kingdoms. The Welsh name for London was Caer Ludd (Lud's town) and Ludgate Hill preserves the name, which is nothing to do with Leicestershire, but we thought it was quite interesting anyway.

The area surrounding Melton Mowbray and its cluster of villages is highly populated with racing stables, so it is not unusual to see strings of fine thoroughbred race horses sedately enjoying the road work which prepares them gently for their early morning, nearby local gallops. What better name for a pub in the vicinity that **The Nags Head Inn** in Saltby. Originally housing the village butcher and baker, this traditional pub serves delicious food at reasonable prices. There is also accommodation, one twin with its own bathroom and a double bedroom, both having tea/coffee making facilities. situated in the midst of delightful countryside The Nags Head will provide you with good food and comfortable accommodation.

The Nags Head Inn.   Saltby.

Five miles away is **Belvoir Castle** which is well worth a visit. It was built in the closing decade of the 11th century by Robert de

Todeni, one of William the Conqueror's standard bearers. The name is first recorded in 1130 as Belveder and in 1145 as Bello Videre - beautiful view. The castle suffered great damage in the Civil War and the 8th Earl built a mansion on the site in 1654, but in 1816 it suffered again in a great fire. The castle was finally completed in 1830 and today is one of the showplaces of the Midlands. There are some wonderful paintings including work by Van Dyck, Reynolds, Hogarth and one of the finest of the Holbein portraits of Henry VIII. We particularly loved the gardens, on the side of the hill, the Duchess' Garden is full of terraces and stone statues; the Duke's Walk is an entire valley filled with flowerbeds and trees and the Water Garden in summer is filled with azaleas and rhododendrons, a marvellous spectacle. A dovecote in the grounds stands on the site of Belvoir Priory founded in 1076 and suppressed in 1539. Only four monks ever lived there.

Belvoir Castle.   Belvoir.

We found the country around Belvoir with its splendid woods, steep and broken hillsides, deep valleys and artificial lakes around **Knipton**, unlike any other scenery in Leicestershire and is justly popular with other intrepid holiday persons.

CHAPTER ELEVEN

Rutland

Normanton Tower, Rutland Water

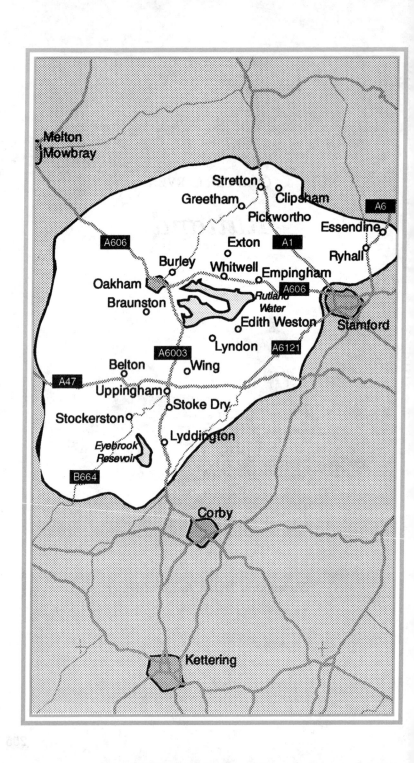

CHAPTER ELEVEN.

Rutland.

For years **Rutland** kept up a vociferous battle to retain its status as the smallest county in England but in 1974 it was forced into marriage with Leicestershire. The bride may have been unwilling but the bridegroom, Leicestershire gained. Rutland, like the counties that surround it has villages of thatch and ironstone, clustered around their churches and the countryside is rich in pasture where once deer were hunted. Its central feature is **Rutland Water**, its 3100 acres making it one of the largest man made lakes in northern Europe. Started in 1971 to supply water of the East Midlands towns, it was created by damming the valley near Empingham. The result is an attractively landscaped lake, around five miles long which also serves as a popular recreational and leisure centre where sailing, water skiing and windsurfing are pursued. There are many picnic sites at **Whitwell, Normanton** and an information centre just south west of **Empingham**. At the west end you will find a nature reserve and for information and access a centre at **Lyndon.** By Normanton you'll see a neo classical church which now houses a Water Museum, orginally built in 1764, extended in 1826 and refurbished in 1911.

Oakham,the former county town of Rutland, is where you'll see some of the beauty of the place and learning something of the old county's history. The infamous Titus Oates was born here in 1649. His ability to create malignant fantasy in order to set the Catholics and the Protestants against each other became well- known as he invented the idea of a Popish Plot against Charles II. Oakham was the home of another oddity too, Jeffery Hudson, a three foot six inch midget. He worked for the Duke of Buckingham at nearby Burley-on-the-Hill where the Duchess treated him like a pet poodle, dressing him up and showing him off to visitors. Once when Charles 1 and his Queen

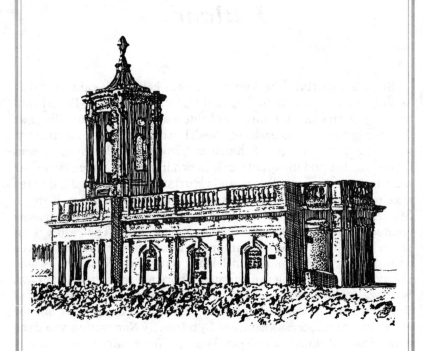

Normanton Tower. Rutland Water.

Henrietta Maria came to **Burley** there was a special surprise for them. A huge cold pie was placed on the table before them at dinner and when the pie was opened, out jumped Jeffery Hudson.

The Queen was very taken with this midget and asked the Duchess to give him to her. Off he went back to court where he became a popular toy but also exceedingly vain thus making many enemies, and finally killing one of them in a duel. That was not all his adventures, he was captured twice by pirates whilst crossing the Channel and was sold as a slave in Barbary. The Duke of Buckingham paid a ransom for him and for a while he returned to Oakham but yearned for London and eventually was thrown into prison, accused of being involved in the Popish Plot conjured up by Titus Oates.

A street market is still held twice weekly in the Market Place which contains an historic Buttercross and a set of stocks. The whole county of Rutland seems to come to these busy markets which are fun. Just off the market place is **Oakham Castle**. A romantic place with a sense of history epitomised by the 12th century Great Hall of this wonderful Norman castle. The pillars supporting its magnificent arcades have carved capitals so much like the ones in the chancel of Canterbury Cathedral that it must have been the same craftsman who were responsible for both. There is a lot to take in but what is especially memorable is the amazing collection of horseshoes. It is a long standing tradition apparently that any peer of the realm coming to Oakham for the first time must present the castle with a horseshoe. You can see them hanging all around the walls of the hall. They are all shapes and sizes, large and small, some wooden some rusty and in amongst them you will see one presented by Queen Elizabeth 1 and one by Queen Elizabeth 11.

Oakham Castle.   Oakham.

It was no distance from the castle to All Saints church with its 14th century tower, a fine parish church and standing watchfully over the town. With the loss of the county of Rutland came the importance of protecting its history. This, you will find, is done admirably at **The Rutland County Museum**, on Catmos Street. The Museum is dedicated to Rutland life and includes agricultural equipment, implements and wagons. There are local craft tools, 19th and early 20th century domestic items and a whole range of archeological finds. The Museum is housed in a splendid 18th century former riding school of the Rutland Fencibles, a volunteer cavalry regiment.

Did You Know...

There is a full

Town and Village Index

at the back of the book?

If you find yourselves in need of replenshisment after visiting Oakhams places of historical interest then we suggest **The Catmose Fish Bar and Restaurant**, situated on Mill Street in the midst of attractive shops, an art gallery and antique shop. The restaurant and take away are very succesful with seating for 40 upstairs if you prefer to eat in. Serving traditonal home cooked food as well as fish and chips you will be satisfied with the substantial portions you have placed before you.

The Catmose Fish Bar and Restaurant.   Oakham.

Taking the little road north out of Oakham we were almost immediately in **Burley -on-the-Hill** where the Rutland Agricultural Show is held in August and a 17th centurt mansion stands close by, considered to be the most attractive mansion in the county. North of here at **Ashwell**, you'll find the **Rutland Railway Museum.**

In a southerly direction from Oakham you'll pass by **Braunston -in- Rutland**, a lovely ironstone village above the River Gwash. The church here has traces of earlier 12th and 13th century buildings. Following the minor roads through attractive country you'll come to **Belton -in- Rutland**, where you'll find a country craft centre.

The Old Rectory.   Belton-in- Rutland. Uppingham. Rutland LE15 9LE.   Tel: 0572 86 279. Fax: 0572 86343

The Old Rectory is a ten bedroomed Victorian house with Bed and Breakfast and Self- catering accommodation standing in gardens and grounds of around 14 acres overlooking the Eye Brook Valley by the tiny hamlet of Belton -in- Rutland. Just a mile off the main A47 in a peaceful and idyllic setting you can enjoy traditional farmhouse bed and breakfast - four course evening meals, packed lunches and snacks by prior arrangement. The majority of rooms have private bath or shower, colour TV and tea/coffee making facilities. Alternatively there is self - catering in five 'cottage style' units, two of which are ideal for families, in the converted stables and outbuildings, all containing ensuite facilities as well as colour TV's. Self- caters are welcome to use the laundry room, ironing board, residents lounge/library in the Old Rectory where breakfast or evening meals will happily be provided by prior arrangement. Guests are also welcome to use bicycles that are available to enjoy the surroundings which are ideal for all types of outdoor pursuits, such as walking, rambling or picnicking. Within 5 minutes drive of Rutland Water and 25/30 minutes drive to Stately homes such as Burghley House, Kirby Hall, Country Parks and historic towns, the Old Rectory is a first class base where friendly hosts Richard and Vanessa Peach provide a country atmosphere and from which you can explore the very attractive and historical countryside.

Medbourne Grange, is an old farmhouse which you'll find by taking the crossroads at the village of **Stockerston**, taking a sharp left hand bend and at the next crossing following the signpost to Nevill Holt. This working farm is a delight. The house was built around 150 years ago and inside you'll find three spacious and light rooms, all beautifully furnished All have tea/coffee making facilties and hot/cold hand wash basins. The dining room is equally elegant where you'll enjoy a full English breakfast. There is a swimming pool which guests are welcome to use.

Please Don't Forget...

To tell people that you read about them in

The Hidden Places

To the west is **Stoke Dry**, which overlooks the **Eyebrook Reservoir.** Sir Everard Digby who was executed for his role on the Gunpowder Plot was born here in 1578 and there are Digby monuments in the church here. Close by lies **Lyddington,** which has the **Bede House**, overseered by English Heritage, it is a 15th to 17th century building that is the remaining part of a manor house that belonged to the Bishops of Lincoln.

Uppingham, standing by the A6003 is a pleasant town where Uppingham School was founded in 1587 to become one of the leading public schools under the headship of DR Edward Tring during the 19th century. North east of here we came to the village of **Wing** where you'll find **The Kings Arms**, in Top Street. It is a pub with a lot of character with one good bar and an attractive restaurant which will comfortably seat 30. The exposed stone walls and wooden beams give the bar a rustic air and the well appointed tables invite one to have a meal. The food is good English fare with everything home made. In the winter months there is a roaring fire whilst during summer you are welcome to sit by picnic tables in the lawned area where children can play on the has swings and slides provided.

The Kings Arms.   Wing.

Continuing via **Edith Weston**, which gets its name from Edith, widow of Edward the Confessor we came to Nomanton. Standing on the south shore of Rutland Water you'll find something very special at **The Normanton Hotel.** This sixteen bedroom hotel has been transformed from its former function as a coach house and stable block of the now demolished Normanton Hall. The building is of the Georgian period and inside the refurbishment defers to this period with its elegant furnishing and decoration. The hotel offers luxury accommodation with its ensuite letting rooms which include TV, direct dial telephones and coffee making facilties. Two of the rooms have been designed with the disabled in mind, with wider doors, handrails, and specially constructed bathrooms and toilets. There is the Galleried Coffee Lounge and The Peacock Room, a licensed restaurant, both of which are open to non-residents.

The Normanton Hotel.   Normanton.

Following the south shore of Rutland Water you'll come to

Empingham, which is dominated by the attractive tower and spire of St Peter's Church. It is a well proportioned building with an eye catching west front. Its interior features include fragments of ancient glass.

Across the A1 stands **Little Casterton** which was a Roman station and beyond is **Tolethorpe Hall.** One of the most beautiful things in the county has to be the 13th century tower and spire of the church at **Ryhall** which stands just beyond the manor. There is a nice little legend about the village which bestrides a little river. In the church St Tibba, niece of King Penda of Mercia, is said to held up by two flying horses and surmounted by a helmet and eagle crest, the whole being supported by cherubs. Inside the house there are panelled room. The road leads through the pretty countryside to **Essendine** where the church forms a wonderful background.

Back across the A1 is **Exton,** situated in one of the largest ironstone extractions ares in the country. It is a charming village and the Old Hall, now ruined, is thought to have been built during the reign of Elizabeth I. It was burned down in 1810 and was replaced by a New Hall in the middle of that century.

On the B668 you'll come to the village of **Greetham** where **The Plough** will catch your eye set on the main street opposite the village school. It has a charming rustic air and is a suitable base from which to tour the area. Accommodation is in one double room and one twin room with a shared bathroom. The rooms are pleasantly decorated, in keeping with the rest of the pub. Although The Plough caters primarily for bed and breakfast, lunch and dinner are available on request. Bar snacks, a children's menu and vegetarian food are also on offer.

The Plough.   Greetham.

Featured in most of the best guidebooks such as Johanssons, RAC is the very famous inn and landmark on the west side of the Great Old North Road (A1) by Stretton, **The Ram Jam Inn.** This 4 Crown recommended probably began life as the humble Winchilsea Arms in the 18th century. The then landlord, a Charles Blake, in common with other publicans of the time brewed his own ale and it is thought that he produced 'Ram Jam Ale', which he advertised outside the inn. After his death in 1791 his recipe was lost but the name continued. In 1811 a prize fight between the Englishman Tom Cribb and Thomas Molyneux from America was fought close by at Thistleton Gap attracting 15,000 spectators and a replica of the commemoration stone hangs by the reception in The Ram Jam today. When the present owners took over it the inn was in a bad state of repair but after the refurbishment they have turned it into a marvellous place with good old fashioned values. There are eight ensuite bedrooms, all but one overlooking the garden and orchard,with full facilities including TV, tea/coffee facilities and direct dial telephones - all beautifully furnished. A cosy delightful restaurant, bar and breakfast area where real ales, bar snacks and palatable meals with an international flavour awaits the hungry and thirsty visitor. This friendly inn has something for everyone including facilities for meetings, private parties and where you discover that The Ram Jam much different than your usual inn.

The Ram Jam Inn.   Stretton. Oakham LE15 7QX. Tel: 0780 416776 Fax: 0780 410361

The most precious possession of the little hamlet of **Clipsham** is the heraldic glass in the north chapel. As you look at it remember that it was shattered in the Wars of the Roses and brought here; when you see the sun glisten on it, it gives one an eerie feeling to think that the same sun was lighting the glass in the war that drove the Plantagenets off the throne and put the Tudors in their place. It was from the ancient church at **Pickworth** by the Lincolnshire border that this glass came and where you can still see some 14th century wall paintings. Which brings us to the end of this chapter of our journey that revealed amongst other things that despite being 'absorbed' into

a greater county, the name of Rutland is still very much alive and
kicking in this delightful area set in ' The Heart of England '.

CHAPTER TWELVE

South Lincolnshire

Mud & Stud House, Thimbleby

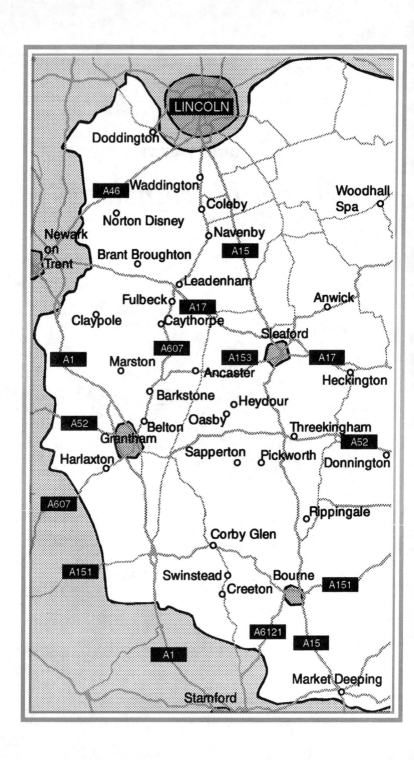

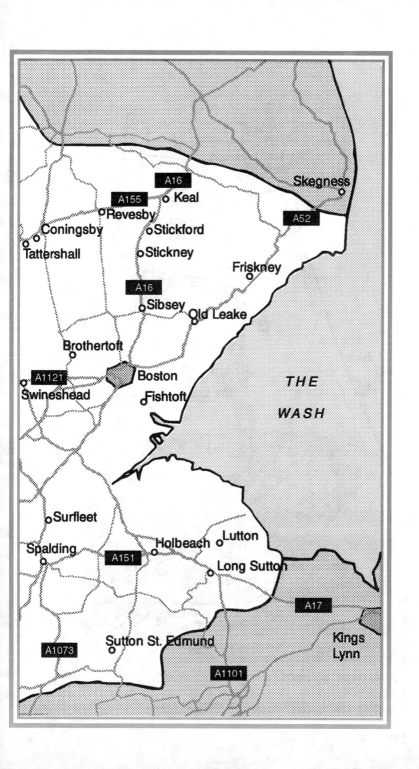

Mud & Stud Cottage. Thimbleby

CHAPTER TWELVE.

South Lincolnshire.

The Danes began their campaign in England sometime before 800 AD, and they broached this part of the country through the Humber and the Wash. The village place names ending with 'ing' and 'by', so common in Lincolnshire, can be traced back to the Danish settlements. Under their rule, this part of the Midlands became known as The Danelaw and Lincoln, Stamford, Nottingham, Derby and Leicester were the five Burghs or administrative centres of the region. The Danes were to stay in England for some three hundred years before being routed during the Norman Conquest under William the Conqueror around 1066.

We decided to start our personal 'campaign' at **Grantham**. Having in recent times become well known through its links with Margaret Thatcher, who was born here, and rather unfairly being voted 'the most boring town in Britain', you'll in fact find it to be a very pleasant town. Its most famous son is Sir Isaac Newton, and in front of the Guildhall, the large bronze statue of one of our most renowned scientists stands to remind us of this great man's influence. He was born on Christmas Day 1642 at Woolsthorpe Manor, in the village of **Woolsthorpe** near **Colsterworth**, seven miles south of Grantham. He attended King's School in Grantham, where his name can still be seen carved into one of the window sills. It was at Woolsthorpe Manor that he is said to have had his inspirational encounter with a falling apple! **The Grantham Museum** near the statue houses local archaeological finds and a Newton collection.

Grantham's coaching inns were used as a stopping place for those travelling on the Great North Road. One of the oldest inns in Britain is said to be the Angel and Royal Hotel, and can be found in the High Street. King Richard III reputedly signed the death warrant for the Duke of Buckingham here in 1483. Another eye- catching pub is the Beehive Inn, where a lime tree outside the building has a genuine bee hive up in its branches, acting as a 'living sign' for the establishment.

You'll find the 2 Star AA and RAC, 4 Crown Commended, **Kings**

Hotel on North Parade in Grantham, despite being a large establishment, a very warm and inviting hotel. Overlooking the Kings School which Sir Isaac Newton attended and originally a Victorian gentlemans residence, called Diana Lodge and later Hotel Diana, it has been refurbished by owners since 1974, Anne and Roger Blakeman, who have many years experience in the hotel trade. There are twenty one, comfortable ensuite bedrooms with full facilities, three of which are on the ground floor and suitable for the disabled. Two restaurants

The Kings Hotel. Grantham Lincs NG31 8AU. Tel/Fax: 0476 590800.

cater for all the different tastes of guests and visitors. The Victorian, featured in several good food guides because of its highly commended service and cuisine, has ' The Kings Bill Of Fayre' which changes weekly and an innovative a la carte, all featuring fresh local produce and complimented by an extensive wine list of over 80 choices. The restaurant is open every lunch from 12.30pm - 2.00pm and dinner 7.00pm - 9.30pm (Sunday 8.30pm). The Orangery, a more informal restaurant is ideal for a quick bite, imaginative meals, cold buffets and includes a full vegetarian menu, is open from 7.30am - 10.30am 12.00pm - 2.30pm and 6.15pm - 10.30pm daily. To entertain diners and for those who enjoy dancing live music is also a feature at weekends. The hotel has facilities for banquets, conferences and meetings which the management are only too pleased to advise and organise. The spacious and comfortable public areas also include a relaxing Victorian lounge bar serving real ales. With good hospitality in an inviting atmosphere, aided by the friendly staff who help make guests feel as if they are at home and the hotels location to the many places of interest in and around the Grantham area make it a perfect base for touring this lovely part of Lincolnshire, which has been made famous by the 'Middlemarch' television series. Special Bargain Breaks are available mid-week and at weekends.

272

Built in 1822 as a private dwelling the Tourist Board registered, **Red House,** stands proudly on your left as you enter Grantham from the north on the A1.The impressive Grade ll listed Georgian House is beautifully decorated throughout, oozing character and warmth from the moment you experience the wonderful welcome given by hosts David and Gillian Parnell. Although in their first season the Parnells are certain that guests will be extremely satisfied by the comfortable three room accommodation, all ensuite with full facilities,and substantial breakfasts served in the characterful dining room. Children are catered for and there is a ground floor accommodation which is suitable for the partially disabled. Evening meals are happily prepared by prior arrangement, and with the excellent personalities of the owners, who have made the Red House a delight through their sheer hard work and determination, your stay here will be a memorable one.

The Red House.   74 North Parade, Grantham. Lincs NG31 8AN.
Tel: 0476 79869.

St Wulfram's Church, with its lofty steeple rising some 280 feet above the ground, has been described as one of the finest churches in England. It has some beautiful windows and feels more like a cathedral. A library from the 16th century over the south porch has books that are chained and the 14th century crypt is though to have been the shrine to St Wulfram. Westgate has some of the best preserved streets in Grantham, and nearer the Market Place are some wonderful old shops, like the wine merchants which boasts a real coal fire inside for when the winter chill sets in.

Set in the heart of historic Grantham, on Welby Street, is the very impressive **Belvoir Gallery** owned and personally run by Roy and Annette Williams for over nine years. Much more than your usual Gallery, it has lots to offer. Crafts of all kinds are delightfully displayed for all to see and the gallery contains original artwork, limited edition prints, pictures of old Grantham, by mainly English

273

artists. We were surprised but pleased to see world famous Moorcroft Pottery on display and for sale as well as numerous Bradford Exchange Collectors Plates. Framing is undertaken in this interesting place where there is something to suit all tastes and pockets.

The Belvoir Gallery.   Grantham. Lincs NG31 6DY. Tel: 0476 79498

To the south-west of the town just off the **A607**, **Harlaxton Manor** stands at the end of its long drive reminding one of a Disneyland palace. Towers, turrets, arches, spires, gables and chimneys, all these architectural delights seem to vie with each other to catch your attention first. The great arched gateway is the only survivor of the original manor, which was pulled down in 1837. The new house has passed through a succession of owners, and is now the British campus of the University of Evansville in the United States.

From Grantham, we took the A607 northwards to **Belton.** Here we found one of those lovely mansions that you will always remember, **Belton House.** Standing in beautiful parkland, it was built somewhere in the late seventeenth century for Sir John Brownlow. The house stayed in the same family until 1984 when it was left to the National Trust. The mellow stone which gives the house its warm elegance came from the local quarries at Ancaster. Inside, the house is rich in lovely furniture, tapestries and porcelain. The gardens contain an orangery, a sunken garden and a fountain pool. The house and gardens are open to the public during the Summer.

You'd miss at your peril the beautifully laid out **Belton Garden Centre** near the National Trust owned, Belton House on the A607, just a couple of miles from Grantham. Set in 10 acres, with a Victorian walled garden -which was part of Belton House, and famed for having propagated ' Newton Apple Trees' from grafts of the original tree associated with Newtons discovery of the laws of gravitation, before it died in 1814 in Woolsthorpe Manor - an aviary, aquarium and displays from trees, shrubs,bedding plants to Conservatories and other horticultural needs, this centre is a delight for the professional or amateur gardener. Having built this magnificent garden centre up from nothing through sheer hard work and determination, Peter, Wendy and Ann Coaten have thirty years experience at your disposal. The atmosphere of the friendly and helpful owners and their staff make a visit to this Garden Centre, a member of the Horticultural Trade Association, a truly enjoyable experience where you can round your visit off by relaxing in their Tea Rooms with a choice beverages, cakes and light lunches. Open all Bank holidays, Tuesday - Friday 9.00am - 6.00pm and weekends 10.00am - 5.00pm with parking for five hundred cars.

Belton Garden Centre.   Belton, Grantham Lincs. NG32 2LN. Tel: 0476 63700.

A couple of miles further up the road, we came to **Barkston** village with the River Witham flowing nearby. Barkston House opposite the village green was a former farmhouse but has since been converted into a country house hotel. The site of an ancient fort can be found on the nearby heathland. If you ask anyone their impressions of Lincolnshire, their first comments will probably be 'flat and marshy'. And while the land is low, only rising to some five hundred feet above sea-level near the Wolds, it does have its own unique beauty. The beautiful sandy coastline attracts many visitors, while the fens and marshes are sanctuaries for many rare breeds of birds. Seeming to slope away into the distance, the Wolds are chalky uplands and few trees grow there. One thing that impressed us about the scenery was the sheer amount of sky over our heads! Man and all his works seem insignificant when seen against the great panoramic views of Lincolnshire.

Veering off to the west is the village of **Marston** with its fourteenth-century Hall, a lovely Tudor manor house. We carried on through the villages of **Hougham, Dry Doddington** -the name refers to the villagers' former dependence on the river for water - **Stubton** and **Fenton.**

Just a mile off the A1 in the village of **Claypole** you'll find **The Five Bells,** an inn that has been mentioned in the 'Good Beer Guide' for the last four years. Dating back to the mid 19th century the inn took its name from the five bells of the village church, St. Peters. The owners, Bob and Jilly Crowther, have refurbished this charming and inviting inn with character in which you can enjoy from a choice of at least four real ales and appetising bar meals served every day, apart from Tuesday lunchtime. Good car parking alongside it and a pleasant Beer Garden with a childrens Play Area make it ideal for family days out. The Crowthers have also converted the old stable block into four first class, homely rooms with local hand made furniture and full facilities for those looking for overnight accommodation.

The Five Bells.　　　*Claypole. Lincs NG 23 5 BJ　Tel: 0636 626561*

The countryside around here is flat, and the villages tend to stand out rather aloof from the land. However, we could not fail to notice **Loveden Hill,** a limestone outcrop to the north of Marston. Because of its prominence it was used as a Saxon burial place, and the Wapentake, or shires councils, met here. Excavations have discovered over thirty skeletons, and there is evidence of over 1,000 cremations on the site. Besides the Witham, the other river in this area is the Brant, and at **Brant Broughton** (pronounced 'Bruton') there is a well preserved Quakers' Meeting House dating back to 1761. The magnificent church with its graceful spire owes some of its stained glass to a local family, the Suttons. Augustus Sutton, who served as a canon at Lincoln Cathedral, was a passionate clockmaker. He and his son Arthur made many clocks for the poorer parishes, and the rectory at Brant Broughton boasted forty working clocks at one time.

North-west of here, close to the Nottinghamshire border, is the village of **Norton Disney.** We could not help wondering if there was a connection here with Walt Disney, that master cartoonist. We discovered that he did in fact claim descent from the family of d'Isigny who came here originally from the French region of Bayeux. The village, which is surrounded by woods, once had a castle and manor house belonging to the family, but time has effectively erased them. The lovely church has fine brasses to the Disney family.

Off the **A46** Newark to Lincoln road or the A17 to Sleaford and in the heart of this picturesque village you'll find a real 'hidden gem' in the **St. Vincent Arms.** This 17th century inn, formerly called the Hare and Hounds, is owned by Neil and Pam Cleveland who go out of

St. Vincent Arms.   Norton Disney. Lincs.   Tel: 0522 788478.

their way to make all visitors welcome in their beautifully decorated and furnished establishment. Walt Disneys ancestors originate from this area and you'll find pictures of him playing darts in the inn when he was visiting in 1949 tracing his family roots. The St Vincent serves excellent ales and delicious food from their Daily Specials which also include a choice from seven starters, six steak dishes and choices of fish. Childrens menus are available, as well as bar snacks and all food is home prepared with fresh produce. The Clevelands don't serve food on Mondays evenings during the winter and to avoid disappointment bookings are preferred for their forty seater restaurant. This lovely,popular inn really does have everything for the visitor except small portions but that can't be bad!

We continued northwards to the remarkably pretty village of **Aubourn** with its Tudor Hall. This contains some beautifully panelled rooms and a splendid oak staircase. From here we passed through **Haddington**, crossed the A46 and came to **Thorpe-on-the-Hill.** On the old railway line is a delightfully ornate railway station. The village's earlier name was 'Thorpe super Montem' which seems very grandiose. Needless to say, the village boasts no 'super hills', only pleasant slopes. From these rises we could see a surprising amount of woodland, although this was mostly new plantations. At **Eagle,** a village a little over from Thorpe, there is still some impressive old woodland. The name of the village was derived from 'ac leah' or 'oak wood', which certainly indicates that this tree thrived here at one time.

On the **B1190** is the village of **Doddington,** and it has one of the most beautiful Elizabethan houses in the county. **Doddington Hall** was built for Thomas Tailor in the 1590s and is now owned by the Jarvis family. The house and grounds are open to the public during the Summer months, and the formal walled garden and four acres of wild garden are particularly enjoyable. There is also a nature trail which gives the public access to some lovely woodland walks on the estate.

The owner of the Hall in the late 1700s was Sir John Deleval, and he rebuilt the nearby Church of St Peter as the last resting place for his daughter. Shortly after her death, Sir John's son died too, and in his grief he ordered that the stonework of the church be painted black. Here and there, you can still see traces of this mournful covering today.

Intending to save Lincoln itself for another part of our tour of the county, we travelled through the southern outskirts of the city, then headed south on the A607. The main road heads through **Waddington**, which is dominated by its enormous RAF base. It really comes as no surprise that the flying service still rules supreme over the skies of Lincolnshire. Connections with the county go back as far as 1914, when a Royal Naval Air Service base was established at **Skegness**, and later at **Killingholme.** From the latter, brave men flew out to intercept the Zeppelin airships which undertook night-time bombing missions during 1916-18. A new church has replaced its medieval predecessor in the village, the original having been completely devastated by a landmine during the war. Although a few attractive houses remain, rows of bungalows line the main road, tempting the traveller to press on to more attractive villages.

If you want to find the **Bell Inn** in the little village of **Coleby,** which is situated off the Lincoln to Leadenham road, you will have to seek it out because it is hidden in Far Lane at the back of the church. Keep this in mind because it is not the easiest place to get to. The pub is over two hundred years old and is renowned for its good food and friendliness. Much of its success can be attributed to Robert and Sara, whose ten years in the area and knowledge add to the ambience.

Perhaps one reason for its reputation is the skill with which they have managed to achieve the continuity of menu's that is to say in the

Bar, the Cold Carvery or the popular Restaurant. Beautifully decorated in an olde worlde style with comfortable pew seating and soft lighting the intimate atmosphere adds to freshly cooked to order food. Log fires welcome you on cold nights and you can reserve tables in the carvery and the restaurant which is advisable particularly at weekends.

The main menu offers some ten starters and that is followed by a variety of Charcoal Grills, fish, chicken and beef dishes as well as traditional pies. Vegetarians are also catered along with childrens meals. There is also a blackboard special which changes daily and includes food such as Beef and Horseradish pie, Roast Duck and much more.

The Bell Inn.   Coleby, Lincs.   Tel: 0522 810240

The Bell Inn got its name because it is on the site of a field where they cast the bell for the village church, which was too big to transport from anywhere else. Going back in its history the pub has acquired an active ghost! The story goes like this, once upon a time it was an alehouse, which is now the restaurant. Above there was living accommodation and alongside three cottages one of which used to be a butchery shop. Two butchers hooks still hang from the ceiling of this part of the pub. Sixty five years ago the butcher hung himself from one of these hooks and his spirit has not left The Bell since. There is no doubt that glasses leap off shelves all by themselves and the chef has been known to refuse going down into the cellar after experiencing icy draughts and hair rising on the back of his neck!

The Bell is close to Coleby Grange which was a World War II airfield and many visitors call in at The Bell after visiting the site and evoking memories of the past. There are two double rooms, one ensuite for those who wish to enjoy the hospitality of this friendly pub whilst in the area.

Just west of **Coleby** are the **Boothby Graffoe** Low Fields, and here the towers of **Somerton Castle** can be seen. The castle was built in 1280 by the Bishop of Durham, and the captive King of France, John I, was imprisoned here by the Black Prince around 1356. The king had a sizeable retinue of some forty servants with him, and wine from estates in Bordeaux were transported to Boston so he could raise some revenue to keep himself in luxury!

The Kings Head.   Navenby.Lincs.   *Tel: 0522   810367.*

In the heart of **Navenby** on the **A607** Lincoln to Leadenham road you'll discover the 17th century, **Kings Head**, an inn when once visited you'll want to return to again. The excellent, down to earth hosts Cliff and Beryl Freeman have made this inn a place that feels like home as you enter and step back in time. Each area of the inn is decorated in different styles with old bygones, wooden floors and characterful seating that combine to give it a homely and warm atmosphere. Serving four excellent ales and delicious food in its 45 seater restaurant, The Kings Head, has a tempting menu that will satisfy all tastes. Look out for their home made daily specials and ever changing sweet selections. Friday and Saturday evenings and Sunday Lunches are popular so the Freemans suggest booking to avoid disappointment. No food is served on Sunday evenings but live folk and Jazz music are on for your entertainment. There is outdoor seating and a boules pitch for the more energetic during those long summer evenings and the Freemans can arrange overnight accommodation for those who decide that they need go further that this inn that extends its friendly welcome to all.

The land here is limestone heath, and between Lincoln and Grantham the rock formation is really a series of 'steps'.   At **Leadenham** there are some surprisingly steep hills. This is the main crossing point between the Grantham and Sleaford roads, and the two Georgian inns here would have provided welcome refreshment for travellers.

We found **Fulbeck** to be a charming village. Set amongst trees and cliffs, its stone cottages, lovely manor house and distinguished church make it a very desirable place. **Fulbeck Hall** is one place that is not only beautiful and much loved but it serves another great purpose, hosting Country House Arts and a remarkable programme of Courses and Seminars. The Fane family have lived in this house or a house on this site since 1632.

Over the last decade the main house and domestic wing have been substantially re-roofed with the aid of English Heritage grants. In return for this help, the present owner opens the house daily during part of July, from 2 pm to 5 pm, and if you are lucky enough to be in the vicinity during that month, do take a look at this lovely house, with its fine furniture and paintings.

Further down the A607, we soon came to the village of **Caythorpe**. The church has a distinctive 'hump' to its spire, and unusually, the spire itself stems from the crossing point of the cruciform shape of the building. Another feature of the village is the Georgian Hall set amongst parkland, while the fine eighteenth-century rectory near the western end of the church is particularly attractive.

South-east of Caythorpe on the **B6403** lies the historic village of **Ancaster**. There have been many associations with the Roman occupation here, and excavations have revealed mosaic pavements, coins and foundations. Ancaster was formerly the Roman settlement of Causennae, and at that time, the B6403 was part of the famous highway known as Ermine Street. This Roman road would have stretched from Chichester through London, Stamford and Lincoln, to the River Humber. A valley near the village is said to be the site of an early race course - for chariots! Ancaster stone comes from local quarries near the main break in the limestone below Lincoln, which is known as Ancaster Gap. The limestone has been used in such well known buildings as St Pancras Station, St John's College Chapel in Cambridge, and the House of Commons. There is evidence that Stone Age man settled in this area, and the main Iron Age camp in the county was at **Honington** to the west. Much of Ancaster village today lies along Ermine Street, and is of course built of the local stone.

We headed east on the **A153** to **Sleaford,** and found it to be a very attractive market town. There are some lovely buildings here, like the fifteenth-century timber-framed vicarage standing beside the fine church. Built in the late twelfth century, the Church of St Denys has one of England's earliest stone spires. The Corn Exchange in the Market Place is very elaborate. It was built by Messrs Kirk and Parry, who contributed a lot of other fine building work in the town. Sleaford would have been the most important meeting place for the Fenland farmers to come and check their prices and exchange gossip.

T/4/2.   Sleaford.Lincs NG34 7HD.   Tel: 0529 307521

Situated within a converted 18th century stables is the outstanding **T/4/2 Tearooms** and restaurant where all are welcome. It is a dream come true for mother and daughter, Sonja and Diana Pescott. Sonja had been seriously ill for many years when last year she took a turn for the worse. Through days and nights of nursing her daughter, they talked about what they would do on her recovery. T/4/2 was dream and with their own skills, Diana cooking and Sonia in the front, they have made a lovely restaurant where people travel miles to taste their wonderful fare. There's no menu, when Diana arrives in the morning she then decides what the menu will consist of but there is always five or six choices of main meals. Besides them there are oodles of delicious home made cakes and other exciting foods, including a wide range of exciting vegetarian dishes and other special diets that are catered for e.g. Diabetic, Gluten free, egg free. T/4/2 can seat up to 28 and are happy to cater for small functions as well as for outside dinner parties, cocktail parties and such. Above the restaurant and with the help of consultant Victoria they have opened a Health and Healing Department for homoeopathic and other alternative therapies. Situated in Cross Keys Yard, Eastgate in Sleaford you'll find T/4/2 open during the week from 9.00am - 4.30pm and later in the summertime and on Saturdays and Sundays 12.30pm - 4.30pm.

In the heart of Sleaford in Mill Court on Carre Street, you'll find the Les Routiers recommended **Millers Wine Bar.** Rowina Drowley came here five years ago to manage the Wine Bar and was so impressed that after six months she bought it! Through sheer hard work and determination she has turned this old 19th century coach works into a wonderful, relaxing establishment, enhanced by tasteful background music. The interior is full of character with its pitched timber frame and beamed ceiling, exposed brick walls, wooden and part flagstone floor. With traditional wooden tables and chairs and surrounded by bygone farm implements you'll be served by the friendly and helpful staff who'll help you decide from the amazing choices on the varied and reasonably priced menu which consists of all home cooked, delicious food, suited to all tastes. There is seating for 70 in the restaurant and booking is advisable for this popular meeting place. The Wine Bar is open Monday to Friday 11.00am - 3.00pm and 7.00pm - 11.00pm. Saturday 7.00pm - 11.00pm and Sundays 7.30pm - 10.30pm. The restaurant Monday to Friday 12.00pm -2.00pm and 7.00pm - Midnight. Saturday 7.00pm - Midnight and on Sundays (booking only) 7.30pm - 11.30pm.

Millers Wine Bar. Sleaford. Lincs Tel: 0529 413383.

The 'modern' part of the town evolved around Sleaford Castle, which was founded in the twelfth century by Bishop Alexander of Lincoln. Sadly, there are no remains of the castle to wander round today. In the south of the town is the enormous Bass Maltings. The central tower which stands four storeys high is quite a landmark, and we could hardly believe the sheer size of this building. Nearly 1,000 feet long, it is double the length of Lincoln Cathedral, and we thought it rather appropriate that this monument to one of man's favourite tipples should be of such 'noble' proportions!

On the edge of Sleaford, adjacent to the Railway station lies the **Carre Arms Hotel**, a place mentioned in many guide books. A building has stood on this site since the mid 17th century but the present Hotel was built between 1907 - 09 by the Carre family, one time directors of Bass Brewery, whose original maltings still stand nearby. Three years ago owners Jean and Paco Cunago, along with their daughter Lisa decided the Carre Arms was for them. Since then they have created a wonderful hotel, with thirteen excellent ensuite rooms, and a Restaurant with old fashioned values at heart. A magnificent enclosed courtyard stands in the centre of the hotel and is adorned with old carts, flowers and foliage. In the sixty seater restaurant and along with their chef, Philip Baker, who has been with them over seventeen years, the Cunagos serve the most delicious and interesting food such as Mushroom Pate wrapped in Filo Pastry, Crepinette Scampi, Medallions Algerienne to name but a few. Washed down by the real ale, wines or spirits from their tastefully decorated bars which compliment the atmosphere you'll know you've discovered something a little special.

Carre Arms Hotel.   Sleaford. Lincs NG34 7JP.   Tel: 0529 303156

By the **B1394** at **Heckington** stands **The Pearoom Craft Centre**, a former pea sorting warehouse that now houses a craft shop and twelve workshops of traditional and contemporary craftspeople. Woodwork, ceramics, embroidery, beautiful textiles, garments, bags and jewellry are on display in the gallery which also puts on touring exhibitions, shows and craft demonstrations. A tearoom offers light refreshment daily from Easter to September and at weekends throughout the year. Run under licence by North Kesteven District Council the craft centre, which opened in 1979, provides and interesting and worthwhile stopover for visitors to the area.

Close by at Sleaford sitting between the A52 and A513 is, **Cogglesford Mill**, another place of interest restored by the District Council. There's evidence that milling has been carried out on this site since the 800's but the present building was last used in 1885. The mill has been owned in the past by amongst others the Bishop of Lincoln until 1547 and later Lord Clinton who then re-sold it Carre family. Leased to millers who ground local produce it was one of several mills in the area. Perhaps Cogglesfords heyday was at the height of the canal days in the late 18th century when vessels passed by the mill and unprecedented amounts of milled corn could be supplied to

284

Boston,Lincoln and places on the Trent and beyond. As with many other industries of the time the advent of steam engines and particularly railways bought about the mills gradual decline. The Slea Navigation which had helped provide the impetus for change fell into neglect as the cheaper and faster railway attracted the business despite the mills conversion to steam some time in the middle 19th century. The careful and considerable restoration work which began in 1989 has now left the area with a wonderful legacy of a bygone era that is well worth a visit. It is open Monday - Friday 10.00am - 4.00pm (closed 12.30 - 1.00) and Sundays 1 - 4pm up to the end of October. Between October and the end of April it is open on Saturdays between 1 - 5pm. Arrangement can be made for guided tours by prior arrangement but remember that access to the first and second floors is by way of ladder type stairways.

Before the formation of the College at Cranwell, the Royal Naval Air Service formed a flying training station there for officers and cadets. On the April 1st 1918 the Royal Flying Corps and the Royal Naval Air Service amalgamated to form the Royal Air Force. Beyond Sleaford you can visit the **Cranwell Aviation Heritage Centre** just off A17 and learn of the aviation history through a series of displays of the famous RAF College Cranwell from its early days up until the present day.

North Kesteven District Council. Sleaford. Lincs NE34 . Tel: 0529 414155

Also whilst in the area the **Billinghay Cottage and Craft Workshop** just off the A513 from Sleaford is an attractive and charming centre that has been restored by the District Council in traditional methods of 'mud and stud'. The house dates from the 1600's and now contains models of how the interior would have looked in the past as well as a changing exhibition of archive photography. The Workshop adjoins the barn and is used by blacksmith Ian

285

Caudwell who displays some of his interesting practical and sculptural work close by.

Lincolnshire Road Transport Museum is also supported by North Kesteven District Council. Situated about three and a half miles out of Lincoln centre,off the Whisby Road which links the A46 with the B1190 in North Hykeham, the museum contains a collection of 35 super vintage cars,buses and commercial vehicles that span fifty years of road transport history. The museum is open (to be confirmed) and group bookings are accepted by prior arrangement - Tel: 0522 689497 for information.

To the west of the Royal Air Force College, near the junction of Ermine Street and the A17, there is a rather odd memorial. Three sets of enormous metal horseshoes set in the earth mark the spot where a local man named Abner confronted a notorious witch known as Old Meg. Sitting astride his blind horse, Bayard, Abner wounded the witch with his sword, but undeterred she leaped onto the horse's back and dug in her claws. In an effort to shake her off, Bayard gave three tremendous leaps which are now commemorated by the horseshoe markers. Abner twisted round in his saddle and plunged his sword into the witch with so powerful a thrust that he inadvertently killed his unfortunate steed as well. There are inevitably, many versions of the story.

South west of Sleaford is **Heydour**. The village church has a sad and somewhat grotesque epitaph to the infant son of the Countess of Coningsby and Sir Michael Newton. The eight week old baby was apparently thrown from the upper storey of the family home **Culverthorpe Hall** by a pet monkey. With this tragic loss of his heir, the direct male line expired with the death of Sir Michael in 1743.

Nearby, the lake belonging to Culverthorpe Hall almost encroaches on the roadside. Built by Sir John Newton in 1680, the house was extended under the guidance of Sir Michael from 1734. It is a popular place for picnickers from where you can enjoy the tranquil views of the house and lakeside.

The little village of **Oasby** boasts a pretty manor house made from local stone which dates back to Tudor times. Oasby is the home of the **Oasby Pot Shop.** The shop has been run by John and Kate Evans for the past eleven years as a village store. However,in the past five years they have also established a Craft Pottery Gallery. There are over 1200 pieces of hand thrown pottery which have been carefully chosen from small potteries scattered across the UK including some from local Lincolnshire potteries. We were pleasantly surprised to see a display, not only of everyday pottery, but also 'one-off' individual pieces, all beautifully painted or decorated by hand. Since the pots are collected from over 40 potteries, there is an unusually wide and varied selection from which to choose. Although it is principally a Craft Pottery Gallery, there is a section devoted to other quality gifts so that there is something to suit everyone's fancy as well as pocket.

Passing through the gallery you can either relax in the newly constructed conservatory where tea, coffee and biscuits are available or on warm days sit outside and admire John and Kate's pleasant garden. The shop is open all week except Wednesday, but it is advisable to check weekend afternoon opening times if you are planning a special visit.

Did You Know...

The Hidden Places Series

Covers most of Britain?

For our full list see back of book

Standing next to the already mentioned Oasby Pot Shop and blending in perfectly with the rest of the village is the very impressive mid 18th century **Houblon Arms.**

The Houblon Arms Inn. Oasby. Lincs NG32 3NB. Tel: 05295 215.

Formerly part of the Culverthorpe Estate, it was once called the Red Lion but was renamed after Houblon, the first person to sign Bank of England notes. Jon (the chef) and Maxine Montague have only been here a few months but have already stamped their own personalities on the place. Inside there are roaring fires,very low beamed ceilings, an exposed feature brick fireplace and exposed brick walls. In the past the inn brewed its own beer but now serves traditional cask and guest ales in a delightful bar area where you can enjoy their varied choice of bar snacks. Complimented by a cosy 34 seat restaurant,where bookings are advisable, you'll find an extensive choice within their menu. There are also five first class ensuite letting rooms with all facilities, two of which contain four poster beds. For those wanting to enjoy more of this delightful area of Lincolnshire you'll find a warm welcome for all at this smashing and homely place.

From Oasby, we dropped down onto the **A52** and headed south - east. Renowned throughout the county, **The Red Lion Inn,** is an inn with a difference. Standing in the picturesque village of Newton this Lincolnshire stone built 17th century inn is truly remarkable. Bought by Graham and Christine Watkin, it now boasts probably the finest cold carvery for many a mile. You can put pounds on just looking at it! But there is a difference, Graham, a pork butcher by trade, has built within the complex a bakery and butchers. The food prepared there comes straight to your table and it is harder to get fresher food than that. The interior of the inn is like a Victorian front room, packed with antiques giving the place character and warmth. That is not all, adjacent to the inn there are two squash courts with all facilities available for those who want to work off the substantial portions you'll get at this inn where the hosts actually do care about their customers. The Red Lion is situated off the A52 Grantham to Boston road, about a mile from its junction with the A15.

The Red Lion.   Newton nr Sleaford. Lincs.   Tel: 05297 256.

Across the **A15** along the A52 we turned off to the tiny village of **Threekingham.** It is situated just beyond the Roman road called Mareham Lane (later named King Street), and is near the site of a great battle that took place in 870 AD. Two Saxon noblemen, Earl Alfgar and Morcar, Lord of Bourne, mustered an army against the Danish invaders. An appalling slaughter ensued, and the Saxons are said to have succeeded in killing the three Danish kings after whom the village is reputedly named.

Legend would have us believe that the Danish kings were laid to rest in the churchyard under several huge tombs. Unfortunately, the tombs have been more accurately dated to the fourteenth century, which rather spoils the romance of the story! And as the alternative spelling of the village's name is Threckingham, place-name experts will put a further damper on things by telling you that it more likely originates from a Saxon tribe called the Threckings who settled here.

Folkingham can be found nearby on the A15, and was once an important coaching station. At one time, the village could play host to as many as seven fairs throughout the year. Inside St Andrew's church with its lofty steeple are the village stocks and whipping post. The House of Correction once stood to the east of the village, but now all that is left of the building is its rather ugly nineteenth-century gatehouse.

The villages of **Pickworth** and **Sapperton** to the west made us feel that we were miles and centuries away from our nearest neighbours. The confines of the villages have hardly grown since the middle of the last century, which made a refreshing change from the urbanisation of rural areas which we had witnessed elsewhere in our travels.

Ropsley was the birthplace of one of our leading men in the field of education. Richard Fox, born in the village at the Peacock Inn some time around 1450, was one of Henry VII's most loyal ministers. He is credited for bestowing funds on the grammar school at Grantham. He was also appointed Bishop of Exeter, Wells, Durham and Winchester, was Chancellor of Cambridge University, and founded Corpus Christi College at Oxford. An impressive array of credentials indeed! Fox lost favour under Henry VIII and retired to Winchester, where he died in 1528. The village sits in a veritable 'basin' with high ground, one could almost say hills, surrounding it. Here, the **Ropsley Rise Wood Trail** will give you access to some lovely country walks.

Some five miles south of Ropsley, we discovered the hidden village of **Irnham**. Lying in a beautiful dell, this is a truly idyllic place. Standing by the large pond with its geese and ducks, we gazed across at **Irnham Hall** which is framed by oaks, beeches and willows. A wooden bridge and little waterfall complete the pastoral scene.

To the east by the A15 you'll find a 'gem' of a find in the picturesque village of **Rippingale** is the 3 Crown recommended, **The Manor House Hotel**. It is delightful in every way; characterful, peaceful, classy and owned by Steve and Sue McDermott, this homely and welcoming hotel goes out of its way to make your stay enjoyable.

The Manor House Hotel.   Rippingale. Lincs.   Tel: 0778 440546.

The excellent accommodation consists of three ensuite rooms - a further four are to be added soon - all which have direct dial telephones, TV, tea/coffee facilities, hair dryers and trouser presses. Downstairs there is a small intimate bar which is comfortably furnished and serves excellent ales. The 80 seater restaurant is well set out and perfect for enjoying the delicious, freshly prepared table d'hôte and a la carte menu's where as far as is possible produce is used from the hotel's own garden and greenhouse. In the delightful grounds there is a tennis court for enthusiasts. The hotel offers visitors a limousine service where guests can be met from the train or taken to and from special appointments. Situated close to Boston, Grantham, Lincoln, Peterborough, Spalding and Stamford you will find an the hotel an ideal place for tours and visits to these and other attractions in the area .

Corby Glen sits by the **A151**and between the two branches of the Glen River, West and East. At one time, Corby's annual sheep fair was one of the largest in Lincolnshire. The village no longer holds a weekly market, but the large market place and the market cross point to its previous importance as a busy trading centre.

Seven miles east of Bourne on the A151 you'll find a place of interest that makes a perfect day out, **Grimsthorpe Castle and Park**. Situated in the midst of rolling pastures and woodland, the medieval deerpark and Tudor oak park are havens for wildlife. The Castle was granted by Henry Vlll in 1516 to the 10th Baron, Willoughby de Eresby on his marriage to Maria Salinas, lady -in waiting to Queen

Catherine of Aragon. The North Front is the last work of Sir John Vanburgh, commissioned by Robert Bertie in 1715, the 16th Baron. The de Eresby family still live in the Castle which has a magnificent collection of furniture associated with the 10th Barons hereditary office as Lord Great Chamberlain to the Palace of Westminster and includes thrones and articles from the old house of Lords as well as family portraits. The Castle stands in beautiful gardens with a formal flower garden, topiary garden and an ornamental vegetable garden and orchard.

Grimsthorpe Castle & Park. Bourne,Lincs PE10 0NB. Tel: 0778 32205. Fax: 0778 32259.

The Park has an spot ideal for picnics beside the Chestnut Drive, where you might see one of the three species of deer - Red, Muntjac and Fallow. Alternatively try a home made tea in the Coach House close by the Castle. The Castle is open on Sundays and Bank Holidays at Easter and then 29th May - 11th September from 2.00pm - 6.00pm. The Park and Gardens are open on Easter Sunday and Monday, and then Thursdays, Sundays and Bank Holidays 1st May - 11th September from 12.00pm - 6.00pm.

From here, the approach past trees and open fields to **Swinstead** is delightful. Situated on the **B1176**, this lovely village with its mellow grey stone buildings is most pleasant. The church has some particularly frightening gargoyles and inside, the church are some fine monuments to the Ancasters.

The B1176 follows the course of the West Glen River across some lovely sweeping countryside. We continued on the road to **Creeton**, then took a minor road across country to **Castle Bytham.** The countryside around Castle Bytham is very reminiscent of the Cotswolds, and cock's a geographical snook at all those who dismiss Lincolnshire as being 'flat as a pancake'. The cottages with their grey stone are most charming. All that now remains of the castle which gave the village its name is the Castle Mound. Built as a fortification for Morcar, the last of the Saxon lords, the castle would have been of wooden construction. Ownership was granted to William the

Conqueror's brother-in-law, Albemarle, sometime after 1066. Destroyed in 1220, it was then rebuilt of stone. During the War of the Roses, the castle was again demolished, and the stones were then used for building the village houses. Most helpful to visitors, the local conservation society and youth club have produced a small village guide. This is very informative, and well worth buying from the Post Office & Village Stores in Pinfold Road. The Village Trail set out in the guide takes you past the Water Keeper's Cottage, the ancient Wheat Sheaf dwelling house, and many other sites of interest.

Just west across the A1 and without doubt one of the most impressive Inns we've come across in Lincolnshire is **The Blue Cow Inn**. Situated on the borders of Lincolnshire, Leicestershire and Rutland this impressive inn stands in the picturesque village of South Witham just over half a mile off the A1 between Grantham and Stamford. Owned and personally run by Dick and Julia Thirlwell, who left their native Yorkshire over a year ago to take over the then boarded up Blue Cow and now with plenty of hard work have created an olde worlde English Inn of true character, charm and old fashioned values. This hospitable inn, formerly on the Tollemarche Estate, with its exposed stone walls, beamed ceilings and slab stone floors provides well kept ales, excellent reasonably price food from a set menu and changing daily specials in warm and intimate surroundings. A beer garden, which overlooks fields with grazing goats and horses, invites you and those with children to taste their fare, especially on warm days and evenings. Stables are available for those wanting a riding holiday and beautifully appointed letting rooms are available for those wishing to stay overnight where your visit will be well rewarded and you'll want to return time and time again.

The Blue Cow. South Witham Lincs NG33 5QB. Tel/Fax: 0572 768432

We continued passing through **Little Bytham** to **Witham on the**

Hill. Witham appears to have had its fair share of minor disasters in the past. During the eighteenth century, the spire and part of the tower of the church crashed to the ground, then the vicarage, the inn, and several other buildings were destroyed in a fire. It is hard to imagine anything so dramatic happening in such a peaceful village.

We continued through **Manthorpe, Wilsthorpe** and **Braceborough**, until we reached **Greatford**. The River Glen runs through the village, and in the churchyard we found an interesting monument to Doctor Willis, a local man. Successfully curing George III of his insanity, he opened an asylum for 'afflicted persons of Distinction and Respectability' in the Elizabethan Hall next to the church. Presumably if you were an afflicted person of no distinction and desolate of character you had no chance of being cared for!

South of Greatford is **Stamford**. The town lies in the heart of the Welland valley and has many historic associations. Roman and Saxon settlements and great religious orders were founded here. In the fifteenth century the town became wealthy through the wool trade, and in the sixteenth century Queen Elizabeth granted a manor house to Lord Burghley. **Burghley House**, a mile or so south east of Stamford stands as testimony to this. Built in in mid 16th century, with the influence of the Renaissance and palatial exterior, the House is regarded as one of Englands greatest mansions. The interior doesn't seem to match the exteriors grandeur but is worth a visit none the less, with the richly furnished rooms and a large collection of art. The well-known Burghley Horse Trails are also held in the grounds.

The town is rich in houses dating back to this time, all extremely well preserved. In the eighteenth century, the Assembly Rooms were built, and the addition of the Georgian houses made it an elegant town of consequence along with its town hall and theatre. **Stamford Museum**, on Broad Street is surrounded by many 18th century houses and contains exhibits of local archeology and crafts. Across from the museum stands the vey impressive almshouse, Browne's Hospital, founded around 1480. Across from the early English, All Saints is the old brewery which has been refurbished and is now a **Brewery Museum.**

If it's good ale, food, accommodation and company you are after, then you need look no further than the Tourist board recommended **Lincolnshire Poacher** on Broad Street in the heart of historic Stamford where all are welcome. Dating back to the early 19th century, the inn was the former home of the original Lowe, Son and Cobold Brewery and still retains many features of its old business. Mike and Fay Wainer have turned the place into 'the' place to be in Stamford. It is very characterful indeed with wooden floors, excellent decoration and furnishings. The inn is open all day and you can order a meal anytime from their extensive bar, a la carte menus or simply look out for the Daily Specials. Mike is rightly proud of the excellent way he keeps the beer which attracts both locals and visitors who mix freely in this friendly place. There are four lovely and comfortable letting rooms with hot/cold water, TV and tea/coffee facilities for those wishing to stay overnight in this lovely part of Lincolnshire.

The Lincolnshire Poacher.   Stamford 0780 64239.
The Danish Invader.   0780 64409.

Mike and Fay also own and run the Danish Invader and Saxon Restaurant, a newly constructed establishment which you'll find on Empingham Road, towards the edge of town. This wonderfully decorated and pleasant restaurant has parking for over 100 cars and welcomes coaches parties. Inside you can choose from an delicious menu,well presented and reasonably priced and served by friendly, helpful staff. Both establishments cater for all tastes including vegetarian. Miss this opportunity to eat well whilst in Stamford at your peril!

Set within the old Corn Exchange on Broad Street opposite the Lincolnshire Poacher is **Stamford Antiques Centre**. It was opened by Cathy Turner some four years ago and she now has over forty dealers who display a vast range of antiques from all different periods. The centre is very characterful with all the displays of quality antiques and collectables tastefully arranged.

The staff are knowledgeable and very helpful and there is always one or two dealers in attendance at this fascinating place where you'll not be disappointed as there is something to suit everyone's taste and pocket. There is on street parking and pay and display parking close at hand.

Stamford Antiques Centre.   Stamford. Lincs.   Tel: 0780 62605

On St Mary's Hill you will find a marvellous place which will undoubtedly tempt you to stop for a while in the form of Truffles, a shop with a difference, run by Sue Kennedy. Truffles,as the name suggests, sells the most delicious hand made Belgian and English chocolates, beautifully made and presented,they make the perfect gift, and are also an excuse to spoil yourself with something a bit special . If the lucky recipient of your kindness lives some way away, or you don't think you will resist the temptation to break into the box, Sue has the answer in Interchoc her mail order service which will send calories to parts other confectionery cannot reach! This haven for chocaholics also serves no less than 15 special chocolate drinks which you can enjoy in the tea room at Truffles. You are also encouraged to choose from dozens of varieties of teas and coffees which are then freshly prepared to order as is the food if you feel like a bite to eat. A must on your tour of Stamford.

Truffles Chocolates and Tea Room, St.Marys Hill, Stamford.
0780 57282.

Burghley House.

In the pedestrian walkway of Ironmonger Street in Stamford is the very well known **Paddingtons Coffee Shop and Restaurant.**

Paddingtons.   *Stamford,Lincs. PE9 1PL.*   *Tel: 0780 51110.*

Set in an early 18th century listed building, Terry and Alison Banks have created a wonderful eating and meeting place which is delightfully decorated both up and downstairs (non- smoking) and adorned with pictures of Paddington Bear. Here you can enjoy the delicious food in a homely and friendly atmosphere where there is a set menu of snacks or you can choose something more substantial from the Daily Specials of meals and sweets which are on the blackboard. Seating 60 Paddingtons is open six days from 9.00am - 5.00pm but note that hot food is not normally served after 3.30pm and also on Sunday afternoons from 2.00 - 5.00pm Easter until September.

In what was the stables for the local post house coaching inn is the very impressive **Tuppenny Rice Restaurant** in Castle Street. Tricia Findlay opened Tuppenny Rice as a health food shop some nine

296

Tuppenny Rice. Stamford. Lincs PE9 2RA.   Tel: 0780 62739.

restaurant three and a half years ago. Here you will find health foods and more - ingredients for cooking Chinese, Indian and Italian food, herbs and spices, local honey, jams, biscuits amongst its very good range. The restaurant is situated to the rear of the frontshop and tastefully decorated with exposed brick walls making it cosy and cheerful. Open six days a week from 9.00am - 4.30pm for delicious home made vegetarian foods which are advertised on the chalkboard - Dish of the Day, salads, jacket potatoes, lentil croquettes, homemade soups plus lots of homemade delicious cakes.

Stamford has produced some notable musical personalities, such as John Taverner who became one of Henry VII's court composers and produced the mass entitled 'The Western Wind'. Involved in the Lutheran movement, he was imprisoned for a time in Oxford but was released and retired to Boston's church to continue composing. Someone we may all be familiar with is Sir Malcolm Sargent, the conductor of so many enjoyable 'Prom' concerts from 1950 to 1967. He was born in Stamford in 1895 and is buried here.

If it's music that's to your liking, you need go no further than **Stamford Music Shop** situated in an impressive 18th century building on St Mary's Hill in the heart of town. This is a friendly shop run in the traditional family manner where musicians of all abilities can find helpful advice and inspiration. With tape and CD, instrument and sheet music departments there's something for all ages. The staff are helpful and knowledgeable and it has earned its reputation as one of the leading shops in the country for sheet music. In the unlikely event that your preferred items are not in stock, be assured that the staff will try their hardest to get it for you. However, for those without a specific aim, it's as wonderful place in which to escape for a while and have a browse. This is a veritable treasure trove which no music lover can afford to miss.

The Stamford Music Shop Stamford. Lincs . Tel: 0780 51275.

In St Mary's Street, situated within a 17th century, grade 2 listed building you'll find a unique shop full of creative gifts and unusual cards. Everything is superbly displayed in **Perfect Presents**, a shop full of character, with original beams and stone walls.

As the name suggests, here you will find perfect presents such as handmade greeting cards, silverware, jewellery, Liberty giftware, crafts and gifts for every occasion. Upstairs, you are in for a big surprise! 'Room for Bears' has everything for the teddy bear collector. World famous bear makers like Steiff, Herman, Merrythought and Deans to name a few, are combined with most leading British bear artists, teddy bear cards, ceramics and accessories are everywhere. On this floor you will also find a 'Perfect Setting Room' with candles, napkins, silk flowers and tableware. This is a shop, not to be missed, a must for those looking for gifts and greetings cards with a difference.

The building that houses **Warunee's Thai Restaurant** dates back to the late 17th century and is as delightful as the food served inside. The interior is full of character being decorated and furnished

Warunee's Thai Restaurant.   Stamford. Lincs.   Tel: 0780 572921

thoughtfully - look out for the huge bellows that hang on the wall - in this intimate and cosy restaurant with seating upstairs and down. Warunee is an excellent Thai cook with ten years experience before arriving here and helping to open the restaurant two years ago. The taste of Thailand is found in the all delicious items on the menu where each meal is cooked to order in traditional Thai style with the result that before you is food that is unique, fresh and savoury. Warunee's is open 6.00pm - 11.00pm Monday to Saturday but it is imperative to book on Thursday, Friday and Saturday if you don't want to miss a wonderful culinary experience. You'll find the restaurant on St Mary's Street in Stamford close to the already featured Tuppenny Rice.

The Candlesticks Hotel & Restaurant is set in a building that dates back from around 1730 and stands in the oldest part of Stamford in Church Lane.

Candlesticks. Stamford. Lincs. Tel: 0780 64033.

This RAC and Les Routiers recommended hotel is a family run by Mr and Mrs Pinto who have been here for eighteen years. The hotel has a comfortable lounge bar where you can relax and enjoy a drink whilst you choose something from the extensive and varied menu which consists of fresh and superbly food prepared by chef Americo Dias. You can enjoy your meal with a wine from their comprehensive list, in the intimate surroundings of the restaurant, a top rendezvous for diners from the area and frequently attracting gourmets from London. There are eight bedrooms, each with a bathroom/shower, TV, telephone, a stocked fridge, toaster sand kettle. Beautifully furnished and decorated you will enjoy your stay in this charming and up market establishment.

On a darker note, Stamford has a history of Bull Running, a custom which saw the luckless bull being chased around the town by all the inhabitants - men, women, children and dogs! This 'sport' was described as early as 1645, and though many attempts were made to stop the cruel event by humanitarians, it was not until the early nineteenth century that the Prevention of Cruelty to Animals Society took active steps to ban it.

A cattle market held in the Broad Street area of Stamford encouraged many pubs to open during the 18th century. On East Street in Stamford you'll find a gem of a pub and a rare survivor of those pubs that flourished at, **The Dolphin.** The original pub was opened in 1717 and described in 1724 as a large house with a good yard, styes for keeping swine, a pair of gates leading into a field, a cellar 20 hogshead of drink and stables for 60 horses. By 1826 it was the meeting place of the Trademans Benefit Society and a year later on Friday, February 16th was the centre of a highway robbery incident. In 1863 the site was bought by the Roman Catholics for a new church, schoolroom and presbytery. However, by 1865 The Dolphin had re-opened just behind the old Broad Street site and has changed little over the years. The original rooms still survive, including a brick floored snug and back room containing on old painted wooden settle.

Now a 3 Crown recommended Inn and Guest House with five comfortable and modern ensuite letting rooms; all with TV, coffee machine, shoe shine and hairdryer, you'll find a warm welcome for all given by Mik and Tina Maksimovic in their characterful and cosy inn. To start the day you can choose between a full English or a Continental breakfast, evening meals are provided upon request. The Dolphin also has an excellent reputation for its fine ales and quality guest beers, they hold an Annual Beer Festival with up to 18 different casks of ale. Another feature is the availability of their delicious food- the inn is famed for its Big Steaks and large helpings - from a varied menu, including daily specials which are all reasonably priced. Just two minutes from the town centre and within easy reach of the Bus and Railway Stations, the inn is in an ideal situation for visitors who come to Stamford for either business or pleasure.

The Dolphin . Stamford.Lincs. Tel: 0780 55494. Fax:0780 57515. Mobile: 0850 567424.

Little Casterton Lodge. Little Casterton. Lincs. Tel: 0780 64289.

Little Casterton Lodge is a magnificent turn of the last century property standing in one and a half acres and surrounded by lovely countryside where all will find a homely and friendly welcome given by Marian and John Croucher. This Tourist Board recommended country house accommodation has four excellent and spacious letting rooms where guests are asked not to smoke - all differently decorated, one which is ensuite, with terrific views and where peace and quiet is high on the list. Open all the year round you'll find the Lodge has lots of facilities which include well stocked and tended gardens to enjoy and being only five minutes drive out of Stamford, is an ideal base from which to tour this delightful area.

The Oak Inn is an outstanding 18th century inn standing proudly on the Kettering Road just two miles south of Stamford at Easton -on-the- Hill.. A picture to look at with its wonderful four cartwheels at the front and well decorated and furnished inside, the main aim here is to please the customer. This is certainly done in this friendly inn with lots of atmosphere where hosts Val and George Kerr and their staff provide 7 days a week lunchtime and evening extensive, delicious and reasonably priced meals and excellent well kept real ales. With good off road parking on the edge of this picturesque village all are welcome at The Oak where the separate restaurant seats up to 40 and it is best to book to avoid disappointment.

The Oak Inn.   Easton-on-the-Hill. Lincs Tel: 0780 52286.

We left Stamford on the A16, to explore the many 'Deeping' villages. The lovely names like **West Deeping, Deeping Gate**, and **Deeping St James,** refer to the 'deep meadows', and much of this area has been reclaimed from marshes. **Deeping Fen** to the north is still a place of vast open spaces, cornfields where the larks soar overhead, and few trees. But it still has plenty of appeal, especially to the cyclist and walker. The country here looks especially charming in the Spring with its soft cover of young green corn.

Market Deeping is an attractive little town where once the monks of **Croyland** built the fourteenth-century rectory. The church is dedicated to St Guthlac, the hermit who lived at Croyland (or Crowland). This village, just off to the east of Market Deeping, was surrounded by water for a great part of the year. In 699, Guthlac, a Mercian noble, sought refuge here from the rigours of military life.

The Goat is one of those olde worlde English country pubs that you come across once in a blue moon. Situated on the main A16 Stamford to Spalding Road at Frognall with good parking and beautiful views of the surrounding picturesque countryside with all modern facilities it still retains its olde worlde character, charm and friendship. Peter and Valerie Wilkins and son Nigel, have been here for virtually seven and a half years and through hard work have made The Goat an excellent establishment in every way. The decoration and furnishings are delightful as are the delicious meals. A comprehensive menu is available plus many daily specials. The ale is just perfect with six different real ales in the winter and eight in season - two from the wood. Food is available every lunchtime and evening but booking is advisable on Fridays, Saturdays and Sundays.

The Goat.   Frognall,Deeping St James.Lincs   Tel: 0778 347629.

Heading north from Market Deeping on the A15, we ended this part of our tour at the town of **Bourne**. One of the most interesting buildings here is the **Red Hall,** a brick building dating back to the Elizabethan age, which at one time was the station master's house. Following the closure of the railway, the future of the hall came under threat. Thanks must go to the Bourne United Charities Society, which undertook the preservation of this historically important house.

Bourne is thought to be the birthplace of Hereward the Wake, son of Lady Godiva and the Earl of Mercia. Famed for his exploits and forays against the Normans, his manor is said to have been on the site of Bourne Castle opposite the church. His rebellion against William the Conqueror made him a virtual outlaw as he led his men to battle. There are tales of his exploits with a giant, a bear, and a magical suit of armour from Flanders.

However tenuous his mythical exploits were, he was chronicled in an eleventh-century manuscript following his attack on an unscrupulous abbot at Peterborough.

The town was named after the supply of water that made it such an important spot. The water had an outlet at Well Head, which would have fed the castle moat. The Bourne Eau flows through the town and across the fens in an easterly direction, heading towards Spalding.

Cawthorpe House.   Bourne. Lincs PE10 0AB.   0778 423223

Just a mile out of Bourne in the village of **Cawthorpe** by the A15, and standing in 3 acres of well stocked garden, is the delightful **Cawthorpe House.** David and Deborah Bowers own and run this characterful country house accommodation which also has Conference and Training Facilities. It is hard to imagine a more beautiful setting than this house, first built in the 17th century and added to in the 18th and 19th centuries, to pursue learning or enjoy a break away from it all. The centrally heated House, open all year round, has 16 individually furnished guest rooms with facilities and two tasteful drawing rooms for guests - one non-smoking. Breakfast is a variety of choices to suit all appetites, lunches and evening meals are provided by prior arrangement, the latter from a table d'hôte menu with a selection of around twenty wines. Real ale is served in the residents bar. Active guests can enjoy croquet, an outdoor swimming pool,badminton and lawn tennis or indoors table tennis,darts,cards and board games. All are welcome at this magnificent yet homely House which is an ideal base for sightseeing being close to the abbey town of Bourne or slightly further afield the Fens and historic towns such as Stamford, Boston and Grantham, to mention but a few.

We mentioned earlier the strong Dutch influence that can be seen in some of the architecture of the county, but there is another feature of Lincolnshire quite startling in its associations with the Dutch. That is - tulips. Not simply a few garden centres that specialise in the flower, but acres and acres of vibrant colour. **Spalding** is the tulip capital of Britain, and as you first enter the town, the acres of flowerbeds and displays which feature mainly tulips in April and May are breathtaking. This area is said to be the largest bulb growing

304

centre in the world, and with 2,500 acres devoted to them we could well believe it.

May is the month for the flower parades, and the floats decorated with millions of flower heads are a sight worth seeing. The parade is led by a float with 'Miss Tulip land' waving gaily to the visitors, and in case you are wondering why only the flower heads are used, it is done for good reason. The growers remove the heads to ensure good strong growth for the bulbs which will be ready to sell in Autumn, so you have to be quick to see them on the stem!

To the north-east of Spalding is Springfields Gardens, established by the Horticultural Association in 1966. There are 25 acres of woods, lawns and flowerbeds here for the public to enjoy, and the displays of daffodils and tulips in Spring are quite stunning.

It is not all that often that one finds a Museum set in a house dating from 1430 and surrounded by the most beautiful gardens but in Spalding at Churchgate this is exactly what we found. **Ayscoughfee Hall** was purchased by a consortium of the citizens of Spalding in 1897 from Isabella Johnson, the last of the family who had lived here since 1658.

The consortium though this purchase a fitting tribute and a practical manner in which to celebrate Queen Victoria's Jubilee. In order to acquire the money, a meeting was called and half the purchase price of £2,000 was raised. The remainder was borrowed but by another royal occasion, the Coronation of Edward V11 the debt was paid and the house passed out of the hands of the Johnson family who in their lengthy residence had played an important part in the life of the district, ranging from stewards and landowners to incumbents of local churches, including Spalding Parish Church.

Well displayed exhibits depict local history give the visitor an in depth understanding of South Holland and its people. In addition there are regular and very good art exhibitions and of particular interest is the permanent display telling the story of local hero Matthew Flinders R.N. and his charting of the coast of Australia. The citizens who purchased Ayscoughfee Hall would be very proud at what has been achieved and especially as their reason for buying was give pleasure to local people.

At one time the spectacular gardens were all that were open to the public and that was only on specified dates during the year. Since the beginning of the century the gardens have been open all the time but it is only in recent years that the final dream has been realised and the Museum opened.

To have a background knowledge of the building and its owners lends more interest to any visit, anywhere. This great merchant's house which has grown and evolved over many centuries retains many of its medieval features making it one of the most important buildings of its kind in Lincolnshire.

It has always been known as Ayscoughfee Hall but there is no proof so far to connect it with the family of Ayscough who owned land in North Lincolnshire in the Middle Ages and who played an important part later in the Civil War but surely there must be a connection. There are two relocated monuments to the members of the family in Stallingborough Church, a small brass to Sir William Ayscough dated 1541 and the other an imposing 17th century marble monument to Sir Edward Ayscough.

As one would suppose the house has been altered as successive owners followed fashion and their own whim. Richard Alwyn, the first owner, is thought to have built the north wing running at right angles to the river which at the time probably came close to the entrance of the house. This brick built hall with its timber framed roof was built about 1430 and shortly afterwards a two storey square building was built on the north side with a vaulted cellar which was possibly used as a woolstore; Richard Alwyn was a wealthy wool merchant and bales were often stored in this manner. There are steps leading up from the cellar to what was probably the quay.

Slightly later a hall built at right angles to the first building created a cross wing. This, now hidden under later 18th century plasterwork, is the finest part of the medieval house and its survival, in excellent condition, is remarkable and very important; it is one of the finest roofs in the country. It is probable that this was open to the roof with smoke from an open fire rising to the rafters, evidence for a louvre was found when the building was re-roofed.

The present south wing is also 15th century and of a similar date to other parts of the house. It has been suggested that it may have been built about the same times as Richard Alwyn's Hall and then acquired by him and a single house created by the construction of the superb hall which joins the two wings.

The house was left in peace until the 17th century when Bevill Wimberley was the owner and it is thought that he was responsible for the internal divisions in the hall and perhaps the insertion of floors in the north and south wings, certainly a service wing was created about that time as the door to it is visible in a late 18th century drawing in the Banks Collection. fortunately this sketch by Nattes and a similar one of the rear of the house are excellent, remarkable survival of documentation for the medieval house; what is particularly important is that the Nattes sketch showed an oriel window in front of the house opposite the surviving one, no trace of this now remains.

Within a very short time the front of the house was drastically altered by the Reverend Maurice Johnson, Incumbent of Spalding, one of the innumerable Maurice Johnsons who occupied the house until the late 19th century. He removed the medieval windows and replaced them with wooden ones creating a provincial Strawberry Hill effect. The house had then been thatched, it is recorded that it was removed in 1772 and replaced by slate.

The 19th century saw more alterations including moving the service and kitchen wing to the north side where a 19th century range still survives and buildings were added on that side; the use of old bricks helps to make a sympathetic union of medieval and later periods.

The west front is the part of the house that has changed most often and in the 1840's the present ornate stone windows and doorways together with the porch and coat of arms were added to the house. The tower too, was altered, it was heightened and a pierced Gothic parapet added creating the appearance the house now has.

Ayscoughfee Hall. Churchgate, Spalding. Tel: 0775 725468.

Marry all this information with the interesting items on display and we're certain you'll enjoy your visit. Should you hunger for more history of the area you'll find close by, **The Pinchbeck Engine.** Here you will be able to see a working example of a steam engine - once a familiar sight in this area as many powered scoop wheel pumping stations - that helped drain the surrounding land for agricultural use. Land reclamation and controlling the waters of the Fenlands has been going on since Roman times, the displays at the Museum inform the visitor of this constant fight to contain nature.

In addition to the title we have already mentioned, Spalding can also claim to be the banana capital of Britain! A small family-run business that started in the town more than fifty years ago has grown into the well known company, Geest Industries, which supplies over 60 per cent of the bananas eaten in the country.

You can be sure of an enjoyable stay at the beautifully refurbished,grade two listed 18th Century **Red Lion Hotel** in the centre of the market town. Owned by the Wilkins family since 1973 and for the last seven years managed by Nigel Wilkins, this delightful three storey, Les Routier recommended Hotel has replenished the thirst and appetite of visitors and provided accommodation for many travellers in its fifteen individual and homely ensuite rooms with full facilities. Delicious food is served in the traditional mahogany panelled Restaurant or Lounge bar between 12.00pm and 2.00pm and 6.00pm to 9.00pm Monday to Saturday, changing slightly on Friday and Saturday with 7.00pm to 10.00pm servings, from a tempting menu that considers the needs of health conscious with its Light Luncheon menu and many low fat choices from the daily menu. Daily specials are put up on the blackboard and the very palatable evening menu changes monthly. Ground floor disabled facilities means no one need miss out as all are welcome at this lively hotel which also contains a superb Blues and Jazz Club which claims amongst its many famous acts an appearance by the legendary Jimi Hendrix. Overnight car parking for the Red Lion Hotel is in the Market Place, except on Mondays and Fridays due to a market the following morning, or on a nearby Public Car Park.

The Red Lion Hotel.   *Spalding, Linc .*   *Tel: 0775 722869 Fax: 0775 710074*

After owning and personally running a bar in Lanzarote and another inn in Nottingham, Bruce and Ellen Wainwright -Bateman purchased the derelict **Lincolnshire Poacher** situated on Double Street, opposite the River Welland in Spalding. With sheer hard work, this Tourist Board registered inn is now,without doubt, one of the most impressive we have come across. This popular place has lots of character and olde worlde charm throughout and is adorned with old metal advertisements boards. Excellent meals and bar snacks, as well

308

as childrens meals, are available from an extensive menu which is very reasonably priced and where there is seating for 50. It is, however, advisable to book at weekends especially during the summer. The inn is included in the 'Good Beer Guide' and has three Theakstons Real ales, I C Old Peculiar and three guest ales,all well kept, each week. Over 500 different ales have been handled in the Poachers in the last three years! The five letting bedrooms are warm and cosy with all facilities and after tasting Bruce's beer, sleep is the least of problems for guests. There is free parking opposite from 6.00pm to 8.00am.

The Lincolnshire Poacher. Spalding Lincs. Tel: 0775 766490.

Out of Spalding on the A16 towards Pinchbeck stands, **The Royal Mail Cart,** with an old Mail Cart Garage sitting across the road from the inn. On the road that was once used by mail coaches on their way to Spalding and Donington, and for virtually one hundred and fifty years known as the Mail Cart, the 'Royal' was added by command of Queen Elizabeth in 1989.

The Royal Mail Cart. Spalding, Lincs .   Tel: 0775 722931.

For the last five years owned and run by Sue and Dick Stoker you'll discover, the homely atmosphere and beautiful decor inside this old staging post - the lounge was once the stables - a delight. The inn is a Free House were Courage and Guest Ales are on tap along with Bar snacks every lunchtime and the pride and joy of the Stokers, the sixty seat restaurant,which is open seven days a week for lunch and evening meals. The extensive menu which has an excellent reputation locally, and not surprising with over 60 palatable choices, including Salmon, Scampi, lobster and grills, is prepared by the highly regarded chef, John Bright. A bowling green and childrens play area are added features which combine to make the inn an ideal stopping off point for all in this friendly, family pub where all are welcome.

We took the **B1165,** Spalding to Wisbech road, and right in the middle of nowhere surrounded by open Finland, we came across the tiny village of **Weston Hills.** The lonely Fens seemed to befriend the village and welcome its presence. Further on we came to **Sutton St. - Edmunds** 8 miles away from Wisbech and only 16 miles from Spalding. The village, which lies in Tydd St Giles Fen, can be approached from the south off the B1166, or as we did, from the north off the B1165. Making our way back to this road, we passed through **Sutton St James,** then headed north to **Long Sutton** on the B1390

Long Sutton grew up as a market and centre for local trade, and derives its name from the incredibly long street around which it is based. It is said to be where Dick Turpin practised the art of the butcher! This apparently was his chosen trade before he opted for a more lucrative 'profession'.

One of Lincolnshires premier attractions,**The Butterfly and Falconry Park,** is tucked away in the village of Long Sutton and attracts up to 200o visitors on a busy day. You'll understand why when you visit as there's something for everyone within its 15 acres - Nature Trails, a Falconry Centre, a Butterfly World, farm animals and a museum, and a childrens play area. The Butterfly garden is one of the largest tropical houses in Britain and you'll see colourful butterflies in a wealth of flora and fauna. A small Insectarium contains scorpions, tarantulas and stick insects, all safely housed behind glass! In the Falconry Centre you can see Falcons, Hawks, Buzzards, Eagles and Owls and the resident Falconer, Martin Foulds gives flying displays daily at 12.00pm and 3.00pm. A Tea room and garden serves beverages, light lunches,cream teas and other delicious home prepared food. Gift and Country Fayre Shops have an excellent range of gifts with wildlife themes, pickles, preserves, local honey and garden plants amongst their stock for those wanting a memento of their visit to this interesting and educational place. The Park is open from March 12th - Oct 31st daily from 10.00am - 6.00pm but during September and October 10.00am - 5.00pm and does take group bookings provided they are made in advance.

Butterfly and Falconry Park. Long Sutton,nr Spalding. Tel: 0406 363833.Fax: 0406 363182.

Taking the **Lutton** sign on the outskirts of Long Sutton and following this road until you see a sign Colleys Gate, a quarter of a mile further on you'll come to a real 'hidden gem' the homely, **White House Farm**.

White House Farm. Lutton nr Spalding. Lincs Tel: 0406 364125.

The owner, Mrs Robin Ward came here about eight years ago and has been providing Bed and Breakfast for the past seven and a half years in her lovely home. Built in 1660 and a working farm until around 20 years ago, Robin provides accommodation,all year round,in five homely and comfortable rooms and serves up the most delicious food. This charming lady will provide evening meals on request for guests who want to enjoy the scenic views that surround the farm and take advantage of its easy location to other attractions in the area. On

311

a one and a half acre site Robin keeps horses, a shetland pony, donkey, wildfowl and friendly dogs.

From here, the **A17** would lead us to the town of **Holbeach,** but first we decided to explore the strange area to the north known as Holbeach Marsh. The roads to the villages around here are a veritable maze, so in some ways it is not easy to give directions even by the compass point! Twisting lanes between dykes led us ever nearer to the sea. The marsh, which stretches all the way to the coast, can almost be described as an 'island'. The land is only a couple of feet above sea level here, due to silting and reclamation of the marshes which began in Roman times. This accounts for the presence of sea banks inland which were once been many miles further out on the coast.

The marshes extend for miles, but if you follow a track with persistence, you will end at a high bank of earth, and peering over it, the sea will be there. Well, almost there - you may have to walk some miles over sparse ground before dipping your toes in the briny! But the marsh is rich in bird life, and watching out for these together with the treacherous bogs and channels keeps you on those toes. North of Holbeach Hurn, further reclamation went on as recently as 1948 when 1,500 acres of land were drained.

Built in 1737, the Tourist Board registered **Whaplode Manor,** was until quite recently a working farm on the Duke of Portland

Whaplode Manor. Holbeach. Lincs PE12 7PP. Tel: 0406 422837

estate. Quite near to the house was the railway junction where potato trains off the Fens would transfer their loads to the main line for delivery to Holbeach and beyond. Set in 12 acres, Whaplode Manor is really an idyllic and picturesque place. Its eleven rooms with full facilities in the house and adjoining converted stables includes facilities for the disabled, all expertly refurbished by the owners and including a wonderful honeymoon suite. The owners Dave and Sandra Wood are planning further extensions in 1995, when the barn will be turned

312

into a bar and 100 seater restaurant. Currently, evening meals are gladly prepared for guests by prior arrangement. Dave, incidentally, is one of the few registered Autogiro pilots and uses an adjacent field for flying where there is free air space for other Autogiro or Microlite flyers. For the more sedate pleasure seekers the Manor is situated in beautiful countryside which is ideal for bird watchers, anglers and walkers. Campers and Caravanners are also welcome at Whaplode Manor which lies three miles north of Holbeach off the A17 near Saracens Head village.

Heading west from Holbeach on the A151, we came to the village of **Weston.** Further north on the A16 is **Surfleet**, a pretty place which lies on the banks of the River Glen.   The sparseness of the fens surrounding it only serves to set it off. At **Gosberton,** a magnificent octagonal spire rises from the church of St Peter and Paul. We noticed some amusing gargoyles around the top of the tower, including what appeared to be an elephant's head.   The road her turns sharply to the east towards **Boston**, and the **A152** will lead you through the village to the small market town of **Donington.**

Donington was the birthplace of Captain Matthew Flinders, and it was through his endeavours as an explorer that much of the Australian coastline was mapped in the 1800s. Many of the names given to natural features there were inspired by towns and villages in Lincolnshire. A monument in the church depicting a sailing ship is dedicated to him, as is a beautiful stained-glass window.

The A16 from Gosberton continues through what was at one time some of the best grazing land in the country. But the countryside between **Kirton** and Boston takes on a whole new appearance. The unexpected advent of trees is in some ways a relief after the low vistas, which we sometimes felt could only be admired from a worms-eye view!

The sudden sight of the Boston Stump rising out of the fens made us sit up a bit straighter in our seats and pay attention! The Stump is a colossal tower rising above St Botolph's Church in three stages, with a plethora of buttresses, enormous windows, a parapet, more pinnacles, flying buttresses - and so on! The immense edifice soars above the town, the fens, and the River Witham to an amazing 272 feet. One could not be more impressed if it were the Eiffel Tower! Building of the church began in 1309, but the tower itself was not finished until 1460.

A short stroll from the Town Bridge over the Witham will take you into the large market place, and most of the town's finest buildings can be seen in this area. Fydell House was saved from demolition by the Boston Preservation Trust in 1935, and opposite Ye Olde Magnet

Tavern in South Street in the heart of Boston you'll find **The Guildhall**, a fine brick structure dating back to 1450. Once the Hall of St Mary's Guild and later the Town Hall, this building has further interesting history in that on the ground floors are the original cells in which the religious separatists, later known as the 'Pilgrim Fathers', were imprisoned in 1607. The Courtroom, used until 1841 and still in its original state, is where they were tried in September 1607. Beyond the cells there is an ancient kitchen equipped as it would have been in the early 17th century. The Maritime Room, formerly the Mayor's Parlour, now houses a display of ships models and custom house artefacts. The Council Chamber which saw the election of every Mayor of Boston from 1545 to 1887 still retains a 15th century deed cupboard with linenfold carved doors. The Banqueting Hall has a Musician's Balcony and a stone-mullioned west window with ancient stained glass depicting the twelve apostles. As the Borough Museum, the exhibits include displays of archeology, costume and textiles, ceramics, militaria and much more reflecting the local history of the borough. There is a small shop in the entrance hall selling a wide variety of gifts and souvenirs. The Guildhall is open Monday to Saturday 10.00am - 5.00pm all year and Sundays 1.30pm - 5.00pm April to the end of September. It is closed Christmas and New Year Holidays. Entry includes the use of a personal audio guided tour.

Boston Guildhall.   Boston,Lincs .   Tel: 0205 365954.

St Botolph, the founder of the town, established a Benedictine order here in 654. No less than seventy churches have been ascribed to him throughout England. Although there is no mention of the town in the Domesday Book, by the middle of the fourteenth century it attracted merchants and traders of all descriptions from around England and the Continent.

It is hard to believe as you approach the attractive exterior of Forte owned **The New England Hotel and Restaurant** in Wide Bargate,

314

that this was once a public house - Cross Keys - of ill -repute, favoured by visiting seamen. Also used by Carrier Carts who stayed on Market Days the present building dates from around 1830 although the Licenses list for 1784 reveals that an inn was in existence on the spot before. This homely hotel with its grand appearance is a delight as inside you'll find charming and comfortable decor and furnishings, whilst the staff managed by Gloria Sands are on hand to welcome you in this 2 Star RAC and AA recommended hotel. Its twenty five comfortable rooms, all ensuite and other amenities combine to make this an ideal place to stay. Its eighty seat restaurant with a tempting A la Carte menu and extensive daily specials is open every lunch and evening all year round. Booking is advisable though at weekends. All are welcome, bar meals and snacks are also available along with John Smiths ales for the visitor who wants rest and replenishment as they discover the historic attractions, such as 'The Stump', Guildhall or Shodfairs Hall, that dot the ancient market town of Boston and the surrounding area.

The New England Hotel & Restaurant. Boston. Lincs . Tel: 0205 365255 Fax: 0205 310597

At one time, Boston was the second largest port in Britain after London. Wines from Bordeaux and Gascony were brought here for the monasteries, while salt and hides were exported. Naturally the fens have been used for salt production for centuries, and we will talk more about this as we come to the coast. Despite its earlier prosperity, by 1571 the borough corporation were muttering that the town was in a recession, with little trade or shipping putting in there. Although its importance continued to fluctuate through the centuries, the port always managed to struggle on, and with the inland water-ways providing better communications, the town went through a revival.

South-east of Boston is the village of **Fishtoft.** The aforementioned St Guthlac is commemorated here in a stained glass window in the

315

church. Depicted as brandishing a whip that was a gift from St Bartholomew, the legend goes that as long as he had a grip on it, the village would be free of mice and rats!

North-west of Boston is **Brothertoft**, formerly known as Goosetoft, and from here the great goose drives would have left for the markets of London. The poor creatures were forced across beds of hot tar to toughen up their feet for the long trek. One can only feel for the doomed birds having to endure scorched feet followed by a hundred mile route-march south, only to be slaughtered for the table! It wasn't only their meat and eggs that were valuable, but also their feathers, not least for quill pens and presumably pillows.

We headed west from Boston on the **A52**, then joined the **A17** at **Bicker Bar.** The road north from here led us to **Swineshead.** It is here at the ruined Abbey, that King John, in no good mood after having lost the Crown Jewels in The Wash, died after overindulging himself. Peaches and ale is what killed him, although the story goes that a monk poisoned him. In conversation with the monk, the King hinted that he might force the poor to pay more money for their humble loaves. The monk, indignant at this injustice, poisoned the King's ale, sipping from it himself to give the impression that it was safe.

Continuing north on the A17, we passed through **East Heckington** and **Garwick**, then turned onto the **B1394** to **Heckington.** This delightful little village is perched on the edge of the Fens. One of the outstanding features of the village is the eight-sailed windmill, the only one of its kind in this country. It was built in 1830, and the eight sails were added in 1891. With an increased surface area, the sails were able to catch the merest breath of wind, and were very effective. The mill ended its commercial career in 1942, but is open today for the public to enjoy as the miller still uses it once a fortnight.

The other main attraction in Heckington is the church, which is said by some to be the finest in England. The interior of the church is wonderful, with its 'visions' of demons, monsters and mortals peering out of stone flourishes and leaves, while in the Easter Sepulchre, angels and saints in devotional attitudes create a more peaceful setting. There is also a fine monument to Richard de Potesgrave, who was probably responsible for the building of the chancel where he now lies.

North of Heckington on the A153, the village of **Anwick** is home to a strange legend. Embedded in the entrance to the churchyard are two large rocks known locally as the Drake Stones. The legend has it that a farmer working in a local field lost his horses in a patch of bog. As the horses submerged, a drake flew out of the mire. The next day, the farmer discovered a massive stone shaped like a drake, lying on that very spot. In 1832, attempts to move the stone failed, as the chains snapped and a drake flew away from the underside of the stone. In 1913, the rock was dragged to the churchyard, where it broke into the two pieces we see today. Villagers will tell you that two drakes are frequently spotted sheltering under the lee of the stones.

Continuing northwards on the A153, the ground rises slightly around **North Kyme** with the fens spreading out all around. At **Tattershall Bridge**, a right-hand lane led us to **Dogdyke**. Here, the River Witham joins the little River Bain, which flows some twenty-four miles through Horncastle to Ludford. This part of the river is well known for its coarse fishing, and at the Packet Inn, the river authority offers fishing permits for an amazing 250 miles of riverbank.

Back on the A153, we caught an arresting glimpse of rosy-red **Tattershall Castle** rearing up above the tiny town of **Tattershall**. The bricks were originally thought to be Flemish, but it is now understood that they were made at Edlington Moor. Over 320,000 bricks were used, and they were all hand-made. The keep, which is rather like a toy-town castle, was built between 1433 and 1443 for Ralph Cromwell, the Lord Treasurer of England. It stands four storeys high, and the base walls are twenty feet thick. Despite its impressive scale, it was not built primarily as a defensive castle, but as a private dwelling. It stands up like a red toy box with four small octagonal turrets at each corner. On each of the four floors lies a massive room with a carved stone fireplace and mullioned windows. Owned now by the National Trust, the castle is open to the public daily, and if you are blessed with clear weather during your visit, you will be able to spot both Lincoln Cathedral and Boston Stump from the top of the tower.

If you stand outside the shops in the market place and look across at one of the houses opposite, you will see an odd-shaped tile sitting on its roof. This is supposed to be a 'scale model' of the house of Tom Thumb, who apparently lived in the village. Talking to the locals, we heard several strange stories relating to this character. When the tile was taken down to be cleaned some years ago, several level-headed villagers swear that it appeared to be much bigger when on the ground. Indeed, one of them told us that a lady visiting the village at that time claims to have gone inside the 'house' to take tea with Tom and his wife!

Local theories as to who or what Tom Thumb actually was range from a mischievous sprite to a sad little man shunned by the villagers, but protected by a local landowner as a lucky 'mascot'. It would be easy to dismiss his existence altogether, were it not for an inscription on the floor near the font in Tattershall church, which implies that he is buried there. The dedication would put him at over a hundred years old when he died, and if the size of the inscribed stone is anything to go by, he must have been a very small fellow indeed!

Further along the road is the small town of **Coningsby.** Its most memorable feature is the remarkable clock face of St Michael's Church. Visible for miles around, the enormous white face of the clock measures sixteen and a half feet in diameter, and its single hand is fifteen feet in length. This makes it the largest single-handed clock in the world. Going back further in 'time', there is evidence that mammoths roamed the area during the Ice Age, and there was also a Roman settlement here.

The White Bull.   Coningsby. Lincs. .   Tel: 0526 342439.

Situated on the main street in historic Coningsby, where the RAF have a base, is the mid 19th century inn, **The White Bull,** which is open all day. Mick and Judy came here seven years ago and have, during this time, turned it into a very popular family inn with a 3 Crown Tourist Board recommendation. With the River Bain running adjacent to the inn and one of the best childrens play area's we have come across, it really is a smashing place. Here you will find excellent ale, food and accommodation. The menu has a range to suit everyone's taste, including vegetarian and over twenty choices for children, who will no doubt also enjoy the large bird aviary in the gardens. There are four letting rooms, two ensuite and all tastefully furnished and decorated with good facilities, one room has a four poster bed. The inn is a real credit to the owners. The White Bull is in idyllic situation in Coningsby, on the A153 Sleaford to Skegness Road, with a large car park and a warm welcome when you enter.

Today, the town is home to the Royal Air Force, and at RAF Coningsby, the **Battle of Britain Memorial Flight** can be seen. The Flight Memorial was established here in 1976 to commemorate the heroic battle, and the one and a half hour guided tour will show you

318

Spitfires, Hurricanes, and the last surviving Lancaster Bomber in Britain. These marvellous old planes are still flown in special displays up and down the country, but it is the Lancaster which is perhaps most closely associated with Lincolnshire.

Woodhall Spa now lay before us, an elegant Edwardian resort that has been referred to as 'Lincolnshire's Unspoilt Gem'. Thanks for putting the town on the map must go to John Parkinson, who came to Woodhall in 1811 and initiated the planting of many of the fir and oak trees we see today. He then began to prospect for coal, but at a depth of 550 feet, clear briny water flooded into the bore chamber. The plans for a coal mine fell through, not least because it was discovered that several of the workmen had smuggled in coal as 'samples'. But all was not lost, as the waters, which contained large amounts of iodine and bromide, soon gained a reputation for curing rheumatism and gout. A little town then grew up around the spa, and the future of Woodhall was assured.

It was from Woodhall that the 617 Squadron, the 'Dam Busters', flew on raids with the bouncing bomb, and there is a memorial to them in the town. The Petwood Hotel was the Officers' Mess for the Squadron, and the bar that they frequented has remained largely unchanged to honour the heroes of Bomber Command.

For the golfing enthusiast, Woodhall Spa boasts its own famous golf course. Overlooking the links is the Tower on the Moor, a fifteenth-century edifice that was probably part of the hunting lodge erected by Ralph Cromwell on this site. The height of the tower made it a useful beacon to warn of invaders in the Wash who might be heading for Lincoln.

Bainland Country Park, classified as one of the top Parks in Lincolnshire is set in 40 acres of magnificent countryside and only a mile and a half from Woodhall Spa. It is a first-rate park offering recreational opportunities that are an added extra to the delights of the Lincolnshire Wolds. The park has bungalows, static caravans for hire and pitches for touring caravans. The main park area is flat, grassy and extensively hedged giving privacy and seclusion where all pitches are numbered and well spaced. The high standard facilities included toilets and showers, suitable for the disabled, a laundry, a baby washing and changing room. There are fully serviced pitches which include hard standing and electricity plug ins. The recreational facilities include an indoor heated swimming pool, jacuzzi, sauna, exercise room, tennis courts, a golf course, crazy golf, amusement room, childrens Adventure Playground, and much more. You can enjoy delicious meals in the Bistro or visit the elegant Poachers Restaurant and Bar for a drink or dinner. Situated as it is in the midst of beautiful countryside and near to the many historic attractions this superb holiday park which is open all year round is ideal for all the family.

Bainland Country Park.   Woodhall Spa. Lincs Tel: 0526 352903.

A lane from Woodhall took us through the heart of the wood originally planted by John Parkinson, but now known as 'Ostler's Plantation' after its second owner. The A153 took us south to **Tumby,** where we joined the **A155** and headed east through Tumby woods and **Mareham le Fen.** We then came to Revesby. **Revesby Abbey** (although not the original building, nor the one that exists today), was the home of Sir Joseph Banks, an explorer, an agricultural expert, and a leading figure in the reclamation of the fens. Born in 1743, he was President of the Royal Society, the man who persuaded Cook to make his famous voyages, and was quite possibly the first European to 'discover' modern Australia. He has in fact been called the 'Father of Australia'. Banks is also thought to have been instrumental in encouraging seafarers to eat citrus fruits in order to combat scurvy.

At the end of the A155 we found **West Keal**, which sits on the extreme southern edge of the Lincolnshire Wolds. The capitals in the nave of the village church have some particularly amusing carvings, depicting a goose being chased by a fox, buxom country lasses, and dragons in combat. There is evidence of settlement in this part of the county going back as far as 10,000 years. Small flint tools have been discovered near the village, most likely used by hunters and fishermen during the Mesolithic Age.

From here we headed south on the A16, the road that divides the East Fen and the West Fen. The villages of **Stickford, Stickney** and **Sibsey** were all early settlements, built on a series of 'islands' that rise above the surrounding fen country. A mile west of Sibsey stands **Trader Mill.** This is a fine six-sailed windmill, and one of the last mills to be built in the county. It was built in 1877, and operated up

320

until 1958. Having been restored by the Department of the Environment, it is now open to the public during the Summer.

Just south of Sibsey, we headed east on the **B1184** through **Old Leake** with its magnificent church tower. Just 200 hundred yards off the main A52 in the picturesque village , you'll find a warm welcome for all waiting at **The White Hart** given by owners Mr and Mrs G Little. Dating back to the early 18th century, the White Hart is beautifully decorated and furnished throughout with pleasant table arrangements and an open fire for cold evenings. The timber framed, partitioned restaurant serves delicious food from a varied menu that caters for all tastes, including vegetarian. Besides a lovely beer garden and childrens play area you'll find to the rear, 25 touring pitches with toilet and shower facilities, which is open all year round for both campers and caravanners. This friendly inn should not be missed for those seeking a friendly place to stay whilst touring this lovely area or for those who simply want to enjoy good food, fine ale in a homely, family atmosphere during a day out.

The White Hart. Old Leake near Boston, Lincs. Tel: 0205 870783.

Off the main road across the fens is **Friskney**, where the French poet, Paul Verlaine, was once a teacher at the village school. Up until the late nineteenth century, this part of the fens was well known for supplying the London markets with geese for the tables of the gentry. A Decoy Pond can still be seen near the village today, and would have worked as follows. Decoy ducks swam on the pond which was surrounded by trees, enticing the wildfowl to land and feed. Once in the water, the decoys would lure them along channels which radiated out from the pond, following trails of seed. If this didn't work, small dogs were sometimes used to drive them into the required position. At the end of each channel, the geese, teal and widgeon would find themselves trapped in the nets, where the wildfowlers stood ready to bag them.

If you had desired cranberry sauce to serve at table with your roast goose, the fens had acres of wild cranberry bushes. Unfortunately, with the drainage and subsequent enclosure of the countryside, these have largely disappeared. However, our discoveries had unleashed an appetite that even progress could not halt, so we pushed on with our journey, hungry to find the 'Hidden Places' of North Lincolnshire.

CHAPTER THIRTEEN

North Lincolnshire

Lincoln Cathedral

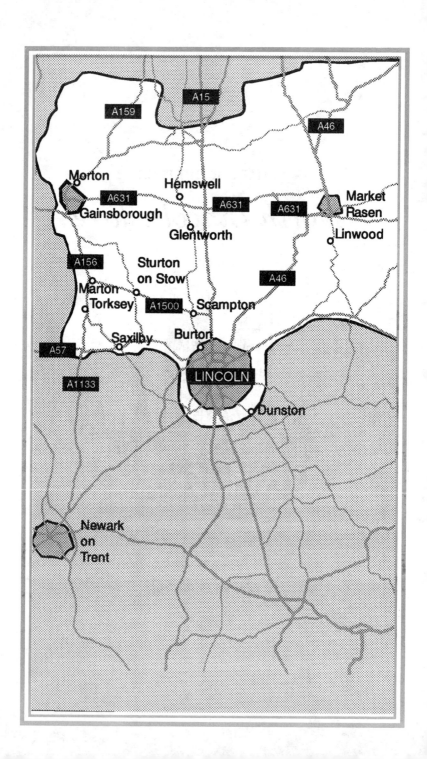

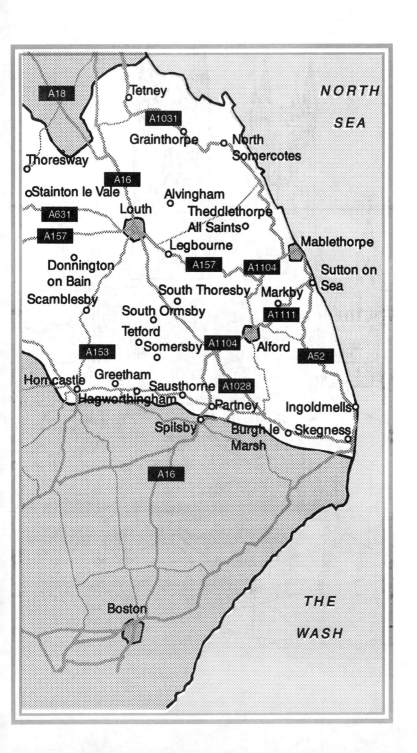

Lincoln Cathedral.

CHAPTER THIRTEEN.

North Lincolnshire.

Among the many attractions in this part of Lincolnshire is **Gainsborough Old Hall**, an enchanting medieval manor house which has been beautifully preserved,retaining the original kitchens and butteries, the magnificent great Hall, a tower and two wings which are virtually unchanged since the visit of Richard 111 in 1483. To accompany you as you explore this splendid building, there is a free Soundalive! taped guide.

Standing proudly on Castle Hill, **Lincoln Castle** is another place well worth a visit, for this was the birthplace of the city. William the Conqueror came here in 1068 and evicted 166 Saxon families from their homes to build his castle, which now stands as a monument to Norman architecture. You can follow the wall walk, explore the towers and stroll around the beautiful gardens. Inside,among the many exhibits, you can see the original Magna Carta issued by King John in 1215.

Lincolnshire is an area with a rich aviation heritage. The county's connections with the RAF date from the Great War and by 1945 there were 49 airfields in Lincolnshire, 28 of them bomber bases, more than any other county in Britain. RAF Coningsby is the base of the already mentioned, **The Battle of Britain Memorial Flight**, a team of five Spitfires, a Hurricane and a Lancaster, which regularly tour major airshows in memory of the RAF crews who gave their lives during the Second World War.

Walkers will find a real haven at Snip Dales which lies on the southern edge of the Wolds. Comprising a nature reserve and pine wooded country park, there are various waymarked trails to follow,leading you through some wonderful countryside which is home to a wealth of bird and plant life.

Lovers of art in its finest forms will delight when they visit the **Usher Gallery** on Lindum Road,Lincoln. Founded by the Lincoln born jeweller James Ward Usher, it contain various art collections, including Chinese Export Porcelain of the K'ang Hsi period (1662-1722), a nationally important collection of paintings and drawings by the Staffordshire born artist Peter de Wint (1784-1849) and a comprehensive collection of English coins. This is just a sample of what's on view, so a visit is a must.

The Museum of Lincolnshire Life on Burton Road is in a listed building that once housed the Royal North Lincoln Militia. This award winning museum gives the visitor the opportunity to gain a comprehensive insight into life in the past. Displays cover areas of transport, agriculture and industrial life as well as the recreation of homes and shops from bygone times.

Elsewhere in the county the Recreational services overseer the Church Farm Museum in Skegness, Grantham Museum. Stamford Museum and the three windmills of Burgh le Marsh, Alford and Heckington.

Lincolnshire County Council Recreational Services. Newland, Lincoln. Tel: 0522 552809.

We began this journey of North Lincolnshire at **Wainfleet** once a port, but now lying some five miles from the sea. The Romans first established the port of 'Vainona' here, but drainage of the East Fen caused the town to lose its navigable waters and thus become the land-locked port of today. Nevertheless, it is a handsome town with elegant housing and some fine buildings, most of them centred around the market-place.

Magdalen College School was founded in 1484 by the Bishop of Winchester, William of Waynflete. He was also the founder of Magdalen College in Oxford, and was largely responsible for Wainfleet being granted its market charter in 1458. The school building is rather similar to Tattershall Castle (albeit on a different scale), which is not surprising, as William went on to complete the building of the castle after Ralph Cromwell's death.

One of the earliest industries of this part of the coast-line was the extraction of salt. All around the Wash throughout the marshes and fens, 'salt-hills' can be found which point to an earlier industry that thrived in this region.

It is extremely rare today to find a totally independent, family run brewery, but this is what emerges in the nice small town of Wainfleet. **Batemans Salem Bridge Brewery** was started by the Bateman family in 1874 to satisfy the thirsts of the ploughmen and land workers of the area and for the farmers who gave their harvesters beer as part payment during the summer. During the ensuing years the Batemans acquired over one hundred of their own public houses and in each they have tried to ensure all the traditional aspects of the pubs. The Royal Oak in Wainfleet is an excellent example of a well-run pub serving really fine ale, hard to believe it was once the local asylum! Not too far away at Boston is The Ball House where Oliver Cromwell spent some time planning his campaign.

To have such a fine brewery you would think would be reward enough for this family but no, they are also lucky enough to have the perfect setting, at the base of a disused windmill on the edge of the Haven River, where the water for brewing was once taken. It is surrounded by fields and rural life with the sea just one and a half miles away.

Mark you, it has not all been plain sailing - or should we say brewing, for this industrious and dedicated family. The first blow they suffered was when the brewery was becoming established in the late 19th century; suddenly they found themselves faced with a compulsory purchase order from the Railway Company who wanted to put track right through where the brewery then stood. The present site is only three hundred yards away from the new railway through to Skegness. Not a family to be fainthearted in adversity, the present Chairman's grandfather managed to purchase the new site at the windmill - hence the company logo.

From that time onwards they expanded steadily purchasing some of the small traditional pubs in the Lincolnshire area. George Bateman handed the reins to his son Harry and he to his sons George and John Bateman.

John Bateman wanted to get out of the industry, which caused another hiccough, leaving this profitable and envied company wide open to larger predators, but after a three year fight sufficient money was raised and the brewery has remained in George's family control.

Since then there have been large steps forward with the beers winning more top national prizes than any other in recent years. Not surprising really because the Batemans still use the traditional raw materials,brewing process,vessels and hand crafted tools. There is very little stainless steel to be seen, only copper,wrought iron and wood.

Getting to look over the brewery is not easy unless you are an organisation or a regular at a pub and join a party wishing to visit - but nil desperandum, there are always ways and means. For starters,do what we did, enquire about a conducted tour at one of the many Bateman pubs,or ring George's secretary on 0754 880317. It is well worth the effort to find out. If you are not fortunate enough,just down a pint or two of their brew and enjoy some of the first class food served in their pubs. You will not be disappointed.

Batemans Brewery, Wainfleet, Skegness. Tel: 0754 880317.

From Wainfleet, it is a short trip to the end of this particular stretch of the A52, and here we would arrive at the coast at last. **Skegness** has been the butt of a hundred jokes, and will probably continue to be well into the future. If you love penny arcades, the frantic pace of fairground rides and the smell of frying on the air, then Skegness will appeal to you. If you like sandy dunes that stretch for miles, fresh air and solitude, then Skegness will still appeal, for it is quite possible to find yourself a quiet spot along the beach away from the masses. It is a rather odd phenomenon that a seaside resort which absorbs coach-loads of frenzied tourists can still have peaceful stretches, but it is true. We have found that those who wish to station themselves near the hot-dog kiosks, the ice-cream parlours and the novelty toy booths, seem to travel no further than 200 feet along the foreshore.

Attracted by the bracing air, holiday trippers have come to 'Skeggie' for over a century, and the twenty miles of sand warrant exploration by young and old alike. It is easy to be disparaging about the simple pleasures to be found at this resort but even the most cynical visitor is bound to succumb to an ice-cream cone.

The town boasts a pier, which was built in 1878 and opened to the public in 1881. A superb example of Victorian architecture, this splendid pier is a marvel of columns and girders. One thing that has always intrigued us is how the columns were sunk into the sea bed, a considerable feat with the sea levels rising all around. In fact, it took twelve tides to ebb before the main structure and pile supports could be installed. The builders, Head, Wrightson & Co, built many of the best loved Victorian piers, some of which still stand today. The pier entertainment consisted of a Saloon and a hall for brass bands and concerts, and the cost of building was estimated at 20,840 pounds, eleven shillings and fourpence!

Natureland, the Marine Zoo and Seal Sanctuary, are situated on the North Parade, overlooking the sands. They give many of us a rare opportunity to look at seals and penguins, an aquarium, and exotic butterflies. There is also a reptile house, where you have the chance to walk over a bridge with basking Nile crocodiles peeping up at you with their malevolent gaze. An ideal place for a chilly day! Another is the **Church Farm Museum**, where you can see displays of agricultural equipment over the years and interiors created to give an idea of how life was for farmworkers in the past.

Just five minutes walk from the beach at Skegness is **The Vine Hotel.** Recently refurbished to a very high standard, it is housed in a building that has withstood the test of time for 350 years and gained a pleasant sense of maturity in doing so. Situated in the quiet Seacroft area, it is far from the madding crowd, with a golf course just 150 yards away and yet the town centre is within ten minutes walking distance.

We drove up the tree-lined drive which overlooks some really beautiful gardens and bowling greens, and then found ourselves at the entrance. Inside it is totally olde worlde, with massive oak beams and huge fireplaces in which fires roar merrily in the winter months. The oak panelling has been preserved over the years and lends distinction to this Les Routiers and Tourist Board recommended hotel. We found the bedrooms to be attractively and individually furnished and all en-suite, whilst downstairs there was a comfortable residents' lounge plus two bars selling real ale which comes from the Batemans Brewery who also own the hotel.

Whatever meal of the day you choose to eat at The Vine, you will find the food excellent and served in a warm and friendly dining room which has up to 45 covers. There are fresh flowers on the table which are set with nice china and glass and crisp table linen. The choice on the a la carte menu is quite large - 21 dishes in fact and the table d'hôte is sensibly priced and well selected. It attracts businessmen which does not surprise us. The staff are a nice, cheerful bunch who obviously enjoy their work and seem to be especially happy when they have something like a wedding or a conference to handle. These sorts of functions are quite a large part of The Vine's business and it is growing because the prices are reasonable and the setting is good and conveniently situated in this now upgraded 3 Star Hotel.

Tennyson stayed at The Vine quite often, he was born at Somersby just fifteen miles away. Under the weeping elm tree in the garden he is reputed to have written the poem, ' Come into the garden Maud', which in the earlier part of this century was set to music and became one of the most popular of ballads. If you happen to be a Customs and Excise Officer you might meet a spiritual colleague whilst staying at The Vine! It is rumoured that one such gentleman disappeared completely after visiting The Vine of tax matters. The legend has it that he never did leave and was bricked up in the wall. His skeleton was found eventually behind a wall still wearing his chains of office - or so it is said.

The Vine Hotel, Vine Road, Skegness, Lincs. Tel: 0754 763018.

Just south of the town, a road takes you to the **Gibraltar Point Nature Reserve.** Bought by Lindsey County Council to thwart development, some 1,500 acres has been designated a reserve. There are marvellous expanses of dunes, beaches and salt marshes. The plant life here is diverse, with samphire and sea purslane jostling with the sea lavender, which forms a beautiful living carpet from August onwards. For the bird lovers among you, some species we have spotted include whimbrel, sky larks, pink footed geese, terns and many more. One rare 'visitor' to the dunes some years ago was a hoopoe, while an arctic skua was noted by one lucky individual.

Situated at **Ingoldmells,** just beyond Skegness and found off the main A52 - follow the brown signs - is the very impressive and premier tourist attraction, **Hardys Animal Farm** where all are welcome. Set within a 500 acre mixed working farm is the 15 acre attraction now open for its third season. If animals interest you then this is the place to visit. It has a pig breeding unit where you can see, in different stages, the life of a pig from Boars to newly born suckling piglets. It is a sight we have seldom seen before. You can even watch them being born should your visit be at the right time. There's a calf rearing house, a free range laying hen house and lots of rare breeds of sheep, cattle and goats. Rabbits and guinea pigs are here whilst poultry and birds walk about the farm. In season Worzels Tearoom is open offering the visitor beverages, sandwiches and ploughmans lunches. There is also a magnificent children and toddlers play area all combining to make this interesting farm a place you'd be sorry to miss!

Hardys Animal Farm. Ingoldmells, Skegness.   Tel: 0754 872267

We headed west from Skegness on the **A158** and soon arrived at **Burgh le Marsh**. Here, you can see the immense five-sailed windmill standing five storeys high, that was built in 1833. It is operational one Sunday in every four and the sails are most unusual in that they rotate in a clockwise direction. If you happen to be in the village between Michaelmas and Lady Day, listen out for the church bells of St Peter and St Paul. An ancient custom demands that they be rung at 8pm during this period of the year, but on one famous occasion the custom was ignored. In 1629, a ship in The Wash was driven perilously close to the shore during a storm. The villagers, hoping to profit from the wreck and its victims, made no attempt to sound out a warning bell.

Luckily for the survivors, the sexton locked himself in the church and rang the bell, warning Captain Frohock and his crew of their danger. The Captain rewarded the sexton with a length of silken rope to ring the bell, and also with a portion of land which is known locally as Bell-String Acre. In another version of the story, the sexton, far from being rewarded for his efforts, died of a heart attack because of

333

them! Nevertheless, this version has its happy ending too, as Captain Frohock decided to settle in the village, and married the sexton's daughter.

Further along the A158 is **Gunby Hall,** which was built in 1700 by Sir William Massingberd. There is a strange tale concerning Sir William, who at his previous residence of Bratoft Castle had shot and killed one of his servants, who had attempted to elope with his daughter Margaret. Charged with the murder, Sir William was sentenced to come to London once a year, where the family coat-of-arms were covered with blood.

Candlesby sits amongst some of the prettiest countryside in this eastern part of Lincolnshire. The River Lymn and its streams flow through hills and valleys. Some of the views, particularly the one from Candlesby Hill, are quite breathtaking. You are really able to take in the sprawl of the land here, a varied patchwork of fen, marsh and pasture. **Partney** village lies at the junction of the A158 and the A16. This is a pleasant place with a lovely church, where we found a memorial to Captain Flinders who we met earlier at Donington.

Heading south from Partney on the A16, we came to **Spilsby**, or as it was once affectionately known, 'Spilsbyshire'. Here, and in some of the surrounding villages, the local squires with their 'small' pockets of land usually around 500 acres, preferred to have them referred to as parishes. Sir John Franklin was born in Spilsby in 1786, and the town celebrated the 200th anniversary of his birth with a Franklin Festival in 1986. This celebrated explorer sadly perished with his crew of 130 men when they were trapped in the Arctic pack-ice for over two years. Franklin had previously explored over 500 miles of Canadian coastline from Hudson Bay, which took an exhausting three and a half years to achieve.

The two ships involved in the fateful Arctic expedition were the 'Erebus' and the 'Terror' and were last seen in May 1845. It was to be a further ten years before the tragic news finally emerged of their last stand against the frozen wastes. Although the expedition ended so tragically, Franklin and his men are remembered for their success in establishing the existence of the North West Passage.

Spilsby Theatre (0790 52936) was built as a court house, complete with basement cells for malcontents and a robing room for judges, but has converted well into an auditorium of a different kind whose outworks are are dressing rooms and recreation area, including the ubiquitous theatre bar. Nothing can prepare the visitor for the shock of coming upon, in this comparatively remote Fenland town, the theatre's huge classical facade, with its fluted Doric columns and the architrave's proud engraving 'Spilsby Theatre' together with the 30ft high doors reminiscent of a Waterloo church, which conceal the

334

intimate 130 seat interior. In this landscape the external scale is breathtaking, rivalling the 13th century church it faces. The theatre is owned by the Dandelion Trust, which rescued it from disuse and threatened conversion into an industrial building for its present artistic, musical and educational programme and purposes.

North-west of Spilsby, we did not find the North West Passage but we did find **Sausthorpe** on the A158. Sausthorpe church spire is a distinguished landmark, and although it looks as if it were made of white icing, it is in fact built of brick. A particularly fine house can be found just north of here at Harrington. **Harrington Hall** is a charming residence dating back to the seventeenth century, and is privately owned. It was here that Alfred, Lord Tennyson, beseeched 'Maud' to 'Come into the garden.' 'Maud' was said to have been based upon Rosa Baring, who lived at the Hall. The hall and gardens are open occasionally in the Summer, and The Wolds here are as lovely a sight as you could wish for. Dips and dells, hollows and woodland, it is a beautiful setting for the Hall and its occupants.

Tennyson's family were Yorkshire born and bred. However, his father was appointed rector to the churches of **Bag Enderby** and **Somersby**, where the poet was born in 1809. The family took up residence at Somersby in 1808, and they lived in the rectory (now privately owned) for almost thirty years. Those years were not entirely happy ones. Dr George Tennyson, the poet's father, was prone to bouts of depression, brought on by epilepsy and heavy drinking. At least one of Alfred's brothers was an opium addict. His father died in 1831, and Arthur Hallam, an old Cambridge friend, was drowned two years later. After a failed business venture, the family departed from Somersby in 1837 under a gloomy cloud.

This area is sometimes referred to as 'Tennyson Valley', and one of the largest villages we encountered was **Tetford**, which lies just over a mile away from Somersby at the foot of The Wolds. The White Hart Inn was the meeting place for the Gentlemen's Literary Club, and was frequented by Tennyson. The church of St Mary's dates back to the fourteenth century, and was built on the site of a much earlier church, recorded in the Domesday Survey of 1086. In the churchyard is a memorial to two gypsy travellers who were 'Slain by Lightening' in 1830.

To the east, **South Ormsby** is almost hidden away in wooded countryside, and **Ormsby Hall**, which dates back to 1752, is most charming. The church, which is surprisingly large for this part of the county, stands on a small hill at the edge of the park.

The village of **Calceby** is easily found on a road map, but much harder to discover in reality! At the southern end of the Blue Stone Heath Road, the ruin of the parish church sits forlorn on a hilltop. And in a road just off the A16, several mounds are visible which show the position of this 'lost village'. That it existed we know from the Domesday Book, which records that it had part-ownership of salt pans near the coast. The Black Death visited the village, but it survived, and in 1563 some eighteen families were still in residence. By 1621, following the demise of their last vicar, all that remained of this once busy community were a few cottages and a farmhouse.

Just over the A16, we came to **South Thoresby** and just beyond sitting high up on the wild moor land is **Haugh**, comprising a Tudor manor and a small, ancient church. The latter is partly built of chalk, and although it has no spire or tower and may escape the attention of the passer-by, it is well worth a visit. Inside the church are memorials to the Bolle family, who left this seat when Sir John Bolle built Thorpe Hall near Louth.

The small market town of **Alford** has many attractions for the visitor to enjoy. The five-sailed windmill with its charming 'onion cap' and dramatic black wood is truly a beauty. The thatched Manor House is one of several thatched buildings to be found on West Street. It now contains a folk museum with a police cell, a maid's bedroom, a sweet factory, and other exhibits of bygone days. The town is also well known for its Craft Market, which is held every Friday throughout the Summer, as well as on Bank Holidays and the Christmas period. The Market has brought large numbers of visitors to the town since it began in 1974, and provides an opportunity for the many craftspeople living in the district to display their talents and wares.

In addition to crafts, the Bank Holiday entertainment include displays of many other traditional country customs, including a veritable National Convention of Morris Dancers.

Alford was where the explorer and adventurer Captain John Smith first attended school. With all his escapades, the person most closely associated with him and probably best known is Pocahontas, the daughter of an Indian chief. The twelve year old princess rescued him from the Indians while he was exploring the area of North America which he named New England. She later went on to marry another settler called John Rolfe, after being convinced that Smith was dead. Rolfe brought her back to England where she died of smallpox in 1617, and she now lies in a Gravesend churchyard in Kent. Smith was born in the village of **Willoughby** to the south of Alford, and you can see his various exploits depicted in the windows at the church.

Three miles north-east of Alford on the A1111 is **Markby** with its charming, highly photogenic thatched church. We pressed on to join up with the A52 at **Sutton on Sea**. This is a charming resort, quieter and more refined than boisterous Skegness. The sandy beaches, which are well-kept and provide excellent bathing, are a favourite 'launching site' for small boats and windsurfers.

Robin Hood Leisure Park. Chapel St Leonards. Tel: 0754 874444

Situated in over forty acres of land at Chapel St Leonards, seven miles north of Skegness, is the **Robin Hood Leisure Park** which has received the Rose Award from the Tourist Board since 1988. Arrival here will make you see why, as this leisure park has literally everything the holidaymaker requires. Between 750/800 caravans are housed in the park, most are privately owned and let out and around 60 are owned by the park for static hire, along with 24 chalets and 120 touring pitches with electrical hook ups. You could spend all your time here as the selection of activities is amazing, to mention some on offer - a heated outdoor swimming pool, junior pool, sunloungers, footpaths to long sandy beaches, a floodlit crazy golf course, children's play parks, amusement centre, take away food shops, a supermarket, off licence and the Maid Marion Club where there is live entertainment for all the family with Resident Artistes and a visiting artiste virtually every night. Should you have the wanderlust then the park is close to some beautiful countryside in the Wolds, Tennyson country and attractive towns such as Boston, Louth, Alford and Lincoln.

The road carries on up the coast through **Trusthorpe** to **Mablethorpe.** The town has more lovely beaches, a motor museum, a sea front theatre, and an animal and bird garden. The Tennysons were once regular visitors here. In the heart of this popular town, on Victoria Road, you'll find **Leicester Guest House and Restaurant.** This turn of the century building owned by Sue and Graham Allen who run it with the help of daughter Glenis and son in law John serves three different functions. Firstly, as a lovely, family guest house with ten letting rooms, all ensuite and with full facilities. Pets are allowed by prior arrangement. Then a licensed seventy seat restaurant that serves appealing homecooked A la carte and standard menus that also caters for children and is open in season and at weekends only in the winter. Attached to this is Ye Olde Curiosity Museum, built and created by the Allens which exhibits thousands of everyday items from this century but specialises in lightshades, having over two and a half thousand types and their materials. The museum has been open for five years and in the opinion of many matches and exceeds many council owned museums.

Leicester House & Restaurant / Ye Olde Curiosity Museum. Mablethorpe. Tel: 0507 472406

A few miles out of Mablethorpe in the village of **Theddlethorpe All Saints** you'll find everyones dream of an old fashioned country pub when you pull up at the large car park of **The Kings Head.**

The Kings Head Inn. Theddlethorpe All Saints . Tel: 0507 3385655.

This thatched roofed building, mentioned in several guide books, with low beamed ceilings - beware those of you taller than 5' 9" - and decorated with bygone memorabilia is owned by friendly hosts Cyril and Julie Robinson who are helped in their quest to make your visit enjoyable by mum and dad, Bill and June. You can enjoy popular, home prepared and delicious food from an extensive menu in this Free house with its fine cask and guest ales or if you prefer from their extensive wine list. Children are also catered for but be advised,to avoid disappointment, that food is not served on Sunday night and Monday lunchtimes (from November 1st to March 1st). This real eye opener with its excellent gardens and beautiful views is a truly friendly place with character and charm that matches all your ideas of a country pub.

Inland we continued through **Legbourne** village, which although comprised mainly of bungalows and modern housing, has an abbey set in its own expanse of park-land. Outside Louth and between the A16 to Boston and the A157 to Mablethorpe you'll find the 5 Crown, **Kenwick Park Hotel** standing within the grounds of the 500 acre Kenwick Park Estate, an area of ' Outstanding Natural Beauty '.

The Kenwick Park Hotel. Louth. Tel: 0507 608806 Fax: 0507 608027

This superb country hotel, which is approached through an avenue of broadleaf trees, was converted in 1992 from Georgian style Kenwick Hall, country home for several families over the years. Its nineteen large and spacious rooms with every facility to meet the travellers needs are beautifully fitted with style and elegance. The Fairway Restaurant overlooks the Kenwick Park Golf course and offers a thoughtful a la carte menu for lunch and dinner which you can enjoy with a wine from their extensive list. All dishes are freshly prepared to order as are the Bar Meals in the Keeper's Bar. This well stocked bar also looks over the Golf Course and is designed and constructed in a relaxing conservatory theme. Golfing holiday packages are available for the enthusiast and country lovers can use the hotel as a base whilst they enjoy the surrounding wonderful Wolds countryside. The hotel is ideal for a tasteful break away but it also has facilities for conferences, functions and meetings. An added attraction will be the soon completed Kenwick Health and Leisure Club, a luxurious members club designed

Westgate. Louth

for health,fitness and leisure. Swimming pools, jacuzzi, sauna, gymnasium, tennis and squash courts, snooker, beauty salons and more are some of the many facilities available for members and their friends. Whatever your needs the friendly and helpful staff are on hand to ensure your stay is comfortable, enjoyable and memorable.

The road took us into **Louth**, a delightful market town. With its narrow streets, old inns and the lovely church of St James, it is a very pleasant place and really captures the spirit of these peaceful market towns which are so steeped in history. The church spire is the highest in England, and at 295 feet, it is a truly magnificent sight as it soars above the town. It contains the 'Sudbury Hutch', a chest from around the 16th century with portraits of Henry VII and Elizabeth of York. Most of the buildings here are of red brick, and there are many fine examples of 17th to 19th century buildings in Westgate.

The Pack Horse.   Louth Lincs.   Tel: 0507 603848.

Situated on Eastgate in the heart of historic Louth, **The Pack Horse,** a Tourist Board award pending inn, has been serving the needs of locals and visitors for well over 200 hundred years. Recently taken over by Midland Taverns, it has undergone complete refurbishment. The new decor is excellent in every way, with deep carpets and plush seating helping to retain the character and charm which oozes from within. Downstairs is the public bar and restaurant, whilst upstairs there are five superior ensuite bedrooms. Fine ales are served along with bar snacks and sandwiches whilst in the restaurant, a delicious and varied set menu along with a changing Daily Special and Sweets board, all at reasonable prices, caters for every taste. Car parking is close at hand on the street or public parking places and for the traveller looking for a convenient base from which to explore Lincolnshire,The Pack Horse, offers a warm and friendly welcome where all your needs are catered for.

It was in Louth that Tennyson had his first work published by J &

J Jackson, the booksellers. Entitled 'Poems by Two Brothers', the publication was a joint effort with his brother Charles. The Bookshop still stands, although it has been renamed Parkers, and can be found in the Market Place.

There is a local folk saying about the town - 'Sleaford for Sleep, Boston for Business, Horncastle for Horses, Louth for Learning. ' There is a grammar school where Captain John Smith and Sir John Franklin as well as Tennyson were pupils. Around 1856, the town could boast an amazing twelve private schools, a charity school and two church affiliated schools.

On Victoria Road close on the edge of this charming market town stands the RAC, AA and 4 Crown highly commended, independently run, **Beaumont Hotel.** Built in 1936 as a childrens homes this splendid building was purchased in 1977 by present owners, the Would family. Initially run as a retirement home until three years ago when it was turned into one of the best family run Hotels and Restaurants in this area of Lincolnshire.

The Beaumont Hotel. Louth.Tel: 0507 605005. Fax: 0507 607768.

Beautifully and tastefully decorated throughout, the emphasis here is on traditional comfort and the seventeen bedrooms confirm this with their private bathrooms, TV, radio, telephone, hair dryer, trouser press and refreshment tray and where Room service is also available. Morning coffee and afternoon teas are served in the snug by the comfortably furnished Cocktail Bar which has an open fire for the winter and during the summer, French windows open onto a secluded terrace. The forty seat Terrace Restaurant is open both lunch and evenings and serves a high standard of traditional food using the best of local produce for its a la carte, table d'hôte and on Sundays, traditional lunch menus. With such temptations as Bavarois of Smoked Trout in a mild horseradish with tomato vinaigrette or Roast Lonsdale Duckling on a bed of caramelised apples with Calvados to mention but a few choices, it is hardly surprising that Mrs Would recommends booking for this highly reputable restaurant. The Grosvenor Suite is an ideal and elegant venue for conferences, weddings and private functions which is serviced with its own bar. The Woulds are only too happy to furnish you with details of these or other facilities at their hotel. Open all the year round and situated in close proximity to the Wolds and other attractions in the area, The Beaumont Hotel, makes an ideal base for business and pleasure where a you can be sure of a warm welcome in a pampered, homely atmosphere.

To the north-east of Louth is **Alvingham** with its watermill and museum. The mill is a large three-storey building which sits above the millstream, and visitors are welcome on special days throughout the summer. The church of St Adelwold can be found in a distant corner of the village, and is the only church dedicated to this Saxon saint in the country. The churchyard stands beside the Louth canal, and is shared by St Mary's which is the parish church of nearby North Cockerington.

Out of Louth on the A16 towards Grimsby if you turn right after a couple miles and follow the Covenham signs until you have passed through the two small **Covenham** villages of **St Mary** and **St Bartholomew** you will find a real gem at the thatched **The Mill House.** Thought to have originated in the 16th century and attached to a mill which ground corn for the Benedictine Priory - William the Conqueror founded the cell for the Abbey of Karalephut in Normandy - that until the Dissolution of Monastries in 1536 stood nearby.

The Mill House.   Covenham near Louth. Lincs   Tel: 0507 363652

The Mill House was built as a bakehouse and produced bread for the neighbourhood for three centuries. The village was swept by the Black Death in the late 17th century - a mass grave has been unearthed on the neighbouring farm - but the Mill House baked bread up until the last war. Now owners Fred and Pat Verity have extensively refurbished the inn whilst keeping its original character with wooden ceilings and wall beams. All are welcome at this charming place where you can enjoy their hospitality and renowned bar meals which are available every lunchtime and evening. It's first come, first served so early arrival is recommended at this popular place. Seating 150, part of which is in the delightful old living quarters upstairs and is reminiscent of a Minstrels Gallery, the picturesque Mill House stands in lovely gardens and has a patio area as well as ample car parking space for the passing traveller.

South of here on the **B1200**, you can find the villages of **Saltfleetby St.Peter**, **Saltfleetby St. Clements**, and **Saltfleetby by All Saints**, all indicating the importance of religion in these coastal areas. Saltfleetby on the **A1031** has five miles of dunes which make up the **Saltfleetby and Theddlethorpe Dunes National Nature Reserve.** Although there are many tracks to explore, we must point out that the sands on the shore can be dangerous. The tide turns fast here and sandbanks are rapidly formed which can surprise the unwary visitor. The reserve is famous for its natterjack toads which thrive in the marshes, as well as dunlin and redshank, linnets and heron, and dunnock and whitethroats. The plant life is very diverse with sea buckthorn, elder, dog rose and willow acting as a windbreak along the sandy ridges.

Further north on the A1031 is **North Somercotes**, which means a place of huts or sheepcotes. This was where the shepherds stayed when their flocks were brought down from the Wolds to graze on the coastal marshes.

Now a marsh village, **Grainthorpe** was once a port, and at Grainthorpe Haven the River Lud comes to its final outpouring. We were much taken with the simple church here. The base of the cross in the churchyard depicts a rock which is said to represent Golgotha. The road took us through **Eskham** and **Marshchapel** to **Tetney**, which is the last village on this coastal road before you cross the border into Humberside.

Its proximity to the coast ensured that it became an important area for salt extraction, and the Domesday Book records that there were once thirteen salt pans in operation. Between the villages of Marshchapel and Grainthorpe there was a salt track that led up into the Wolds.

When we reached **Tetney Haven,** we had come to the end of the Louth navigational way, but you can still follow the canal through the marsh to the sea. The waters were once deep enough here to take large cargo ships along the twelve mile stretch of river to Louth. Tetney Lock, once so vital for the shipping that came up here in its heyday, is now derelict but still an important land mark for this coast. Sluice gates have been fitted on the lock, and it stores water for the reservoir at **Covenham** to the south, which covers an area of 218 acres and is Lincolnshire's largest lake.

An interesting natural feature of this area are the Tetney blow holes, or wells. Water comes up from the springs below under enormous pressure, passing up through chalk and clay until it bursts forth on the surface. As the underlying water-table drops, many of the wells are sadly drying up. The wells are said to be bottomless, and whether they are or not, pike and eel thrive in them. Industry in this region has been varied over the years. The willow trees in the area have long been used in the craft of making cricket bats, while watercress beds can still be made out, although they have long since been abandoned.

There is a nature reserve near Tetney Haven run by the Royal Society for the Protection of Birds. The ground is often treacherous here, and if you wish to visit the reserve you should first contact the Warden for details : c/o The Post Office, Tetney, Grimsby, South Humberside.

Further up the coast road you'll come to **Cleethorpes**, more or less a suburb of Grimsby now but developed as a resort in the mid 19th century along with the growth of the railways. This was certainly an improvement on earlier Cleethorpes history when the area was known for piracy and aggressive competition, particularly with Grimsby. The pier was completed in 1873 and opened on August Bank Holiday that year. Ten years later the promenade and gardens were laid out as more peolpe came to enjoy its safe beaches and other holiday attractions; these include golf,boating, fresh and sea water fishing. There are shops to satisfy most needs and weekly markets are held on Wednesdays with occasional Sunday markets.

Situated on Balmoral Rd in Cleethorpes you will find the **Crows Nest Hotel**, a welcoming establishment run by friendly hosts Bill and Sheila Hayward. Built approximately 30 years ago, the hotel offers first class hospitality, comfortable accommodation and well kept ale. The 6 attractively furnished guest rooms are available all year round and in the Summer, visitors can enjoy a refreshing drink in the beer garden which contains an aviary. To find the Crows Nest, take the A46 towards Cleethorpes to Loves Corner Roundabout. Turn right here, signposted Mablethorpe and continue along the road for about half a mile turning left into Davenport Drive. Take the next right into Balmoral Rd and you will find the hotel on your left.

The Crows Nest Hotel, Balmoral Rd., Cleethorpes. 0472 698867

Dating back to the late 19th century, **The Cliff Lodge Hotel**, formerly two private houses, stands proudly overlooking the Humber

Estuary and only yards from the sandy beach at Cleethorpes. Found on High Cliff Road, between the Leisure Centre and the Pier, this family run Hotel, where all are welcome, offers homely comfort at affordable prices. All thirteen letting rooms are differently decorated, warm and cosy with excellent facilities, three of which are ensuite. Licensed, the hotel offers a friendly and relaxing atmosphere, where the comforts of home are there for you to enjoy during your stay. Evening meals for residents only are served in intimate dining area which like the rest of the hotel is delightfully decorated. A private car park is to the rear of the building.

The Cliff Lodge Hotel.   Cleethorpes. Lincs.   Tel: 0472 691583.

Immediately opposite Grimsby Town Football Club on Grimsby Road, **Blundell Park Hotel** makes a comfortable and convenient holiday base for visitors to Cleethorpes and the surrounding area.

Blundell Park Hotel, 140 Grimsby Rd. Cleethorpes . 0472 691970 .

Although it was built over a century ago as a doctors surgery, Blundell Park has been a hotel for many years providing a warm welcome to all who visit. There are 18 attractively furnished rooms 15 with en -suite facilities, while downstairs in the cosy atmosphere of the restaurant you can choose from an extensive menu which caters to most tastes. Exposed brick and York stone floors in the bar add a country pub feel and if you prefer a more informal meal,you can sample a tasty bar snack with your drink, or enjoy a lunchtime selection from the carvery.

Grimsby, although in the county of South Humberside is included in our journey, has continued to be a fishing and trading port since the the middle ages. Catches aren't what they were in the past and the size of the fishing fleet has been reduced, particularly in recent years, but the town is still the chief fishing port in the country. The Royal Docks built in the 1850's, the Dock Tower, a copy of the town hall of Siena in Italy, and the Victoria Flour Mill stand as reminders of the heyday of the port. A visit to the National Fishing Heritage Centre, in Heritage Square by the docks, will help you appreciate the long and difficult history of the fishing industry in this area.

Did You Know...

There is a full list of

Tourist Information Centres

at the back of the book?

Lovers of smoked fish will find it hard to pass by the factory of **Alfred Enderby Ltd.** which lies on the aptly named Fish Dock Road in Grimsby. One of only a few independent family run traditional Fish smoking firms left in the country, sixty years experience shows in the quality and flavour of the fish sold here and the choice available ranges from smoked Scottish salmon, haddock and cod to kippers, ensuring everyone's tastes are catered for.

Enjoying a riverside setting in Alexandra Road in Grimsby, **Leon's Family Fish Restaurant** is exactly what its name describes - a superb fish restaurant where you can enjoy a family meal out. Leon Marklew is the friendly proprietor who has been in the fish business for over 45 years. The restaurant is Egon Ronay Recommended and really is outstanding. The building itself is modern and clean, situated by the side of the River Freshney and close to the Fishing Heritage

Centre. Together with his dedicated team of staff, Leon goes out of his way to ensure you get exactly what you want. There is a wide variety of fresh fish to choose from and a special children's menu at reduced prices. The additional side dish menu means you can make up your plate to suit yourself and afterwards what better than to finish off your fish and chip meal with a traditional helping of apple pie or ice cream.

Leon's Family Fish Restaurant, Riverside, 1 Alexandra Road, Grimsby Tel: 0472 356282

Formerly a famous brewery, Abbeygate in the heart of town is now a charming pedestrianised shopping mall. Great care has been taken to preserve the splendid architecture and old-fashioned atmosphere whilst combining it with the best of modern shopping facilities. One of the many wonderful establishments here that you must not miss is **Abbeygate Antique and Craft Centre.**

Abbeygate Antique and Craft Centre, 14 Abbeygate, Grimsby Tel: 0472 361129

Divided into three main areas, there is an antique section where you can view the fine wares of over twenty quality antique dealers, with something to appeal to every taste and pocket. Another area is the Craft Centre which houses the beautiful creations of over 25 craftsmen and women, with items ranging from paintings to cuddly toys, dried flowers to needlework. You name it, it's here and you can easily while away an hour or so, browsing at your leisure. Afterwards, you can relax in the pleasant surroundings of the third section which is a spotlessly clean tearoom serving a variety of hot and cold snacks.

Situated just 5 minutes walk from the centre of Grimsby on the main A46 on Bargate you will find **Millfields**, a superb hotel where

Millfields, 53 Bargate, Grimsby . 0472 356068 Fax 0472 250286.

the old has been successfully blended with the new to provide excellent accommodation and leisure facilities in beautiful traditional surroundings. Millfields was originally built in 1879 as a private house for a local fish baron and became a hotel early this century, but returned to being a private residence before the present owner Charles Mountain bought it in 1979 and turned it into an 8 court squash club. Having dispensed with 4 of the squash courts, an extension was added for accommodation, and a further extension now

houses a beautifully decorated orangery restaurant.

Attractively furnished throughout , the hotel retains the original floor of the entrance hall, stone mullioned windows, and the original staircase, all of which enhances an air of grandeur. The 22 en- suite guest rooms are well equipped and for those who feel the need to work off the excesses of the restaurants mouthwatering menu, there is a comprehensive health and fitness club including sauna, jacuzzi, sunbed, and dance studio.

About six miles further along the **A180** lies **Immingham**, a deep water dock built originally in 1912 to ship coal from the Yorkshire coalfields now contains an oil refinery and chemical industries. A monument stands in the midst of this, at South Killingholme Haven, to mark the spot where in 1609 the Pilgrim Fathers left for Holland.

The Old Chapel Hose and Restaurant. Habrough 0469 572377
Fax 0469 577883.

A couple of miles across the A180 lies Habrough and if you are in the area and looking for somewhere to stay , you would have to go a long way to beat **The Old Chapel Hotel** and Restaurant. Dating back to 1836, this converted chapel enjoys a beautiful location in the heart of South Humberside countryside, yet is easily reached via the M1 or M62 motorways. You are immediately aware of a cosy welcoming ambience which is enhanced by a friendly personal service so often lacking in larger hotels. The Old Chapel is well furnished throughout and all 14 guest rooms are en-suite and equipped for maximum comfort.

The small licensed restaurant provides the perfect setting for an intimate dinner , with the emphasis placed on the finest English fare cooked to the highest standards. Alternatively you can opt for a lighter bar meal in the pleasant surroundings of the Victorian conservatory which boasts magnificent country views. David and Christine Wilson are super hosts whose hard efforts have created a lovely place to stay, well deserving of its AA 2 star and ETB 4 crown rating.

Continuing on the **A1077** you'll come to **Thornton Curtis**, where the church here is Norman and early English and slightly to the east stand the remains of **Thornton Abbey.** Founded in 1139 for the Austin Canons, English Heritage maintain the buildings where you can still see five original statues in the gatehouse and parts of the chapter house.

Barton-upon-Humber, is another small town that is trying to come to terms with a changing role that was once based around its port. North of town stands the magnificent **Humber Bridge**, opened in 1981, stretching north across the Humber, where there is a viewpoint and Tourist Information. In the town St Peter, has one of the earliest church towers in England with Saxon arcading dating from the early 12th century as is the west porch. Nearby, St Mary is an early English church that contains a brass to Simon Seman, the Sheriff of London in 1433.

Baysgarth House Museum. Baysgarth Leisure Park, Barton -upon-Humber. Tel: 0652 632318.

Situated on the B1218 at Barton -upon- Humber, **Baysgarth House Museum** provides a fascinating day out for the whole family. Dating from the late 17th and 18th centuries, the museum forms part of Baysgarth Leisure Park and is set in over 30 acres of grounds. Within the museum there are various displays relating to the geology,archeology and later history of the surrounding Glanford district. The many attractions here range from a magnificent 18th century panelled room with costume models to the skeleton of an Anglo-Saxon warrior. There are also impressive collections of 18th and 19th century English and Oriental pottery and porcelain and during 1994, three rooms will be transformed to show Victorian Baysgarth, Georgian Baysgarth and 17th century Baysgarth. There is so much to see here, a day is easily filled, making this one place not to miss.

We followed Ermine Street down its straight road and situated just off the A18 at **Broughton, The Briggate Lodge Inn** provides a luxurious and peaceful holiday base for the discerning traveller. Awarded 3 stars by the AA and RAC and the prestigious Five Crowns Highly Commended grading by the English Tourist Board, this superior establishment stands in 200 acres of which 195 are soon to be turned into an 18 hole golf course. Built seven years ago by its present owner, The Briggate Lodge Inn has everything you could possibly need for that relaxing break away from it all. Each of the fifty en-suite guest rooms is equipped to the highest standards and for those with children there is a baby listening service. The elegant restaurant serves the finest international cuisine accompanied by a select wine list, while in the comfortable surroundings of the Buttery you can enjoy the informality of a tasty bar meal. With beautifully landscaped grounds and a variety of leisure activities within easy reach, your holiday is complete.

The Briggate Lodge Inn, Broughton, South Humberside. Tel: 0652 650770 Fax: 0652 650495

The industrial landscape of iron and steel works as you approach **Scunthorpe** might be initially off putting and perhaps hardly one where you'd find 'hidden places' but its location is ideal for those pursuing business or pleasure. **The Borough Museum and Art Gallery**, situated in Oswald Road contains an interesting and important collection of archeology along with displays on local history.

The Larchwood Hotel, Scunthorpe Tel: 0724 847517 Fax/Tel: 0724 864712

Situated in the heart of Scunthorpe, close to the Police Station,

The Larchwood Hotel makes a convenient and very comfortable holiday base from which to explore South Humberside and its many attractions. Formerly a number of cottages dating back to the turn of the century, The Larchwood is a very homely establishment where guest comfort is of paramount importance. John and Shirley Fisher are smashing hosts whose hard efforts have won the hotel Highly Commendable awards in the Scunthorpe Landscape Competition for the past two years. In fact, almost all year round the exterior of the building is adorned with numerous beautiful hanging baskets. There are eleven attractively furnished guest rooms, four of which are en-suite and situated on the ground floor, making them ideal for disabled visitors.

We decided to head for **Normanby Hall Country Park** which is 4 miles North of Scunthorpe on the B1430 to Burton on Stather. The Hall is decorated throughout in the Regency style, with a marvellous collection of paintings, costumes and furniture depicting a family home of that period. Leaving the Hall you then have a staggering 312 acres of garden and parkland to explore, with deer parks, a picturesque lake with tickets for fishing, and plenty of country walks.

Normanby Hall Country Park, Laundry Cottage, Normanby Hall, Scunthorpe. 0724 720588

One could spend from dawn till dusk wandering around discovering the plentiful wildlife, indeed the grounds are open all day all year round. There is also a farming Museum which offers a fascinating display of farming equipment and views of rural life in the area as well as an authentic farm kitchen, saddlers workshop, smithy, rural crafts and transport displays, which feature the estates original 19th century fire engine. The Gift Shop offers a wide variety of books and gifts with a countryside theme. A wide selection of snacks is available at the Woodland Cafe, while at the Hall, Edwardian Cream Teas are served every Sunday to give you a taste of high living.

Throughout the Summer, regular events include craft demonstrations, the recently revived Normanby Country Show, a miniature railway and group guided tours. There are also facilities for group camping and caravanning, a childrens play area and a golf course. With so much for all the family to do and see, your visit to Normanby Hall will no doubt be the first of many, especially as the modest car parking charge covers admission to all parts of the Park.

Heading back inland, passing via **Brigg** and standing beside what is probably the busiest freight line in the country, **The Station Hotel** in **Barnetby -le-Wold** is an excellent place to stay, particularly for railway enthusiasts.

The Station Hotel , 10 Railway St. Barnetby le Wold . 0652 688238

To get here follow the A18 through Brigg towards Grimsby and you will see Barnetby signposted. Originally built in 1854 as a doctor's house, it was converted into a hotel when the railways came and has remained thus ever since. The main accommodation is housed in converted stables and a coach house. The upper part of the coach house was used for many years as a meeting place for railwaymen, where such things as tribunals took place. Tastefully decorated throughout, there are 14 guest rooms altogether 11 with en-suite facilities. As The Station is a free house there is a wide choice of well kept ale available, including the highly popular Theakstons range. Pub lunches are available and evening meals can be provided for residents if required.

We made for **Caistor**, where there is a local legend around that should deter anyone who has a miserly nature! St Paulinus, a companion of St Augustine, was riding along a track near the village when he spotted a farmer sowing his fields. When Paulinus requested some grain to feed his ass, the man curtly refused, saying that he had no more. Paulinus pointed to a sack lying on the field and asked if there was any grain in it, and the man replied that it was no sack, but

354

a stone. Paulinus retorted 'Then stone it shall be', and today the Fonaby Stone stands as a tribute to the farmer's meanness.

Caistor is a small market town that lies at the northern tip of the Wolds, and was once the site of Roman occupation. Some of the walls of this settlement still stand, however it was most probably an administrative or commercial centre rather than a military outpost.

We then headed south on the **B1225,** and took a leisurely drive through some lovely hill country to arrive at **Thoresway** which was once a rabbit farming community on a grand scale. Some 1,700 acres of warren were held by the parish, and the rabbits from the Wold warrens were highly prized for the silvery colour of their fur which was used mainly in the hat trade. One man could run an extensive warren at little cost, and the effective 'crop' rotation employed here went as follows. One year a rabbit warren, the following year corn, the next turnips, finally clover or grasses, and then back full circle to rabbits. Eventually rabbit farming on this scale died out, mainly due to low cost-effectiveness and the constant threats from poachers and natural predators.

South of Thoresway is **Stainton le Vale,** a charming hamlet and very isolated. It has an odd custom associated with it, called 'Mumping'. On the 21st December the 'mumpers', a group of village women, went around requesting gifts and giving some in return. We then headed east on the **B1203** to **Binbrook**, a comfortable village with a pleasant square. Very different from when the practice of poor working conditions, little pay and long hours was widespread throughout the nineteenth century. The particular plight of the agricultural labourers at Binbrook aroused much public concern, and this certainly helped prompt the formation of the National Union Of Agricultural and Allied Workers in 1872. Now you are rewarded by the familiar sight of a 'Marquis of Granby' pub sign, while the Plough Inn offers an alternative place for refreshment. During World War II the Royal Australian Air Force was stationed here, and chaps from the nearby RAF station must have swelled the pub's capacity quite considerably.

Situated on the B1203 at **Swinhope** near Binbrook you will discover a truly relaxing holiday haven at **Hoe Hill**, the charming home of Ian and Erica Curd. As a guest here you are immediately made to feel at home and your hosts go out of their way to ensure you have everything just as you like it, even down to the strength of your tea! Dining is a veritable pleasure, with an amazing choice of breakfast dishes and, with prior arrangement, a homecooked three course evening meal. Awarded a One Crown Highly Commended grading, Hoe Hill has three comfortably furnished guest rooms and you are welcome to relax in front of the sitting room fire, where you can choose to read, play board games or simply watch TV. In addition to pointing out the best local walks, Ian and Erica will happily fill you in on the history of the house and the surrounding area, including the Neolithic long barrow which lies in a copse 500 yards in front of the house.

Hoe Hill.   *Swinhope near Binbrook. Tel: 0472 398206*

We continued south through **Burgh on Bain** on the A157, then arrived at **Donington on Bain.** If you begin to spot signs featuring Viking helmets, then you will know you are on the Viking Way. This stretch of the footpath runs for five miles over the Lincolnshire Wolds, following the course of the River Bain. You are able to join the path in the village by the old water mill.

In the hamlet of Donington -on- Bain, you will discover a delightful 'hidden' 18th century coaching house, **The Black Horse Inn.** It really does have everything as character and charm exude from its low beamed attractive snug and lounge with a roaring open fire in the winter, as well as the spacious comfortable forty seat restaurant.

The Black Horse   *Donington -on- Bain. Lincs Tel: 0507 343640*

The owners Tony and Janine Pacey are rightly proud of their inn, a Free House that serves Courage ales and appetising, freshly cooked locally produced food to order, from its main menu and blackboard specials for both lunch and evening meals. Visitors are welcome, including the disabled, to stay in one of their eight twin rooms, all ensuite with TV and Tea/Coffee making facilities and take advantage of the surrounding beautiful countryside, panoramic views and easy location to the many attractions in the Lincolnshire. The Inn is open all year round and you can be certain of a friendly and warm welcome and where you will be well looked after.

Near **Stenigot** is the Red Hill Nature Reserve. Once a quarry, the great red gash on the hill reveals the layers of rock which make up these lovely Wolds. Sandstone, red chalk and white chalk make dramatic bandings, and we discovered that the red chalk owes its colour to the iron deposits found in the area. This band of red chalk is known to stretch from South Yorkshire to North Norfolk, and can only be seen to surface here in the Wolds. The path is fairly steep, but quite manageable if you go carefully - however, visitors are advised not to climb the rock face. The views from the summit of Red Hill are quite lovely, with the valley floor looking rather like a map as it spreads beneath you. A walk through the reserve may reward you with a glimpse of a number of birds common to the area, such as the meadow pipit and the red-legged partridge, and an abundance of wild flowers carpets the hillside.

South-east of here at **Scamblesby,** the A153 gives you a marvellous view as you descend the road towards **Horncastle.** To the east lies the Blue Stone Heath Road which wends its way across the Wolds for 14 miles. Today, no villages can be seen along the route, although a number of them existed a few centuries ago. The lost villages of **South Cadeby** and **Calcethorpe** have long since disappeared. On this road, just east of **Belchford,** you are afforded a lovely view of the River Waring and the old beacon point of Nab Hill.

We continued southwards through **Greetham,** then headed east on the A158 to **Hagworthingham.** Just off the A158 Horncastle to Skegness road near the village of Hagworthingham, in the Lincolnshire wolds is **Stockwith Mill.** Tennyson has a very strong influence on this part of Lincolnshire, he always refused to say that any of his poetry referred to any specific place but sometimes he gives it away in his poems because they are full of images of the countryside he walked around when at his childhood home of Somersby, less than two miles from here. Stockwith Mill is sometimes referred to as 'Philips Farm', which is mentioned in Tennysons famous poem 'The Brook'. Stockwith Mill is open from March to November, Tuesday to Sunday 10. 30 to 6pm. The mill is closed on Mondays except bank holidays.

West of here on the **B1195** is the village of **Winceby,** that witnessed some of the bloodiest fighting during the Civil War. The Battle of Winceby took place at Slash Hollow in 1643. The fighting between Cromwell's men and the Royalists, led by Sir Thomas Fairfax, was particularly fierce. Sir Ingram Hopton felled Cromwell with a blow, but before he could finish him off, Hopton was pushed aside by the wall of men and horses. The Royalists were defeated, and Hopton was killed in the battle. Cromwell arranged for him to be buried at Horncastle church, where a painting commemorates the brave soldier.

A footpath in the village will lead you to the **Snipe Dales Nature Reserve.** This 120 acre conservation area is one of the few places where you can see a surviving wet valley system. This is a place where many streams abound, attracting grasshopper warblers, snipe, kestrel and woodcock. The lovely vivid marsh marigold thrives here, and it is heartening to see that many deciduous trees have been planted in amongst the conifers.

South-east of Winceby is the village of **Old Bolingbroke.** Few remains of Old Bolingbroke Castle can be seen today, but this was the birthplace of Henry IV in 1367. His father, John of Gaunt, the Duke of Lancaster, occupied the castle in the fourteenth century. Following its capture by Cromwell's men, the castle fell into disrepair and has been crumbling away ever since.

To the west is **Scrivelby** on the **B1183,** where the Sovereign's Hereditary Champion comes from. The Champion would have ridden into Westminster Hall (where regents were previously crowned) and dared anyone to challenge the impending monarch's right to rule. Then the Champion rode a white steed and was fully clad in armour, today in these 'less violent' times, the Champion bears a standard at the coronation ceremony at Westminster Abbey.

We took the A153 to Horncastle, which sits on the furthest south western edge of the Wolds and is a most attractive market town. The name probably derived from 'Hurncastre', which means 'the camp at the horn', as the town lies on a peninsula between the Bain and Waring rivers. Despite the 'castle' of the name, none has ever stood here.

The delightful **Crowders Garden Centre** sits on the main A158 road into Horncastle from Lincoln. Beautifully set out, the centre caters for the needs of everyone from the professional to the keen amateur gardener. Items for sale are displayed clearly and arranged attractively. The centre has a comprehensive range of shrubs, garden plants, a smashing display of garden and leisure furniture and a fine Gift shop. Well designed and suitable for the disabled, you can enjoy a stroll around the centre and end your visit with tea, coffee and light meals in the Botts Cafe which is part of the Garden Centre. The staff are extremely knowledgeable and the service excellent. All are welcome, including coach parties at the centre which is open daily from 8.30am - 5.30pm.

Crowders Garden Centre.   Horncastle. Lincs . 0507 525252 Fax: 0507 524000

At one time there were 48 public houses in the town, and although today their numbers are considerably reduced, the Red Lion and the Bull are still going strong. For a chance to see a really old building, the sixteenth-century King's Head is well worth a visit as it was built of 'mud and stud'. A building at the end of Wharf street boasts another 'Tom Thumb's House', a similar ridge tile to the one we discovered earlier in Tattershall Thorpe. St Mary's church dates from the late twelfth century, and here we were able to see Sir Ingram Hopton's memorial.

Horncastle was widely renowned for its horse fairs and it must have been a great sight to see horses of all shapes and sizes being paraded in the markets. Today, antiques have replaced the horses, and the town has a good reputation amongst the dealers who come from far and wide.

Set within an attractive 19th century property which over the years has housed many businesses, such as upholsterers, a funeral parlour, coffin makers, is the very impressive **Lincolnshire Antiques Centre**. Within it over thirty different antique dealers display their outstanding and very varied goods. Three floors ensure that there is something for everyone at prices to suit all pockets. Outstanding period furniture, exciting collectables, impressive brasswork, old toys; you name it and you'll probably find it here. All displays are beautifully arranged and you'll find the very knowledgeable staff willing to help you in your search. There are memories of bygone days at every glance and the centre is the sort of place you could find yourself staying at all day. Situated on Bridge Street in the centre of

Horncastle which is off the A158 Skegness to Lincoln road, you'll find it hard to miss.

The Lincolnshire Antiques Centre. Horncastle. Lincs 0507 527794.

From Horncastle, we took the B1190 through **Thimbleby** with its white thatched houses, then **Horsington** and **Bucknall**, until we came to **Bardney.** Its most dominant feature is the large sugar-beet factory which lies close to one of the bridges that cross the River Witham.

From Bardney we headed north on the **B1202,** past **Wragby, Holton cum Beckering** and **Lissington** to the village of **Linwood.** This is a richly wooded area with many varieties of trees, including the lime (or linden) which gave the village its name. The wildlife is equally varied, and the rare red squirrels have been spotted from time to time.

Bleasby House.   Legsby, Market Rasen   Tel: 0673 842383

Set within a 1200 acre mixed farm estate just four miles south east of Market Rasen you will find a lovely place to stay at **Bleasby House.** This magnificent 130 year old farmhouse is Highly Commended and provides a peaceful holiday base surrounded by beautiful countryside. John and Janet Dring are super hosts who enjoy sharing their home with their many guests. The decor and furnishings are outstanding, reflecting the period elegance of the house and the three guest rooms are equipped for maximum comfort, two with en-suite facilities. Guests can make use of the hard tennis court or try their hand at trout fishing in the adjacent reservoir. If you prefer self-catering, the Drings also have a lovely self-contained holiday cottage in the village of Legsby, which sleeps six and is available all year round.

The road eventually led us to **Market Rasen.** This is a small town with excellent shopping facilities, and it has the only racecourse in Lincolnshire. National Hunt Racing occurs here on seventeen days of the year, and a particularly useful service provided is the supervised children's enclosure. The town is situated on the western edge of the Wolds, and though there are several elegant Georgian houses, most of the buildings here are Victorian.

The Rase, a tributary of the River Anchholme, links the town with the neighbouring villages of **Middle Rasen** and **West Rasen.** The church at Middle Rasen is said to have some of the county's finest Norman decoration in its chancel arch, and at West Rasen, a lovely three-arched packhorse bridge has spanned the tiny river since the fourteenth century.

The A631 from West Rasen took us through **Bishopbridge,** and just off the road at **Glentham,** we came upon 'Molly Grime'. At Glentham church, there is a stone effigy of the fourteenth-century Lady Tournay. Up until 1832, seven old maids were each paid a shilling to scrub the figure clean every Good Friday. The custom of washing holy images was known locally as 'malgraen', and this was corrupted to Molly Grime. Although the practice no longer exists here, a child discovered with a grubby face is still referred to as 'a Molly Grime', so the name lives on.

From here, we journeyed north and then west on the **B1205** through **Waddingham** with its village green, past **Grayingham,** then turned off the road and headed north to **Scotton.** The River Eau flows near to the village and heads on towards the Trent. The Lincolnshire Trust owns forty acres of Scotton Common, and they have successfully reintroduced the grayling butterfly, which had previously disappeared from the area. The reserve which the Trust established here is now a haven for lizards and adders, harvest mice and tree pipits.

In **Kirton-in-Lindsey,** just a few miles off the main A46 Lincoln to Grimsby road, you will find **Kirton Lodge,** a small and very comfortable hotel and restaurant run by welcoming hosts, Maxine and Steve Walker. Set within a converted 300 year old barn, Kirton Lodge provides excellent and somewhat unique accommodation, well deserving of its Three Crowns Commended grading. There are four individually styled and beautifully furnished en-suite guest rooms all equipped for maximum comfort. Steve is the chef here and he has developed a reputation throughout the area for his superb culinary expertise. However, the restaurant only seats sixteen, which whilst making it ideal for that intimate dinner for two, also makes prior booking essential if you don't want to be disappointed. The menu is both imaginative and extensive which can be a problem - which dish to choose? They all sound so tempting!

Kirton Lodge. Kirton-in-Lindsey, Gainsborough Tel: 0652 648994

The road north passes by a deserted medieval village, **Gainsthorpe Village**, which is overseered by the English Heritage and on towards **Scotter** on the **A159.** Once a market town, but now demoted to a fairly large village, Scotter still has some pretty cottages and an impressive church near the village green. It lies close to the edges of Laughton Forest, where the Forestry Commission has been busy planting trees in the hitherto rather poor sandy soil.

We continued south on the A159 town of **Gainsborough**, which lies on the far western side of the county, alongside the River Trent which marks the border with Nottinghamshire. The town is well endowed with parks and open spaces, and with the wooded slopes that descend almost into the town it is a very pleasant place. Its name derived from the earliest settlers who were known as the Gainas and came here in the sixth century. The Danish king, Svein Forkbeard, took the town in 1013 and although he died soon after, his son Canute took control. Already ruler of Denmark and Norway, the succession to England's rule was the final prize needed to make Canute the most politically important ruler in the northern kingdoms.

We heard an interesting anecdote regarding Canute, who is

generally remembered as the king who tried to hold back the sea. Gainsborough folk reckon that history has got it wrong, and that it was in fact the River Trent which he attempted to master. The Trent here is well known for its tidal 'wave' that rises with the spring tides. The bore, or 'Aegir' as it is known by the locals, rolls down the river several feet above the normal level. They say that Canute sat on the bank of the river and commanded the tidal wave not to splash his royal personage. Nevertheless the tide swept by and drenched him, and he leapt back with the immortal words, *'Let all the world know that the power of monarchs is vain. . . . '*

From the seventeenth to the eighteenth century, Gainsborough prospered mainly through its river trade, together with ship and boatbuilding and allied trades. As an inland port, it was conveniently situated to import and export goods to Hull and inland to Nottinghamshire and Derbyshire. With the advent of the railways the river trade fell off considerably, but the town survived and prospered thanks to its connections with agriculture and engineering.

The White Hart Hotel has been sitting proudly in the centre of historic Gainsborough since the early 17th century, although there has been a building on this site since a century earlier. A former coaching inn , the White Hart blends all the charm of a bygone age with excellent present day facilities. Awarded a 3 crowns rating, the hotel provides very comfortable accommodation in 14 en-suite guest rooms, including a romantically decorated Bridal Suite complete with four- poster bed. The pleasant Fleur de Lys restaurant offers an extensive and varied menu at very reasonable prices, with dishes to suit every taste, and as the White Hart is a free house, there is also a wide range of beers to choose from, including three traditional hand -pulled ales. While you are here, keep an eye out for the hotel's ghosts -a man dressed in black who has been seen on several occasions by different people.

The White Hart, Lord St, Gainsborough. 0427 612018

Historically, the town has its links with the Pilgrim Fathers, but the main attraction for the visitor is without doubt **The Old Hall.** This stunningly beautiful fifteenth-century manor house stands in the heart of the town, and its splendid Great Hall and medieval kitchens should definitely not be missed. With its beautifully maintained gardens, five sets of chimneys, black timbered gables and huge arched beams, it represents most people's idea of the perfect medieval building. Some of history's most interesting characters have stayed here, including Richard III, and Henry VIII who possibly met Katherine Parr here for the first time.

Just a few minutes walk from the famous Gainsborough Old Hall on North Street in the centre of this historic town you'll discover **The Sun Hotel.** This former 18th century inn was boarded up when Ann and Terry Wynn set their hearts on it but with sheer hard work and determination they have now turned it into an attractively decorated hotel with a lovely homely atmosphere. 3 Crown commended and open all the year round there are fourteen nicely decorated and furnished rooms to let, three of which are ensuite. A Free house that serves Bass beers and lunches from Tuesday to Saturday with evening meals by prior arrangement, all their food is freshly prepared and the Specials Board changes daily. There is off road car parking for visitors who can be sure of a warm welcome by the lovely down to earth hosts at this characterful hotel.

The Sun Hotel.   Gainsborough.   Tel: 0427 616916

From Gainsborough, we took an easterly route on the A631 to **Corringham.** Built over 300 years ago, **The Beckett Arms** in Corringham is an impressive looking building, and is an ideal stopping off point, whether it is food, drink, or accommodation you are after. Refurbished just over 3 years ago, the facilities are of the highest standards, with a particular feature being the front conservatory where customers can both eat and drink in pleasant surroundings.

There are 4 first class en-suite guest rooms and families are most welcome, as are the wheelchair bound, with a disabled toilet provided in the restaurant.

Barry and Alcija Carr are super hosts and people come from quite a way to sample Barry's excellent cooking which has earned him a well deserved reputation in the area. A free house, the Beckett Arms serves a wide selection of Bass and Youngers beers, as well as a regularly changing guest ale.

The Beckett Arms ,Corringham, Gainsborough. 0427 838201.Fax 0427 838479

Further east, **Hemswell** is situated on the old RAF base, on which Lancasters and Blenheims were once regularly seen, and here you will find a hidden gem at the eye opening **Hemswell Antiques Centre**. Bought by Nepi and Rex Miller in 1985,the first building housing antiques was opened just one year later. Today within three large buildings, over 285 antique dealers have their magnificent wares on display. Antiques of every description can be found here, all beautifully arranged to enable you to browse at your leisure. The centre exports throughout the world and is renowned among antique collectors. In addition to beautiful period pieces of furniture, wonderful paintings and prints, and antique books and silverware,there are also many collectables, ensuring there is something here to suit every taste and pocket. Having spent some time admiring the wonderful displays and lingering over some long wanted item, you can enjoy welcome refreshment at the centre's excellent restaurant which serves delicious homemade food every day. There is parking space for over 450 cars,plus plenty of overspill in adjacent fields. The centre is open every day of the year apart from Christmas and Boxing Day, so when the weather puts you off outdoor pursuits, you know you can spend an enjoyable few hours here.

Hemswell Antiques Centre. Hemswell Cliff . Tel: 0427 668389.

Close by lies the oddly-named **Spital in the Street.** No more than a hamlet, it was once an important stopping place for the London coach runs as they transported various members of the judiciary to the Quarter Sessions. A glance at your road map will show you that the importance of the village was purely due to its proximity to the nearby crossroads, where the road is intersected by Ermine Street. Now prosaically called the A15, this road slashes across the country in an uncompromising way with hardly a village along its route.

South of here, on the **B1398** around **Glentworth,** we had some splendid views over the surrounding countryside. The castle at **Fillingham** was built by Sir Cecil Wray, and was the setting of a curious feud between him and a member of the Whichcot family. When Wray had built the castle and enclosed the parkland with a wall, he had effectively cut off access on a public right of way that Whichcot frequented. Whichcot's response was to take a gang of labourers to the site to break down the wall, then to ride his coach through the gap and continue on his way. Sir Cecil had the wall rebuilt, and Whichcot broke it down again, and so they continued year after year until Whichcot's death.

From Fillingham we headed south to **Scampton.** Both the **B1398** and the otherwise ruler-straight A15 suddenly develop bulges here, and if you look at a map you will see why. The large RAF base which is situated here thrusts the roads apart. The 617 Squadron were based at RAF Scampton before they moved to Coningsby, then later to Woodhall Spa.

We then took the **A1500** west to **Sturton by Stow,** then the **B1241** north to **Stow** itself. The church of St Mary's at Stow is so splendid that it is known as the Mother-Church to Lincoln. Looking more like a castle than a church, the magnificent Saxon arches and the splendour of the interior somehow made us feel quite humble. The tiny hamlet clusters almost insignificantly round this great building, and most of the local population lives in Sturton.

At the end of the A1500, we came to **Marton** where a fine herring-bone tower rises from the eleventh-century church, then headed south on the A156 to **Torksey.** The village lies by the side of the River Trent, and it is here that the **Fossdyke Navigational Canal** starts its journey eastwards to Brayford Pool in Lincoln. The Foss Dyke was built by the Romans, and is the oldest navigable canal in the country.

Although Torksey was once a strategic settlement, today it's importance is quite possibly measured in the membership of its golf course, the Elizabethan mansion of **Torksey Castle,** and an oil terminal. The mansion belonged to the Jermyn family, and was by all accounts quite lovely at that time. Sadly, it was burnt by Royalists from Newark during the Civil War, and all that we can see of it today is a hollow shell which stands overlooking the Trent.

A short way south of Torksey, we joined the A57 and headed east towards Lincoln. We came almost immediately to **Saxilby**. Roughly three miles south of the village is **Doddington Hall,** dating from the end of the 16th century for Thomas Tailor, the Registrar of Lincoln. The architect is thought to be Robert Smythson who was responsible for Hardwick Hall, Wollaton and Worksop Manor. The interior was redesigned in the mid 18th century by a Thomas Lumby who was also involved in the village church. The Hall has never changed hands and this is reflected inside with collections of textiles, porcelains, furniture and family portraits. Set in interesting grounds the Hall is open to the public.

Mentioned in the 'Where to Stay' guides, **Garden House,** is a three hundred year old magnificent property that was once the gardeners cottage on the estate of Lord Monson. It was sold off in 1953 and since 1970, present owners Paul and Jane Blackburn have kept the character of the house. The Victorian walled garden and lovely gardens to the front and rear are in keeping with the interior which has been upgraded to contain the high class facilities of its three room accommodation, two of which are ensuite. Special features inside include beamed rooms and a stone fireplace. Although the Blackburns don't provide evening meals the house is only a few minutes drive from the centre of Lincoln and this 2 Crown commended, 3 Cheveron for the disabled country house is a haven of peace and tranquillity where you will feel immediately at home as the hosts pamper to your needs. Garden House can be found off the B1398 from old Lincoln in the hamlet of **Burton**.

Garden House. Burton by Lincoln 0522 526120 Fax: 0522 523787.

At last our travels brought us to the lovely, picturesque city of **Lincoln,** a place rich in heritage and with two very distinctive faces.

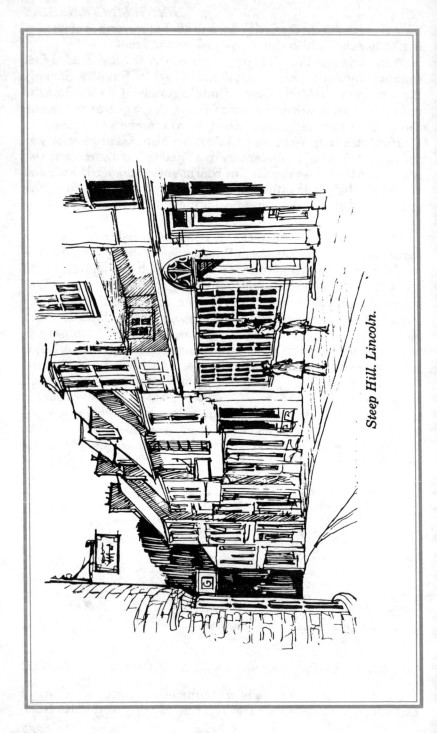

Steep Hill. Lincoln.

Indeed, it is difficult not to think of Lincoln as two towns in one. A simple, but inadequate description would be that 'historic' Lincoln sits high on a hill, dominated by the Cathedral and Castle, while the modern city lies on the valley floor two hundred feet below, with the River Witham flowing through it on its way to Boston. ' Below hill ' Lincoln certainly has all the conveniences of a modern city centre, but it also has its fair share of fine buildings and historic associations too.

It was the history and not the establishment that took us to St. Catherines Hotel, 21 St Catherines, in Lincoln. St Catherine's was once the site of the most important and interesting of the religious houses. It was the Gilbertine Priory and stood between the High Street and the Witham. It was founded about 1148 for canons, that is, religious men who lived together in a community, but who also acted as parish priests in the parishes belonging to the house. Lay sisters, or religious women, who had not taken the vows of a nun, were soon introduced to look after the sick and the children in the hospital of St Sepulchre, which was attached to the Priory.

It was here that Queen Eleanor's body was prepared for burial in 1290, and the first of the famous Eleanor Crosses was erected just outside the Priory on Swine Green. King Henry VII once stayed here and after the dissolution the house was known as St Catherine's Hall and was used as a residence by its various owners and as a place of entertainment for distinguished guests. One one occasion James I stayed there, and among the guests was a young man, John Hutchinson, who later signed the death warrant of James' son Charles. In the 18th century the building was allowed to fall into ruin and was pulled down, and now the only reminder we have of it is the name St Catherine's, by which the district in which it stood is known today.

To see the lower town at its best, you have only to follow the course of the Witham. A good place to start your walk would be at the on Waterside North, where a carefully restored fourteenth-century timber-framed building stands which was formerly a merchant's house. There are a number of good watering-holes along this stretch of the river, and in the Summer you will need to skirt around the scores of patrons who sit at tables outside on the footpath, soaking in the atmosphere.

You can follow this course for half a mile west of your starting point, sometimes straying away from the river into the town, until you come to **Brayford Pool**. This is a wide stretch of water where the Foss Dyke meets the Witham, and from Roman times to the early nineteenth century it was the centre of activity for Lincoln's role as an important inland port.

Jews House.

Today, Lincoln can still claim to be the inland waterway centre for the East Midlands, and along with the numerous pleasure craft anchored here, you will still see working boats making their way from Brayford Pool to join the thousands of miles of canals and rivers that it is linked with.

Walking up the long High Street, you can cross the Witham at High Bridge. Built in the twelfth century, it carries sixteenth-century half-timbered buildings on its span, the oldest bridge in the country still to do so. A few hundred yards along the street, you pass under the main arch of the Stonebow, which was the southern gate of medieval Lincoln. Around and above this archway, Lincoln Guildhall was built, and the Mote Bell on the roof, which dates back to 1371, is still rung to summon the City Father before each Council meeting.

To get to the historic, ancient heart of this city you should make your way to the end of the High Street, where The Strait will take you to the bottom of Steep Hill. On our travels we are sometimes fortunate enough to come across a place which is both interesting from an architectural or historical point of view and which also has something extra to recommend it to the traveller. In this respect the **Jews House** is truly a gem.

The building itself is a fine example of a Norman house, which as the name suggests was originally the property of one of the members of the Jewish community in Lincoln and indeed it is reputed to be the oldest inhabited domestic dwelling in these Isles.

Take warning that this ascent to 'Up-hill' Lincoln is extremely aptly named! Although you will see elderly local residents fairly charging up and down the hill, you should bear in mind that their legs and lungs are acclimatised to the gradient. At the top of Steep Hill, all your efforts will be amply rewarded as you come to the delightful cobbled **Castle Square**. To your right is the Cathedral, and to your left is the eastern gateway to the Castle.

Lincoln Castle is steeped in history. Commissioned by William the Conqueror in 1068, it was built on the site of a former Roman fort. Originally very primitive with earth banks and a timber stockade, the castle was eventually rebuilt of stone. It has often been under siege, first in the 1140s when the Empress Matilda invaded England and disputed King Stephen's throne, and later during the Civil War. In 1644, the Parliamentarians took the Castle, and the Royalists were thrown out of the city. The Castle's main role from then on was as a seat of law, and within the walls is Lincoln County Gaol and a Prison Chapel. Near the prison buildings is another cross commemorating Queen Eleanor, who died nearby in the small village of Harby.

The Gift Shop is situated in the centre of the old Roman City of Lincoln, between the Cathedral and the Castle. For the last 400 years

371

Newport Arch, Lincoln

there has been a shop on this site and certain parts of the building date back to the 16th century.

The shop is very much a family business with everyone lending a helping hand. The original olde world charm of the shop remains very much alive and unchanged. We found an extensive range of gifts available from toys to ladies outerwear, and could not fail to sense the friendly atmosphere that filled the air. It made us feel relaxed and welcome.

Over the years the tea room has become a very successful part of the business and has an almost magnetic charm to it. We could not resist the temptation to stop and have a bite to eat. The tea room has an excellent menu, all of the food is home cooked, with a variety of homemade soups, meat and fruit pies all at extremely reasonable prices.

To add to the delight of this little shop there is a pleasant courtyard which is full of beautiful flowers. During the summer months customers are able to eat out side which gives one a chance to appreciate the heavy scent of the gorgeous blooms.

No visit to this historic town would be complete without a visit to The Gift Shop.

The Gift Shop, 5, Bailgate, Lincoln. 0522 523161

Lincoln Cathedral is said by many to be the finest in the country, and is certainly most impressive. Over nine hundred years old, the massive front tower stands proud, while the two towers at the southern end are splendid monuments to man's ability to put heart and soul into these ecclesiastical buildings. The interior is marvellous, and no few words can do justice to the carvings and soaring columns which meet the eye.

If you look carefully you will spot the Lincoln Imp, unofficial symbol of the city and a cheeky little devil, who sits cross-legged on top of a pillar overlooking St Hugh's shrine. Apparently carried on the

373

east wind, he caused a lot of damage in the cathedral, ripping up the vestments and generally hindering progress on the building of the shrine. When the angels saw the disruption caused by his mischievous behaviour, one of them threw a stone at him, hitting his leg. The imp immediately turned to stone, and he has sat on the spot ever since, rubbing his injured limb.

Opened in 1990 by HRH the Prince of Wales, **The Lawn** is Lincoln City Council's major new development, providing an ideal venue for conferences and entertainment, as well as housing an attractive shopping mall of specialist shops. The Lawn dates back to 1820 when it was known as The Lincoln Asylum. It was the country's first purpose-built mental hospital and pioneered the idea of removing physical restraint and isolation as forms of treatment for the mentally ill, and thus it became known as a caring hospital. It closed in the mid-1980s when it became surplus to health authority requirements and Lincoln City Council saw the potential of this vast building set within 8 acres of grounds and bought it. Following a multi-million pound renovation and restoration programme, a new Lawn has emerged, although the Council have retained much of the building's history within the new centre, with an interpretative gallery depicting the history of The Lawn since 1820.

The Lawn.   *Union Road, Lincoln*   *Tel: 0522 560330*

The facilities here are suitable for any major conferences, meetings, banquets, live entertainment, concerts and much more besides. Apart from these uses, The Lawn is a lovely place to wander, with 8 acres of attractively landscaped grounds to stroll in and picnic tables and a small children's play area to make use of. The Sir Joseph Banks Conservatory is a delightful tropical glasshouse with running water and a small aquarium, while the Lincoln Archaeology Centre has a fascinating public display area with 'hands-on' exhibits.

Another fascinating place to visit whilst here is the National Cycle

374

Museum, Britain's premier collection of cycles and associated artefacts. Here you can discover the changes in cycle design from 1820 onwards from old-fashioned boneshakers to modern racers and mountain bikes, and is something that will appeal to the whole family.

Among the specialist shops you'll find in The Lawn is The Fudge Factory, a haven for the sweet-toothed. Owned and personally run by Mrs. Williams, this is not the place for people on diets, although for the rest of us, it is sheer heaven. The Fudge Factory offers over 15 different varieties of fudge, all personally made by Mrs. Williams on the premises and only available here. However, this is not just a place that sells fudge - other delights are sold here including individually made chocolates, candy and ice cream as well as numerous quality crafts that make ideal mementos of your visit.

The Fudge Factory, The Lawn Visitors Centre, Lincoln

Bailgate takes you through the heart of 'Up-hill' Lincoln, and was the original main street of the Castle's outer bailey. We do not intend to present a blow-by-blow account of the wealth of splendid architecture and history to be enjoyed in this Roman and Medieval part of the town. One thing that impressed us strongly was that not only are the buildings or the sites on which they stand of great historical interest, but the shops and eating places which now occupy them offer such an interesting and varied choice.

Situated at the northern end of Bailgate, we discovered the **Duke William Hotel** which is reputed to be the 3rd oldest public house in Lincoln, dating back to the 16th century. It attracts a wide range of visitors who come to visit the Cathedral and Castle and potter around the Bailgate shopping area. Near to the hotel stands the Newport Arch, which dates back to the 2nd century and is the only Roman gateway in Britain open to traffic.

The hotel is very atmospheric, with original beams, stonework and fireplaces throughout the public rooms and bedrooms, some of which

offer splendid views of the cathedral. We were amazed at the enormou
bellows which are suspended from the ground floor ceilings and th
massive oaken door which lies against the restaurant wall is said t
have come from Lincoln prison. One wonders where the inmate
escaped to!

The Hotel offers 11 en-suite bedrooms and a function room suitabl
for informal dinners, meetings and receptions. A residents bar i
available throughout the evening for those of you who require
nightcap.

The restaurant speciality is homecooked fare with the Steak an
Real Ale Pie being a favourite among regulars. A good selection o
vegetarian dishes including Mushroom and Nut Fettucinni can b
washed down with an excellent range of traditional ales . The Duk
William is run by Peter Docherty and his friendly team of staff and yo
are assured of an informal and relaxing stay here with the emphasi
placed on you, the individual. While chatting to staff we discovere
that the hotel boasts its own ghost, although there is some confusio
as to its sex! It prefers to keep himself to herself apparently.

The Duke William Hotel, Bailgate, Lincoln. 0522 533351

If you are a connoisseur of fine whisky the **The Whisky Shop** o
the Old Bailgate, is the place to indulge yourself. Sandy Steel runs thi
highly successful and unique business and he or his assistants ar
always only too willing to help you in making a decision. This can b
a trifle difficult when their stock contains 250 - 300 different types o
whiskies!

We found that this shop is well worth a visit especially for educate
whisky drinkers who appreciate a good rare malt and who don't hav
the desire to travel all the way to Scotland in search of the 'rea
McCoy'. Until you start talking to experts like Mr Steel the uneducate
like ourselves haven't the slightest idea what a huge subject whisk
is.

376 The tiny little shop is stacked with every conceivable single mal

hisky and this forms a collection which even the most discerning
xpert would find hard to match, anywhere outside Scotland. This
mber nectar is available in full,half and miniature sized bottles. The
iiniatures we bought were ideal gifts for our malt loving friends and
e still have one or two left for stocking fillers at Christmas.

We enjoyed our little adventure into the whisky world enormously
nd will return next time we are in the neighbourhood to sample more
nd replenish our stock. For those who can't visit Lincoln on a regular
asis or wish to send someone a gift,the shop runs a mail order service
whisky often being sent back to Scotland!

The Whisky Shop, 87 Bailgate, Lincoln.   0522 537834.

Situated at the Northern end of Bailgate, we discovered the Duke
Villiam Hotel which is reputed to be the third oldest public house in
incoln, dating back to the 16th century. It attracts a wide range of
isitors who come to view the Cathedral and Castle and potter around
ie Bailgate shopping area. Near to the hotel stands the **Newport
rch,** which dates back to the second century and is the only Roman
ateway in Britain open to traffic.

For visitors to Lincoln, one excellent place to stay is **Minster Lodge
Iotel,** which is situated just 50 yards from the famous Newport Arch
the only remaining Roman Arch still in use and spanning a main
ioroughfare. Five minutes walk from here will bring you to Lincoln's
ther major attractions such as the Cathedral and the Castle. At
Iinster Lodge, one thing you can be sure of is that your comfort is of
ie utmost importance. All six of the guest rooms are en-suite and
Illy equipped, with the usual facilities plus radio, hair dryer and
censed bar to ensure you have all you need. Beautifully furnished
iroughout, there is a well appointed dining room where you can enjoy
 full English breakfast each morning to set you up for a day's
xploring.

377

Minster Lodge Hotel, 3 Church Lane, Lincoln. 0522 513220

We approached the end of our journey through Lincolnshire, an what better place to do so than in this beautiful 'dual' city. If you approach deposits you 'Up-hill', you could easily be forgiven fo imagining that the city stretches no further than this upper leve However, we do have a another recommendation for those wishing t learn something of the history and present day Lincoln but still enjo time in the surrounding countryside.

The Red Lion.   Dunston. Lincs.   Tel: 0526 322227.

Well known throughout the area for its excellent food and ale is th very impressive **Red Lion Country Inn and Restaurant** in th picturesque village of **Dunston** on the B1188. Dating back to the 17t century, it was formerly a row of farm workers one up, one dow cottages. The Inn now oozes character and style with stone expose walls, a stone inglenook fireplace and low wooden beams enhancin its charm. A free house, the inn boast a variety of well kept ales an

378

food second to none. Besides the set menu, there is a large choice of daily specials. The Red Lion also has a supper licence and on Sundays you can enjoy their special lunch menu. Whether you eat in the lounge or the 40 seater restaurant, you'll not be disappointed. Outside there is a large car park, a smashing childrens play area, well tended gardens where barbecue's are held in the summer when the exterior of the inn is awash with colour from the hanging baskets and splendid arrays of flowers. Friendly hosts and staff go alongside the first class facilities making the Red Lion a place you will want to return to time and time again.

So our meandering journey through Lincolnshire came to an end. Despite its flat appearance the county proved to have a deep and rich history with many places of interest awaiting your visit. We hope that we have increased your curiosity with our journey and whetted your appetites so we can only urge you to visit this county that decieves the eye in many ways.

The Lancaster Bomber of the Battle of Britain Memorial Flight

CHAPTER FOURTEEN

North Nottinghamshire

Welbeck Abbey

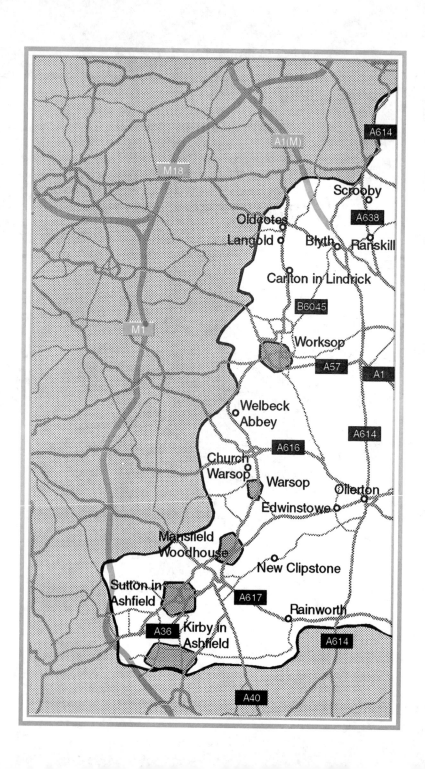

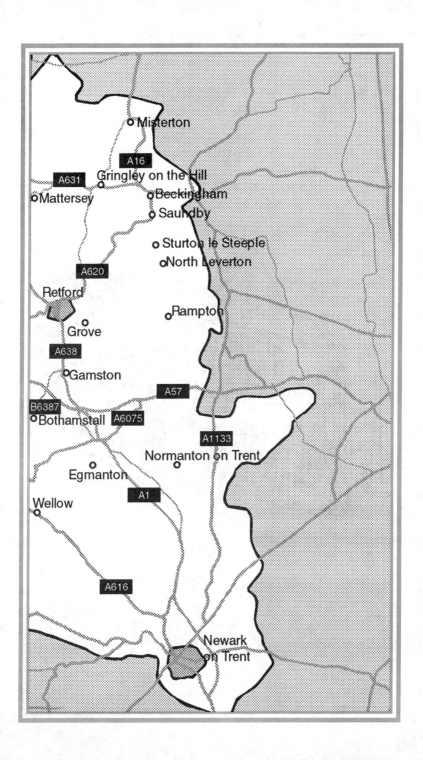

Wellbeck Abbey.

CHAPTER FOURTEEN.

North Nottinghamshire.

North Nottinghamshire is the land of the Pilgrim Fathers, and in the central part of the county you will find the great Dukeries, the collective name for the four estates governed by the dukes who owned these lands. There are lovely houses to discover throughout the county like **Newstead Abbey, Hodsock Priory**, and the beautiful **Wollaton Hall.** There are large tracts of parkland to explore, and you will come to love the forests of Clumber and Sherwood with their timeless atmosphere and the sense of parts played in the myths that are woven into the history of these Isles. The hills and vales seemed to ripple like a tablecloth that has been spread upon the ground as we drove. The pretty, nestling villages lie like tiny becalmed islands in this lovely expanse. If one could see the country with a bird's eye view, the gently undulating swells of land would appear to slope down to the horizon and tip into the Lincolnshire wolds. Not a geographical accuracy, but an instinctive feeling that this land lies secure between its larger western neighbour Derbyshire, and the sea-bound Lincolnshire.

The area we decided to visit first was the district of **Bassetlaw**, which begins just above **Warsop** and extends up to Nottinghamshire's northern borders. Its name is derived from the Old English word 'wapentake' which was the name given to the division of a shire. However, we failed to see how the intervening years have changed that word into the present day 'Bassetlaw'.

The four ducal estates which make up 'The Dukeries' are **Welbeck, Worksop, Clumber** and **Thoresby.** Welbeck, the first of these estates, was our starting place. Just off the A60 to the east of Creswell Crags, stands **Welbeck Abbey**. It was founded as a house for the religious order of the Premonstratensians in 1153. In 1597 after the dissolution of the monasteries, it passed into the hands of Sir Charles Cavendish, the third son of Bess of Hardwick. Still owned by the Cavendish-Bentinck family today, it is unfortunately not open to the public. Entrance into the estate grounds is through the beautiful Lion Gate just outside Worksop, and one of the most impressive sights here is the Great Lake which sprawls across the estate. It is fed by the River Poulter, which approaches from the west then goes on to feed the lake at the neighbouring estate of Clumber.

The small hamlet of **Norton** is situated in the heart of the Welbeck Estate, part of Sherwood Forest, and can be reached off the A60 Worksop to Mansfield Road. It is here, tucked away on a no-through road that you will find **Norton Grange**, a 170 mixed arable farm run by Fernie Palmer, a welcoming host who has been providing bed and breakfast for his many guests for the past 23 years. The impressive ETB Listed Georgian stone farmhouse has a cosy, homely atmosphere and provides a peaceful setting for a relaxing break away and there are 3 spacious and well equipped guest rooms to choose from.

Norton Grange Farm, Norton, Cuckney. 0623 842666

We continued south on the A60 until we came to the village of **Cuckney**. In the village, we were able to see some of the lovely cottages that were part of the Welbeck estate. The church has a splendid thirteenth-century tower and was seriously threatened by subsidence. Because of this, some of the bays and arches have been strengthened by iron supports. Just outside the village, you can see the huge arched doors of the eighteenth-century barns at Hatfield Grange Farm.

A few miles further on we reached **Church Warsop** which, sitting on top of the hill, is separated by the River Meden from the town of Warsop itself. Although the town has little to offer the tourist, Church Warsop is worth a visit. The church with its Norman tower has an elegant arcade, and numerous monuments dedicated to local dignitaries. To the west of the church, we saw a group of buildings that really epitomised the charm of the village, with a seventeenth-century converted barn which now functions as the parish hall.

386

Situated on the main road at **Old Clipstone** you will discover a welcome stopping -off point at **The Dog & Duck**. This former farmhouse dates back to the early 19th century and is a fine example of a traditional family pub with old fashioned values. Mike and Maria Coleman are super hosts who make all of their customers feel welcome, locals and visitors alike. There is a wide selection of ale available, including regular guest beers and an excellent menu of homecooked food is provided each lunchtime and evening with a choice of blackboard specials. The restaurant seats 46, but it is advisable to book Sunday Lunch. Outside there is ample off-road parking and two children's play areas to keep younger family members amused.

The Dog & Duck, Main Rd. Old Clipstone. 0623 822138

Picking up the A6075, we found ourselves getting ever nearer to Robin Hood country. Inevitably, once we arrived at **Edwinstowe,** all the signs pointed to Sherwood. The church dates back to the twelfth century, and it is said that Robin and Maid Marian were wed here. King Edwin, who gave the village its name, died in battle in 633 and his burial place is close by. The village became the most important settlement in the forest, and as one of the main routes to Sherwood passes through it, it still attracts a fair number of 'pilgrims' today.

Not far from Edwinstowe off the A6075 you will discover **Sherwood Forest Farm Park**, a naturalist and animal lover's delight. Enjoying a peaceful setting in a secluded valley within Sherwood Forest, the Farm Park boasts no fewer than 30 rare and threatened species of farm animal and is beautifully laid out, with ornamental ponds, two wildfowl lakes, a pets corner and a delightful aviary full of exotic birds. There is so much to see and do that a fun day out for the whole family is guaranteed. Younger family members will appreciate the adventure playground and everyone can enjoy the guided nature tours on the tractor and trailer which takes you around the farmland adjacent to

387

the Park. With a tearoom, gift shop, picnic area and much more besides, there is too much to list here, so your best bet is to visit and see for yourself.

Sherwood Forest Farm Park.   Edwinstowe.   0623 823558/822255.

Adjacent to Sherwood Forest Farm Park, holidaymakers will find a peaceful retreat at **Sherwood Forest Caravan Park** which stands in over 20 acres of beautiful countryside which has been tastefully landscaped very much with the environment in mind. This 5 Tick graded park offers a haven to various forms of wildlife and there are many picturesque walks which bring you into the farm park, for which residents can obtain half price entrance tickets. There is a boating and fishing lake for guests use and plenty of childrens play areas all close to the caravan plots. There are a few static caravans, but this is a park mainly for tourers.

A little way up the road is the Visitor Centre; Sherwood - The Shire Wood - was once a great woodland mass, stretching from Nottingham to Worksop. Although only relatively small pockets of the original forest remain today, it is still possible to lose yourself amongst the trees, both figuratively and literally! Whether or not Robin and his Merry Men ever did frolic in the 'greenshawe' is debatable. Arguments still rage as to which particular historical figure gave rise to the legend of the famous outlaw. Records from the twelfth century suggest a number of possible candidates, including the Earl of Huntingdon.

Undeterred by the vague foundations upon which the legend is built, visitors still flock to see the great hollow tree which the outlaws purportedly used as a meeting place and as a cache for their supplies. The Major Oak, which is located about ten minutes walk along the main track in the heart of the forest. This huge tree, which is not so much tall as broad, with its massive wooden 'crutches' and supportive iron corsets presents a rather forlorn sight. There is no denying that

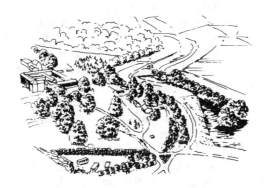

Sherwood Forest Caravan Park, Nr.Edwinstowe. 0623 823132

it is at least 500 years old, and some sources would claim it to be more than double that figure. Yet despite its appearance, the tree is still alive thanks to careful preservation. Recent tests have established that some parts of the tree have successfully taken to grafting, and one hopes that at some stage a whole colony of 'minor oaks' may be produced.

The Visitor Centre houses a display of characters from the Robin Hood stories, with appropriate scenes of merry making. This theme has been more successfully translated to the city of Nottingham in the Tales of Robin Hood exhibition, and the children certainly enjoy it.

The ruined **Rufford Abbey** is screened from the **A614,** although through the massive gates you can see a tantalising glimpse of the house from the road. Built of a soft red stone, this former Cistercian Abbey was founded in 1148. Following the Dissolution, the lands passed into the hands of the 6th Earl of Shrewsbury, Bess's husband. The church and related buildings were dismantled and the great Elizabethan house we see today was erected. The sad fate of the house was to pass down through many generations until in this century following military occupation, it was abandoned. Left to deteriorate, it was eventually bought by the County Council, and most of the house including the staircase and staterooms was demolished.

Said to be haunted by the ghost of a giant monk with a skull-like face, there is written 'evidence' in the parish register for Edwinstowe that a man died of fright after catching sight of this unholy visitor! Although the ruins are inaccessible, you are able to wander around the lovely parkland with its 25 acre lake and crafts centre.

Heading north on the A614 towards Worksop, we crossed the River

Meden and turned left down a lane which brought us to the Victorian mansion of **Thoresby Hall**. It was built for the Pierrepont family by Anthony Salvin in 1864, and was completed in 1871. It is the third house to have stood on the site and presents a wonderful show of furniture and weaponry. The Great Hall is 64 feet long and its interesting mixture of styles can be seen to advantage from the galleries. In its heyday, the house was said to have required an indoor staff of nearly fifty, and looking at the wonderful Blue Drawing Room with its Louis XVI chairs, it still presents a very regal air. There is a deer park and a riverside walk, and the extensive grounds of 12,000 acres are lovely to walk around.

Back on the A614 and just a few miles further north, we came to one of the several entrances to **Clumber Park.** The Normanton Gate is opposite the Normanton Inn on the main road, and the long drive eventually took us to the estate village of **Hardwick.**

The first building we noticed was the magnificent Victorian Gothic Revival chapel, built of pink and grey stone by Bodley and completed in 1889. Standing alone beside the 85 acre lake, its spire pointing majestically upwards, you can immediately understand why it is often referred to as a 'cathedral in miniature'.

The building of **Clumber House** began in 1760, and was the home of the Dukes of Newcastle. After a series of fires, the house was demolished in 1938, and all that remains of it today is the foundations.

However, any sense of disappointment is quickly dispelled by the charm of the buildings that remain in this lovely setting. The estate houses with their high pitched gables and massive chimneys are most impressive. The red-brick stables are particularly fine, as they are surmounted by a clocktower crowned by a domed cupola. The inset clock in the tower dates back to 1763, and the stables now house the cafe and visitor centre.

The park is owned by the National Trust and attracts many visitors, especially throughout the summer when special events are arranged. However, with the huge area of woodland and riverbanks to explore, you can always escape from the masses. The lake is particularly lovely, and away from the main walks, you can watch the swans and ducks go about their daily chores unaware of your presence.

One of the other entrances to the park is through the Apleyhead Gate, farther north on the A614. This will take you on a marvellous ride along a double row of limes, planted over a century ago with a total of 1,296 trees. Known as the 'Duke's Drive' and stretching for a distance of two miles, it is now established as the longest avenue of limes in Europe.

The **A57** runs along the north side of Clumber Park, and it was this road which took us into the town of **Worksop**. One of the important duties of the Lord of the Manor of this ancient town is to provide a glove for the coronation of a new monarch. Despite the unattractive modern houses that lead into the town, there are some fine Georgian buildings in Bridge Street. A real attraction of Worksop is the **Priory Gatehouse**. The best place to approach this from is Potter Street, where you can see the full glory of the fourteenth-century building. Its great niches house large and beautifully carved statues, and the immense entrance is rather reminiscent of a cave opening. Originally the portal to a large Augustinian monastery, the gatehouse together with the church of St Mary and St Cuthbert is all that remains. There is also a wayside shrine, which makes it a unique ecclesiastical attraction. Today, the upper floor of the gatehouse houses an art gallery, and exhibitions are put on here regularly .

In the heart of Worksop, across from Worksop Market, **The Lion Hotel** has been looking after the needs of weary travellers for over 400 years. Although completely modernised, it still oozes with charm and character from years gone by. Luxuriously decorated and furnished throughout, there is an excellent lounge bar, an elegant restaurant, a function rom and 32 wonderful bedrooms, all en-suite and equipped for maximum comfort. This is definitely a place fit for a King, but frequented by all walks of life, with welcoming and friendly staff soon putting you at your ease and ensuring your stay is pleasurable and relaxing.

The Lion Hotel, 112 Bridge St., Worksop.   0909 477925

A recent acquisition by the National Trust in Worksop, 7 Blyth Grove, is unusual, quite unique and also well worth a visit. The familiar looking house and a million pounds was left to the Trust by William Straw, who were surprised to find upon inspection of the Edwardian semi-detached house that they were actually stepping back in time. Inside, everything had been preserved from 1932 when

391

William Straw, a grocer and seed merchant in Worksop died. Seven years later their mother died and the two sons, William and Walter lived a bachelor exsistence. Walter taking on the family business, died in 1976; William after first teaching at the City of London College eventually returned to look after the house, died in 1990. In all those years, little changed, their parents bedroom was closed up and everything left as it was; a 1932 calender still hangs on the wall, their father's hats still perch in the hall and his pipes and tobacco pouch are ready by the fireside. During this time William documented passionately and was known for his dislike 'anything new' as well as a reluctance to throw things away, including bills. Now the Trust have a unique record of social history of those times with a display of items that reflects life as it was in the 1930's and the earlier decades of this century.

Heading north from Worksop on the **A60,** we came to the ancient village of **Carlton-in-Lindrick.** The name has a delightful meaning - 'the freedmen's enclosure in the limewood'. The church with its massive Saxon tower is quite awe inspiring as it soars above the village. In Church Lane, we spotted the **Old Mill Museum** which is a converted eighteenth-century water mill. It houses some unusual linen pictures which were used by the Victorians as educational 'material', as well as farming implements and mill machinery. You will have to make arrangements to view in the spring and summer months, but admission is free.

Although the next village of **Langold** does not have any inherent attractions, there is a magnificent quadrangular farm building just off the main road, known as Hodsock Grange. This is not to be confused with the other lovely house of Hodsock Priory in nearby Blyth which we will come to later.

Just off the A60 on the **A634** is the small village of **Oldcotes** with its cluster of stone cottages and houses. A pretty brook runs through the village, and we saw an unusually styled farmhouse with Gothic windows. Another building with Gothic hallmarks is Hermeston Hall a rather plain house. The Roman Catholic church with its lovely interior was built in 1869 for the owner of Hermeston, on the site of a Roman villa.

Situated between Blyth and Oldcotes on the A634, **The Charnwood** is an impressive hotel and restaurant owned and personally run by friendly hosts Nick and Liz Williams. Although only some 30 years old, this AA and RAC 3 Star establishment has a certain grandeur and style. The Charnwood stands in 3 acres of land with magnificent scenic views, and in the 9 years since they came here, Nick and Liz have tastefully extended the building to incorporate

20 beautifully furnished en-suite guest rooms. There is ample off-road parking, which is just as well, because The Lantern Restaurant is open to non-residents and proves highly popular. Seating up to 65, the intimate ambience is enhanced by exposed brick walls and alcove seating. The menu is simply mouthwatering, with a vast range of gastronomic delights to tempt every palate and the Sunday lunch menu offers a selection beyond the traditional roast.

The Charnwood, Blyth, 0909 591610 Fax 0909 591429

Approaching **Blyth** on the A634, the first thing we noticed was the great tower of the Church of St Mary and St Martin, which looms above the village and commands your immediate attention. The eight tall pinnacles are linked by a delicate tracery of stone that gives a surprising grace to the tower. 900 years old, it is one of the most important Norman buildings in this country. Although the first impression is of a gothic structure, the Norman windows give its origins away. The church epitomises the French love of dignity and simplicity, rather solemn, but still quite lovely.

There are many other buildings of distinction in the village, including a handsome stable block and the former rectory which is surmounted by a cupola. Among the red-brick Georgian houses you will discover a number of coaching inns, a reminder that Blyth was once an important staging post on the Great North Road.

From its pretty exterior to its cosy and welcoming interior, **The White Swan** in Blyth is everything you would expect of a typical country pub.Situated opposite the village green, this charming inn is 17th century in origin as is apparent from the timbered ceilings and walls. A warm, friendly atmosphere is enhanced by roaring log fires for those chillier days and Peter and Elaine Franklin together with their daughter Lorraine have developed The White Swan into an establishment renowned for fine ale and excellent food with a varied menu that always includes fresh fish dishes.

At the far end of the village is **St John's Hospital**, which was originally founded as a leper hospital in the twelfth century and later converted into a school. The former schoolhouse stands on a diamond shaped 'island' of grass, obviously dating back to a time when these poor unfortunates (the lepers, not the pupils!) would have been kept isolated from the villagers.

Whilst in the area, don't miss the chance of a visit to **Hodsock Priory** and its beautiful gardens. This is situated only a mile and a half south-west of Blyth, and stands within its own parkland and meadows. Although this would make a perfect setting for a medieval monastery, no priory ever stood here. The present house was built in 1829 in a brick Tudor style to complement the marvellous sixteenth-century gatehouse.

The gatehouse is approached across an ancient rectangular moat, and within this area the gardens have been laid. The southern arm of the moat was made into a small lake around 1880. The gardens are well known for their shrub roses, and the owners Sir Andrew and Lady Buchanan are more than happy to welcome the public into their lovely grounds.

Leaving Blyth on the **B6045** we came to **Ranskill**, then headed north on the **A638** towards **Bawtry.** Our route took us through the village of **Scrooby,** which has close associations with the Pilgrim Fathers. The settlement of 'Scroppenthorp' existed here before 958 AD. In that year King Edgar granted the land rights to Oscytel, the Archbishop of York. But Scrooby's greatest claim to fame is through William Brewster, who was a founder member of the Pilgrim Fathers.

It was at Cambridge that his radical ideas on religion were formed, and his spell in the Netherlands with its toleration of religious views gave him a new perspective. In 1598 he was summoned before the ecclesiastical court for poor church attendance, which was to lead him on the path to Separatism. This eventually forced him to resign his post and he became outlawed for his views. He was imprisoned for a short time in Boston in Lincolnshire, but eventually resurfaced in Amsterdam. After some years he returned to England, and in 1620 he left again on board the 'Mayflower'. He was by now an elder of the Separatist Church and the group later became known as the Pilgrim Fathers. He and his colleagues founded a colony in Plymouth, New England. He died in America in 1644 aged about 77.

For such a small village, Scrooby has a wealth of other interesting features. There is a stone walled pinfold near the churchyard where straying cattle or sheep were rounded up and released on payment of a fine. The Pilgrim Fathers Inn dates back to 1771, although it was originally called The Saracen's Head. The Monks Mill, which stands

The White Swan, Blyth. 0909 591222

on the old course of the River Ryton, is now a private dwelling and despite the name it has never had any close associations with a monastery.

Scrooby was also the scene of a particularly grisly murder. In 1779, a shepherd from North Leverton called John Spencer murdered the local tollbar keeper, William Yealdon, and his mother Mary. Caught in the act of trying to dispose of the bodies in the river nearby, Spencer was later executed at Nottingham Assizes. His body was then taken back to Scrooby to hang in chains from a gibbet, specially erected near the scene of the crime.

The Old George and Dragon, Scrooby, Nr.Doncaster 0302 711840

`Situated adjacent to the Great Northern Road in the village of Scrooby, the home of the original Pilgrim Father, you will find a lovely holiday base at **The Old George and Dragon**. This former public house was built in 1738 and had its first landlord in 1832. Today it is the charming home of Georgina and John Smithers who provide first class bed and breakfast accommodation in 3 comfortable and well equipped guest rooms, two with en-suite facilities. The house is beautifully furnished throughout and one of the bedrooms is very unusual and quaint, but wait and see for yourself because this is definitely a superior holiday base in every way.

South-east of Scrooby, just off the B6045, look out for a rough lane at the end of **Mattersey** village. The lane leads down to the ruined **Mattersey Priory**, which was founded in 1185 for the Gilbertine Order. It was the only monastic order to be founded solely by the English. This site is rarely visited by tourists and with the River Idle nearby, it is one of those quiet spots that you will always remember.

Just a few hundred yards off the main A631 Bawtry to Gainsborough Road, **The Griff Inn** at Drakeholes is the perfect place to pause your journey, whether you fancy a refreshing drink, a first class meal, or a comfortable place to spend the night. Built 200 years ago by the then owner Johnathan Acklom, to serve the increased trade brought about by the new Chesterfield Canal, the inn, then known as The White Swan went into decline some years later with the arrival of the railway system, until it was rescued in 1982 and restored to its former glory. Its present owners Norman and Barbara Edmanson now run it with the help of their son Mike. Beautifully furnished throughout this is a super country inn with a cosy snug full of character, a comfortable lounge, and a terrific dining area called The Peach Room. The menu is both extensive and imaginative, far above the usual pub fare and the guest rooms are again superior, being very spacious and equipped with full facilities for maximum comfort. You would have to go a long way to find another pub to match this one, so don't miss it.

The Griff Inn, Drakeholes,Nr Everton,Bawtry. 0777 817206

At the end of the B6045, we turned right onto the A631 which led us to the village of **Gringley-on-the-Hill.** The hill stands proud of this rather flat landscape, and from here we caught a glimpse of the

396

Idle and the Chesterfield Canal as they meander across the southern lowlands. With its lovely houses and dovecotes and its picturesque farms, the village is the sort of photogenic place that is often reproduced on postcards and the jigsaw trade.

From Gringley we took the **B1403** to **Misterton.** Through the village, the Chesterfield Canal passes on its way to West Stockwith, where it joins the River Trent. We were able to walk along the towpath, nodding to the barge-owners and 'river-rats' who make for the Anchor Inn. Surrounded by old cottages and farm buildings, the church has a rather stumpy spire, which rises from its tower without a parapet - known in the trade as a 'broach spire'. A notable feature of the church can be found in the Lady Chapel. This is the stained glass window designed by John Piper, which depicts the Crucifixion using the symbols of hands and feet and the Sacred Heart.

To the east lie the villages of **West** and **East Stockwith**. West Stockwith is the most northerly village in Nottinghamshire, and was once an important inland port with warehouses and boat building yards. The Canal, Trent and Idle join here, and although some of the bustle of the port has died down, the rivers are full of boats and barges jostling for mooring space. There is plenty here to entertain you - the towpath walk to Misterton, a narrow boat ride along the canal, or a fascinating visit to the dolls' museum next to the White Hart pub in the main street. Neighbouring East Stockwith is just over the border in Lincolnshire standing on the east bank of the Trent.

The Blacksmiths Arms & Wiseton Restaurant Clayworth 0777 818171

Following the A161 southbound, we by-passed **Beckingham** and headed down towards **Saundby** on the **A620**. This tiny village has a lovely church tower, which is almost hidden by immense yews and cedars. In the tiny hamlet of nearby **Clayworth** you will discover a rare gem when you call in at **The Blacksmiths Arms and Wiseton**

Restaurant. Dating back to the 17th century, it was formerly a smithy and a license was granted in the early 19th century. Roger and Katy are welcoming hosts who in the short time they have been here, have refurbished the premises to the highest standards. This is very much a restaurant first and an inn second. Original beams and timber work is now enhanced by designer furniture and fabrics and all the tables are beautifully laid out with the finest crystal and crockery. The 'a la carte and table d'hote menus provide a varied choice of the finest cuisine, accompanied by an excellent wine list, all of which makes this one place you are sure to return to time and again.

We followed a minor road through **North Wheatley** to **Sturton-le-Steeple.** 'Sturton' is a corruption of the word 'Stretton', which means 'the town on the street.' The origin of the second part of the name is immediately obvious once you approach the village. The splendid tower with its twelve impressive pinnacles rises above the houses, and is quite the highest point for miles around in this flat landscape. It was formerly part of the church, which was destroyed by fire in 1901. Apart from the steeple, little survives.

The Reindeer, Sturton-le Steeple, Notts. 0427 880298.

Situated in the tiny hamlet, **The Reindeer** pub enjoys an idyllic and picturesque setting beside the village church with the green and duck pond to the front. Formerly called The Stag Inn, there has been a building here since the 18th century and a licence was granted in the early 19th century. Terry and Kath came here 6 years ago and their careful efforts at refurbishment have not detracted from the building's original character and charm. Three things make The Reindeer a very special place; the cosy, welcoming atmosphere, the excellent homecooked food served lunchtime and evenings (except Tues Evenings) and the excellent range of ale which includes 3 cask brands.

We noticed several windmills in the vicinity as we drove around, but one of the loveliest in our opinion is the one at **North Leverton.**

It is particularly attractive, and is the only working windmill in the county. The great irony is that it stands almost overshadowed by two massive power stations, a meeting of two completely diverse sources of power. The windmill was built in 1813, and despite some rebuilding has always looked pretty much as it does today.

The windmill is open to visitors most days except Tuesdays, and if you would like to make bread from freshly ground flour, Mr Barlow who runs the mill will be glad to oblige. Admission is in the form of a voluntary donation, or you could become a member of the Friends of the Windmill Association.

From North Leverton - North Leverton with Habblesthorpe, to give the village its full name - the land rises noticeably with gentle hills. To the south east one of the premier attractions in Nottinghamshire has to be **Sundown Adventureland** at Rampton which is a truly magical place for children up to the age of about ten. Set in 10 acres, what started off as a hobby 25 years ago for owners Mr. and Mrs. Rhodes, grew and developed into the wonderland that it is today. Here children can immerse themselves in their favourite stories and fairytales, for this is the place where nursery rhymes, cowboy and indians, knights and dragons and every other childhood fantasy come magically to life. When they have had their fill of thrills, spills and adventure they can enjoy the more sedate activity of meeting the friendly animals in the Pets Garden and before leaving can pick up the perfect memento of their visit in the souvenir shop.

Sundown Adventureland, Rampton near Retford. Tel: 0777 248274

In the picturesque Trent side village of **Laneham** stands **The Old Cottage Guest House**, a delightful house believed to date back to the late 17th century and judging by its style and appearance, this is probably so. Having served a variety of different purposes over the years, among other things it has previously been a smithy, petrol station and restaurant. Since Mike and Anne Hardman bought it ten years ago they have gradually developed The Old Cottage into a super holiday base, with four lovely beamed guest rooms providing very comfortable en-suite accommodation. There is a pleasant garden with ample parking space and Mike and Anne have created a Post Office and Shop within a converted barn. If required, in addition to a full breakfast, they will provide guests with excellent homecooked evening meals with drinks available from the licensed bar.

The Old Cottage Guest House, Main Street, Laneham. 0777 228555

Situated on the A57 Retford to Lincoln road at Dunham On Trent, **Wilmot House** is ideally situated as a touring base for visitors to this

Wilmot House, Church Walk, Dunham on Trent. 0777 228226

lovely part of Nottinghamshire. This Georgian listed building was the village shop until the early 1970s and the name Wilmot comes from the name of the grocer who ran it. Now the charming home of Ruth and David East, guests here are immediately aware of a warm, homely atmosphere and will soon find themselves relaxing. There are 4 attractively furnished guest rooms, one with en-suite facilities, and the Easts are happy to provide packed lunches and evening meals on request. The beautifully laid out gardens are a picture and the house lies only a short walk away from the River Trent, all of which makes this a super place to stay.

Coming via minor roads to **Grove** village with it's noble church spire, we were struck by the peacefulness of this rather solitary place. Situated within the old walled gardens of the old Grove Hall Estate in the small village of Grove,you will discover **Grove Garden Centre and Nursery**, a place where you can browse at your leisure and can be sure of finding just what you are loking for. Since he started the centre, the present owner Mr Wallwin has developed it into a thriving business, with a large selection of quality trees, shrubs and plants for the home and garden, including specialities such as Camellias, Hydrangeas, and Conifers.

In addition to various garden sundries, you can choose from a range of lovely terracotta, porcelain and stone plant containers. Having made your purchases, the real treat of your visit has to be relaxing in teh delightful tea garden with its palms and fountain, and sampling the range of mouthwatering homemade cakes and scones with a fresh pot of tea.

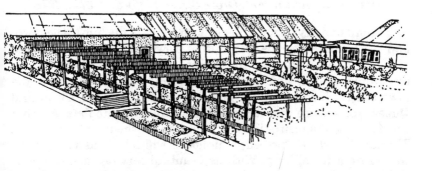

Grove Garden Centre, Grove Hall Gardens, Grove. 0777 703182

Three miles west of Grove is the lovely old market town of **Retford**. The town has grown in importance over the centuries, from the granting of its charter by Henry III in 1246, to the prosperity bought to it by the railway and canal links. The town is divided by the River Idle, and as you approach it, the churches seem to vie with each other for attention as they rise above their respective parishes.

Visitors to this quaint town will find the perfect place to stop for lunch or a tasty snack when they call in at **Boaters Family Restaurant**, a licensed establishment run by John and Angela Tetley. This attractive listed building is situated on Grove Street,itself a listed street, just 70 yards from the market square. As you walk through the door, you can be forgiven for thinking you have just entered a beautiful garden, for all around you is a wooden lattice with shrubbery and flowers that enhance the 'garden' theme. The menu is so varied and imaginative, including a vegetarian 'Dish of the Day', a childrens menu and special ice creams, so there is sure to be something to appeal to the most particular palate and the reasonable prices make this is a very popular eating house.

Boaters Family Restaurant. Grove Street, Retford.   0777 701818.

Retford has a typical market square which is the hub of the town, and is dominated by the magnificent Town Hall. As we wandered along Rectory Road near the parish church of St Michael's, we discovered a farm, which seemed a strange location so near to the town centre. Just beyond the farm is West Retford Hall, a beautiful Queen Anne house that has now been converted into flats. Another charming building can be found opposite the almshouse in Churchgate. This is a tiny white-stuccoed gothic house, which looks as if it has been carved from Royal icing. With its beautiful carvings and exquisite 'frill' under the roof tiles, it looks rather like a wedding cake. One of the town's most infamous visitors was the highwayman Dick Turpin, and several historic inns still stand to remind us of the old coaching days. Another man who 'stood and delivered' here in a more respectable fashion was John Wesley, who conducted many of his open air meetings in East Retford.

The Market Hotel in Retford, formerly known as the Cattle Market Hotel, stands on the historic site of the old cattlemarket with the now disused Harwich to Liverpool Railway running alongside it. To one side of the Hotel where there were once piggeries and a tack salesroom, there is now a magnificent function room, ideal for wedding receptions and private parties.

This delightful hotel has been in the Brunt family for 20 years and is now run by Ray and his son Graham. Ray prides himself on the wide range of real ales he stocks in the cosy bar, having no less than 14 different varieties at any one time. He is also justifiably proud of the superb and extensive menu which includes a wide range of mouthwatering fish dishes- watch out for the size of the Scarboro' Haddock!

The Market Hotel, West Carr Rd, Retford. 0777 703278.

On the A620 which is Gainsborough Road 10 minutes walk from the town centre, is the delightful **Tanamara Guest House.** Owned and personally run by Dee and Wally Craig if it is homeliness coupled with first class facilities and good cooking you are after, you will find it here. The interior is a picture, beautifully furnished and individually styled bedrooms, some with en-suite facilities, a lounge, breakfast room, and a packed lunch and evening meal can be provided by prior arrangement.Smoking and non-smoking rooms are available.

Tanamara, 167 Moorgate Cottage,Retford. 0777 706447

Standing on the edge of Retford in its own Magnificent grounds, the **West Retford Hotel** is an impressive 18th century manor house which offers the discerning guest a luxurious retreat for thet relaxing break away from the hustle and bustle of everyday life. The grand exterior is matched by the beautiful interior decor and furnishings and the ornate ceilings are simply breathtaking. The whole place exudes an air of elegance and class, yet the atmosphere is warm and friendly and you can immediately feel your cares falling away. Each of the 60 guest rooms is attractively furnished and equipped to the high standards one expects of a hotel with a 4 Crown rating. Dining is a treat, with a restaurant menu that will have you lingering as you savour the finest cuisine accompanied by an extensive wine list. If it's the finer things in life you are after, you will find them all at the West Retford Hotel.

West Retford Hotel . Retford. 0777 706333 Fax 0777 709951

Somewhat hidden but well worth seeking out, **The Barns** in **Babworth** can be found by taking the A620 out of Retford towards

The Barns, Morton Farm, Babworth, Retford. 0777 706336

Worksop, turning left at Babworth on the A6420 and this splendid 18th century former barn stands about 200 yards on your right Formerly a barn within a farm long since gone, The Barns is the charming home of Rosalie Brammer who enjoys sharing it with her many guests. She provides superb accommodation in 6 individually styled and beautifully furnished en-suite guest rooms. A warm welcoming atmosphere is immediately apparent and the immaculate decor is in keeping with the exposed oak beams and roaring log fires which lend The Barns so much character. One professional gentleman came to stay for one night and has now made return visits for the past three years, which must be the best recommendation you can get.

We headed south from Retford on the Old North Road, or the **A638** to give it its less romantic name! The River Idle runs parallel to the road, and we passed through the village of **Eaton**. All the communities in this area have a feeling of tranquility and timelessness about them. In **Headon,** however, the inhabitants bestir themselves once a year to carry on the custom of Well Dressing - the only village outside of Derbyshire to do this. With only the occasional droning of light aircraft at Gamston airfield and little else to distract you, this gentle landscape is ideal for the walker.

Run of the Mill Restaurant &Hotel, Rockley.   0777 838669.

Despite its name, **The Run of the Mill Restaurant** in **Rockley** is far from that, in fact it is a top class establishment, renowned for its excellent cuisine. Enjoying an outstanding location, the restaurant is set in 10 acres of scenic countryside and straddles the River Maun. The existing mill dates back to 1796,although there was mention of a mill on this site in the Domesday Book. Sympathetic restoration by the owners has created a wonderful place full of character and history,with old mill stones and other relics from its former mill days making attractive ornaments. The tables were made from a cedar of Lebanon tree belonging to the adjoining house,which blew down in 1989 and personal touches add to what is sure to be a superb meal. The menu is imaginative and extensive, offering something to suit every palate, but as the restaurant only seats up to 50, it is preferable to book to avoid disappointment. Ensuite accommodation is available and the restaurant is located only half a mile from the A1 Markham roundabout.

After **Gamston** we took the **B6387,** crossed the A1, and headed towards **Ollerton.** Situated on the A616 Newark to Sheffield road, a mile and a half from Ollerton, you will discover an excellent stopping -off point at **The Durham Ox** . An attractive 17th century former coaching inn, it has been refurbished and extended over the years, yet still retains its individual character and charm. David and Julie Preston bought the Durham Ox some 4 years ago you would be hard put to find a more cosy or friendly pub. Roaring log fires greet you on cold wintry days, enhancing the delightful decor, with smart comfortable seating, a stylish bar area and walls adorned with brass and bygone memorabilia. david has been in catering since the age of 15 and has gained many qualifications, which explains why the Durham Ox has such a fine reputation for food. Children are most welcome and have their own menu with the use of a well equipped play area.

The Durham Ox, Wellow, Notts. 0623 861026

Just before reaching **Bothamsall** the two rivers the Meden and the Maun finally merge to become the River Idle. This pretty village with its twisting lane has a pleasant church that looks much older than it is, only dating back to 1845. There was a church on this site originally which dated back to the fourteenth century, but the only relics of this that remain are a few monuments and the font.

A road to the west of the village took us up Castle Hill. The ruined outer wall of a castle and an artificial motte formed part of the defences here, although no other evidence points to it being a large fortification. The views from this hill allow you to see the lovely plantations forming Clumber and Thoresby to the west. To the east, almost hidden in its wooded grounds, is **Lound Hall**. This neo-Georgian house was rebuilt in 1937, and is now open to the public as a **National Mining Museum** as well as serving as a training centre.

Thaymar Dairy Ice Cream is produced at Haughton Park Farm near Bothamstall, easy to find, it is just a short distance from the A1. A most attractive and well kept farm, it offers a real treat to the traveller. The Ice Cream produced by Thelma Cheetham is truly superb. Real home produced Ice Cream made only with the best natural ingredients. The variety is enormous and ingredients come from as far afield as Italy and Mauritius. An exceptional treat for warm Summer days or indeed dessert, flavourings such as Marsala, Rum and Raisin, Coconut Creme, Caramel, Coffee Truffle, Kiwi, and pure Mediterranean Lemon or Tangy Orange sorbets are enough to complement the most formal of dinner parties. Other flavours available range from Vanilla through to Blackberry.

Now a successful wholesaler to restaurants and commercial premises covering a wide area, all are welcome to call into the farm and sample these delicious treats. The tea room situated in an attractive farm cottage, is spotlessly clean and offers vistors a large selection of snacks ranging from freshly made sandwiches to jacket potatoes with a variety of tempting fillings. Extra special homemade gateaux and dairy desserts offer visitors the opportunity for further indulgence. The young visitor is also able to enjoy the play slide and the close proximity of farm animals. The farm has been in the Cheetham family since 1923 and is mainly a dairy farm supporting 80 pedigree Friesians. If you call into the farm we are convinced you will be unable to walk away without resisting the temptation to purchase some of these mouthwatering desserts.

Thaymar Dairy Ice Cream, Haughton Park Farm, Nr Bothamstall,
0623 860320

Making our way back to the A1, we headed south to **Tuxford**. This

17th century market town was once an important staging post on the Great North Road, and is ideally situated for travellers today using the M1, A1 and A57 routes.

The Newcastle Arms Hotel can be found in the heart of the old market square in Tuxford, and offers that traditional English hospitality typical of old coaching inns. Margaret Tudor, sister of Henry the Eighth, stayed here in 1503 on her northward journey to marry King James IV of Scotland, and todays visitors will receive no less a royal welcome! Traditional decor and antique furnishings, help create an elegant, yet informal and friendly atmosphere throughout the hotel. The comfortable bedrooms are all en-suite and offer the full range of amenities. There is a fully licensed a la carte, French cuisine restaurant which has won the RAC award for outstanding food for 3 consecutive years. Excellent bar snacks and coffee are provided in the bar where both residents and non residents alike can relax. If you are travelling for pleasure the Newcastle Arms provides an ideal base from which to discover the many leisure attractions of Nottinghamshire's Robin Hood Country. The businessman is also well catered for with a special lunch menu and full conference facilities.

The Newcastle Arms Hotel, Market Place Tuxford. 0777 870208.

We continued our journey east of Tuxford, in a village just off the **A1133,** right on the Lincolnshire border, **North Clifton.** Like its neighbour **South Clifton,** also on the east side of the Trent, the two

villages are quite separate, with the church lying just between them. The nearest crossing point to the other side of the river is on the **A57** north of the villages. Once over the toll bridge, we left the main road and headed south along the network of by-roads that lead you from one peaceful village to another.

The Pureland Meditation Centre in North Clifton offers a haven of peace for all ages who wish to come and experience the benefits of relaxation and meditation. Buddha Maitreya, a former Zen monk from Japan, has devoted the last 14 years to creating a Japanese garden and centre where we can seek refuge from the pressure of the 90s.

The garden reflects the natural landscape of Japan with its large central pond, bridges, a small pagoda where visitors can meditate, and an abundance of flourishing plants and trees. Images are certainly conjured up of authentic Japanese gardens. The Buddha hopes that after leaving, visitors will have a sense of inner peace and self awareness and feel at one with nature. The garden is open Tuesday to Saturday 1pm to 5.30pm, Sunday and Bank Holidays 10.30am to 5.30pm between April and October. The garden is closed on Mondays. Light Refreshments are served.

Buddha Maitreya teaches meditation at the centre and is available for individual tuition and group relaxation and meditation. The centre also provides accommodation and is an ideal base for anyone wanting to explore Lincoln and Nottingham and the surrounding area while at the same time learning meditation and relaxation techniques.

The Pureland Meditation Centre & Japanese Garden, North Clifton
0777 228567

At **Normanton on Trent,** we really felt we had stumbled upon a place that few know about. The secluded village has a seventeenth-century Grange, and a stuccoed Hall from the early 1800s standing next to the church.

Goosemoor Hall in neighbouring **Weston** is a magnificent 300 year old former coaching inn standing in 5 acres of beautiful grounds. Run by the Bellamy family, this super Grade II listed building provides a peaceful and relaxing holiday retreat for those who want to " get away from it all ". At present there are 10 luxurious and well equipped en-suite guest rooms, but plans are under way to extend the property to include a further 10 bedrooms and additional luxuries such as a jacuzzi and sauna. The hotel has quite a history, indeed Queen Victoria used to stay here while journeying from London to York and many of the guest rooms are named after her children. The outstanding decor and beautiful furnishings are matched only by the quality of the food served in the elegant restaurant. The menu is both imaginative and varied, changing weekly and offering the discerning diner a wide choice accompanied by an equally select wine list.

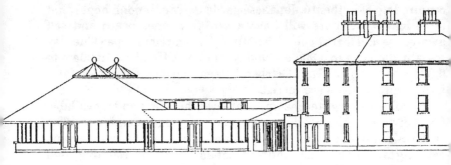

Goosemoor Hall, The Old Great North Rd. Weston. 0777 872110
Fax 0777 871988

West of here, across the A1, is **Egmanton**, which is regarded as a holy place. In 1896 an ancient religious cult was restored by the seventh Duke of Newcastle, and so today we can enjoy the Shrine of Our Lady. The church's exterior is really quite modest, and we were not prepared for the beauty of the interior. The medieval church is a mass of colour, with the light from many tapers and candles giving it a mesmerising atmosphere.

The church is rich with other splendours too - an elaborately decorated and gilded organ, painted panels and pulpit, and many other religious objects. The Shrine, which can be found on the north side of the chancel, houses the figure of the Virgin, surrounded by flowers and candles and protected by a canopy. In the Middle Ages, a local woman was said to have had a vision of the Virgin Mary, and this has consequently been a place of pilgrimage for centuries. As you would expect with pilgrims flocking here, the whole atmosphere issteeped in prayer.

South of Egmanton lies the unique village of **Laxton**. The land here gives a living insight into the Open Field farming system. Devised in the Middle Ages,this system is still in use here today, and in no other part of the country. Since the enclosure of farming-lands from the eighteenth and nineteenth centuries, this is a rare sight of medieval land management.

The fields have been strip-farmed for about 1,200 years. The reasoning behind this was to ensure that farmers had an equal share of both good and poor land. With the dividing of the land, a farmer could have as many as 100 strips, which would have represented about 30 acres. By the seventeenth century, the strips were on average about half an acre in size, but with the advent of more efficent means of ploughing, this increased to three-quarters of an acre. The familiar three-year crop rotation (remember your history lessons!) ensured productive use of the land.

A committee known as the Court Leet handles the administration and meets each year at the Dovecote Inn in the village. At the meeting, the jury is appointed to oversee the marking out of the ditches, and a pinder is elected to impound straying cattle and sheep in the pinfold.

Just north of the village, along a lane close to the church, we came across another fascinating aspect of Laxton's medieval history. This is the Norman motte or castle mound which lies almost hidden beneath the trees. At the beginning of the twelfth century, the stewardship of Sherwood Forest moved to Laxton, and it became the administrative centre for the Forest. As a consequence, the motte and bailey castle was one of the biggest in this part of the country, and the village grew dramatically.

Over the years, however, the size and importance of Sherwood Forest dwindled, and Laxton suffered a similar fate. Although no ruined keep or crumbling walls exist today, the castle earthworks are still the largest and best preserved in the county. All the information you need on the history of this fascinating village can be found at the Visitor Centre, which we discovered next to the charming Dovecote Inn.

To the west of Laxton on the **A616** is the village of **Wellow.**

Wellow is located on the site of an early settlement, and an earthwork still surrounds the village. Known as Gorge Dyke, villagers still have the right to graze their cattle on this land. Other notable features of this surprising village include a ducking-stool and stocks, and the seventeenth-century case clock in the twelfth-century parish church. The clock face was made locally to commemorate the coronation of Elizabeth II in 1953.

West of Wellow on the other side of the A614, we picked up the **B6030** and headed towards Mansfield. In a field to the side of the road, you can still see the ancient remains of Clipstone Palace, the royal hunting lodge built for King John, and one of his favourite residences.

Nearby stands the Parliament Oak, beneath which it is said that both King John and Edward I held emergency meetings with their respective advisers.

Another unusual piece of architecture in the vicinity is the 'Duke's Folly'. This Gothic arch can be found on the road between Edwinstowe and Clipstone, and was built by the eccentric 4th Duke of Portland in 1842. Using Worksop's Priory Gatehouse as inspiration, it provided lodging below and a schoolroom above. The arch has buttressed walls, and in the niches you can see the figures of Richard the Lionheart, Robin Hood, Maid Marion, etc.

We continued along the road through **Clipstone** and **New Clipstone**. The latter is a mining village which grew up around the colliery in the 1930s, and on this occasion we gladly resisted the normal temptation to depress the accelerator. The cottage-style and terraced designs of the houses makes a refreshing change from the usual unimaginative dwellings associated with the industry. We only wish that more architects of the period had given some thought to the quality of life of miners and their families.

From whichever direction you approach **Mansfield**, the structure which immediately catches your eye is the enormous railway viaduct. Built in 1875, the immense stone arches cut through the heart of the town and dominate the skyline, dwarfing the houses and shops and even the factories. The handsome **Moot Hall** stands in the market place and bears the arms of Lady Oxford. The town has several pleasant churches and a handful of other interesting buildings, but most of the architecture is too solid to inspire great photographs.

North west on the A617 takes you to **Hardwick Hall**, one of the finest Elizabethan mansions in the country. Built in the 1590's for 'Bess of Hardwick', the Hall is said to " have more glass than wall ". Inside, the stone staricase climbs from the Hall to the High Great Chamber and you'll find displays of tapestries,embroideries and furniture. The original layout of the walled courtyards are preserved in the grounds and you'll find the ruins of Hardwick Old Hall nearby,- there is more about the hall in chapter sixteen.

Leaving Mansfield east on the A617, the mining village of **Rainworth** was our next stop. The village has rows of cosy cottage-style houses, the apparently obligatory Robin Hood Inn, and a relatively modern church with some delightful architecture. Rainworth Water has been designated an area of natural beauty, and the naturalist Joseph Whittaker established a bird sanctuary here.

Situated on the outskirts of Mansfield on the A617 road to Newark,

The Fringe Hotel offers much more than just a place to rest your head. Awarded a 3 Crown grading, it has one of the finest leisure complexes outside London, which with a professional manager and qualified instructors provides everything you could wish for. There are six squash courts, out of this world changing facilities, a nautilus gymnasium,dance studio, saunas, a solarium,plus a super olde worlde snooker room and reading room. All these facilities are available to residents at no extra cost which is why staying here is such a treat. The high standards extend into the hotel itself, which provides superior accommodation in fifteen fully equipped,en suit guest rooms. The bar offers a plentiful choice of beers,wines and spirits and you can choose from a wide selection of tasty bar snacks or a full a la carte meal.

The Fringe Hotel. Mansfield 0623 641337 Fax: 0623 27521.

South Nottinghamshire

Belvoir Castle

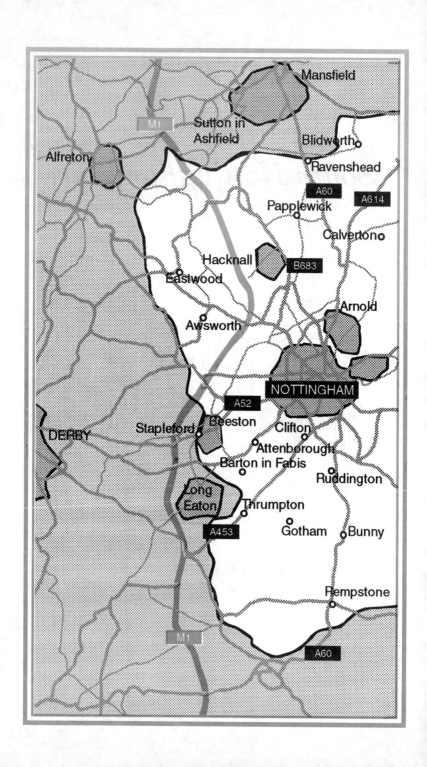

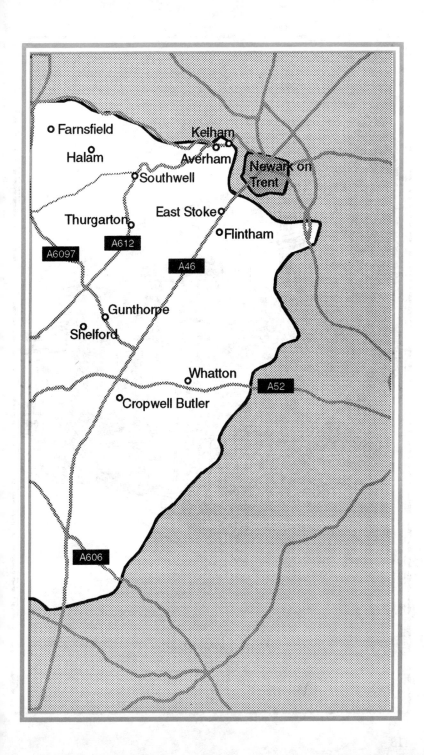

Nottingham Castle.

CHAPTER FIFTEEN.

South Nottinghamshire.

We carried on to **Blidworth**, south of Rainworth on the **B6020**. Here we found a mixture of 1930s miners' homes, stone cottages and a particularly attractive church. Dating back to 1739, it has some interesting items, including continental glass, Jacobean panelling, and more besides. A rather touching monument in the church is one dedicated to a Ranger of the Forest called Thomas Leake, who died there in 1598. The stone memorial has some splendid carvings of stags and dogs, which denotes his role as a Sherwood Ranger. Another of Robin's associates, Will Scarlet, is reputedly buried in the churchyard.

As a peaceful, rural holiday base, **Holly Lodge** near Blidworth really is hard to beat.

Holly Lodge, Rickert Lane, Blidworth.   0623 793853.

Situated just off the main A60, two miles south of Mansfield, this attractive former hunting lodge is the home of welcoming hostess Ann Shipside and her son Simon. The house was built around 1860 and stands in fifteen acres of ground, five of which are woodland and guests can enjoy pleasant woodland walks,or for the more energetic a game of tennis on the tennis court. There are panoramic countryside views on all sides and Ann provides very comfortable accommodation in the four beautifully furnished guest rooms which are housed within converted farm buildings. The atmosphere is very homely and relaxed and in addition to providing a full breakfast each morning, Ann will readily prepare an evening meal by prior arrangement.

Taking the minor road east of Blidworth, we crossed the **A614** and travelled through the villages of **Farnsfield, Edingley** and **Halam.** The latter derives its name from the Anglo-Saxon for 'hidden or secret valley'. In the centre of Farnsfield you will find a super watering hole called **The Red Lion Inn**. Dating back to the era of Charles I , this a typical olde worlde village pub where locals and visitors mix easily, sharing friendly conversation over a pint of fine ale. The Inn won the title of Mansfield Tenants Cellar of the Year, a credit to Martyn and Jaqueline Thorpe the proprietors. There is a lovely warm atmosphere which is enhanced by beamed ceilings, feature leaded windows, and on wintry days a welcoming log fire. Also popular for its excellent restaurant, the Red Lion provides an extensive and varied menu both lunchtime and evening, but popularity makes it essential to book at the weekends.

Red Lion Inn, Main St., Farnsfield, Newark. 0623 882304.

The countryside here is indeed very pleasant, with large expanses of meadow stretching up to the horizon. You may not think the ground is high, but when you start looking around, you are suddenly aware that the fields do roll gently upwards. Alongside Farnsfield and Halam is the Old Railway Nature Trail with a number of picnic sites - a good place to stretch your legs and breathe in some of that wholesome Nottinghamshire air.

On the White Post roundabout where the A614 meets the A617, **The White Post Modern Farm Centre** is a must for children and adults alike. This, as its name suggests, is a modern farm centre, where learning becomes fun and you can meet and make friends with traditional and not so traditional farm animals.

The Centre is set in fifteen acres which includes an outdoor breeding unit, an 8,000 egg incubator, a farmyard mousetown nd more unusually, the Wild World of Farming which is home to a varied selection of insects, spiders, snakes, turtles and fish. There are various picnic sites dotted around the farm,or if you prefer, you can enjoy refreshments in the farm's cafe. The list of attractions is endless and a day here is easily filled, so treat the children and yourselves and spend a 'day on the farm' - you'll be glad you did.

The White Post Farm Centre. Farnsfield.   0623 882977

Situated just off the A614 at Farnsfield in the heart of Robin Hood Country, you will find a super example of a stately home at its best when you stay at the **Dower House**. This splendid house dates back

Dower House, Lr. Hexgreave Farm, Farnsfield. 0623 882020
Fax 0623 882100

to the early 19th century , and is set within the 1100 acre Hexgreave Estate. Bill and Janet Winward are your welcoming hosts who provide luxurious accommodation in 5 elegantly furnished en-suite bedrooms for which they have been awarded a 3Crown ETB grading.   In addition to a full breakfast, delicious home cooked evening meals are available daily, and special diets can be catered for.

As Bill runs a working livestock and stud farm pets are not allowed.

And so we came to **Southwell**, an elegant market town which boasts a cathedral. This may sound implausible to the uninitiated,

Southwell Minster.

but the lovely twelfth century Minster was elevated to the status of cathedral in 1884, when the new Diocese of Southwell was created. This has given rise to the building often being referred to as the 'village cathedral'.

The choir screen is quite stunning, bearing no less than 200 human carvings, while the Chapter house has thirteenth-century carvings of the most beautiful natural objects.

The two west towers with their pyramidal roofs make quite a striking note as they stand proud, dominating the cathedral green. The Eagle lectern which stands in the choir was salvaged from the lake at Newstead Abbey in 1750. It had been thrown there by the monks to protect it from the looting that occured during the Dissolution, and was presented to the Minster in 1805.

The Old Forge, Burgage Lane, Southwell. 0636 812809

Enjoying a central yet peaceful location in Southwell, overlooking the Minster, **The Old Forge** is a simply super place to stay for visitors to this lovely part of Nottinghamshire. This delightful 200 year old forge is the home of Hilary Marston, a charming and experienced hostess who enjoys sharing it with her many guests. Beautifully decorated throughout, the original character and charm of the building is enhanced by antique furniture and exposed beams, creating an inviting and cosy atmosphere. All 5 guest rooms are en-suite and equipped to the standard you expect from a 3 Crowns Highly Commended establishment. Breakfast is enjoyed in the conservatory / dining room or, weather permitting, on the patio beside the fish pond setting you up perfectly for a days exploring.

Southwell has many other fine buildings and a wealth of fascinating places to discover. Among these are the Prebendal houses where the secular canons resided, the ruins of the Archbishop's palace, sequestered alleyways, and charming coaching inns like the Saracen's

Head where Charles I spent his last hours of freedom before his final surrender.

The young Lord Byron often stayed at Burgage Manor while on vacation from Harrow and Cambridge. He was a member of the local theatrical group, and it was his friends in the town who convinced him to publish his first set of poems. One of his earlier collections, 'Hours of Idleness', was published by Ridges of Newark and was to bring him great acclaim.

When you have had enough of the historical and feel the need to indulge in more material pleasures, the shops are wonderful. Selflessly devoting a large proportion of our visit to an inspection of the antiques, fine clothes, glass and china and quality foods available, we found ourselves quite spoiled for choice.

Old National School, Nottingham Rd., Southwell. 0636 814360

Situated on the A612 Nottingham Road in Southwell, **Old National School**,is ideally located as a touring base for Robin Hood Country and , as its name suggests, was formerly a school built in the 19th century . Today it is the charming home of Ben and Mercia Kinchin, and many of their guests who come from all over the world think this is the best B &B in the country. The house carries an ETB 2 Crowns grading. This exceptional establishment is full of character and exudes an atmosphere of warmth and friendship, Guests will find first class accommodation provided in 7 fully equipped and beautifully furnished en-suite guest rooms, some boasting four poster beds. Breakfast, always a substantial affair, is savoured in the lovely beamed dining room. Signs of the houses former academic life still remain, such as the two long corridors which border the guest rooms, one for the boys part of the school, the other for the girls, and the garden is the old school playground. Wonderful hosts combined with its lovely location make Old National School a very special place to stay and one you are sure to return to.

424

Southwell can also be credited as the 'birthplace' of the Bramley apple. The story goes that in the early nineteenth century, two ladies planted some apple pips in their cottage garden in Easthorpe. Nature took its course, and one of the seedlings grew into a tree. By this time, one Matthew Bramley owned the cottage, and the quality of the tree's fruit began to excite public interest.

Mr Henry Merryweather, a local nurseryman, persuaded Bramley to let him take a cutting, which he consequently propagated with enormous success. Permission had been granted on the condition that the apples took Mr Bramley's name and not the two ladies'! Mr Merryweather's descendants still operate a nursery today just outside the town, and here visitors can enjoy an exhibition about the famous apple. Look out for a Southwell Galette, a scrumptious pastry confection of hazelnuts, sultanas and of course -Bramley apples!

Brinkley Nurseries, Fiskerton Rd., Southwell. 0636 814501

Half a mile out of Southwell on the Fiskerton Road, **Brinkley Nurseries** is not a garden centre but a working nursery where visitors can not only purchase plants, but see them in situ and gain first hand knowledge of the plants from owners Celia and Arthur Steven. Celia is in fact the great granddaughter of Henry Merryweather who gave the world the famous Bramley apple. The Stevens specialise in unusual trees,shrubs and plants from all over the world and can also trace plants that you may find difficult to locate yourself. Being a member of a very famous horticultural family, Celia's knowledge is second to none in her field. Beautifully sited in 4 acres, the nursery is a delight to walk around and there is a 'magnificent private garden which is also open to the public under the National Gardens Scheme on certain days or by appointment.

Adjacent to Brinkley Nursery you will find a lovely place to stay at **Brinkley Hall Farm**, home of Ken and Maria Merryweather. Ken is the brother of Celia who runs the nurseries, and as you would expect he is also a keen horticulturalist. Set in 3/4 of an acre, this charming farmhouse dates back to the 17th century and makes a very peaceful and comfortable base to use while exploring this lovely part of Nottinghamshire. Ken and Maria are super hosts who go out of their way to ensure your stay here is memorable. They have 3 beautifully furnished guest rooms, one with en-suite facilities, and for those who require, they will happily provide a packed lunch for you to take with you on your day out.

Brinkley Hall Farm, Fiskerton Rd, Southwell. 0636 812268.

We left Southwell on the A612 and took the pleasant drive past farms and cottages and open fields to **Upton.** Perhaps the most impressive building here is **Upton Hall**, a stylish Grecian villa with a central dome and elegant colonnade, built in the early nineteenth century. The hall is now the headquarters of the British Horological Institute, and inside you can see the National Exhibition of Time - a fascinating display of clocks, watches and other horological pieces. The Institute's Open Days are currently between 14th - 16th September, and groups will need to make a prior appointment.

Upton also boasts a couple of very good pubs, and the nine-pinnacled church is worthy of a visit too. As a point of interest, a famous son of the village was James Tenant, the man who cut the world-renowned Koh-I-Noor diamond.

If you love fine food, you would be well advised, if you are in the area, to seek out **The French Horn,** a super inn and restaurant situated off the main Newark-Mansfield road in the vilage of Upton. Dating back to the 18th century, it was formerly a farmhouse then an alehouse and is now renowned throughout the area for its food. The restaurant seats up to 60 people and is found in the upper part of the building above the stables in what was the old hayloft. It really is a beautiful restaurant, the old wooden beams enhancing its character and cosy intimate atmosphere while the menu offers something to suit

426

every palate. Open every lunchtime and evening, it is best to book to avoid disappointment. The bar area with its log fire adds to the character of the place and its walls are adorned with the work of local artists Penny Veys and John Smith.

The French Horn, Upton. 0636 812394

East of here, just off the **A617**, is the unlikely setting for the Robin Hood Theatre at **Averham**. Starting life in 1913 as a private theatre for opera lovers, it had a fully equipped stage and orchestra pit, and boasted the rare advantage of being lit by electricity. When re-opened as a public theatre in 1961, it could seat 150. In these hallowed walls, the late, great Sir Donald Wolfit gave his first performances.

Further down the road is **Staythorpe,** with its massive power station dominating the village, while beyond is the riverside village of **Rolleston**. Kate Greenaway, the author and illustator of many children's books   spent much of her childhood here. Southwell Racecourse lies to the west of the village and is one of only two all-weather courses in England.

There aren't many pubs that can claim to have been preserved thanks to the commitment of the villagers, but that is exactly true of **The Crown Inn** at Rolleston. On its last legs and due to be sold off by the brewery, local villagers got together and signed a " Save Our Pub " petition which received such attention it was featured on Central television.

A year ago Terry Sowter came along and bought the Crown Inn and together with the support of villagers, turned it into one of the most attractive and welcoming pubs in the area. The atmosphere here is terrific and having savoured a pint of fine ale and a tasty bar meal, or dinner in the restaurant, you can enjoy a traditional game of skittles in the adjacent converted barn.

The Crown Inn Staythorpe Rd.,Rolleston, Southwell. 0636 814358

To the south, **Fiskerton** rests alongside the River Trent with its beautiful quiet waters. Here you are able to stroll along the wharf past the charming houses and meditate on the tranquility of the peaceful setting, a far cry from Fiskerton's industrial days in the mid-nineteenth century.

Back at Averham, we turned right on the A617 and headed for **Kelham**. Coming across the lovely **Kelham Hall** is quite a surprise, and the beautiful towers, pinnacles and gothic windows represent all that is best in Victorian architectural splendour. The architect Sir George G. Scott built the hall around 1860, and comparisons to his other great work, St Pancras Station, are inevitable. The building became well known through the Kelham Fathers, who purchased the house in 1903. Although there is a theological atmosphere to the hall, it was originally built as a private dwelling and now serves as the offices for Newark and Sherwood District Council.

On the A617 Newark to Mansfield road at Kelham, you will discover a great place to stay at **The Red House Country Manor**. Built in 1903 it was formerly a retreat for the use of monks until the present owners, John and June Hand bought it about 9 years ago. Through sheer hard work and determination they have successfully transformed it into an outstanding hotel and restaurant renowned throughout the county. Beautifully furnished ,The Red House has an air of grandeur as befits its impressive exterior, yet an overall atmosphere of peaceful relaxation pervades.The 8 individually styled en-suite guest rooms provide very comfortable accommodation, and in the elegant surroundings of the restaurant with its soft lighting and pleasant piped music, the discerning diner can choose from an excellent selection in both the a la carte and table d'hote menu.

428

The Red House Country Manor, Main St., Kelham. 0636 705266

Our approach into **Newark-on-Trent** took us across the relief road, then over the river up Beast Market Hill. At the top of the hill stands the splendid Ossington Coffee Palace, with its half-timbered upper storey and projecting oriel windows. Built by Viscountess Ossington as a temperance hotel in 1882, the idea was to persuade the public that coffee would be a lot better for them than stronger brew. The building was used as offices for many years, and now operates as a fish restaurant with some accomodation available.

Standing alongside the River Trent, **Newark Castle** was built in the twelfth century and has a long and chequered history. It was initially built for the bishops of Lincoln, and became one of the most important castles of the region. King John died here in 1216, and during the Civil War the castle became a refuge for Royalist supporters, managing to withstand three sieges. You can wander freely around the grounds, and during the Summer an exhibition is mounted in the south west tower. This gives visitors a clear picture of all the events that have made this castle one of strategic importance.

We made our way to the cobbled market place with its lovely architecture, which is set in the heart of the town. This is one of the finest market places in England, and the impressive Town Hall gives it an almost French feel. Classical pillars in the Doric style support the massive pediment, and the balustraded balcony is surmounted with a pair of urns and the figures of Justice, the Lion, and the Unicorn. The great assembly hall with its plaster ceiling and columns contains busts of the 4th Duke of Newcastle and George III, and the whole air is one of elegance.

Narrow streets radiate out from the square with its Georgian houses, while the Clinton Arms and the former Saracen's Head have

429

early eighteenth-century facades. To stand in this square and glance around is a pleasurable experience. Just over the tops of the houses and shops, we could see the parish church of St Mary Magdalene. This lovely church was built in 1227, and Henry III gave permission for six Sherwood oaks to be used in the construction of the tower. With a spire reaching some 237 feet into the blue yonder, this is one of the highest landmarks for some miles.

Of special interest inside is the Fleming brass, one of the largest of its kind in the country. And in the crypt where the Treasury is housed, you will find the largest collection of altar plate in an English parish church. There are some spectacular paintings to be seen, like the 'Raising of Lazarus' by William Hilton, and a font dating back to at least 1660 sitting on a fifteenth-century base. The whole interior is one of richness and colour, and makes it another fine example of the wonderful treasure troves that churches provide for us to enjoy today.

Two of our national banks in the town provide marvellous examples of Victorian banking decor, and it would be quite an experience to cash a cheque in their highly decorative vestibules. One of these, the National Westminster, is on the corner of Stodman Street and was built on the site of a house owned by an alderman during the Civil War. With Newark under siege, the alderman's dreams were three times disturbed by visions of the house burning down. Not one to ignore bad omens, he packed up his family and possessions and left. Shortly afterwards, cannon fire set the house ablaze.

For those of you seeking relaxing entertainment in plush surroundings, an evening at the Palace Theatre in Appletongate could be the answer. It has recently been refurbished and can justifiably claim to be one of the best theatres in the East Midlands, offering a variety of shows that should please most people.

So we left this attractive market town where the Great North Road, the Roman Fosseway and the River Trent converge. The Fosse Way was the last of the great military Roman roads in southern Britain. In its final form, it cut across the country from Exeter via Bath to Cirencester, Leicester, Newark and Lincoln, then northwards to a point on the River Humber above Scunthorpe. As the Romans did not appear to consider it necessary to name their roads in Britain, this task fell to either the Saxons or to modern historians. The Fosse Way comes from the Latin 'fossa', meaning a ditch.

The old road in this particular part of the country has become the main A46. Heading south we arrived at **Farndon,** where there is a slight encroachment of modern housing, but the old village is truly delightful. From behind their high brick walls, the Georgian houses turn their elegant faces to the traveller and look just a little smug, but perhaps with good reason. There is a dignified three-storey Old Hall, and next to the church, Farndon Lodge with its Doric portico poses prettily for the amateur photographer. Wandering down one of the lanes, we came to the banks of the Trent, and it was from this spot that a ferry used to cross the waters between Farndon and Rolleston. This is very much an angling and boating community, and there is also a secluded marina.

East Stoke can be found right on the A46, and is of great historical importance. The site of the last great conflict of the War of the Roses, the battle of Stoke Fields took place on 16th June 1487. It was here that the army of Henry VII defeated the Yorkists in a bloody battle that lasted for three hours and resulted in 7,000 deaths. The defeated army fled to the river across the meadow known today as the Red Gutter, which gives us a horrible insight into what the scenes of carnage must have been like. From this vantage point, one can clearly see **Fiskerton** over the river, and it made us wonder how many soldiers managed to escape there that day. Many of those who didn't do so lie in 'Deadman's Field' nearby, and local farmers have occasionally uncovered swords and other relics from the battle when ploughing their fields.

Further south at **Flintham** we were impressed by the great Victorian house of Flintham Hall. The conservatory has often been likened to the Crystal Palace, but if you are unfamiliar with that structure, the comparison won't mean much to you! Still very much a family home, parts of the building herald back to the seventeenth century, while some of the brickwork dates even further back to the Middle Ages. The conservatory is said to be the finest in England, and though we can only judge by what we could see from the road, it certainly appears quite magnificent.

At the main roundabout, we headed west on the **A6097** Mansfield road. A few miles along the road, the A612 offers you an alternative approach into Southwell. On this road, the village of **Thurgaton** is not only picturesque, but has a Priory dating back to 1187. The setting of the village with its range of gentle hills is quite lovely. All that remains of the priory today is the parish church, and with trees brushing its exterior, it presents a typical picture postcard scene. Although no material sign of the former inhabitants exists, we have it on good authority that one of the Black Canons still haunts the Priory grounds.

A super holiday base awaits you when you stay at **Hall Farm House**, the delightful farmhouse home of Ron and Rosie Smith. Dating back to 1709, the house really is a picture both inside and out, from the ivy-clad brick walls outside to the cosy beamed interior where guests are immediately made to feel at home.

Hall Farm House, Gonalston. 0602 663112 Fax 0602 664844.

Awarded a One Crown Commended grading, there are 3 lovely guest rooms, a well stocked games room, and outside an aviary of tropical birds. There is also a swimming pool and tennis court for guests to use. Dining is a real pleasure with breakfast served 'en famille' style in the warm surroundings of the kitchen/dining room, complete with Aga. Rosie loves cooking and wil happily prepare an excellent homecooked evening meal on request. Self catering accommodation is also available in the The Granary, a converted barn situated within the grounds, which sleeps seven and is equipped with every modern facility including a jacuzzi!

Back on the A6097, the dual carriageway sweeps through the village of **Lowdham,** formerly a peaceful place, the main road does not encourage visitors to linger. Where the B6386 crosses the road a few miles further on, we headed west for the industrial village of **Calverton**. The charming cottages here date back to the early nineteenth century. They were once lived in by framework-knitters, and have been carefully restored by the Nottinghamshire Building Preservation Trust.

Framework knitting was the main industry of the village at that time. The stocking-knitting frame was invented in nearby Woodborough by Reverend William Lee in 1589. His wooden frame so revolutionised the stocking industry that he attempted to seek patronage from Elizabeth I. Unfortunately, the wind was taken out of his sails as she refused to grant a patent for something that would mean great job losses for her loyal subjects!

Somewhat hidden but well worth seeking out, is **Patchings Farm Art Centre** which lies on the edge of the village of Calverton on the

B6386 or can be reached off the A614 or A6097- look out for the brown tourist signs.

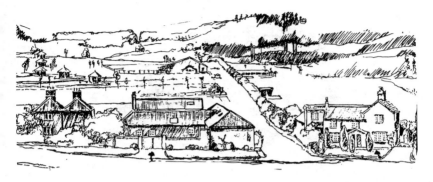

Patchings Farm Art Centre, Calverton. 0602 653479 Fax 0602 655308

This exceptional and award winning centre is set in 500 acres of beautiful Nottinghamshire countryside. Here you will find 2 galleries with monthly changing exhibitions, a working art studio, art materials, framing service, and gift shop. There's also a licensed restaurant serving excellent homecooked food, a pottery studio, a lovely garden and a unique' painters paradise' developed around the idea of Monet's garden at Giverney for the enjoyment of all artists. Patchings holds regular art and craft courses, painting holidays and Monet painting weekends. A real artist's haven, this is one place that has to be seen and experienced.

We took a lane from Calverton which crossed the A614, and a little further north just off Longdale Lane, we came to **Papplewick Pumping Station**. This is unquestionably the best working example of a late Victorian waterworks. We found plenty to marvel at here - not only the steam engines and other exhibits, but the utter beauty of the interior.

The station is no longer in use, but is open to the public at various times throughout the year. Do check the noticeboard by the gates for viewing times, and you may be lucky enough to visit when the station is 'in steam'. Papplewick is situated on the edge of some lovely woodland and heath, and at **Burntstump Country Park** you are able to take advantage of a number of lovely walks on the forest trails.

Travelling along the main A60 Mansfield to Nottingham Road, close to historic Newstead Abbey, you will discover a superb licensed restaurant and ice-cream parlour called **Seven Mile House.** Here the owners, Susan and Harvard Goulborn, have enhanced the olde English atmosphere of their 17th century building with tasteful decor and furnishings. You can savour an excellent menu which caters for every taste, including a range of vegetarian dishes and daily specials.

Seven Mile House. 1 Mansfield Road. Papplewick. 0602 204 204656.

Susan and Harvard are friendly and experienced hosts, who have established a reputation for fine fresh food, and, of course, not to be forgotten are their delicious home-made ice-creams, which have been made on the premises for over fifty years. Which is another reason to pause here during your journey.

Visitors returning to this part of Nottinghamshire might be familiar with **Newstead Abbey** and its associations with Lord Byron. Nottingham City Council owns the Abbey, which now houses the Byron museum containing many of the poet's personal effects. The entrance to the grounds of this historic house can be found off the A60, opposite the northern end of Longdale Lane. A long drive takes you through thickets of rhododendrons, and beyond these the view is over countryside dotted with heather and bracken.

The Abbey in its lovely setting was converted from a medieval priory into a family house in the sixteenth century. To do justice to the many treasures of the individual rooms would be impossible in the space available, so we will leave you to discover them for yourself. Although well-trodden by visitors, the grounds still contain a wealth of hidden places. There is a secret garden, a large lake where the fifth lord re-enacted naval battles, and a beautifully carved fountain decorated with fantastic animals. With over 200 acres to explore, the grounds alone are worth every penny of the entrance fee!

We headed south on the A60 then turned right onto the **B683** towards Bestwood. This took us through the pretty village of **Papplewick,** which is two and a half miles west of the pumping station. With its cottages of pink stone and quiet rural aspect, the village has successfully shrugged off most of the trappings of its industrial past. Back in the eighteenth century, times were much harder. The cotton mills based in Papplewick and nearby Linby were witness to the worst excesses of child labour, and an appalling 42 apprentices now lie buried in Linby churchyard.

A lane from the village will take you past the grounds of Papplewick Hall to the Church of St James. This is a truly beautiful church, rebuilt in the Gothic style by the local squire in 1795. The elegant interior is furnished with a gallery down the north side of the church, and to ensure the comfort of Squire Montagu, a fireplace was installed to warm his pew!

Anyone having stayed in the very special Bed and Breakfast establishments in the U.S.A. will appreciate the extremely high standard afforded in **Cottages in the Square**. Based on this idea, Janice Hill, the proprietor, has spared no attention to detail i.e guests are welcomed with bowls of fresh flowers, luxury towels and toiletries and even slippers by the fire. The cottages are tucked away off the B600 in the village of Selston with lovely gardens to the rear. All 3 cottages are Georgian in origin and have been tastefully restored. The guest list is impressive, particularly with visitors from overseas who perhaps demand such a high standard and enjoy being made to feel special. Cottages in the Square offer nightly rates also for anyone wishing to stay in this type of establishment as opposed to a hotel for short periods of time. The location (just 2 miles from Junction 27 of the M1) makes the cottages readily accessible and offers complete security, privacy, and luxury- the real hotel alternative.

Cottages in the Square, Selston. 0773 812029 Fax 0623 559849.

South-east of Bestwood Village, with the vast ocean of suburbia almost lapping at its feet, a low hill is crowned by the magnificent **Bestwood Lodge**. In the days of Charles II, this was the royal hunting lodge, but his descendant the tenth Duke of St Albans decided to build an altogether more imposing house on the site. Work began in 1862, and today you can enjoy the grandeur of flying buttresses, gables and chimneys, tall bay windows, and best of all, the lofty entrance tower with its high pyramidal roof.

On the outskirts of **Arnold**, on the A614 you will discover a rare and fascinating place called **Greenwood Bonsai Studio**.Run by Harry and Petra and their son Corin, this unique family business has something to interest everyone.

It is one of the largest established bonsai centres in the world and really has to be seen to be believed. Set in over 12 acres of lovely countryside, 3 and a half of which are open to the public, everything to do with bonsai can be found here, from seedlings and cultivars to exclusive bonsai containers and informative books. Harry and Petra are both internatinally known and respected, Harry as a bonsai artist, lecturer, and author, Petra as a bonsai and ceramic artist who makes beautiful, handcrafted bonsai containers. Outside, the extensive nursery area is Corin's domain, whilst in the main studio there is a magnificent bonsai display and a separate studio where regular lectures and demonstrations are given.

Greenwood Bonsai Studio, Greenwood Gardens, Ollerton Rd.,
Arnold. 0602 205757

We have mentioned several famous authors in our travels so far, but the one who is probably most closely linked with Nottinghamshire is **D. H. Lawrence.** You can discover this land through the man and his writings. Many of the places we have visited so far may have directly inspired him, and they certainly gave us an appreciation of his narratives. Lawrence's country is not one of fiction. Although today the mines may be closing down, the men and women are stoical and good humoured. If you love his writings, then Lawrence's Nottingham will definitely appeal to you.

8A Victoria Street in **Eastwood** was the humble birthplace of D. H. Lawrence who was born there in 1885. Now transformed into The D. H. Lawrence Birthplace Museum, the house has been preserved by

Broxtowe Borough Council as a living museum showing how a family might have lived at that time. From the heavy furniture and weak gas light to the flourishing aspidistra, one can sense how D. H. Lawrence lived his early life and possibly had his first stirrings of imagination. Exhibitions in another part of the house show Lawrence's paintings and perspectives of his life, and publications are offered for sale. A craft centre has been established nearby showing visitors the art of traditional skills, and Eastwood Library houses a collection of Lawrence's material as well as the "Phoenix" headstone from his grave.

Awsworth is near to the Erewash Valley, and it is here on the Bennerley Viaduct that we can cross the river. The iron bridge with its sixteen spans was built in 1887 to carry the Great Northern railway between Nottingham and Derby, and efforts have been made to preserve it.

To the south, the pretty village of **Cossal** lies in a conservation area. There are some notable buildings here such as the Willoughby Almshouses, and a farmhouse which includes part of the original home of the Willoughby family. They were a branch of the Willoughbys of Wollaton, a dynasty which was founded by a wealthy thirteenth-century wool merchant from Nottingham named Ralph Bugge. This rather unfortunate name, which meant 'hobgoblin', was understandably changed by his descendants to the more acceptable Willoughby. This was taken from the village Willoughby-on-the-Wolds on the border with Leicestershire, where Ralph owned a fair amount of land.

Cossal was another of D. H. Lawrence's haunts. Used as a setting in his novel 'The Rainbow', the village was referred to as 'Cossethay', where the Brangwen family lived. 'William Brangwen' was said to have been based on a Mr Alfred Burrows, whose daughter Lawrence courted for some time. The Burrows family lived in a cottage near to the charming village church.

Stapleford churchyard has a Saxon Cross which is quite beautiful, with intricate carving winding up the shaft. Interestingly, the carving depicts an eagle standing on a serpent, which is said to be the symbol for Saint Luke. The church, which dates mainly from the thirteenth and fourteenth centuries, has many war memorials to its lost heroes. The village was once a thriving centre for framework knitting, and terraced cottages built specifically for the workers can still be seen in Nottingham Road.

One other feature of Stapleford which made us pause for thought is The Hemlock Stone. The Hemlock Stone is a massive redstone boulder standing 30 feet high and is situated opposite Bramcote Park

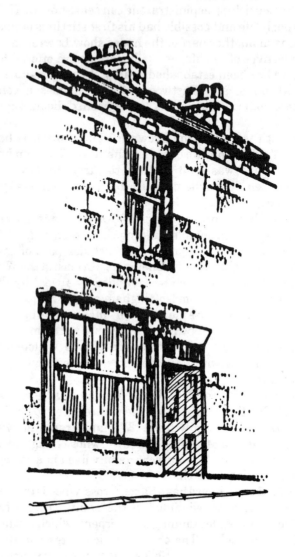

Birthplace of D.H.Lawrence.

ι Stapleford. It has come to be associated with the Devil, who pparently threw the rock at Lenton Priory whilst in a bad mood and ιissed. Despite the inaccuracy of aim, the rock was probably eposited here by glacial action, whilst wind erosion has contributed) its brooding appearance. Its geological make up consists of andstone cemented by the mineral barite, which is found in large ιantities throughout the Stapleford and Bramcote Hills. The rigins of its name are Celtic and undoubtedly the rock has played)me part in witchcraft rituals in its past history.

The approach to **Attenborough** is not particularly attractive but, is worth visiting as part of the old village still stands today. The ιirteenth-century church is tucked down one of the side lanes near) the river, and the former gravel pits in the area have now been ιankfully transformed into lakes. Inside the church, we were greeted ·ith the rather incongruous sight of animal heads gazing down from ιe capitals of the pillars. Some seventeenth-century panels continue ιis decorative theme of the unexpected, with mermaids carved in the ·ood.

From the church, the Strand leads directly to the **Attenborough ſature Reserve**, which was established here in 1966 amongst the ιkes and islands. While gazing at the birdlife in this lovely spot, we ιund our eyes kept wandering upstream to the enormous power ;ation at Ratcliffe. Although it rather detracts from the scene, it ιouldn't discourage the potential visitor.

The village of **Barton-in-Fabis** (or Barton-in-the-Beans) was ιce the scene of some anticlimax, if the writings of Sir Osbert Sitwell ·e to be believed! He described the village in his book 'Tales My ather Taught Me', an account of a retrospective tour made by Sitwell ith his father and brother. Apparently it rained solidly during their ιsit, and several buildings that he hoped to see had been demolished.

South of Barton, right on the border with Derbyshire, lies the idden village of **Thrumpton**. This should not be confused with the istrict of the same name in Retford that we mentioned in an earlier ιapter. This quiet spot lies just off the A453, and is a must for visitors) the area. The main thoroughfare led us past some lovely cottages, ιe church, a splendid turreted gatehouse, and then to **Thrumpton ſall.**

The H-shaped building with Flemish gables is marvellous to ehold, and the interior contains such wonders as a balustrade carved ·ith the acanthus scrolls so loved by the Eygptians. There are some chly carved doors, and an Oak Room displays some fine panelling ating back to Charles II. The eighth Lord Byron inherited the house through marriage, and some relics of the poet Byron are also displayed here.

Just to the south of the A453, the tiny village of **Ratcliffe-on-Soar** has a pretty little church with an eye-catching blackened spire, and a handsome manor farmhouse. These are set picturesquely on the meadow-banks of the River Soar. The massive power station looms over everything and the railway clatters by, and yet this charming village is definitely worth a visit.

The church with its broach spire and four pinnacles houses the splendid tombs belonging to the Sacheverells. A Ralph, three Henrys and their wives lie here under the watchful gaze of the cooling towers. Here too, Sir Osbert found fault with his ancestors' resting places having apparently discovered the church under water when he came to pay his last respects!

Further along the **A453** towards Nottingham, a lane took us to the sprawling village of **Gotham.** Unlikely as it may sound, we have heard tales of the odd tourist turning up in the village, seeking connection with that fabled city of the same name where Batman keeps law and order! As far as we are aware, no caped crusaders stalk the streets, and the name is actually pronounced 'Goat'm'. There are a few noteworthy buildings here, but the village is best remembered as the home of the 'Wise Men'.

Such were the odd tales of this village that a certain Dr Andrew Borde published the 'Merrie Tales of the Mad Men of Gotham' in the sixteenth century. King John had decreed that he wished to build a hunting lodge here in the village. Naturally displeased at having to give up their land to his whims, the villagers devised a plan. They decided that the best way to dissuade the royal presence was to feign madness.

When the messengers entered the village, the inhabitants reacted in such a peculiar way that the King's men returned with the suggestion that the mad men of Gotham should be left well alone.

Sutton Bonnington on the banks of the River Soar has some lovely buildings, including its two churches. It is also home to the Nottingham University School of Agriculture. One of the finest buildings in the village is the Hall, which was built in the eighteenth century by Beaumont Parkyns, the brother of the 'Wrestling Baronet of Bunny'. More of this pugilistic peer later! A few miles down river is the tiny canal village of Zouch, a watering hole for barges, with a lock and an old mill.

At **Stanford-on-Soar,** we found ourselves at the southernmost point of Nottinghamshire. Here the River Soar, the King's Brook and the Grand Union Canal make their individual paths across the

440

ounty. Here also lie the disused railway lines of the Great Central Railway that once stretched from Nottingham to Marylebone - a sad example of the decline of the railways. The church interior has some lovely decorative stencilling and many monuments to the Dashwood family. Stanford Hall, which was built in 1771, is now a Co-operative College, and from here the wonderful views of Charnwood Forest can be enjoyed.

At the junction of the A6006 and A60, is **Rempstone** with its late Georgian Hall. This handsome white building is now a retreat for the Community of the Holy Cross. Founded in London in 1857 this Anglican Benedictine order moved to the village in 1980.

We headed north on the A60 to **Bunny**. This pretty village has a wealth of lovely architecture, and owes much of its charm to the eccentricities of its former eighteenth-century squire, Sir Thomas Parkyns. A man obsessed with the sport of wrestling, he employed two full-time professionals to spar with him at **Bunny Hall.** He also organised an annual tournament in the village to promote local wrestling talent, and this event continued nearly seventy years after its originator's death. In St Mary's Church, which was designed by Sir Thomas, his memorial graphically illustrates his commitment to the sport. It depicts the squire standing victorious over his defeated opponent on a wrestling mat, while Old Father Time stands by, perhaps as referee.

Continuing up the A60, we passed through the small village of **Bradmore,** most of which was destroyed by fire in the early 1700s. The new village was rebuilt to Sir Thomas Parkyns' design. Further up the road lies the historic village of **Ruddington.** Make sure you turn left off the main road when you enter the village, or you may drive through imagining that you've seen all there is to see. Nothing could be further from the truth, as this interesting place has much to offer.

In 1829, a factory and frame workers cottages were built around a courtyard in Chapel Street. This group of buildings now houses the **Framework Knitters' Museum,** showing living and working conditions for the workers of the trade. After your visit, you will be fully conversant with Trick Bars, Jacks, Slurcocks, Griswolds and other mysterious terms of the industry. Of the twenty-three hand frames we can see today, twelve are fully operational, and there is an opportunity to buy samples made at the museum.

The industry reached its height in 1780, with the staggering number of 20,000 frames operating in Nottingham, Derbyshire and Lincolnshire. In 1730, a Mr Draper of Nottingham produced the first pair of cotton stockings to be made in this country using an Indian thread. Throughout the years, there were many experiments to refine

441

the stockings by giving then fewer threads and greater stength. Th cotton industry and the mills really had their renaissance from th time, with Arkwright and Strutt building their empires.

The River Trent at nearby **Clifton** is the scene of a tragic lov story. In 1471, a young squire called Henry Bateman went to th Crusades with his master. When he returned, he discovered that h sweetheart Margaret had fallen for another man and married hir The heart-broken lover threw himself into the Trent from Clifto Grove, a wooded cliff above the river. Some time later, Margar« herself took the same way out, presumably in remorse for her 'sin'

The approach from Clifton into the city of **Nottingham** took u along the A453 and over the world famous Trent Bridge. A bridge ha spanned the river here since medieval times, but the currer ornamental structure dates back to 1871. Of course, it is not th bridge itself which is renowned throughout the world, but the crick« ground to which it gave its name. The first county match betwee Nottinghamshire and Sussex was played here shortly after th ground opened in 1838, and many Test Matches have followed. Ju a few hundred yards from this 'holy' site lies the no less revered grour of Nottingham Forest Football Club. And just on the other side of th river, Notts County hold court.

Nottingham, self-proclaimed 'Queen of the Midlands', is justifiab« said to be one of England's finest cities. It is ripe for exploration b« visitors are regaled with the Robin Hood theme wherever they g with Maid Marian 'caffs', Friar Tuck fish and chips and the lik However, once you begin to discover the city, it becomes perfect obvious that Nottingham has plenty going for it without having to re upon its associations with the popular folk hero.

The settlement of Nottingham was founded by the unfortunate named Snot, chief of a sixth-century Anglo-Saxon tribe. He and h people carved out dwellings in the soft local sandstone, and th settlement thrived to become Snottingaham, 'home of the followers Snot'. The name changed into its currently more acceptable form a some stage in Nottingham's ancient history but when that was ha never been established.

We decided to visit **Nottingham Castle** first, the place so close associated with the Sheriff, the wicked Prince, and the brave ar faithful outlaw, Robin Hood. If visions of crossbow tournaments ar seige towers, swash-bucklers and limp maidens are what you ha« come for - forget it. The current building could not be described as 'castle' in the popular sense of the word at all. In fact, this seventeent century mansion belies its spectacular position on its massive sandstor rock, standing plain and rather disappointingly lacking in majest;

A castle of one sort or another has occupied the site since the Middle Ages, although today only a few ruins of the original can be seen.

In 1831, the castle fell victim to an angry mob who set it ablaze whilst petitioning for the Reform Bill to go through. It remained a virtual shell until 1875, when it was taken over by the Corporation and converted into a museum for public use. It was in fact the first municipal museum in England outside London. Inside there are displays of ceramic, local history, and the picture gallery contains works by Rossetti, Spencer, Crome and others .

The views from the Castle are very fine indeed, stretching far over the city with glimpses of far-off church spires and the occasional sighting of the canal. The towers of lovely Wollaton Hall can be seen some way off, while the distant view of the power station at Ratcliffe marks the position of the M1.

The Castle sits on top of a monstrous bee-hive of pale golden sandstone, a rock formation quite riddled with caves. Some 400 have been discovered throughout the city, and guided tours through some of the eerie passageways start from the top of Castle Rock. At the base of Castle Rock, we discovered the Trip to Jerusalem. The Crusaders are said to have stopped here for a pint to fortify themselves before their jaunt to the Holy Land. Dating back to around 1189, it is said to be the oldest pub in England. Set back into the rock, it was once the brewhouse for the Castle. Another pub in the area which oozes with ancient charm is the Salutation Inn, with its heavy beams and hints that robbers such as Turpin may have dropped in for an ale.

The 'Tales of Robin Hood' which is located along Maid Marian Way is definitely worth taking the time to visit. It may not strictly be called a hidden place, but the adventure is a must for young and old alike. The exhibition has won awards, and quite justifiably, as it is well produced and should please anyone with a romantic notion or two!

Nottingham is of course famous for its lace, and **The Lace Centre** in a 16th century half -timbered building on Castle Road offers a selection of beautiful lace designs for sale. If you want further insight into the lace making process, then **The Lace Hall** in High Pavement is the place to go. The museum displays both hand and machine-made lace, and as well as seeing the designs you can buy samples here.

If you are interested in the history of costume, then you will definitely enjoy a visit to the **Museum of Costume and Textiles.** Situated in a lovely row of eighteenth-century houses, this is a wonderful setting for the beautiful clothes on display. Clothing dating from 1790 to the 1960s will stun you, and the unique Eyre map tapestries of 1632 are splendid. The museum has become one of the most important study centres for textile design in this country.

Nottingham's waterways and canals have played a major part in the life of the city. **The Canal Museum** is situated in an old warehouse on the banks of the Nottingham to Beeston canal, and trips on canal boats can be enjoyed during the Summer season. The big names of Raleigh, Players and Boots have their massive factories in this city. The Boots factory out at Beeston was built in the 1930s and its architectural splendour was featured on BBC 2 in the series 'Building Sights'.

Old Market Square is dominated by the great domed building which is the Council House designed by Cecil Howitt, and reminiscent of that famous London building, St Pauls. Just north of the square Theatre Royal and the Royal Concert Hall provides resident and visitor alike with a variety of stage performances. Nearby is Trent College, which includes the original University College which D.H.Lawrence attended.

The oldest fair in England, possibly going back a thousand years, is Nottingham's Goose Fair. Once a wonderful place for the showman it is held in October and attracts enormous crowds. Originally a glorified goose market, it became at its peak a fifteen-day event with all the side shows you could imagine. Dancing bears, human oddities merry-go-rounds and swing-boats.

A few miles from the centre of Nottingham is **Wollaton Hall,** and what a surprise that such a place lies surrounded by the urban sprawl. Built in 1588 by Sir Francis Willoughby, it is one of the most beautiful Tudor houses in England. Our first sight of the Hall was very early in the morning when the park had just opened, and our immediate impression of the building was of a light and airy palace. Four corner towers richly decorated with niches and statues give the place a pleasing symmetry. There are banks of windows, gables, and countless chimneys, and to crown it all the central belvedere tower rises splendidly above.

Further down the Radcliffe Road and well signposted from all parts of Nottingham, a lane will take you to the **National Watersports Centre.** At the two mile long man-made water course, you can indulge in all sports associated with the pleasures of getting wet! Tucked away from the noise and crowds of the Centre is **Holme Pierrepont Hall.** Built by the Pierrepont family in the early 1700s, the house stood derelict for some years, but is now being carefully restored by the present owner. The attractive pink brick frontage is surmounted by battlements which were added at a later date. The gardens are undergoing transformation with herbaceous shrubs, while yew, beech and box trees strike a lovely contrast. The Hall and gardens are occasionaly open to the public on summer afternoons.

Just a little further along the A52 is **Radcliffe-on-Trent.** Since Victorian times, Radcliffe has almost taken on the dimensions of a small town, yet it retains the atmosphere of a large and sprawling village At nearby **Shelford,** the red cliffs that border the River Trent gave the larger village of Radcliffe its name. There are some pleasant walks in the surrounding riverside villages, particularly at **Gunthorpe,**which stands by the **A6097.** This small village boasts several restaurants and pubs, all a few minutes stroll from the river. The banks of the river are usually festooned with fishermen intent on their hobby, and the pleasure boat brigade that patrol up and down the river usually manage to bring a responsive scowl to the faces of the solitary anglers.

The road over Gunthorpe Bridge led us to the attractive village of **East Bridgford.** The church stands at the crossroads in the centre and was built on the site of an early Saxon church.

Just north of the A52 lies the old market town of **Bingham.** The heart of the village has managed to preserve its charm with a few exceptions; side by side with the pleasant old buildings we found the usual shopping precincts, which lacked in distinction and unfortunately can be found in any town throughout the country.

To the south of the A52 Nottingham to Grantham road, we found a cluster of pretty villages which have fared better against the ravages of the twentieth century. **Cropwell Bishop** and **Cropwell Butler** are close to the edge of the Vale of Belvoir. 'Crop' is the Scandinavian word for a hump, or low hill, one of which lies between the two villages. 'Bishop' refers to the fact that the Archbishop of York once owned this land.

At Cropwell Bishop, we were surprised to see a couple of bottle kilns used to dry gypsum, a sight more associatd with the Potteries. Also in the village is the Cropwell Bishop Creamery, a family-run business where Stilton and Cheddar cheese is made.

The hamlet of **Colston Bassett** was at one time large enough to hold a weekly market. Although the village has considerably diminished in size, the partly medieval market cross can still be seen near the old post office. Owned by the National Trust, it was their first property in Nottinghamshire. The post office itself has featured in several television programmes, most recently in an episode of 'Boon'. Through the village, the River Smite runs its course.

Langar village is situated in the broadest sweep of the Vale of Belvoir. There are several fine buildings to be seen here. The charming Langar Hall which commands a fine view of the Vale is now a very comfortable country house hotel.

Granby village has a very 'well-known' personality associated with it. The Marquis of Granby's portrait and name has been used in countless pub signs all over England. As Colonel-in-Chief of the British Army, John, the eldest son of the third Duke of Rutland, was immensely popular with his troops. The village which was once a market town seems a quiet backwater for such a hero to come from. And naturally enough, the name of the pub is - The Marquis of Granby!

Whatton lies just off the A52, and has therefore mercifully escaped the heavy flow of traffic which heads up and down to Nottingham. The church here has some magnificent carvings, and a Burne-Jones glass window. We also noticed an engraved memorial to Thomas Cranmer, the 'father' of the Book of Common Prayer who died in 1502.

Scarrington has a most unusual man-made edifice, one that we certainly had not come across before. A pile of around 35,000 horseshoes towers fifteen feet high, and was built by the former blacksmith, Mr Flinders. A crown of three upstanding horseshoes finishes this wonderful folly off. Over the years, souvenir hunters have taken the odd shoe here and there, with the result that the monument is bending over very slightly at the top.

However, the obelisk which Mr Flinders began in 1946 stands rock solid, and all he used to bond the shoes was his skill and a great deal of luck! At one time it was coveted by an American visitor who wished to buy it and transport it to the United States. Thankfully, the borough council intervened and this strange piece of heritage can now be enjoyed by us all.

We have explored many of the villages of south Nottinghamshire in a fairly haphazard way - but that is half the fun of travelling, never quite knowing where you may end up! However, our last glimpse is not of a hidden place, rather the opposite. Directions to **Belvoir Castle** are quite superfluous, for the castle dominates the Vale of Belvoir for miles around. The golden turrets rise above a screen of trees and make a delightful picture. From the castle, fields of corn stretch endlessly below the hill, and as Belvoir means 'beautiful view' you will certainly be able to appreciate it.

Our journey through the central and southern part of the county had been an interesting and varied one. Riverside villages, mining communities and historic market towns and cities share the landscape in surprising harmony. Each presents its own insights into the historical and contemporary life of the people who have lived here. We

Belvoir Castle.

wondered what Derbyshire had in store for us as we turned our attention towards that county lying north west of us.

East Derbyshire

Hardwick Hall

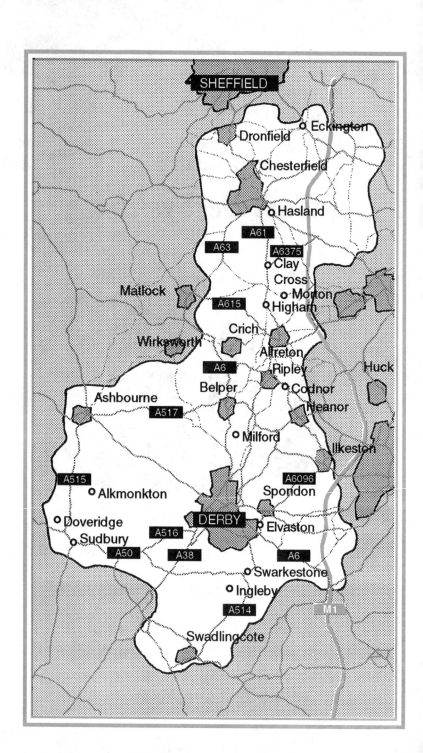

CHAPTER SIXTEEN

East Derbyshire.

Derbyshire is a land of great beauty, with soaring crags, plunging caverns and massive caveworks which pre-date the Industrial Age by thousands of years. It is a place of rugged gorges and uplands, remote moor and splendid isolation as well as boasting its fair share of most beautiful historic houses in the British Isles. This is a water-rich area, with pockets of lush growth in the valleys where coursing rivers such as the **Dove** and **Derwent** flow. High up on the moors where the curlews fly, you will find a vastly different landscape.

We started our journey in this large and varied county in **Doveridge**. This village is close to the border with Staffordshire, and by the banks of the River Dove. Although there is a fair amount of modern housing here, the village still exudes a rural atmosphere. It boasts a distinguished thirteenth-century church, and in the churchyard stands an old yew tree which is reputed to be one of the largest in Derbyshire.

Nearby **Sudbury Hall,** which lies to the south-east of Doveridge on the **A50,** is a splendid example of a late seventeenth-century house. It contains elaborate plasterwork and murals throughout, wood carvings by Grinling Gibbons, and some fine examples of mythological paintings by Laguerre. Of particular interest is the **Museum of Childhood** which is situated in the servants' wing and provides a fascinating insight into the lives of children in history.

Marston Montgomery can be found to the north of Doveridge. It has a half-timbered manor house dating from around 1670, and **Waldley Manor House,** standing on the Doveridge road before you reach the village, is another good example from this period. Further north still, **Norbury** can be found on the **B5033.** The church here is definitely worth a visit, as it houses the alabaster tombs of the fifteenth-century Fitzherberts, one of the oldest families in Derbyshire. It is probable that the family contributed much towards the church building over the years.

Those of you familiar with the works of George Eliot will feel much at home in this part of the county. The characters Adam and Seth from

Limestone Gorge. River Wye.

her famous novel 'Adam Bede' were based on her father, Robert Evans, and his brother. Members of her family are buried in the churchyard at Norbury.

We had great fun map reading in this area, and many times our best efforts found us revisiting villages we had only recently just left! Eventually, this confusion of lanes led us to **Longford**, which has the distinction of being the home of the first cheese factory in England. Opened on the 4th May in 1870, its first manager bore the memorable name Cornelius Schermerhorn. Derbyshire, with its excellent rail and canal links, made it an ideal centre for the mass production of cheeses for foreign markets.

The next village on our travels was **Sutton on the Hill**. Despite its name, this is a sheltered spot, with the church standing above the village on the hill. For those of you who know and love cricket and its heroes, the names G. M. and R. H. R. Buckston should be familiar, as they both captained the Derbyshire team. The Gothic Hall which stands in the village is the home of this famous family.

Following the road which runs parallel to Sutton Brook, we joined the **A516** and headed east on the Derby road. This led us to **Etwall**, a charming place with a fine range of Georgian buildings. These include the seventeenth-century almshouses built by Sir John Port, who founded nearby **Repton College**. The original site of **Etwall Hall** where Sir John lived is now the home of a large comprehensive school which is named after him.

Close by on Egginton Road in the village of **Hilton** you will find an excellent stopping-off point called **The White Swan**.

The White Swan, Egginton Road, Hilton Tel: 0283 732305

Dating back 150 years, this former smallholding became a public house in 1830 and has been providing visitors and locals with welcome refreshment ever since. Paul and Wendy Weston are friendly hosts who through sheer hard work have developed The White Swan into a first class family pub with stone fireplaces and half panelled walls enhancing a cosy atmosphere in which you can sample a range of well-kept ales and a varied and imaginative menu that far exceeds the usual 'pub fayre'. Younger family members will particularly appreciate the assault course and play area outside, making this an ideal place for a family meal out.

East of the **A38**, we joined the **B5008**, and crossed the Trent and Mersey Canal. We drove through the once important river port of **Willington** and arrived at **Repton**. Sir John Port had specifically intended Repton College to be a grammar school for the local poor children of Etwall, Repton and Burnaston. These intentions have somewhat deviated over the passing years, and now Repton stands as one of the foremost public schools in the country.

Interestingly, two of its headmasters, Dr Temple and Dr Fisher, went on to become Archbishops of Canterbury, while Dr Ramsey was a pupil at the school under Dr Fisher's guiding light. If you are a film buff, then the fourteenth-century gatehouse and causeway may be familiar, as they were featured in the 1938 film version of 'Goodbye, Mr Chips'.

Repton is steeped in history. The first mention of the town came in the seventh-century when it was established as the 'capital' of the Saxon kingdom of Mercia. A monastery housing both monks and nuns was founded here sometime after 653, but the building was sacked by the Danes in 874. A battleaxe, now on display in the school museum, was excavated a little distance from the church. It had apparently lain undisturbed for well over 1,000 years.

Brook Farm Tea Rooms, Brook End, Repton. 0283 702215

Enjoying an enviable location in this picturesque and ancient village **Brook Farm Tea Rooms** is the perfect place to call in for some welcome refreshment. Approaching the Cross in the centre of the village, turn left down Brook End and then left at the bridge over

454

the trout brook. Set within a converted sandstone and brick barn, the tearooms are readily accessible to the disabled, with ramps and disabled toilet facilities provided. The original beams and A frame are still visible, which with the Rayburn at the far end of the room retain a cosy farmhouse atmosphere. In addition to an excellent menu of homecooked food, you can buy local crafts and farmhouse ice cream. There is also very comfortable accommodation provided in a lovely en-suite guest room within the main farmhouse.

Situated on the edge of the village in a quiet no through road called Well Lane, **The Bower Lodge** is a delightful somewhat stately looking Victorian house originally built in 1818 and now the charming home of Elizabeth Plant who enjoys sharing it with her many guests. Set in eight acres of lovely grounds, the house is surrounded by beautiful countryside and inside it is a real picture, with lovely antique ornaments, feature fireplaces and beautiful decor creating a rather grand yet welcoming air. You can't help but relax once here and the six guest rooms provide very comfortable overnight accommodation after which you can look forward to Elizabeth's substantial breakfast.

The Bower Lodge, Well Lane, Repton.   0283 702245

South-east of Repton on the A514 we came to the village of **Ticknall.** Its attractive stone cottages are set amongst richly wooded country, and close by lies the great park of **Calke Abbey.** This mansion has been described as the 'House that Time forgot'. It was built in 1701 in the Baroque style, and since the death of Sir Vauncey Harpur-Crewe in 1924, the house has remained largely unaltered. There is a spectacular eighteenth-century Chinese silk State Bed on display.

Further along the A514 you'll find at the **Bull's Head** in **Hartshorne**, an inn full of history and character. The Georgian front, probably the most prominent part of the structure, was built around 1700, while the lower storey of the rear of the inn is much older and probably dates as far back as 1570-1600. This is a true olde worlde inn with beams throughout and a high wooden plinth adorned with a host of bygone memorabilia, all of which enhances the cosy, welcoming ambience that is immediately apparent. The set menu and daily blackboard specials offer a choice of food far superior to the usual offerings, making this a popular venue for eating out with both visitors and locals alike and for those wishing to stay there are four lovely en-suite guest rooms upstairs.

The Bulls Head, 1, Woodville Road, Hartshorne .0283 215299

Heading east towards the Leicestershire border, we reached the pleasant town of **Melbourne** on the **B587**. The name-source of that rather better known area of land 'down-under, Melbourne is equally well-known as a successful market garden centre. A famous son of Melbourne who started his working life in one of the market gardens was Thomas Cook, who was born here in 1808. He went on to pioneer personally conducted tours, and gave his name to the world-wide travel company we all know so well today.

A long yew tunnel flanks the grounds of the delightful **Melbourne Hall**, birthplace of the nineteenth-century statesman, Lord Melbourne. The hall's most notable feature is a beautiful wrought-iron bird-cage pergola built in the early 1700's by Robert Bakewell, a local blacksmith from Derby. We were sad to learn that the creator of this exquisite arbour ended his life in poverty, as such superb craftsmanship surely warranted a better reward.

Every now and then you come across a real 'hidden' gem and in the tiny hamlet of **Kings Newton** which lies a mile from Melbourne you will discover one such place at **The Hardinge Arms.** Dating back to 1645, this is a cosy, traditional inn and restaurant run by super host Mike Johnson. The front of house bar oozes with character, with beamed ceilings and solid oak floor to ceiling stanchions. The original Newton apple is said to have come from here and the oak top of the bar

456

is engraved with apples. This is the epitome of the olde worlde village inn and people come miles to soak up the wonderful atmosphere and savour the outstanding cuisine for which chef Steve Clarke has a well-deserved reputation. No fried food or set menus here; the daily changing menu is listed on a blackboard and offers a mouthwatering choice to appeal to every palate. Treat yourself and enjoy an evening out at The Hardinge Arms, it will leave you with memories to treasure.

The Hardinge Arms, Kings Newton, Melbourne. 0332 863808

After Melbourne, we took the **A514** to **Swarkestone**, and discovered the barrows at **Swarkestone Lowes Farm**. Excavations here have led to the discovery that the district was occupied in Bronze Age and Saxon times. **Swarkestone Bridge,** with its seven arches and three-quarters of a mile long causeway, has been important strategically throughout its history. The advance guard of Bonnie Prince Charlie reached the bridge in 1745, and had they managed to cross the River Trent at this point they would have faced no other natural barriers on their 120 mile march to London. As it transpired, the army retreated, and the rest is history!

Having a passion for motor racing, we welcomed a chance to see nearby **Donnington Park**. This is a late eighteenth-century motor racing circuit not far from **Castle Donnington.** At the Park you'll find a museum housing old racing cars in the area. In the delightful village of **Isley Walton** which lies between Castle Donington and Melbourne, you will find a wonderful holiday base at **Park Farmhouse Hotel,** a very special, homely establishment run by welcoming hosts, John and Linda Shields. Dating back to the 17th century, this former farmhouse is now a lovely country hotel set in 20 acres of beautiful grounds and boasting magnificent views. Roaring log fires and a grand piano in the lounge area make it easy to relax and in the comfort of the dining room you can savour excellent homecooked food. With

457

three choices of accommodation available, ranging from a fully equipped seven acre caravan park, a charming self-catering cottage sleeping six situated within the grounds, and nine lovely en-suite guest rooms in the hotel itself, Park Farmhouse really caters for everyone's needs.

Park Farmhouse Hotel, Isley Walton. 0332 862409

For other pleasurable modes of transport, nothing beats a canal ride. At **Shardlow** on the **A6**, we had a wonderful opportunity to potter round the old warehouses and watering holes. Once so vital as an inland port, cotton and silk that sailed from the Indies in the nineteenth century may well have been unloaded at Shardlow, and a short trip up the road would have deposited the bales at the Victoria Mills in nearby **Draycott**. Having strong connections with the Nottingham lace trade, the mill was built in 1888, and was established as one of the most important lace factories in the world. It is now joining the twentieth-century with a yacht marina, a modern boat yard and numerous pleasure craft taking to the waters.

The Coopers Arms, Weston Hall, Weston-on-Trent. 0332 690002

The small hamlet of **Weston-on-Trent** can be found by turning of the A6 at Shardlow and it is here that you will find a delightful stopping-off point at **The Cooper Arms**. This impressive 17th century mansion hall has been converted into a charming country inn full of character, with large open fireplaces and old timbers carefully incorporated into the renovations over the years. The comfortable lounge bar and carvery prove popular with visitors and locals alike and in the splendid conservatory you can enjoy the fine food and drink as you soak up wonderful views of the lake and surrounding countryside.

Turning off the A6 onto the **B5010**, we came to **Elvaston**. Here you will discover a pseudo-Gothic 'castle', standing in its own grounds which are open to the public. A far cry from the sentiments of the fourth Earl of Harrington, who is quoted as saying, *'If the Queen comes . . . show her round, but admit no-one else'*. The public was in fact admitted to the gardens for the first time in 1851. The magnificence of these grounds can be attributed to William Barron, who in 1830 began the transformation of the hitherto unremarkable gardens. Amongst other things, he created a yew tunnel, planted an avenue of limes, and built an exotic Moorish temple and arch.

Situated between Nottingham and Derby on the **A6005** in the centre of **Long Eaton**, the **Europa Hotel** is a 2 Star establishment which has been completely refurbished over the past ten years and with its delightful front conservatory is a place full of atmosphere and charm.

Europa Hotel and Restaurant, Long Eaton.   0602 728481

Awarded a Three Crowns grading and listed in Les Routiers, the Europa caters for everyone's needs, from the weary shopper in need of a refreshing mid-morning coffee, to the holiday maker looking for a comfortable and relaxing base from which to explore the many attractions in the area. All the guest rooms are attractively furnished and equipped for maximum comfort, all with shower/bath and most

459

with en-suite facilities. The restaurant is licensed and open to non-residents, with excellent lunchtime and dinner menus catering for every taste.

We skirted Derby and headed north on the **A6096** to **Dale Abbey**. Now reduced to ruins, it has quite an interesting history. At its peak, the Abbey housed Augustinian monks, but it started life in a very humble way. Local legend has it that a Derbyshire baker came to the area in 1130, carved himself a niche, and devoted himself to the way of the hermit. The owner of the land, one Ralph FitzGeremunde, discovered the baker and was so impressed by the man's fervour that he bestowed on him the land rights and tithe rights to his mill in Borrowash.

We decided to pay a quick visit to **Ilkeston** further up the A6096. The third largest town in Derbyshire, it received its royal charter for a market and fair in 1252, and both have continued to the present day. Once a mining and lace-making town its history is told in the local museum on High Street. **Little Hallam Hall** and the perpendicular tower of St Mary's Church are both well worth seeing.

In the village of **Trowell** just a mile or so from Ilkeston you will discover **The Festival Inn,** a delightful freehouse run by Keith Bell and his partners. Built in 1956, the inn's modern outward appearance belies the beautifully decorated and atmospheric interior. Renowned throughout the area, this is the place to come if you like Real Ale and good homecooked food, all of which is served at surprisingly reasonable prices. The carvery menu always proves popular, accompanied by a varied wine list and with a separate children's menu. An added attraction of The Festival Inn is the adjacent building which is a busy local nightspot, open three nights a week as a disco and providing live music on Fridays.

The Festival Inn, Ilkeston Road, Trowell Tel: 0602 322691

Between **West Hallam** and the town of **Heanor,** you will discover

Shipley Country Park. In addition to its magnificent lake, it boasts over 600 acres of beautiful countryside, which should keep even the most enthusiastic walker busy. Well known as both an educational and holiday centre, there are facilities for horse riding, cycling and fishing. This medieval estate was mentioned in the Domesday Book, and under the auspices of the Miller-Mundy family it became a centre for farming and coal-mining production during the eighteenth-century. Restoration over the years has transformed former railways into wooded paths, reservoirs into peaceful lakes and has re-established the once flowering meadows and rolling hills, which had been destroyed by the colliery pits. You'll find another fun park in the locality, **American Adventure**,its name explaining the thrills on offer-saloons,gunfights and such.

And so to Heanor. The hub of this busy market town centres on the market place, where the annual fair is held. A market is held in the town every Friday and Saturday, so there are plenty of opportunities to pick up knickknacks, especially if you are dedicated bargain hunters! If you fancy a bit of peace and quiet after the bustle of the market, do pay a visit to the Memorial Gardens. In this peaceful setting, there is always a magnificent spread of floral arrangements, herbaceous borders and shrubberies to please the eye. We were impressed by the massive wrought-iron gates at the entrance to the park, which were formerly the gates to Shipley Hall. Working men and women have helped shape this landscape, and at Heanor there are some good examples of the type of cottage lived in by the nineteenth-century mill-worker, potter, and stockinger.

Loving pottery as we do, we decided to visit **Denby Pottery Visitors Centre** (Tel :- 0773 743641) on the **B6179**. We are always looking for a chance to add to our collection, and here we spent a happy hour or so looking round. Not only do you have the chance to purchase pottery, but you can see the potters hard at work by taking advantage of the guided tours available. The Pottery was established in 1809, and skills used then are still employed by the craftsmen today.

Travelling along the **A609**, about a mile and a half outside **Belper** you will discover **The Spinning Jenny,** a super inn and restaurant run by Kevin and Michelle Barrett. Guests here are assured of a stay to remember, with first class cuisine, fine ale and excellent accommodation in four lovely en-suite rooms provided by friendly welcoming hosts for whom nothing is too much trouble. Kevin has over eight years experience in the catering industry which shows in the extensive and imaginative menu that caters for every palate. Guests with a hearty appetite can face the challenge of a Full Mixed Grill and if they manage to eat it all, are awarded with a Record of Achievement certificate!

The Spinning Jenny, Openwoodgate, Belper.   0773 823900

Further west on the A609 we arrived at the town of **Belper**, where in 1964 the remains of a Roman kiln were discovered. Famous for its cotton mills, the town is situated alongside the River Derwent on the floor of the valley. In 1776, Jedediah Strutt undertook the harnessing of the natural powers of the river to run his mills. Three hundred years later, the mills stand proud and commanding on the river banks, and have played a large part in local history. One of our lasting impressions was the thundering roar issuing from the weir near to the East Mill, as the River Derwent plunged alongside the towering building.

The River Gardens in Belper were established in 1905, and today you can stroll along beautifully tended gardens or hire a row-boat for a jaunt up the Derwent. The Gardens are a favourite with the film industry, having been used in Ken Russell's 'Women in Love', as well as television's 'Sounding Brass' and 'In the Shadow of the Noose'. The riverside walk is very pleasant here, offering meadows to wander in which are particularly rich in bird life. The town was mentioned in the Domesday Book as Beau Repaire, or 'the beautiful retreat'.

There are many places in the area to stay or eat and here are some of our recommendations. Situated in the tiny hamlet of Broadholme and overlooking the beautiful Amber Valley is the lovely **Fisherman's Rest,** a charming country inn owned and run by David and Kathryn Brett. Although it lies only 20 yards from the main A6 as you travel from Matlock towards Belper, be careful not to miss this somewhat 'hidden' gem. The culinary skill of the inn's chef, David Mason, is renowned throughout the area and the Bretts are friendly hosts who have created a wonderful place for families to enjoy a relaxing drink and first class food. The cosy bar has a warm, welcoming atmosphere and the lovely beer garden to the rear with its well-equipped play area is ideal for those fine summer days.

Fisherman's Rest, Broadholme Lane, Belper. 0773 825518

Heading out of Belper towards **Matlock**, if you take the **Alderwasley** turning off the A6 prior to Whatstandwell you will find **Ye Olde Bear Inn,** a superb Tudor Post House and Coaching Inn standing on your left. Resident proprietor Tony Brough has, through sympathetic modernisation, created a very special place where you can experience every modern comfort without detracting at all from the building's original character.

Ye Olde Bear Inn, Alderwasley, Belper. 0629 822585

Set within six acres of land, the views from here are simply breathtaking and the newly developed two acre caravan and camping park that Tony has established makes an idyllic holiday base. There are full facilities including a shower and toilet block and of course you have a ready made pub and restaurant on your doorstep! If you prefer the luxury of in-house comforts, you can always opt to stay in one of Tony's beautifully furnished en-suite guest rooms, some of which even boast four-poster beds. A warm, friendly atmosphere extends through the cosy bar and restaurant areas, enhanced by various original features which retain the inn's olde worlde charm. Renowned throughout the area for its excellent food, the functions room here is regularly booked for parties and special celebrations. The restaurant menu is both extensive and reasonably priced with something to please every palate including a range of vegetarian dishes. With all this and the most spectacular scenery on all sides, Ye Olde Bear Inn is a 'hidden' place not to be missed.

If you are touring the beautiful countryside of Derbyshire and the Peak District, you will discover an excellent place to stay at **Shottle Hall.** Shottle Hall is not in the village of **Shottle**, but is situated off the **B5023**, 200 yards north of its junction with the A517 Belper to Ashbourne road. Over 100 years old, this splendid house is not your run-of-the-mill guest house as you soon discover. Spacious, high-ceilinged rooms are filled with beautiful antiques and lovely furnishings, creating an air of bygone elegance. Philip and Phyllis Matthews are friendly, attentive hosts who go out of their way to make their many guests feel welcome and apparently succeed. Very comfortable accommodation is provided in ten attractively furnished guest rooms, some with en-suite facilities and one ground floor suite with ramped access being particularly suitable for the disabled. Phyllis is an excellent cook and the table and residential licence means you can complement her tasty dinner menu with a drink of your choice. The three acres of beautifully laid out gardens are a riot of colour in Spring and Summer and the surrounding countryside provides a wealth of spectacular walks, making this an ideal touring base.

Shottle Hall, Shottle, Belper.   0773 550203/550276

If you take the **Hazelwood** road off the **A517** Belper to Ashbourne road, about a mile further on your left you will discover a real 'hidden' gem called **The Bluebell Inn** and Restaurant. Friendly proprietors Fred and Winifred Silver have over 30 years experience in the catering industry and since 1987 have developed The Bluebell into a superb establishment, renowned throughout the area as the best place to eat. The sheer quality and variety of food, combined with surprisingly reasonable prices make eating here a real treat, which means booking is advisable to avoid disappointment. In addition to an excellent dinner menu which includes such delights as Poached Scotch Salmon complemented with Asparagus Spears, Prawns and Lemon Butter Sauce, there is also an extensive range of tasty bar snacks, ensuring everyone's needs are catered for here.

The Bluebell Inn and Restaurant, Belper.   *0773 826495.*

South of Belper on the A6 lies the village of **Milford**, which also boasts mills dating from the late 1700s. Milford's first cotton mill was built by Richard Arkwright and Jedediah Strutt using stone transported from nearby Hopping Hill. It was only a year later that the partnership dissolved, and both industrialists went their separate ways to forge their individual empires.

Ideally situated for touring the Peak District National Park and only 20 minutes drive from the M1, **Makeney Hall** is a superb country house hotel, well deserving of its 3 Stars award by the AA and Four Crowns grading by the English Tourist Board. What a luxurious holiday base this is; a former Victorian mansion house built by the Strutt family, it stands in six and a half acres of beautifully laid out grounds with panoramic views of the Derbyshire countryside and the impressive exterior is matched by the elegant decor and furnishings within. Friendly, smiling staff greet your arrival and superior accommodation is provided in 45 well equipped and individually styled en-suite guest rooms. The candle-lit restaurant has been awarded Two AA Rosettes and provides an intimate setting in which to savour the finest gourmet cuisine and after dinner you can relax with a nightcap in the comfort of the drawing room in front of the ornately carved fireplace.

Makeney Hall, Makeney, Milford 0332 842999 Fax: 0332 842777

A little further south on the A6, we entered the ancient parish of **Duffield.** This really is a charming place, with most of its Georgian houses and cottages lining the banks of the Ecclesbourne river. One thing that struck us as odd was the church, which stands proud but rather isolated by the Derwent. Inside, we found an impressive monument dedicated to Anthony Bradshaw, whose great-nephew went on to officiate over the court which called for the execution of Charles I.

There is a castle mound here, but as the castle was demolished in 1266 by Simon de Montfort, you do have to use your imagination to appreciate its scale. However, excavations show that it must have been a massive building, possessing a large keep with walls over sixteen feet thick. Owned originally by Robert de Ferrers, Keeper of the Royal Forest of Duffield, the castle reflected by its enormity the influence and power of the de Ferrers family.

A few miles east by the **A609** and ten miles from the M1 just outside **Horsley Woodhouse, Horsley Lodge** is first class hotel and restaurant, well-deserving of its Four Crowns Commended rating. Originally a derelict farmhouse set in 168 acres of farmland, the land was turned into an 18 hole golf course and the hotel and restaurant was added, creating a central holiday base in wonderful surroundings. Traditionally furnished throughout, the hotel is full of character and class, with four lovely en-suite guest rooms, one boasting a four poster bed. The newly opened celebration suite is ideal for wedding receptions and parties, while the elegant restaurant provides a relaxed setting in which to savour a varied and extensive menu and if you should over-indulge, you can make use of the comprehensive leisure complex to work off your excesses!

466

Horsley Lodge, Smalley Mill Road, Horsley   0332 780838

A few miles further along the road and just north of the village of **Morley,** at the end of a long drive lies **Morley Hayes**, once a farm and now a superb bar, restaurant and conference centre. Set in 200 acres of parkland, including two large lakes and an eighteen hole golf course, deer roam freely and there is a sense of true oasis here, with peace and tranquillity belying the fact that the bustling town of Derby is only minutes away. Old farm buildings have been expertly converted to create the aptly named Roosters Bar and Dovecote Restaurant and all the original character of the buildings has been retained, enhanced by exposed brickwork and beams, hay racks and wagon wheels. Everyone is catered for here and great care has been taken to ensure ready access for the disabled. Renowned throughout the area for its excellent cuisine, the restaurant is a popular venue for locals and visitors alike, making booking advisable.

Morley Hayes, Main Road, Morley 0332 780480

Worthy of a particular mention is **The Abbey** public house which has a particularly interesting history attached to it. Situated just off of the Duffield road on the main A6 it is to be found in **Darley Abbey Old Village**. The Augustinian Abbey of St. Mary of Darley was founded in 1137 and grew to become the most powerful abbey in Derbyshire and possibly in the whole of the Midlands. In 1538 the abbey was surrendered as part of the dissolution of the monasteries. Sadly, few monasteries could have been so completely obliterated, so much so, that what is now known as the Abbey public house is the only building remaining.

The layout is of a simple medieval hall house and is thought to have been used as the Abbeys Guest House for travellers and pilgrims during the 13th century.

Derby is essentially a commercial and industrial city, its position historically and geographically has ensured that it has remained one of the most important and interesting cities in the area and consequently there is much for the visitor to see, whether from an architectural, historical or another point of view.

One of Derby's newest of Museums is **Pickford House**, situated on the city's finest Georgian street at number 41. It is a Grade I listed building, erected in 1770 by the architect Joseph Pickford as a combined family home and place of work. Pickford House varies from the majority of grand stately homes. Unlike most it does not have wealth of priceless furnishings and works of art. Instead visitors are able to gain an insight into everyday middle class life during the 1830's. Pickford House is the epitome of a late, Georgian professional man's residence.

There is an exciting programme of temporary exhibitions as well as other displays which deal with the history of the Friar Gate area and the importance of Joseph Pickford as a Midlands architect. The displays include a late 18th century dining room, a breakfast room, and an early 19th century kitchen and scullery. One special feature of Pickford House is the excellent collection of costumes, some dating back to the mid-18th century. A period 18th century garden is also laid out at the rear of the house.

Just a short walk from Pickford House is the **Industrial Museum**. What better place to house a museum devoted to the preservation of Derby's industrial heritage than the beautiful old Silk Mill; a building which stands on one of the most interesting sites in the country and which preceded Richard Arkwright's first cotton mill by over 50 years. The Silk Mill was badly damaged by fire in 1910 and had to be substantially rebuilt, however it still gives an impression of Lombe's original mill and tower. The whole of the ground floor galleries are

Pickford House.

devoted to the Rolls Royce aero engine collection and illustrate the importance the aeronautical industry has played in the history of the city.

Since 1915 Derby has been involved with the manufacture of engines and this section of the Museum displays model aircraft, sectioned engines demonstrating how aircraft fly. A specially designed annexe houses a complete RB211 Turbo-fan engine. On the first floor of the building there is an introduction to other Derbyshire industries with displays of lead and coal mining, iron founding, limestone quarrying, ceramics and brick making. There is also a railway engineering gallery with a signal box, a model railway and displays on the growth of the railway works in Derby, since the 1840's. Since the coming of the railways in 1389, the railway industry has played a large part in the life of the city. Along with Rolls Royce, British Rail is one of the largest employers in Derby and its development is well documented within the Museum and allows visitors to broaden their knowledge.

The Central Museum and Art Gallery is also well worth visiting. Opened in 1879, it is the oldest of Derby's Museums and the displays include, natural history, archaeology and social history.

Three Museums, Leisure Services Department. Derby 0332 255586

One section of the Museum is devoted to a Military Gallery and relates to Derby's local historical regiments. A relatively new feature is the walk-in World War I trench scene which captures the experience of a night at the front. A ground floor gallery houses the City's superb collection of fine porcelain, manufactured in Derby from the mid 18th century. The Museum is home to a collection of portraits, landscapes, scientific and industrial scenes by painter Joseph Wright of Derby A.R.A. On the second floor of the Museum are temporary exhibition galleries. These change very three or four weeks and cover not only the Museum's own collection but also travelling exhibitions representing

470

Industrial Museum, Derby

an exciting range of arts and crafts both modern and traditional in a variety of styles and techniques.

One must remember that Derby is home to Royal Crown Derby and yuo can arrange to join a tour of the factory (Tel:- 0332 712800) or alternatively visit the Museum and factory shop. Also worthy of a visit is the **Markeaton Craft Village**, acclaimed as one of Derby's newest attractions it is situated in the centre of Markeaton Park. Crafts people and Artists are encouraged to enquire about the possibility of renting a workshop. It provides an ideal opportunity for visitors to browse around the various workshops and gain an insight into how the variety of crafts are made. There is something to suit everyone, using traditional skills members of the public can learn the art of marquetry, pottery and quilting to traditional design and sculpture.

The cathedral possesses a fine sixteenth-century tower, and the tomb of Bess of Hardwick Hall can be found here. We will meet this formidable lady more than once in our travels. In 1840, Joseph Strutt presented the town of Derby with eleven acres of land, and commissioned the landscaping of the **Arboretum,** which resulted in the first municipal park in England. Situated on the outskirts of Derby town centre in Ashbourne Road, **The Georgian House Hotel** is an impressive Grade II listed establishment built in 1765 which offers the discerning guest superior and somewhat luxurious holiday accommodation in an atmosphere of friendly hospitality.

The Georgian House Hotel. Derby   *0332 49806*

RAC and AA listed, the beautiful furnishings and decor reflect the grandeur and style of a bygone era, with a cosy bar full of olde worlde charm and an elegant restaurant complete with chandeliers providing the perfect setting in which to savour the fine cuisine of the extensive à la carte menu. Guests can choose from over twenty exquisitely furnished en-suite bedrooms, some boasting four poster beds and some situated on the ground floor having access to a delightful paved

472

courtyard. As a holiday retreat, this is very much a 'hidden' gem well worth seeking out.

We headed north-west from Derby on the **A52**, stopping off for visit to the church at **Mackworth**. Most of the building dates from around 1300. This was a good opportunity to get first hand experience of the wealth of ancient and modern alabaster carving that is displayed in the interior.

Along the A52, just two miles from Derby city centre at Mackworth you will find a splendid place to stay at **The Mundy Arms Hotel,** a super holiday base where the reasonable prices do not reflect the extent of first class facilities on offer. This is very much a family-run establishment which owners David and Dorothea Prince with the help of their daughter Sheree have turned into a very popular venue with visitors and locals alike. Whether you are looking for excellent homecooked fare, a pint of fine ale in a cosy bar atmosphere, or very comfortable accommodation, The Mundy Arms with its thirty en-suite guest rooms and wonderful ambience enhanced by exposed brick walls, beams and beautiful decor caters for everyone's needs.

The Mundy Arms Hotel Mackworth 0332 824254 Fax: 0332 824519

Passing through the attractive village of **Kirk Langley,** we headed north towards **Kedleston Hall.** The hall has been the family seat of the Curzon family since the twelfth-century, although the present house was originally designed by Matthew Brettingham for Sir Nathaniel Curzon in 1759. Lord Curzon, Viceroy of India from 1899-1905, in turn lived here, and on display in the Indian Museum you can see the silver-ivories, weapons and works of art gathered by him during this period. In nearby Kedleston Church, Lord Curzon's tomb can be found in the family chapel which he had built as a memorial to his first wife. Their two marble effigies can be seen there, along with other Curzon monuments.

The Yew Tree Inn can be found in the picturesque hamlet of

Ednaston, just 1/4 mile off the main A515 Derby to Ashbourne road. The premises date back to the 16th century and careful refurbishment over the years, whilst providing every modern amenity, has ensured that none of its original character has been lost. An atmosphere of warm friendliness greets you the minute you arrive and the interior really is a picture, with lovely stained glass leaded windows and beamed ceilings adding to its charm. The Yew Tree is a freehouse and as such, offers a wide selection of real ales with a regularly changing guest beer. This is accompanied by a range of daily blackboard specials and an extensive and varied set menu which tempts your palate with such delights as Crispy Coated Mushrooms with Garlic Dip, homemade Steak and Kidney Pie and Broccoli and Cheese Bake. Children are welcome and there are ramps and toilet facilities for disabled visitors.

The Yew Tree. Ednaston,near Brailsford.   Tel: 0335 60433

The main A52 road led us into the lovely town of **Ashbourne**. Often called 'The Gateway to the North', it is a treat to visit. Don't think of it as merely some sort of portal into another landscape, Ashbourne deserves more attention than that. It is a pretty town which encourages you to linger and look in the shop windows. To potter up and down its streets is a pleasurable way of spending time.

For instance, many of us have no doubt marvelled at the beauty of handcrafted crystal, a craft which dates back to Roman times and one which has made Britain the leaders in production of lead crystal glassware, but visitors to **Derwent Crystal** in the heart of Ashbourne, actually have the opportunity to watch skilled craftsmen transforming a lump of crystal from its raw state to its exquisite and artistic finish. Here you can watch the different stages of glass blowing, edging and cutting, all essential processes in creating various works of art ranging from crystal fruit bowls and glasses to commemorative plates and highly decorative drinks decanters beautiful enough to take pride of place on anyone's shelf or sideboard. The showrooms are easily accessible from Ashbourne's main car park and are open Monday to Saturday from 9.00am - 5.00pm.

Derwent Crystal Craft Centre. Ashbourne tel: 0335 345219

With its central spire climbing more than 200 feet into the sky, **St Oswald's Church** is generally recognised as being one of the best examples of the early English style. Indeed, George Eliot referred to it as 'the most beautiful mere Parish Church in England'.

Ye Olde Vaults, Market Place, Ashbourne Tel: 0335 346127

Standing proudly in the market place of this delightful spa town, **Ye Olde Vaults** makes a super holiday and touring base. Dating back to the 1730's, this former coaching inn has lost none of its character over the years, although careful refurbishment has provided every modern comfort. Alan and Carol are welcoming hosts who provide excellent accommodation, fine cuisine and well-kept, varied ales, ably assisted by cheerful, smiling staff, a factor often lacking in many establishments. The four en-suite guest rooms are beautifully furnished and well equipped and have their own private entrance separate from

475

the inn. The extensive menu of tasty homecooked fare always proves popular, as does the carvery and the bar with its cosy atmosphere is the perfect place to relax, where visitors mix easily with locals and enjoy quiet conversation.

If you are lucky enough to visit Ashbourne on Shrove Tuesday or Ash Wednesday, you will find yourself a spectator at the famous Shrovetide football game. This is played between the Up'ards, those born north of the Henmore Brook, and the Down'ards, those born south of it. The two goals are situated three miles apart along the brook, on the site of the old mills at **Clifton** and **Sturston.**

Near Ashbourne, you will find outstanding self-catering accommodation at **Yeldersley Hall,** the magnificent 18th century home of Rex and Penelope Sevier. This splendid Georgian manor house stands within twelve acres of beautifully laid out grounds and has a wonderfully regal aura. Within the stable block there are two self-contained apartments, each with one double bedroom, equipped to a standard commensurate with their Four Key Commended rating. The East Wing of the Hall is something special, as its Five Key De Luxe rating suggests. From the bathrooms, which were designed by Pipe Dreams of London, to the two exquisite bedrooms with their lovely antique beds, you have everything you need for that perfect break away from it all. For sheer luxury in idyllic surroundings, a holiday at Yeldersley Hall will leave you with memories to treasure.

Yeldersley Hall, Ashbourne, Derbyshire. 0335 343432

Recommended by various organisations including the AA, RAC and The Camping Club of Great Britain, **Sandybrook Hall Holiday Park,** offers everything the camper or caravanner could need. There are excellent toilet and shower facilities, a fully equipped laundry room, outdoor swimming pool, site shop and the added attraction of a licensed clubhouse where you can enjoy a tasty bar meal. The location of the park is ideal for exploring the picturesque surrounding

476

countryside, with the Tissington Trail just five minutes walk away. For those who prefer more excitement, Alton Towers is within easy reach as are the Blue John Mines and of course there is plenty of space within the park itself for the children to run off their energy.

Sandybrook Hall Holiday Park. Ashbourne .0335 342679

In an easterly direction and situated opposite **Hulland Green** on the A517 Belper to Ashbourne road, **Hulland Nurseries** stands in

Hulland Nurseries, The Green, Hulland Tel: 0335 370052

seven and a half acres of lovely grounds surrounded by beautiful countryside and aside from being a superbly stocked nursery, makes an excellent place to stay. Jean and Martyn Barr are super hosts who provide very comfortable accommodation in two spacious and beautifully decorated guest rooms within their charming Grade II listed house. They also hope to offer self-catering accommodation in the near future. Within the grounds, the nursery specialises in beautiful hanging baskets, plant tubs and window boxes and on fine days you can enjoy one of Jean's delicious cream teas and homemade cakes on the patio.

477

Joining the **B5035,** we travelled towards **Wirksworth.** On our journey we took the opportunity to stop at **The Red Lion** in the tiny hamlet of **Hognaston,** an ideal touring base which caters to everybody's needs. In addition to providing everything you expect of a cosy traditional inn, The Red Lion provides very comfortable accommodation in two lovely en-suite guest rooms and for those who prefer to holiday independently, also provides a licensed campsite which has facilities for up to five touring caravans and plenty of space for campers. What could be better than a campsite with a first class pub on your doorstep providing fine ale and an extensive menu of homecooked food to please every palate?

The Red Lion, Main Street, Hognaston 0335 370396

If you are in search of that special place to stay, you would do well to make your way to **Henmore Grange** which is located in the village of **Hopton,** just off the B5035 Wirksworth to Ashbourne road. AA listed and awarded Three Crowns by the English Tourist Board, Henmore Grange offers superior holiday accommodation in the most picturesque surroundings.

Henmore Grange, Henmore Grange Farm, Hopton. 062 985 420

478

John and Elizabeth Brassington are friendly hosts whose hard efforts over the past ten years have created delightful accommodation within converted 300 year old farm outbuildings. Every room oozes character, with exposed stone walls and old oak beams and a magnificent 15th century fireplace in the lounge, all complemented by magnificent furnishings. Most of the eleven lovely guest rooms are en-suite and there is a licensed guest lounge to relax in. Outside a further attraction is the wonderful garden which has been carefully stocked to attract wild butterflies.

Wirksworth is a town we had been assured was worthy of a visit, so we set off to discover this charming market town. Several attractions caught our eye, mainly the very impressive church. The parish church of **St Mary's** stands in notably pretty surroundings. It is enclosed by almshouses provided by the Gell family in 1584, and the former grammar school founded by Anthony Gell in 1546. Inside the church, we took time to view one of the country's oldest carvings, The Wirksworth Stone. This is actually a coffin lid dating back to the 8th-century which has been magnificently carved from stone. Found under the chancel in 1820, it celebrates various events from the life of Christ and in all, some forty figures are represented.

It is probable that Wirksworth is 'Snowfield', the town depicted in George Eliot's 'Adam Bede'. If you enter the town from the direction of Derby, do look out for the first house on the right. This was the home of Elizabeth Evans, the author's aunt, who was the inspiration behind the character 'Dinah Morris' in the novel.

Leaving Wirksworth on the **B5036**, we headed north and began the steep descent into the village of **Cromford**. Before taking the plunge, however, we do recommend that you stop off at the picnic area at Black Rocks, which is signposted to the right at the top of the hill. The walk up to this famous landmark is fairly strenuous but well worth all the energy you can muster. We promise that your efforts will be rewarded by one of the most panoramic views of the **Derwent Valley**. From these windswept gritstone heights, your eyes are first drawn to the seemingly remote **Riber Castle,** then to the wooded gorge of nearby **Matlock**. On a clear day you can see cable cars wending their way across the gorge from the **Heights of Abraham**, a sight you would more likely associate with an alpine postcard.

We carried on down the hill into Cromford, which was developed by Richard Arkwright into one of the first industrial towns. In addition to housing, he also provided his workers with a market place and a village lock-up. Born in Lancashire in 1732, Arkwright was the inventor of the Waterframe, a machine for spinning cotton that was powered by water. He built his first mill at Cromford in 1771, the

479

Arkwright's Cromford Mill

project taking a further twenty years to complete. In 1792, he commissioned the building of the village church, where he now lies.

The mill proved to be a great success and became the model for others both in Britain and abroad, earning him the accolade, 'Father of the Factory System'. His pioneering work and contributions to the great Industrial Age resulted in a knighthood in 1786 and one year later he became High Sheriff of Derbyshire. **Cromford Mill** is probably one of Derbyshire's premier attractions and provides the whole family with a fascinating day out. This is the home of the world's first successful water powered cotton mill, built by Richard Arkwright in 1771 and today, continuing refurbishment and conservation by The Arkwright Society who bought the site in 1979, ensures that future visitors will be able follow the fascinating history behind this pioneering establishment. Within the complex of the mill site there are a range of craft workshops where you can purchase an ideal memento of your visit and in the Mill Restaurant you will find excellent homecooked refreshment including a wide selection of wholefood dishes.

Cromford Mill, Mill Lane, Cromford Tel: 0629 824297

For lovers of waterways, there is an opportunity at Cromford Canal to potter along a towpath, or better still, to take a peaceful canal boat ride. Cromford has a rather odd fifteenth-century bridge, which has rounded arches on one side, and pointed arches on the other. From this height, local folklore has it that in 1697 a horse and rider took a flying leap from the parapet, plunged into the river twenty feet below and lived to tell the tale. We are pretty sure that this miraculous feat must have kept them in free ale and oats for many years to come. **The High Peak Trail,** which stretches some seventeen miles up to Dowlow near Buxton, starts at Cromford. It is suitable for walkers and cyclists, and horses too if you remembered to pack one!

As you make your way off the main A6 at Cromford and follow the winding road to the small hamlet of Holloway, you will discover a rare gem of a pub called the **Yew Tree Inn.** Deceptively small from the outside, you could be forgiven for feeling as though you have stepped inside Dr. Who's Tardis, since a tasteful extension in 1970 has made this a far larger establishment than first appearances would have you believe. The extension part of the building has a lovely beamed ceiling and a beautiful feature mirror which came from the Lea Hurst home of Florence Nightingale. If it's well-kept ale you are after, there are always three fine traditional ales available plus the occasional guest beer, perfect accompaniments to the extensive and varied bar menu provided, but be warned, popularity makes bookings advisable for Sunday lunchtimes.

Yew Tree Inn, Holloway, Near Matlock.   0629 534355

We turned right onto the A6 and followed the Cromford Canal, heading towards Ambergate. If you take a left hand fork after **Whatstandwell Bridge** onto the **B5035,** it takes you up over a particularly lovely hill which offers some splendid views of the Derwent valley below. The road winds up the hill towards the village of **Crich,** where on the outskirts we found the **National Tramway Museum.** Referring to itself intriguingly as 'the museum that's a mile long', it offers a wonderful opportunity to enjoy a tram ride along a Victorian Street scene. The signposts, stone flags and gas lamps, are all original and come from such diverse places as Liverpool, Oldham and Leeds.

From the top deck of a tram, we had our first close-up of the tower of Crich Stand. We had spotted this landmark some miles before our arrival, and had likened it to a lighthouse. Curious as to why it was some distance from the nearest sea, we discovered that it is in fact a Regimental Memorial for the Sherwood Foresters. Erected in 1923, it stands almost a thousand feet above sea-level. Local people will tell you that you can see seven counties from its viewing gallery. We don't know about that, but the views it gave us of the next part of our journey certainly made us eager to carry on.

Scotland Nurseries Garden Centre. Tansley. 0629 583036
Fax: 0629 583013

The next village we came to on our chosen road was **Tansley**, very near to **Riber Castle.** Having learnt of the local flora and fauna we were fortunate to find a place where we could indulge our recently acquired knowledge. Situated on the **B6014,** a mile further up on the left hand side after its junction with the A615, **Scotland Nurseries** is one place well worth calling in at. Much more than just a garden centre, this a browser's paradise with a coffee shop that comes Egon Ronay recommended. Set in 45 acres at an altitude of some 800 - 1000ft, the interior of the garden centre was formerly an old packing shed set within a Victorian style barn. Outside for the horticultural enthusiast there is a vast selection of very hardy container grown and bare rooted trees, shrubs, hedging, rhododendrons etc. and after making your purchases, no visit is complete without sampling some of the excellent homebaked fare served in the coffee shop parlour, where only the finest fresh produce is used.

We spotted a lane leading to the village of **Dethick,** called a village, but actually comprising no more than a handful of farms. Here was the birthplace of the unfortunate Anthony Babington, who in a time when it was not advantageous to do so, fell in love with the doomed Mary, Queen of Scots. Plotting to secure her release from nearby Wingfield Manor, he and his colleagues were discovered and he was executed most horribly in 1587.

Almost a stone's throw away, is the charming village of **Lea.** The village is famous for its associations with Florence Nightingale. The local pub, the Jug and Glass, was formerly a hospital for the employees of the Nightingale family. It was probably here that she discovered her vocation for tending the sick. Florence spent many happy summers as a girl in the house called Lea Hurst in nearby **Holloway.**

The Coach House, Lea, Near Matlock Tel: 0629 534346

In this peaceful village, lying four miles from Matlock at the gateway to the Peak District National Park, you will find a lovely holiday base called **The Coach House.** Over the past nine years, proprietors John and Valerie Shaw have, through sheer hard work and determined effort, created a place that caters for the whole family. Set around the original cobbled courtyard are pleasures for everyone, from delicious homemade Jersey ice cream, to a delightful craft and gift shop, ideal for holiday mementos. The Harness Room is a super licensed restaurant which oozes with character and provides a wide selection of tasty and reasonably priced homecooked meals and clotted cream teas. With very comfortable accommodation provided in three guest rooms situated within tastefully converted outbuildings, plus two self-catering flats in the former hayloft, The Coach House makes the perfect holiday retreat.

You don't have to be a horticultural enthusiast to appreciate the sheer natural beauty of **Lea Gardens,** a superb collection of rhododendrons, azaleas, kalmias and other wonderful plants located in a delightful woodland setting.

Located in the heart of Lea, the gardens can be easily reached from either the A6 or A615 and provide a stunning visual display to enthral the whole family. Covering an area of some 4 acres, the site is set on the remains of a mediaeval millstone quarry and includes a lovely rock garden with many dwarf conifers, alpines, heathers and spring bulbs. There are several mapped out walks taking visitors through delightful floral displays and when you feel like giving your feet a rest, the cosy tearoom provides welcome refreshment before you purchase a living memento of your visit.

Lea Gardens, Lea, Matlock.   0629 534380

We decided to aim for **South Wingfield** to find out more about the luckless Anthony Babington. Our route took us along country lanes and through the village of **Wheatcroft,** but if you are in a hurry you will find South Wingfield on the **B5035.**

The ruins of Mary Queen of Scots prison, **Wingfield Manor,** is quite haunting in its beauty. Above the village on the rise of the hill, the house stands graceful and serene, while through the open windows, the sky behind can be seen. With the trees dotting the hill and masking parts of the building, we felt that a Sleeping Beauty should reside in a cobwebbed room hidden here.

At the end of the B5035 we turned right onto the **A615,** and a short drive took us to the historic town of **Alfreton.** The town dates back to Saxon times, and despite what you may imagine, Alfred the Great was not immortalised in the naming of the town. There are some splendid old buildings to be seen here, and of these, the most impressive is **Alfreton Hall** at the head of the park. In soft mellow stone, the Hall was built some time in the middle of the eighteenth century. Owned until fairly recently by the Palmer Morewood family who owned the local coal mines, it really is a delightful building. It is now used as an Arts and Adult Education Centre. The park is quite extensive, boasting its own cricket ground, and a horse-riding track around its perimeters.

In King Street there is a 'house of confinement' which was built to house law-breakers, and catered mainly for the local drunkards. The close confines of the prison with its two cells, minute windows and thick outer walls, must have been a very effective deterrent especially to those suffering from claustrophobia!

We ambled round the **Ogston Reservoir** for a while, admiring the techniques of the local sailing club. Covering an area of over 200 acres, the reservoir sits peacefully below Ogston Hall, and looking up to the hills, we noticed the ruins of what proved to be a chapel that has long since been abandoned.

We found our way onto the **B6036** and came to **Ashover**. The name of the village means 'ash tree slope', and we noted that this theme had recurred throughout our travels in the county so far, with names like Ashford-in-the-Water, Ashbourne to mention but a few. Although we certainly had noticed many ash trees, other trees also flourish here such as oak and birch. The village is just outside the Peak National Park, but it still captures the typical character of a Peak village.

Situated off the **B5057** that runs between the A6 and A632 you will find a lovely place to stay at **Old School Farm**, the lovely home of Dawn and Jonty Wootton. RAC and AA listed, this delightful house was built in 1983 and stands within 45 acres of mixed farming land, with wonderful views wherever you look. Set in the picturesque village of Uppertown, the house, despite its fairly recent construction, is full of character and charm. The four guest rooms are all very comfortably furnished and the large guest lounge/dining room provides satellite TV for those quiet evenings in. A homely, welcoming atmosphere is all apparent and in addition to a substantial breakfast, wholesome homecooked evening meals are available by prior arrangement.

Old School Farm, Uppertown, Ashover tel: 0246 590813

Taking the Ashover turn off the A61 at **Clay Cross** and making your way to **Old Tupton**, you will find an excellent holiday and touring base at **Bateman's Mill Hotel.** This magnificent former flour mill dates back to 1831 and was closed during the 1920's, although it has been in the Bateman family for over 100 years. From the time of its closure until two years ago, the Mill spent its life being used as cowsheds and a warehouse, a fact that is hardly credible today when you see the first class hotel that Alan and Isabel Bateman have created here. Oak beams and exposed stone walls plus the unusual feature of the original mill race, all enhance the character and charm of this welcoming, family run establishment. There are eight spacious and attractively furnished en-suite guest rooms, whilst the lovely restaurant proves popular with guests and locals alike, making booking advisable at the weekend. In the cosy pub atmosphere of the bar you can sample a wide range of traditional handpumped ales and to the rear of the hotel, Alan and Isabel cater for campers and caravanners in a small caravan and camping park.

Batemans Mill Hotel, Mill Lane, Old Tupton. 0246 862296

On the outskirts of Clay Cross on the main Chesterfield to Derby road you will find a convenient stopping-off point at **The Cannon,** a

The Cannon Hotel, 4 Thanet Street, Clay Cross. 0246 250078

charming 18th century freehouse where you can enjoy a fine range of ale and beer accompanied by tasty bar meals. A full à carte menu is available in the restaurant. A warm, cosy atmosphere is enhanced by beamed ceilings and walls adorned with bygone memorabilia. Children are well catered for at mealtimes with their own menu to choose from and the Sunday roast always proves popular, making weekend bookings advisable. The Cannon is within a few minutes drive of the beautiful villages of Ashover and Matlock on the fringe of the 'Peak District ' and within easy reach of the M1 motorway.

Just off the A61 on the B6013 overlooking the Amber Valley, you will find a lovely holiday base at **Higham Farm Hotel and Restaurant.** Dating back to the 15th century, this former farmhouse has been sympathetically converted so as to retain all its character whilst offering every modern facility. This is one of the oldest buildings in Higham and inside there is still an original well dating back to 1483. The Cocktail Bar and Lounge have a lovely olde worlde atmosphere enhanced by beamed ceilings and, in the lounge, an open fireplace and comfortable armchairs. There are eleven attractively furnished en-suite guest rooms, one even boasting a water bed and in the pleasant surroundings of the restaurant you can choose from both an à la carte and table d'hôte menu. The Hotel even has its own pub called The Tipsy Toad, which serves a fine range of real ale and tasty bar meals, ensuring everyone's needs are catered for here.

Higham Farm Hotel and Restaurant, Higham. 0773 833812
Fax: 0773 520525

Doubling back on ourselves, we returned to the **B6014,** and about five miles down the road we came to the village of **Tibshelf.** Stretching from here to Grassmoor, the Five Pits Trail had been recommended to us. This scenic walk takes you past the collieries at Tibshelf, Pilsley, Alameda, Williamthorpe and Grassmoor. Maybe at first sight you would not entertain the idea of exploring these old coal workings, but since their reclamation by the County Council, the land has been opened up to provide a seven mile trail. Suitable for walkers, cyclists and horse-riders, the walk is quite lovely, and offers some splendid

488

views. With the closure of the pits, which had been largely developed since the middle of the nineteenth century, the land had fallen into disuse. With the help of the Countryside Ranger Service, Derbyshire County Council manages the trail. There is also a great deal of support from local groups, who have contributed much time and effort to bring this land back to life. The clearing of paths and the addition of plantations, ponds and meadows has ensured that many species of wildlife have been encouraged to return here.

Wild plants to look out for include the Bush Vetch, Meadowsweet, and perhaps our favourite, the Corn Poppy. At one time, these lovely wild flowers could be seen in abundance in so many fields and hedgerows.

The village of **Pilsley,** the second old colliery site on the Trail, has its associations with Chatsworth. During the 1760s, 'Capability' Brown was busy carrying out his reorganisation of Chatsworth Park for the fourth Duke of Devonshire. One small part of this 'tidying up' of the landscape was the demolition of a number of houses in the original village of Edensor -which was later transferred to a new site in the time of the sixth duke. The inhabitants of these unwanted buildings were rehoused at Pilsley, and when Joseph Paxton came on the scene, more houses were built here.

Just across the M1 east of Hardstoft, lies the magnificent Tudor house, **Hardwick Hall**. Set as it is in rolling parkland, you would never guess that a major motorway was nearby. The house, with its glittering tiers of windows, has the letters 'E. S.' carved in stone and surmounted with crowns on the turrets, and is really quite spellbinding. Inside, the silence of the chambers strewn with rush matting, combined with the simplicity of the white-washed walls, gives a feeling of almost overwhelming peace. 'E. S.', or Elizabeth of Shrewsbury, was the jewel in this stone crown. Better known as Bess of Hardwick, this larger-than-life woman crops up in so many places throughout the county that we feel compelled to devote a few sentences to her life.

She was born in the manor house at Hardwick in 1520. The house stood only a little distance from the present day Hall, and was then not much more than a farmhouse. The young Bess married her neighbour's son Robert Barlow when she was only twelve. When her young husband, who himself was only fourteen, died a few months later she naturally inherited a great deal of property. Some fifteen years later she married Sir William Cavendish, and when he died in 1557, she was bequeathed his entire fortune.

She was the richest woman in England, save for one, Elizabeth the Queen.

The Gallery with its gorgeous lavender-hued tapestries, has in pride of place a portrait of this formidable woman. We could not help

489

but compare her with her counterpart Elizabeth the First. The one, a 'Virgin' Queen who commanded so forceably the men around her yet never married, and this Bess, who throughout her life married and survived four husbands. The portrait depicts a woman who could be mistaken for Elizabeth R, and we wondered what their thoughts and words might have been, on the occasions that they may have met throughout both their long 'reigns'.

The property is owned by the National Trust, and if you only have the time to visit one stately home while in this part of the county, this should be high on your list. Whilst in the area some might be interested to know that Thomas Hobbes the philosopher and author of ' Leviathan ' is buried at the church in nearby **Ault Hucknall.**

Although Hardwick Hall and Wingfield Manor proved so delightful, it must be said that the towns and villages from here to Chesterfield are not really places for the tourist. However, this is by no means a criticism of the area as pockets of interest vie for your attention admist the changing skyline.

We were closing in on Chesterfield but not before taking the **B6417** to **Clowes.** Here,dating back to the early part of the nineteenth century, **The Van Dyk Hotel** stands proudly beside the main A619 Chesterfield to Worksop road at Clowne. Run by Frank and Dorothy Smith for over 20 years, the hotel is magnificent in every way, with a stately and elegant air, both inside and out. The beautiful gardens surrounding it make this a popular venue for wedding receptions and the splendid restaurant with its lovely panelled walls provides the perfect setting in which to savour the superb cuisine provided in both the à la carte and table d'hôte menus. As with the rest of the hotel, the sixteen en-suite guest rooms are all extremely tastefully furnished and equipped for maximum comfort, making a stay here an experience you are sure to remember for a long time.

The Van Dyk Hotel, Worksop Road, Clowne . 0246 810219

Closer to Chesterfield and situated in the peaceful village of **Brimington,** just a couple of miles outside Chesterfield is **Brimington Equestrian Centre**, a BHS and ABRS Approved establishment run by highly experienced horsewoman, Tracey Priest-Redford. Horse-lovers of all ages and abilities will find this a super place, whether for a quiet afternoon hack or a full residential holiday. There are plenty of horses of varying size and temperament to suit everyone's needs and the flood-lit all-weather surface means you can enjoy your riding whatever the weather. With a full range of livery services available, private and group lessons, plus camping and own-a-pony holidays, Brimington Equestrian Centre is a veritable horse-rider's paradise.

Brimington Equestrian Centre, Brimington. 0246 235465

With its large bay windows adorned with attractive hanging baskets, **The Brickmakers Arms** in Brimington makes a tempting stopping-off point in any journey.

The Brickmakers Arms, 165 Manor Road, Brimington 0246 27509

The perfect example of a traditional olde worlde pub, it dates back to the 19th century and was at one time used as the stabling area for

Hardwick Hall.

horses transporting wagons of clay to and from a nearby brickworks, long since closed. Alan and Janet Barnes are welcoming hosts who since they bought The Brickmakers Arms, have developed it into a popular place where visitors and locals mix easily and can enjoy a pint of fine ale and tasty bar meal in an atmosphere of warmth and friendship.

Chesterfield is a friendly, bustling town on the edge of the Peak National Park, which grew up around its Open Air Market. The town lies at the cross roads of England, the hub of trade routes from all points of the compass, so it is not surprising to find such a large and colourful market at the heart of the town. Life in Chesterfield has revolved around this market since the towns earliest days, it was earning Royal revenue in 1165, as the Sheriff of Derbyshire recorded in the Pipe Rolls. In that year, the market earned the princely sum of £1.2s.7d for the Crown. The Pipe Roll of 1182 also mentions a fair in Chesterfield. Such fairs were large markets, usually lasting for several days and drawing traders and buyers from a much wider area. Chesterfield's formal Charter however was not granted until 1204, but this Charter made the town one of the first eight free boroughs in the country. Markets are held every Monday, Friday and Saturday, with a flea market each Thursday.

The town centre has been conserved for future generations by a far sighted council. many buildings have been saved, including the Victorian Market Hall built in 1857. These beautiful buildings, many of them of architectural and historical interest were well worth the effort made to save them. The traditional cobbled paving was restored in the Market Place, and New Square was given a complete face lift. Seats were provided along with trees, colourful hanging baskets and the Peace Fountain. Subsequently the Town Council was awarded the prestigious Europa Nostra Award, an award which is internationally recognised.

Situated on a pedestrian walkway in the heart of Chesterfield, the discerning gastronome will discover a superb place to eat at **Mr C's Bar and Restaurant.** Run by the perfect combination of John Cruickshank, a highly experienced chef, and Michael Norton, a front of house manager with a lively personality, the restaurant lies adjacent to the historic outdoor market and is a place full of style and magical ambience where you can sample the finest in mouthwatering cuisine. You can savour John's culinary expertise in the relative privacy of the individual wooden alcoves with lovely stained glass windows, whilst still enjoying the convivial atmosphere which abounds. It is no surprise then, that Mr C's has developed a reputation as the place to eat in Chesterfield and being open from 8.00am Monday - Saturday, it clearly caters for everyone's needs.

Mr C's Bar and Restaurant, Chesterfield : 0246 207070

Visitors to the town are drawn to a peculiarly graceful Spire reaching high into the skyline, twisting and leaning it is totally confusing to the eye. Recognised as one of Chesterfields landmarks the 'Crooked Spire' has dominated the skyline for so long that local folk have ceased to notice its unusual shape. How did it happen? superstition surrounds it and the truth itself has sadly been lost during the intervening years. The truth probably lies in the wake of the Black Death during the 14th century, when the people of Chesterfield were building their beautiful new church and awe inspiring steeple. Many must have fallen to the Plague, and among them skilled craftsmen who knew how to season wood. The survivors built the Spire out of green timber, which over the years has distorted under the heavy lead covering.

This magnificent Spire rises to 228 feet and leans 9' 4" from its true centre point. It is eight sided but the herring-bone pattern of the lead slates trick the eye into seeing 16 sides from the ground. The Crooked Spire of the church of St. Mary's and All Saints is open all year, Monday to Saturday 9am to 5pm and on Sundays at service times only, except by appointment. **Revolution House** is situated in the village of Old Whittington, three miles north of Chesterfield and is another feature which definitely warrants a visit when in the area. During the 17th century the building was part of an alehouse called the 'Cock and Pynot'. (Pynot being a dialect word for Magpie.) It was here that three local noblemen - the Earl of Devonshire, the Earl of Danby and Mr. John D'Arcy met to begin planning their part in the events which led to the overthrow of King James II in favour of his daughter Mary and her husband, William of Orange. Revolution House is now open to the public and features period furnishings and a changing programme of exhibitions on local themes. A video relates the story of the Revolution, and the role which the House played in those fraught and dangerous days. The House is open Saturday and Sunday throughout the year from 10am to 4pm and Easter to October daily, admission is free.

Situated not far from the centre of Chesterfield on Ashgate Road, you will find a very comfortable holiday base at **Little Lonsdale**, the

Little Lonsdale. Chesterfield. 0246 272950 Fax: 0246 271062

delightful home of Angela and Trevor Walls. Awarded a Three Crowns rating, the house motto is 'Where strangers are there none, merely friends we have yet to meet' and you certainly feel like a friend when you stay here, with such warm, welcoming hosts and a relaxed, homely atmosphere. There are nine individually styled guest rooms, three with en-suite facilities and all with satellite TV and hot drinks trays. For that special occasion, you can book the four poster room, with its lovely canopied bed, antique furniture and en-suite bathroom. In addition to a full breakfast, Angela readily provides homecooked evening meals by prior arrangement and happily caters for vegetarians.

If you are looking for somewhere to enjoy a lively night out full of fun and atmosphere, then **The Red Lion** on the A619 at **Brampton** to the west of Chesterfield is ideal. There has been a Red Lion pub on this site for many hundreds of years, although the existing Red Lion was rebuilt here in 1890. Graham and Linda Haslam are the friendly owners of this excellent freehouse and have developed it into a very popular place with locals and visitors alike. In addition to a fine selection of ales and tasty, freshly prepared bar meals, the Haslams also provide super accommodation in seven attractively furnished and well-equipped en-suite guest rooms, enabling you to enjoy a complete 'night out'!

Crooked Spire. Chesterfield.

The Red Lion, 281 Chatsworth Road, Brampton.   0246 207869

Off the **B6051** heading out of Chesterfield towards **Barlow** you'll see on your left **The Olde House Hotel** owned by Mansfield Brewery. This 3 Crown Commended Hotel centres around an original 16th century farmhouse and provides an ideal haven for the weary traveller. Its twelve excellent ensuite bedrooms with full facilities, which includes a newspaper of your choice, are pleasantly and comfortably furnished.

The Olde House Hotel.   Newbold.   0246 274321 Fax: 0246 221853

The intimate restaurant has a landscaped stream running through it and in this calming atmosphere you can enjoy from an extensive and often changing menu of freshly prepared food. Afterwards, relax in the Olde Worlde bar or Bar Lounge with a drink or retire to your room and TV? The Olde House Hotel is a welcoming, homely place with helpful staff that should suit most pockets and with its easy location to Chesterfield, Sheffield, Derby, the Peak National Park, Chatsworth

House, Haddon and Hardwick Halls, makes it ideal for those wanting to discover the area with the help of a comfortable base. The Hotel also has an attractive, 'church style' function room that accommodates up to one hundred and which sometimes holds exhibitions amongst its many events.

Owned and run by David Cook and his son Gary, **The Sandpiper** hotel and restaurant can be found on the A61 about half a mile prior to the village of Unstone. A very attractive building it has been beautifully refurbished and extended over the years to provided very comfortable accommodation, for which it has been awarded 2 Stars by the AA and a Four Crowns Commended grading by the English Tourist Board. Each of the 28 en-suite guest rooms are individually furnished and equipped to the high standard you would expect and in the relaxed atmosphere of the restaurant you can choose from both an à la carte and table d'hôte menu, offering a wide choice of mouthwatering dishes to suit every palate.

The Sandpiper, Unstone. 0246 450550 Fax: 0246 452805

Continuing north along the **B6052** from **Old Whittington** the road took us to the sprawling village of **Eckington**, one of the largest villages in England. Of particular note in this locality is **Renishaw Hall,** situated between Eckington and the neighbouring village of Renishaw. Home of the famous Sitwell family, the hall was built by George Sitwell in 1625, who re-established his lost fortune with the advent of the Renishaw Iron Works.

The massive house was greatly transformed under the first baronet, Sir Sitwell Sitwell (no, that's not a printing error!), and in the grounds can be found the world's most northerly vineyard. The Sitwell family were much given to writing and with Dame Edith, Sir Sacheverell and Sir Osbert all having inclinations that way, there must be something in the wine that promoted such literary leanings.

Just before Renishaw, we turned right onto the B6419 which took us to the fairytale 'folly' of **Bolsover Castle.** The present 'keep' was built for Sir Charles Cavendish some time in the early seventeenth century on the site of a ruined castle that would have dated back to William the Conqueror. Known as the 'Little Castle', it has successfully captured a medieval flavour despite the different styles that have gone into the building over the years. A riding school and gallery built in the Classical style were added by Sir William Cavendish around 1660.

To the east visitors to **Nether Langwith** will find excellent cuisine and first class accommodation at **Goff's Restaurant** which

Goff's Restaurant. Nether Langwith 0623 744538

enjoys a delightful setting within Langwith Mill House. Standing within the vast shadow of Langwith Mill, a six-storey water-powered cotton mill built in 1784, Goff's Restaurant is a superb establishment run by Lynne and Graham Goff. A cosy, welcoming ambience is immediately apparent, with beautiful furnishings and that extra little touch at every table enhancing the restaurant's distinctive character and appeal. The extensive menu offers the discerning palate a choice of mouthwatering and imaginatively prepared dishes, with something to tempt everyone and having enjoyed your meal, there can be nothing nicer to complete your evening, than retiring to one of the two delightfully furnished en-suite guest rooms.

In **Spinkhill** off the A616 and for those seeking a special place for a relaxing break away from it all, **Park Hall Hotel** is truly an oasis within a desert, a hotel and restaurant well-deserving of its Four Crowns, 3 Star grading. Set in over eight acres of beautiful grounds, its peaceful location belies the Hall's close proximity to the M1 motorway. Dating back in parts to the 14th century, renovation and refurbishment has not detracted from its original character and charm, with oak panelled walls, large open fireplaces and four poster beds all enhancing an air of timeless elegance. Jan and Tony Clark are

499

superb hosts who have successfully combined outstanding facilities and professional service with a warm, welcoming hospitality. Each of the eight en-suite guest rooms is exquisitely furnished and equipped for maximum comfort, while in the cosy restaurant, you are assured of the finest cuisine, imaginatively prepared and beautifully served, accompanied by a carefully selected wine list.

Park Hall Hotel and Uplands Manor Restaurant, Spinkhill, Sheffield 0246 434897

We decided that our last port of call would be to Creswell, a few miles north-east of Bolsover. Once a sleepy hamlet nestling amongst peaceful farming country, the character of **Creswell** was irreversibly changed at the end of the nineteenth century. It was then that Creswell Colliery was opened, and now the village is one of the biggest in the county.

The Crags were formed thousands of years ago with the erosion of the river forming a gorge through the limestone. This rock, which is porous and subject to erosion underground as well as on the surface, by its very nature contributes to the forming of natural chambers. The subterranean movement of water created a vast network of caves. These were subsequently exposed and today we can see some of them along the river gorge. The animal remains found here dating back over 70,000 years.

Testimony to the artistry of the later inhabitants of these caves was the discovery of a bone carved with the head of a horse, which is about 13,000 years old, and can now be seen in the British Museum. The largest cavern, Church Hole Cave, extends some 170 feet into the side of the gorge, and it was in here that hand tools were found.

Our final chapter required our retracing our steps across to Matlock. We did so with eager anticipation, sure that Northwest Derbyshire would have as much if not more to offer the visitor looking for more ' Hidden Places '.

CHAPTER SEVENTEEN

North West Derbyshire

Chatsworth House

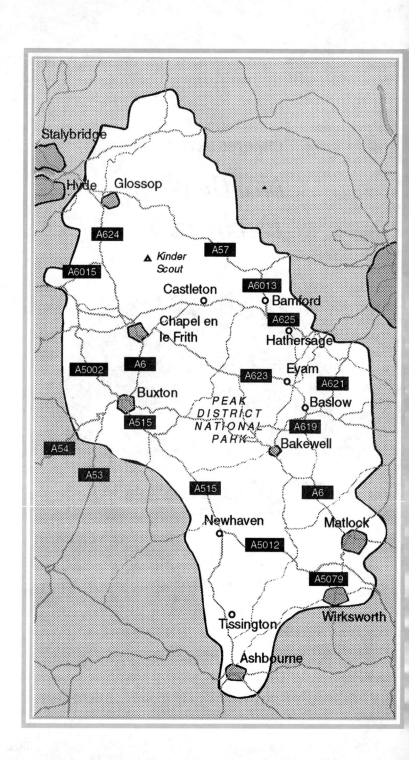

CHAPTER SEVENTEEN.

North West Derbyshire.

Fish And Chips, a bandstand, amusement arcades and a tranquil river. Motor-cyclists, the soaring tree-covered ravine and trippers buying ice-cream cornets. There can be no other place in the British Isles that so harmoniously blends this incongruous mixture of English pleasures than here in **Matlock Bath.**

The entry into Matlock Bath is lovely. A pleasant drive heading north along the A6 brings you past Cromford, which we visited in the previous chapter. On your right, the splendid **Masson Mill** by Arkwright and above the road, clinging like kagoule clad flies, rock climbers try out their clamps and ropes and defy gravity on the 1110 feet of Masson Hill or across the river on High Tors 673 feet.

The town today is essentially a holiday resort, and yet it still possesses an air of Victorian charm, left over from the days when it was a popular spa. Walking along South Parade, the oddity of this town struck us, as we came upon a line of gaily painted cottages. Built into the sides of the gorge, they would not have looked out of place in a Cornish fishing village.

Non-smokers would have to go a long way to match the comfort and hospitality of **Sunnybank Guest House**, a licensed establishment which enjoys a peaceful location on Clifton Road, off the main A6 at Matlock Bath. Awarded a Three Crown Commended grading by the English Tourist Board, Sunnybank is an impressive Victorian house dating back to 1883 and is the home of Peter and Daphne West. There are five well-appointed guest rooms, three with en-suite facilities plus a comfortable TV lounge to relax in. The dining room with its lovely view along the Derwent Valley provides a lovely setting for both breakfast and an optional evening meal which can be provided by arrangement. With the centre of Matlock Bath just a short walk away and many local attractions within easy reach, Sunnybank makes an ideal holiday and touring base.

Sunnybank Guest House, Matlock Bath. 0629 584621

The River Derwent is the heart of Matlock Bath. The buildings of the town cling tightly to the side of the road, and the road itself hugs the river, following its twists and turns through the gorge. On the hill above you, houses partly hidden amongst the trees climb up into the dizzy heights. Hidden away in a narrow twisting gorge of the River Derwent, the **New Bath Hotel** at Matlock Bath makes a luxurious base from which to explore the beauty of the surrounding Derbyshire

The New Bath Hotel, Matlock Bath 0629 583275 Fax: 0629 580268

countryside and its many attractions. Set within five and a half acres of well-laid out grounds, this impressive Regency hotel provides all you need for a relaxing break away from it all. Each of the 55 en-suite guest rooms is beautifully furnished and equipped for maximum comfort. Downstairs in the cosy atmosphere of the Spinners Bar and Lounge you can enjoy a refreshing aperitif before making your way to the Lamp and Seam restaurant where stone archways enhance a quiet, intimate ambience in which to savour superb cuisine and fine wines. With full leisure facilities including outdoor swimming pool, sauna, solarium, indoor plunge pool and a hard tennis court, it seems your every need is catered for.

Set high up off the A6 at Matlock Bath with wonderful panoramic views, **The Temple Hotel** is an idyllic holiday base. Awarded a Four Crown rating by the English Tourist Board and AA and RAC Commended, this splendid hotel is run by welcoming hosts, Mr. and Mrs. Essl. The beautiful exterior with its pretty window boxes is matched inside, with grand yet comfortable furnishings throughout. There are fourteen well-appointed en-suite guest rooms and two pleasant lounge bars to relax in, while in the cosy atmosphere of the restaurant you can choose from an extensive menu which incorporates both traditional English and authentic Austrian dishes. With various local attractions within easy reach and a variety of events going on throughout the year, this really is a hotel for all seasons.

The Temple Hotel, Matlock Bath. 0629 583911

The Aquarium is housed in the Matlock Bath Hydro, and where once a visitor to this thermal spring would have received treatment for gout, lumbago and nervous disorders, it is now the fishy residents who benefit from the stimulating waters! Sharing the same building is the Hologram Gallery, and these two diverse attractions seem to sum up the odd mixture of entertainment on offer in the town.

For spectacular views of Matlock Bath, nothing beats a walk on the High Tor Grounds. There are sixty acres of nature trails to wander around, while some 400 feet below the Derwent appears like a silver thread through the gorge.   Surrounded by historical villages this former Spa town developed during the Regency period, it now enjoys several more up to date attractions, such as Cable cars, which allowed us to witness the beauty of the Derwent Valley. There are plenty of ideas for family outings in and around the town. The Pavilion houses the Peak District Mining Museum, and nearby you'll find Gullivers

Kingdom,a fun park for younger children,Chatsworth House,the Tramway Museum, Haddon Hall and Denby Potteries.

Leaving the town along North Parade, we couldn't fail to notice the cable cars which we had previously sighted from our precarious perch on Black Rocks. From the foot of High Tor, a dramatic 350 foot precipice, the cable cars cross the limestone gorge of Matlock Dale. The ride takes you to the Victoria Prospect Tower at the top of the **Heights of Abraham** and magnificent views.

Along the main A6 towards Matlock Bath you will come across an excellent stopping-off point called **The Boat House Inn.** It really would be hard to find a more welcoming place, this is hospitality at its best. Dave Whitehurst is a super host who has developed this 18th century inn into a very popular venue with visitors and locals like. Attractively furnished throughout, in keeping with its age and character, the inn provides a cosy, relaxed setting in which to enjoy fine ale and a wide selection of homecooked food at very reasonable prices and in portions to satisfy the biggest appetite. For those wishing to stay, there are five lovely guest rooms and you can choose to have a continental breakfast served in your room, or make your way to the dining room for a full English breakfast, with the emphasis firmly placed on the 'full'!

The Boat House Inn, Dale Road, Matlock. 0629 583776

Just a few minutes further along the road brought us into **Matlock** itself, a testament to the lasting attraction of Victorian architecture. Situated off Jackson Road in Matlock, you will find an ideal place to stay at **Jackson Tor House,** a delightful family-run hotel set high up overlooking the town with just over an acre of beautiful gardens to the rear. Run by friendly hosts Mick and Sheila Newman for the past twenty years, this Two Crown establishment provides a comfortable touring base from which to explore this lovely part of Derbyshire. All 29 guest rooms are fully equipped and beautifully furnished, four with en-suite facilities. You can't help but relax in the cosy, welcoming atmosphere of the spacious lounge and bar and the restaurant serves an excellent range of homecooked fare with a weekend carvery proving popular with residents and non-residents alike.

Jackson Tor House, Jackson Road, Matlock. 0629 582348

A bustling town that nestles in the valley, Matlock is the administrative centre of Derbyshire, with the County Council headquarters based in the former hydropathic hotel at Matlock Bank. John Smedley founded the establishment in 1853. This was at a time when Victorian values demanded stringent regimes, and the people considered that puritanical methods were vital for their curative powers. The hydro proved overwhelmingly successful throughout the next century.

Abid Tandoori Restaurant, Matlock 0629 57400/55915

Lovers of traditional Indian food will discover a real haven in the centre of Matlock at the **Abid Tandoori Restaurant** which can be found on the A6 as you travel towards Matlock Bath, just prior to the railway bridge. Mohammed Bashir is a welcoming host who, together

507

with his friendly team of staff, has created a superb establishment here. As soon as you walk through the door, you are hit by an atmosphere of class, enhanced by the elegant decor and furnishings and you are immediately made to feel as though you are someone special. Flowers on the tables, soft lighting, unobtrusive background music and air conditioning create a warm, relaxed ambience and provide the perfect setting in which to savour a very extensive and varied menu. The range of dishes leaves you with a real dilemma as to which to choose, each freshly prepared to the highest standards and if you can't decide on individual dishes, then you can always opt for one of the Abid Tandoori set menus. The restaurant is fully licensed and also offers a take-away service. Open evenings only, Sunday - Thursday 6.00pm - midnight, Friday and Saturday 6.00pm - 1.00am.

High up on the hill behind you stands the brooding 'ruin' of **Riber Castle.** Built in 1862, this was another of John Smedley's memorials. It was the family home for many years. Now established as a sanctuary for rare breeds and endangered species, the Wildlife Park has been particular successful at breeding lynx, and boasts the world's largest collection of this magnificent animal.

Once over Matlock Bridge, we turned left at Crown Square roundabout, and headed north on the Bakewell road to **Darley Dale** One of the most unassuming heroines of this part of Derbyshire must be Lady Mary Louisa Whitworth, or 'Lady Bountiful', as she later came to be known. She was the second wife of Sir Joseph Whitworth the famous Victorian engineer whose name is associated with the Great Exhibition of 1851. Following Sir Joseph's death in 1887, Lady Mary undertook to bring sweeping changes to the lifestyle of the local poor and needy. She allowed the grounds of her home, **Stancliffe Hall,** to be used for school outings and events. In 1889, the Whitworth Cottage Hospital was opened under her auspices.

The Whitworth Institute was opened in 1890, this project bringing to the community a wide range of facilities including a swimming pool an assembly hall, a natural history museum, and a library. At a time when a woman was required to take a secondary role, she was determined to credit her late husband with these changes, which so benefited Darley Dale. Lady Whitworth died in France in 1896, and is buried next to her husband at the parish church of St Helen's.

Turning off the A6 onto the **B5057**, we crossed over the Derwent once more, on the fifteenth-century Darley Bridge. Dating back to 1735, **The Square and Compass** in the village of **Darley Bridge** is a delightful pub situated beside the River Derwent, with lovely scenic views on all sides. Although obviously refurbished and modernised over the years, it has lost none of its charm and character or of course its hospitality. Mark and Anita Singleton are friendly hosts who pride
508

themselves on offering their many visitors fine ale and first class food. As Mark is the principal trombonist in the Darley Dale Brass Band, concerts are a regular attraction here. Across the road, the inn also provides a certified caravan and camping site for caravans and tents, making The Square and Compass an ideal stop-over point.

The Square and Compass, Darley Bridge. 0629 733255

On the main A6, at the edge of Darley Dale you will come across **The Grouse Inn**, a welcoming and well run family pub owned by Philip and Susan Rogers. Dating back to the 1840's, this former coaching inn was once used as a place for changing teams of horses and there is still evidence of a blacksmith's shop in what is now the garage. Particularly popular during the summer are the large beer garden with children's play area and the boules pitch and barbecue. In a warm, friendly atmosphere you can enjoy fine, well-kept ale and excellent homecooked food and should you need somewhere to stay, bed and breakfast accommodation can be arranged for you locally.

The Grouse Inn, Dale Road North, Darley Dale. 0629 734357

At **Wensley,** we entered the Peak District National Park, which is controlled by the Peak Park Authority. The Peak District was the first of Britain's ten National Parks, and covers an area of over 540 square miles. Thanks to the efforts of the Park Authority, we all have the opportunity to roam freely through some spectacular countryside.

Although the term 'peak' is used often when referring to the Derbyshire highlands, with the exception of a handful of places, the district has few real peaks in the common sense of the word. The origin of the name probably comes from the Pecsaetans, or 'hill people', a primitive tribe who are thought to have settled in the area around the seventh century.

Wherever you cross the borders of the Park, you will notice millstones standing on their edge on stone plinths at the side of the road. These are used as boundary markers by the Park Authority, which has also adopted the millstone symbol as its logo.

Further along the B5057, we came to the village of **Winster** with its splendid seventeenth to eighteenth-century **Market House.** This building was the National Trust's first acquisition in Derbyshire, and is open to the public several weekend afternoons during the Summer. If you happen to be in the village on Shrove Tuesday and hanker for sport a little less vigorous than Ashbourne's football match, you will be able to enjoy Winster's annual Pancake Race. Situated in the village of Winster, you will discover **The Bowling Green Inn,** renowned as the oldest pub in Derbyshire. Dating back to 1473, this Crook building is reputed to be the 313th of its kind to be built and it is thought to have once had its own bowling green.

The Bowling Green Inn, Winster, Near Matlock. 0629 650219

Inside, a cosy, welcoming atmosphere is enhanced by traditional furnishings and a beautiful arched stone fireplace. Les Routiers Recommended, this is a freehouse in the truest sense, with four different brewer's ales plus over sixty malt whiskies to choose from. Open evenings only during the winter, but lunchtime and evening in

510

the summer months, The Bowling Green complements its fine range of drinks with an extensive menu of excellent homecooked food.

You will also find **The Dower House**, a charming Grade II listed Elizabethan country house which between 1737 and 1861 was owned by the Curzon family of Kedleston Hall. Today it is the lovely home of Helen Bastin and Geoff Dalton and can be found by taking the B5057 off the main A6 to Winster village. Passing through the village, The Dower House faces you as the road forks. Awarded a Two Crown Highly Commended rating by the English Tourist Board and Four Q's by the AA, all three guest rooms are beautifully furnished and have en-suite or private facilities and the beamed guest lounge with its polished wooden floor leads into a cosy breakfast room. With a beautiful walled garden surrounding the property and warm, welcoming hosts tending to your every need, staying at The Dower House is a real treat.

The Dower House, Main Street, Winster. 0629 650213

Although our planned route would take us south from here, don't miss the opportunity of visiting some of Winster's neighbouring villages. Around **Stanton-in-the-Peak** and **Birchover** you will find a number of diverse attractions, including **Rowter Rocks, Robin Hood's Stride** and the **Nine Ladies.** The Rocks contain caves which were carved out at some stage in the seventeenth-century. Not only the living space, but tables, chairs and alcoves were made to create a cosy retreat for the local vicar, Reverend Thomas Eyre. Prior to these home improvements, the caves were reputedly used by the Druids, who did not believe in such creature 'comforts'.

If you are not yet weary of your brush with the past, we suggest you make tracks for **Stanton Moor**, site of the Nine Ladies Stone Circle. This is not really a stone circle at all, but the remnants of a sizeable barrow, with nine standing stones encircling a small cairn. Also in the area is the site of an Iron Age hillfort known as Castle Ring, and in all, some seventy Bronze Age barrows are dotted over the moor. Many of the artifacts from this area can be seen at the museum of **Sheffield.**

Still following the past, we left Winster and headed south on the B5056, passing through Grangemill, where once the Romans may have travelled on the ancient Portway. This trackway predates the Roman occupation, as it was used to link a network of Iron Age forts, and was vital as a highway for centuries.

Here set in 40 acres of picturesque countryside within the Peak National Park and boasting some of the finest views in Derbyshire, **Middle Hills Farm** is owned and run by Linda and Joe Lomas, a welcoming couple who cater for everyone's holiday needs. Within their attractive stone-built farmhouse accommodation is provided in three lovely guest rooms, two en-suite, awarded a Two Crown rating by the English Tourist Board. There is a guest TV lounge to relax in and Linda's substantial breakfast gives guests the perfect start to the day. Within the grounds there is also a fully equipped static caravan, which sleeps up to six and, new this year, a barn conversion into two luxury self-catering cottages. For camping enthusiasts there is a level grassy site complete with toilet block, water tap and disposal point. Taking the A6 turn right onto the A5012 for about 3 miles, past the Hollybush pub for 300 yards then take the first left over the cattle grid.

Middle Hills Farm, Grange Mill, Matlock. 0629 650368

Visitors to this area will be well aware of **Dovedale** and the beautiful walks along the River Dove and its sister river, the Manifold. At Dovedale there is a large car park, but as you would expect, such a beauty spot does tend to get rather chock-a-block, especially at weekends. Much work has been undertaken by the local ranger service to resurface the paths, which take a fair amount of wear and tear throughout the year. You can cross the Dove over a small bridge while a little further along, there are stepping stones spanning the river. Great limestone rocks rise out of the ravine in strange formations

512

of pillars and spires. **Lion Rock, The Twelve Apostles, Tissington Spires** and **Reynards Cave,** these are just some of the fabulous places to be explored.

As mentioned in the previous chapter Izaak Walton used to stay with his friend and later adopted son Charles Cotton, who owned Beresford Hall. The Dove flowed through the estate, giving him a first hand opportunity to fish from this pleasant water. 'The Compleat Angler' was written here and first published in 1653. The book was a great success, and has enjoyed a virtually uninterrupted print run since that time. Although Dovedale can get over-crowded at times, don't despair, as **Thorpe Cloud** offers plenty of open space to explore. This incredibly odd-shaped peak stands out offering you the opportunity to escape and some pleasant walking.

We left this wonderful spot, and crossed the **A515,** heading towards **Tissington** which sits in the foothills of the Pennines. Before our arrival there we discovered **The Bentley Brook,** a delightful half-timbered inn situated within the Peak District National Park at **Fenny Bentley** two miles north of Ashbourne on the A515.

Bentley Brook Inn, Fenny Bentley. 033 529 278 Fax: 033 529 422

Formerly a medieval farmhouse, then a private country residence of some style, now careful renovation by the Allingham family has retained all the building's original character whilst providing every modern amenity. Set in two acres of gardens, a further five acres of meadow and woodland includes a 270 yard stretch of Bentley Brook, a tributary of The Dove. A warm, welcoming ambience greets you in the cosy bar where you can savour a fine selection of ales and choose from an extensive bar and à la carte menu. Awarded a Three Crown Commended grading, there are nine very comfortable guest rooms, seven en-suite, as well as two fully equipped self-catering cottages, ensuring everyone's needs are met. During the warmer months visitors can make use of the large beer garden and enjoy a game of boule or croquet and sometimes a barbecue.

Tissington village is perhaps famous for its ancient festival of Well Dressing, a ceremony which possibly dates back to 1350 or earlier in this particular area and is celebrated by many villages in the area. This takes place in the last week of May and draws many crowds who come to see the spectacular folk art created by the locals. Using natural objects like mosses, flower petals, nuts, leaves and pebbles, the well heads are beautifully decorated with pictures favouring religious events. The significance of the event in Tissington may have been to commemorate those who survived the ravages of the Black Death when it raged throughout the villages of Derbyshire. This was attributed to the purity and plentitude of the local spring waters, and the villagers were extremely lucky to have no less than five wells to choose from.

Another good reason to stop at the village is that from here you can walk the **Tissington Trail**. The route takes you through some lovely country as you follow the former railway line that at one time stretched from Ashbourne to Buxton. Leaving Tissington, we crossed over the **B5056** through **Bradbourne** with its notable Norman church and Saxon cross, then headed for **Brassington.**

This grey stone village has its past firmly entrenched in the leadmining and quarrying traditions of this part of Derbyshire. Protected from the wind by the limestone plateau that soars some 1000 feet above sea level, the village sits by strange shaped rocks, with names like **Rainster Rocks** and **Harbourough Rocks.** Stone Age man found snugs amongst these formations, and there is evidence that animals like the sabre-toothed tiger, brown bear, wolf and hyena also found comfort here in the caves.

The Miners Arms, Miners Hill, Brassington, Matlock. 0629 85222

In the heart of Brassington we discovered the **Miners Arms**, a

514

delightful inn which during the 18th and 19th centuries was the centre of lead mining activity here. The charm and character of this lovely establishment is immediately apparent and while you soak up the warm, relaxed atmosphere, it is worth talking to Vicky and Rob who are the 23rd recorded landlords, and discovering the fascinating history of the Miners Arms. A traditional inn in the truest sense of the word, visitors here can be sure of fine ale, good food and comfortable accommodation. The lunchtime and evening menu offers a variety of dishes to suit every palate, ranging from Mussels in White Wine and Vegetable Stroganoff to Sausage and Onion Yorkie, and homemade soups are a popular speciality. With three lovely guest rooms, each with colour TV and hot drinks facilities, the Miners Arms offers everything the passing traveller needs.

The road from here takes you ever nearer to the High Peak Trail, a vantage point which gives the visitor a superb insight into the beauties of this limestone county. A strange land where farmsteads and villages, lead workings and quarries, rock-piles and gentle hilltops do not intrude on the overall picture of a restful landscape.

Veering off to the north-west on the **A5012**, we really felt that we were on top of the world. This area of the **White Peak** is a windswept landscape, with small farms set amongst the rugged grasses and clusters of boulders. This initially bleak and tough looking countryside under its covering of scrub and gorse is strangely uplifting when the sun shines down as was the case when we drove by.

We eventually came to the A515 and headed north towards **Buxton**. Our road took us near to the remote stone circle of **Arbor Low** often referred to as the 'Stonehenge of the Peak'. Arbor Low was built 4,000 years ago using a total of forty stones, each weighing at least eight tons. Although the stones were originally stood on end, they now all recline on the ground except for one.

Ivy House, Newhaven, Biggin-by-Hartington, Buxton.0298 84709

Situated on the A515 Ashbourne to Buxton road at Newhaven, **Ivy House** is the charming home of Patricia and Michael Flint who offer a very warm welcome to their many guests. This former coaching inn, now a Grade II listed building, has been carefully restored to its former glory and visitors will find very comfortable accommodation in four beautifully furnished guest rooms, three with en-suite facilities. Television and tea and coffee trays are also included. Meals are available by arrangement and vegetarians are well catered for. It is a non-smoking house, as is the cottage and dogs are most welcome. This Georgian house really is a picture enjoying lovely views towards the Tissington Trail. There is also self-catering accommodation provided in a delightful, fully equipped cottage adjacent to the house, which with its oak beams and attractive furnishings provides an equally restful holiday base.

In the picturesque village of **Biggin-by-Hartington,** which is signposted off the A515 Ashbourne to Buxton road, you will find a real gem called **Biggin Hall**. This beautiful 17th century house is Grade II listed as a Protected Building of Historic Interest and offers the discerning guest a very special holiday base. Delicious homecooked meals accompanied by fine wine are served each evening at 7.00pm, in a relaxed and convivial atmosphere reminiscent of a friendly dinner party. Featured in Off The Beaten Track and Johansens, the house itself boasts a wealth of original features including a lovely stone fireplace, exposed oak beams and flagstone floors. There are fourteen en-suite guest rooms, all beautifully furnished with antiques, five of which are housed in a nearby converted 18th century stone building and form self-contained 'studio' apartments. For peace and tranquillity in stunning surroundings, Biggin Hall is very hard to beat and having stayed once, you are sure to return time and again.

Biggin Hall, Biggin-by-Hartington, Buxton. 0298 84451

One 'hidden' place well worth seeking out has to be **Biggin**

Grange, the elegant historic country home of Sandie and Arthur Flower which was once a monastic sheep farm. Situated 1000ft above sea level in 450 acres of traditional limestone farmland, visitors here can choose from first class self-catering accommodation in a delightful 18th century cottage, which carries a Four Key De-Luxe grading, or extremely comfortable bed and breakfast accommodation provided in three lovely en-suite guest rooms in the main farmhouse. Travelling north, turn left off the A515 towards Biggin, pass under the railway bridge, now the Tissington Trail, and follow the Liffs Road for a mile and a half. Continuing downhill past the right turning for Biggin village, the entrance to Biggin Grange lies 100 yards on your left. The farm is centrally situated within the Peak District National Park and offers magnificent countryside views. Part Georgian, this impressive Grade II listed farmhouse also has a large 19th century addition on the west side and is steeped in history, retaining all its original character and charm, as you will discover when you stay here.

Biggin Grange, Biggin by Hartington, Buxton Tel: 0298 84772

Further north on the A515, a left-hand lane opposite the **Monyash** turn-off led us to the village of **Earl Sterndale**. Here we found an inn called The Quiet Woman, with a rather strange pub-sign. It depicts a headless woman, and the motto above her reads, 'Quiet words turneth away wrath'. 'Chattering Charteris', as she was known, drove her husband to distraction with her nagging. The final straw came when her never-ending carping continued unabated in her sleep. In desperation, her spouse cut off her head. He evidently had the sympathy and gratitude of his fellow villagers and sufferers, for they organised a whip-round to raise the money for her headstone which was inscribed with a firm warning to all would-be chatterboxes.

Back on the A515, we travelled the last few miles into Buxton, temporarily leaving the Peak District National Park. To the west of this approach lies Axe Edge, and the moorlands below are the source of the Dove and Manifold rivers. The highest point of Axe Edge rises 1,807 feet above sea-level, and from this spot the panoramic view of Derbyshire is overwhelming. Just beyond the Cat and Fiddle Inn stands 1690 feet above sea level as the Cat and Fiddle pass itself runs by the head of the Goyt Valley.

Further on in Buxton Country Park you'll find **Poole's Cavern**, a natural limestone cave which as the Visitor Centre will inform you was used by tribes from the Neolithic period onwards. Guided tours are provided for visitors who might remember should they decide to visit that temperatures can be quite cool inside. The Cavern is open from Easter to November, for more information Tel :- 0298 26978. About twenty minutes walk from the Cavern you will be rewarded by lovely views of the area from **Solomon's Temple.** This folly built in 1896 is 25 foot high stands on a tumulus from the New Stone Age at an altitude of 1440 feet.

Referred to as the heart of the Peak District, **Buxton** provides a wealth of things to do. The current popularity of the town is attributable to the fifth Duke of Devonshire. The Romans were here naming the place *Aquae Arnemetiae* - The Spa of the Goddess of the Grove - and later Buxton became a place of pilgrimage. In the 18th century the Dukes intervention and commission of such beautiful buildings as **The Crescent** ensured that visitors would flock here. Designed by John Carr the building is similiar to the architecture found in Bath in Avon. At the time of writing the building is undergoing renovation .

Other notable architectural features are the octagonal **Pump Room,** a marvellous construction in glass and iron. Here, visitors can discover the Micrarium, the only exhibition of its kind allowing you to use microscopes to view the amazing structures that surround us in the natural world. **The Colonnade**, and the **Devonshire Royal Hospital**, originally built as stables then converted in 1859. The attractive **Opera House,** restored in 1979 has a comprehensive and popular programme . The nearby and attractive **Pavilion Gardens** have a Conservatory and Octagon within their grounds - there are often Antique Markets and Art Shows here. At **Buxton Museum** we saw displays of artifacts from local caves, Roman treasures housed within a reconstructed Roman shrine, and specimens of Blue John, the mineral which you can discover more about when visiting Castleton. Within striking distance you'll also find the **Transport Museum** and **Peak Rail Steam Centre.**

Hartington Hotel, 18 Broad Walk, Buxton. 0298 22638

Over a period of years the luckless Mary, Queen of Scots came to Buxton to take advantage of the beneficial waters. Whether or not you

518

visit Buxton to take the waters, enjoy some first-class opera or simply to relax, we feel sure you won't want to leave it in a hurry. Overlooking the Pavilion Gardens and River Wye, you will find a lovely place to stay in Buxton at the **Hartington Hotel.** Originally built in the 1860's as a doctor's house, this charming establishment has been run as a hotel by the same family since 1958. The present owners, Jacqui and Michael Whibberley are welcoming hosts who provided very comfortable accommodation in 17 attractively furnished guest rooms, seven with en-suite facilities. The dining room with its beautifully laid tables and freshly cut flowers provides a cosy setting in which to enjoy a daily changing dinner menu and the relaxed, informal atmosphere throughout makes you feel as if you are staying in a friend's house rather than a hotel.

Further up the A6, we came upon the picturesque hillside town of **Chapel-en-le-Frith**, or 'Chapel-in-the-Forest'. Dating back to 1225, it was in this year that the guardians of the High Peak's Royal Forest purchased land from the Crown and built a chapel here, dedicating it to St Thomas of Canterbury. Now the parish church, a curious legacy has been passed down, allowing owners of freehold land in the district the right to choose their vicar. In 1648, the church was used as a gaol for 1,500 Scottish prisoners. The dreadful conditions arising from such close confinement caused unimaginable suffering. Their ordeal lasted for sixteen days, and a total of 44 men died.

The Renaissance. Chapel-en-le-Frith. 0298 812030

The Renaissance is a superb restaurant recently opened in Chapel-en-le-Frith which enjoys a unique location in the 19th century Old Station Masters House adjacent to the Buxton to Manchester line. Lovers of good food will not be disappointed when they book a table here, for friendly hostess Rozalind Roberts has create a real gem of a place where the beautiful surroundings and warm, friendly atmosphere are surpassed only by the excellent gourmet menu. The Renaissance oozes class and elegance and a cosy intimate ambience is enhanced by candlelit tables, complete with freshly cut flowers and for those chilly evenings, a roaring log fire. Open lunchtime and evenings Tuesday - Saturday and for Sunday lunch, this is one 'hidden place' not to be missed.

Deciding to leave the A6 for a while, we headed west on the **B5470**. The road passes by **Combs Reservoir,** and at one end of it you will find the curiously named Dickie's Bridge. There cannot be many bridges in this country that have been named after a skull! 'Dickie' is said to have resided at a farm in Tunstead, where in his mortal life and still attached to his body, he was Ned Dixon. Apparently murdered by his cousin, he continued his working life as a sort of guard-skull, alerting the household whenever strangers drew near. Various strange occurrences are said to have ensued when attempts were made to move the skull.

Situated on the B5470 at **Tunstead Milton** between Whaley Bridge and Chapel-en-le-Frith, the **Rose & Crown** is an ideal place to pause in your journey. Built during the 17th century, this charming, ivy-clad coaching inn was once the stopping point for coaches en-route from Manchester to Sheffield and is full of character. There are three very comfortable guest rooms, one en-suite and two with private bathroom, while downstairs, the cosy bar boasts the unusual feature of two rowing oars on the ceiling which are engraved with the names of the crews of the New College Eight from 1900 and the New College Second Torpid from 1904. With a fine range of ales, a superb à la carte menu and a lovely beer garden and children's play area, this is one place not to be missed.

Rose & Crown, Tunstead Milton, Near Whaley Bridge.0663 732145

Our road intersected the **A5004** at **Whaley Bridge**. To the south lies the beautiful **Goyt Valley,** where the river was dammed to form

520

the twin reservoirs of Errwood and Fernilee. This area is wonderful for walks, picnic and watersports. At the crossroads at Whaley Bridge where the **B5470** meets the **A5004**, you will discover **Edwardo's Bistro**, a delightful place to eat. Complete refurbishment has created a restaurant full of character, where a superb menu is complemented by beautiful beamed surroundings, creating a cosy, intimate atmosphere. Eddie and Carol Sumner are excellent hosts whose experience in the catering trade is immediately apparent. Once here, there is no rush to eat your meal, you can savour it at your leisure, a pleasure which may well take all evening. Not only will you find your meal, whichever culinary delight you choose, absolutely delicious, but the warm friendly ambience makes an evening out here a real treat that you are sure to want to repeat.

Edwardo's Bistro, 110 Buxton Road, Whaley Bridge. 0663 732002

North of Whaley Bridge we rejoined the A6 once more, only to leave it again at **Newtown**, where the **A6015** took us to **New Mills**. Built on the River Sett, it has several note-worthy old buildings, and provides the starting point for the Sett Valley Trail. Walkers, cyclists and horse riders can all enjoy this pleasant two and a half mile trail, which lies on the site of the old New Mills to Hayfield railway line. The route takes you past the remains of buildings related to the once prosperous textile industry, and veering off the Trail along footpaths and bridleways, you can discover a number of unspoiled villages set in attractive countryside.

If you are searching for somewhere that little bit special for a relaxing break away, you would be well advised to make your way to the quaintly named **Waltzing Weazel,** a cosy traditional country inn which offers superior accommodation and food in an atmosphere of friendly hospitality. Situated on the A6015 New Mills to Hayfield road, it lies amidst beautiful grounds and is surrounded by breathtaking countryside views of The Peak District, just half a mile outside

Hayfield. Michael and Lynda Atkinson are first class hosts who succeed in providing their many guests with all the facilities associated with a top city centre hotel and yet retain the personal touch which makes staying here such a treat. The bedrooms are all en-suite and furnished to the highest standards while the restaurant with views towards the dramatic landscape of Kinder Scout provides an elegant setting in which to savour the outstanding cuisine of acclaimed chef George Benham whose culinary creations are sure to please the most discerning palate. It comes as no surprise therefore to learn that The Waltzing Weazel is Johansens recommended. With various country pursuits such as fishing, shooting and golf all readily available, not to mention a wealth of beautiful walks literally on the doorstep, this is a country retreat you will want to return to time and again.

The Waltzing Weazel, Birchfield, Hayfield. 0663 743402

At **Hayfield**, we turned left on the A624 and found ourselves back in the Peak District once again. Referred to as the Dark Peak, this area is not as foreboding as you may imagine from its name. These high moors are ripe for exploring on foot, and a walk from the Kinder Reservoir will eventually lead you to the western edge of **Kinder Scout**. This whole area of the High Peak is really a series of plateaux that we had been driving across, without realising how much the ground level was rising. The highest point on Kinder Scout is 2,088 feet, and attracts many people who wish to experience the thrill of these remote spaces. Here the walker can really feel a sense of freedom. However - do remember to respect these wild places. Moors, with their treacherous peat bogs and unpredictable mists that rise so quickly in the summer, are not to be dismissed as places for a casual ramble.

There are not many natural waterfalls in Derbyshire, so Kinder Downfall must definitely be on your list of places to visit. Three miles north-east of Hayfield, this is the highest waterfall in the county.

When temperatures are very low, the fall freezes solid, and this makes for a memorable sight. It is also renowned for its 'blow-back' effect, when the wind blows the fall back against the rock, almost making it appear to run uphill. Towards the southern end of the Pennine Way close to the Kinder Reservoir is the picturesque village of **Little Hayfield.** The village is made up of stone terraced houses many of which were old mill houses.

The A624 eventually led us to **Glossop,** where we found an interesting mixture of styles. First, the industrial town of the nineteenth-century with its towering Victorian cotton mills, and then the seventeenth-century village of Old Glossop with its charming old cottages standing in the cobbled streets. Further back in time, the Romans came here, establishing a fort known locally as Melandra. High above the point where the River Etherow meets Glossop Brook, you can still just see the remains of the fort, which the soldiers abandoned as they moved northwards.

Situated on the **A626** in the heart of the pretty village of **Charlesworth**, just a few miles from Glossop, **The Grey Mare** is a charming olde worlde inn with a fascinating history. Built in 1812, it got its name following a horse race between the parish vicar and Sam Higginbottom, a local brushmaker who rode a little grey mare. If you wend your way to this lovely inn, friendly hosts Bob and Julie Rigby will happily relate the full story as you relax with a pint of fine ale and a tasty meal from the extensive menu. The half-panelled walls and open stone fireplaces with roaring log fires in the winter months, enhance the wonderful character of this cosy establishment and you are sure to find yourself making a return visit.

The Grey Mare, 2, Glossop Road, Charlesworth Tel: 0457 852056

It would be hard to imagine a more picturesque and idyllic location than that of **Woodheys Restaurant,** which stands in 18 acres of beautifully landscaped gardens and woodland on the main A626 where the counties of Derbyshire and Cheshire meet at **Chisworth**. Owned and run by the same family since 1964, today John and Vivienne Bouchier, John's brother Paul, Vivienne's sister Ann Revington and Fiona Kendal are the well-matched team who make this superb restaurant tick. With such beautiful surroundings, this is the perfect place for a wedding reception or special celebration and makes a relaxing change for an out of town conference. The mouthwatering menu is both extensive and varied, with something to suit every palate, while for those who prefer traditional fare, the carvery menu proves a popular alternative.

Woodheys Restaurant, Glossop Road (A626), Chisworth 0457 852704000

In contrast to the Roman legions, our campaign took us in an easterly direction on the **A57.** This road with its hair-raising bends can tax any driver, but the exhilaration of slowly motoring along Snake Pass is an experience hard to beat. At one stage, we found ourselves edging past Kinder Scout. Here, the Pennine Way comes into the picture as it crosses the road on its way to Bleaklow Moor, heading for the Scottish border. The road is frequently made impassable by landslides, heavy mist and massive snowfalls in Winter. At the top of the pass, The Snake Inn offers a welcome respite if you wish to fortify yourself before continuing your journey. The Inn was built in 1821 by the sixth Duke of Devonshire. The Cavendish family, whose main seat is at Chatsworth Hall, have a coat of arms depicting a serpent, and the Duke presumably felt the name would be appropriate.

At 2,060 feet, **Bleaklow** is only a little less high than Kinder Scout, but it covers a greater area. This seemingly featureless plateau is a cheerless place to the casual observer. Dark peat bogs extend for many miles, and the predominant colours to be seen in this harsh environment are from the belts of purple heather and tufts of white cotton grass. **Ladybower,** which lies at the bottom of the Pass, is part of a chain of three massive reservoirs, known collectively as 'the Peak's Lake District'. Although recognised as a great feat of civil engineering when it was opened in 1945, the building of this giant man-made lake claimed the villages of **Ashopton** and **Derwent** which were drowned in the process.

Once the old lake house to the Duke of Norfolk's Derwent Hall, **Derwent Lodge** offers a truly idyllic holiday location beside Derwent Reservoir and set in the most picturesque and peaceful surroundings imaginable. Thanks to the hard efforts of owner Carmen Turner, this charming house is a picture both inside and out. The four acres of beautiful grounds provide the perfect venue for summer musical evenings and the character of the house is enhanced by a stone mullioned fireplace, flagstoned floors and lovely antique furniture. The two en-suite guest rooms she provides are a delight and Carmen serves excellent homecooked food to her many guests who having discovered this magical retreat, return time and again.

Derwent Lodge, Derwent Water, Near Bamford tel: 04336 51771

Hugging the southern end of Ladybower, we turned on to the **A6013** and arrived at **Bamford**. Situated on the main A625 at Bamford, **The Rising Sun** is a delightful former coaching inn dating back to the 17th century. Standing proudly at the roadside, this impressive black and white timbered building entices the passing traveller in and once here, you will find it very hard to leave. Set in over an acre of beautiful grounds with secluded and well-tended gardens, this is a popular venue for wedding receptions and family celebrations. The interior is equally impressive, with lovely oak furniture and richly coloured furnishings enhancing the air of olde worlde elegance. All the guest rooms are en-suite and beautifully coordinated with all the facilities you would expect of this Three

Crowns Commended establishment and in the comfortable surroundings of the restaurant which is open to non-residents you can choose from an extensive menu which will appeal to the whole family. With various local attractions within easy reach, including the Blue John and Speedwell caverns, Haddon Hall and Chatsworth House, The Rising Sun makes a relaxing base from which to explore the delights of Derbyshire.

The Rising Sun, Castleton Road, Bamford 0433 651323

Less than a mile off the A625 and within the Peak District National Park at Bamford you will find **Ye Derwent Hotel,** an English Tourist Board member which is featured in Les Routiers and BHRCA.

Ye Derwent Hotel, Bamford. 0433 51395

Just over 100 years old, this charming building oozes character, enticing you inside to a warm, welcoming atmosphere. Angela and David Ryan are the proud owners of this freehouse establishment and the attractive oak bar provides a cosy setting in which to choose from a wide selection of fine handpumped ales plus an extensive menu which is Good Pub Food Guide recommended. The ten bedrooms are all very comfortably furnished and well equipped, two with en-suite facilities, and downstairs, the lounges are full of fascinating old pictures and knickknacks.

For a peaceful,relaxing self-catering holiday in beautiful surroundings,you would be well advised to seek out **Shatton Hall Farm** in Bamford. To reach this idyllic haven,take the Shatton turning off the A625 (almost opposite High Peak Garden Centre) and continue straight ahead over a ford whereupon the road becomes a single lane track. Shatton Hall Farm lies about half a mile further on. Set in 100 acres of combined moorland,woodland and pasture,this Elizabethan farmstead boast panoramic views. This is certainly not your run of the mill farm,as soon becomes apparent when you see the three delightful cottages. Each has been tastefully converted from stone barns,creating holiday homes of character which also have the benefit of every modern convenience including heating and double glazing for maximum comfort. Facilities within the farmstead include a hard tennis court and a summer house, plus ample parking space and places to sit out or play. A wealth of beautiful walks are literally on your doorstep and various leisure activities such as pony trekking,fishing or climbing are available locally.

Shatton Hall Farm Cottages. Shatton Hall Farm,Bamford.
0433 620635

At the end of the **A6013**, we faced a difficult choice. We could either head east on the A625 to **Hathersage**, or west to **Castleton**. Compromise was the answer as we decided to visit Hathersage first. Once a centre for needle-making, it is difficult to know whether to classify Hathersage as a large village or a small town. In either event, it is a pleasant place, and has two interesting literary connections. Charlotte Bronte stayed at Hathersage vicarage, and the village itself was later to appear as the village of 'Morton' in Bronte's novel 'Jane

Eyre'. The name 'Eyre' was probably gleaned from the church of St Michael's, where it figures prominently with various monuments to this local family.

In the churchyard lie the reputed remains of Little John, Robin Hoods renowned companion. Whether or not you choose to believe the legend, it is worth mentioning that when the grave was opened in the 1800s, a 32 inch thigh-bone was discovered. This would certainly indicate that the owner was well over seven feet tall. The inscription on the gravestone indicates that he was a local man, while a great yew bow hung in the church before it was removed to Cannon Hall near Barnsley.

Little John or not he probably enjoyed his food and for us contemporary lovers of good food, a trip to **Longland's Eating House** is a real treat. Situated in the centre of Hathersage above the 'Outside' Shop, this lovely restaurant has a distinct European feel as you climb the spiral staircase to be faced with a wonderful display of food in a glass fronted cabinet behind which is a wide selection of wines and spirits to accompany your meal. Longland's is one of those rare establishments where the character and atmosphere undergo subtle changes according to the time of day. Throughout the week it is run more as an up-market café which offers an even balance of meat-based and vegetarian dishes. On weekend mornings you can enjoy a hearty breakfast here, but on Friday and Saturday evenings it becomes a very cosy, intimate restaurant, with a dinner menu to match and popularity makes bookings advisable.

Longland's Eating House, Main Road, Hathersage. 0433 651978

Set in the heart of the Peak District National Park and with many fascinating places to visit within a short driving distance, **Highlow Hall** is an excellent touring base for visitors to the area. This splendid 16th century manor house is reputedly the most haunted house in Derbyshire, a fact which has never deterred friendly hosts Philip and

528

Highlow Hall, Hathersage.   0433 650393

Julie Wain. Enjoying a rather grand and somewhat secluded setting, this imposing farmhouse stands back a short distance from the quiet lane running from Hathersage to Abney and Great Hucklow and there are panoramic countryside views on all sides. With six very comfortable guest rooms, three with en-suite facilities, visitors here will find Highlow a peaceful and relaxing base, with fine homecooking provided both at breakfast and at the optional three course evening meal.

Back on the A625 heading west towards Castleton, we first came upon the village of **Hope**. The village lies at the entrance to the Vale of Edale. This is one of the loveliest valleys that we have visited. The River Noe flows through it, and the scattered farmsteads and patchwork of fields present a restful picture of the gentler side of rural life.

Underleigh, Off Edale Road, Hope. 0433 621372

About a mile and half outside Hope village in tranquil rural surroundings you will discover superior country house accommodation when you stay at **Underleigh**, the delightful home of Anton and Barbara Singleton. Originally built as a barn in 1873, sympathetic conversion has created a house of character and charm, standing in 3/4 acre of lovely gardens. Beautifully furnished throughout, the house carries a Three Crown Highly Commended grading by the English Tourist Board and provides quality accommodation in six well-equipped, en-suite guest rooms, two with elegant corner baths. Two rooms are situated on the ground floor, making them readily accessible to partially disabled guests. Stone flagged floors and beamed ceilings enhance a peaceful, olde worlde ambience and the Singletons can provide their guests with a wealth of local information and have even devised programmes of walks and tours in the vicinity. After a day's exploring, guests can look forward to an evening meal of gourmet standards which completes a perfect day in beautiful surroundings.

In **Edale** village you will find the Nag's Head Pub, opposite which the Pennine Way begins. The path here passes through lush meadows, with sycamore, oak and beech adding their charm to the scene. However, the moment you pass over the little brook which runs out of Golden Clough, the country becomes altogether wilder, and pasture gives way to a barren landscape. Many travellers have spoken of Derbyshire as being a county of contrasts, and this seemed to us to be a perfect illustration of the point.

We decided to investigate the caverns around Castleton, which were to prove fascinating. Having spent so long exploring above the ground, we felt it was high time we found out what attractions lay underneath it.

Blue John Caverns, Castleton tel: 0433 620638

There are a wealth of caves to investigate, all with their own unusual features. Situated in the heart of Castleton, the **Blue John Mine and Caverns** are probably one of Derbyshire's most popular attractions which have been in the hands of the Ollerenshaw family for many years. Having experienced amazing trips down into the caverns themselves, where you will find incredible natural beauty and unique rock formations plus original 19th century mining tools, you can then explore the two first class gift shops, one of which is sited at the cavern and the other in the main street in Castleton. Each stocks a wide selection of Blue John crafts, which make an ideal memento of your visit, as well as a wide variety of other arts and crafts which will have you browsing for ages.

To explore **Speedwell Cavern**, you will have to brave a ride on a boat through the old lead mine. We have mentioned the 'Blue John' stone earlier on in the book, and in the cavern of the same name you will find the only known veins of the mineral in the British Isles. 'Blue John' or 'Bleu Jaune' is a striking flurospar with purplish-blue to yellow colouring.

Once prized highly by the Romans, it is said that Petronius paid the equivalent of around £40,000 for a wonderfully ornate vase carved from the stone. In a fit of supreme petty mindedness, he preferred to smash the vase rather than relinquish it to the Emperor Nero. The veins now produce only small amounts, but you can still purchase smaller pieces of jewellery or bowls from the craft shop in Cross Street. Next door the Ollerenshaw Collection can be viewed at the Museum of Derbyshire. Here you can see some fine examples of the larger pieces, including an ormolu table of one metre in diameter.

The descent into the cave itself is fine as long as you don't have a heart condition or are even mildly unfit. Although a struggle do beware of the steps which have a tendency to be very slippery. **Treak Cliff Cavern** boasts some spectacular stalactites and stalagmites. **Peak Cavern** along by a delightful riverside path as the gorge rises spectacularly above has the widest opening of any cave in Europe. Up until the seventeenth century, little cottages used to stand within the entrance. The ropemakers who lived in these dwellings used the entrance for making ropes, and the ropewalk may still be seen, The guided tours will give you a good insight into the techniques used, one of the guides can even lay claim to making these ropes himself when a younger man. Most recently, the cave was used by the BBC, who filmed an episode from their 'Chronicles of Narnia' series. The cave was originally known as 'The Devils Arse, but the Victorians refused to take that sitting down and promptly changed the name. Above the cave is **Peveril Castle** with its spectacular views over Castleton and its surroundings. The castle was originally built as a wooden stockade in 1080 by William Peveril, illegitimate son of William the Conqueror. It was later rebuilt in stone, and the keep was added by Henry 11 in 1176.

Castleton is a delightful and busy village, with pleasant walks, interesting shops, and plenty of good places to eat and drink. You will find a super touring base at **Ramblers Rest Guest House,** the magnificent 17th century home of Mary and Peter Gillott. Situated just a short walk from the centre of this delightful village, Ramblers Rest has five fully equipped and beautifully furnished guest rooms, three with en-suite facilities and three on the ground floor lending greater accessibility. The interior is simply delightful, with high and low beamed ceilings adding to the charm and character of this super house and Mary and Peter are excellent hosts who treat their many guests as welcome friends and go out of their way to make you feel at home. With ample parking space provided alongside a babbling brook, Ramblers Rest is aptly named indeed.

Ramblers Rest, Mill Bridge, Back Street, Castleton. 0433 620125

Always a haven for tourists throughout the Summer months, perhaps its busiest day of the year is on the 29th of May. This is Oak Apple Day, when the Garland Ceremony can be seen. The ceremony commemorates the Restoration of Charles II, and a Garland King and Queen in Stuart costume lead a procession through the village on horseback. The King wears a bell-shaped garland of leaves and flowers, which covers him from head to waist and weighs around 60 lbs.

We could not leave this part of the Peak District National Park without mentioning **Mam Tor**. The name means 'Mother Hill', and locally the tor is referred to as 'Shivering Mountain'. This latter name comes from an immense cliff face near the summit which is constantly on the move owing to the seeping of water. Standing up on the ridge you'll see the marvelously contrasting views of those two diverse rock formations, the White and the Dark Peak. To the south is the White Peak, where the limestone lends the hills a bright, gentle aspect. To the north, the gritstone of the Dark Peak creates a far different landscape, which appears sombre and massive.

Our road out of the area would take us through the **Winnats** (or 'Wind Gates') Pass. Speedwell Cavern is at the entrance to this steep but spectacular route through a deep ravine. Occasionally, the Pass is closed to motorists at weekends in the Summer. If you do get the chance to use it, please note that it is a steep incline and should be negotiated carefully.

Joining the **B6061** we reached **Sparrowpit**, then headed east on the **A623**. A short way down the road, we came to the village of **Peak Forest**. Rather disappointingly, the only signs of forest we spotted were a few elms huddled near the church. We took a short walk north-east of the village to see the 'bottomless' pit of **Eldon Hole**. Once thought to be the Devil's entrance to Hell, stories abound in which sundry characters were lowered down on increasingly longer pieces of rope. They all returned in various states of mental instability, never having reached the bottom. Seasoned pot-holers, who view the hole as no more than a practice run, will tell you that it is in fact a 'mere' 180 feet deep.

Tideswell is one of the largest villages in the area and can be found just south of the A623. The magnificent fourteenth-century church has a wealth of splendid features. With its impressive tower, beautiful windows, and fine collection of brasses, the sheer size of the church deservedly earns it the title 'the Cathedral of the Peak'.

Situated in the heart of Tideswell next to the beautiful Parish Church, stands **The George Hotel**.

The George Hotel, Tideswell, Near Buxton.   0298 871382

Formerly a coaching inn on the Manchester to Derby turnpike road, the character and style of The George has changed little since it was built back in 1730 and its attractive stone-built exterior adorned with pretty windowboxes can't help but entice you in. Good food, fine ale and first class accommodation are all readily available and a homely, old-fashioned pub atmosphere prevails. The original stables still stand within a lovely walled courtyard where you can enjoy a relaxing drink, weather permitting. With an excellent menu of homecooked fare and four lovely guest rooms, two en-suite, The George Hotel has all you expect of the perfect olde worlde inn.

Across the A623 in **Little Hucklow** you'll find a typical old English village pub at the **Old Bulls Head.** Dating back to 1661, this delightful country pub is full of character with exposed oak beams, bygone memorabilia and brass decorations throughout. The lovely period fireplace provides crackling warmth for those chilly winter days, while during the summer months, visitors can sit outside and take in the picturesque views. In addition to fine ale, this wonderful freehouse serves an excellent menu of homecooked food which is superior to the usual pub fare one comes to expect and makes a visit here even more special.

Old Bulls Head, Little Hucklow, Near Tideswell 0298 871097

Further along the A623, we turned off the main road to pay a visit to the 'plague village' of **Eyam.** In 1665, a local tailor received a bundle of plague-infected clothing from London. Within a short time the infection had spread, and the terrified inhabitants prepared to flee the village. However, the local rector, William Mompesson, persuaded the villagers to stay put, and thanks to his intervention, neighbouring villages escaped the disease. Eyam was quarantined for over a year, relying on outside help for supplies which were left on the village boundary. Out of a total of 350 inhabitants, only 83 survived.

Enjoying a central location in the historic village of Eyam, opposite the sheep roasting spit and the plague cottages, **Delf View House** is a charming holiday and touring base. Steeped in history, this beautiful Grade II listed Georgian house carries a Two Crown Highly Commended grading by the English Tourist Board and provides superb accommodation in two lovely guests rooms, one with en-suite shower, the other with an adjacent bathroom. Exquisite antique furniture abounds and one bedroom boasts a fourposter bed. The house stands within four acres of beautifully laid out grounds and guests are welcomed with tea in the drawing room on arrival. Breakfast is a substantial treat enjoyed in the magnificent surroundings of the oak beamed dining room, at one time the servants' hall of this great house. For safety and out of consideration to other guests, this is a non-smoking establishment.

Delf View House, Church Street, Eyam. 0433 631533

Doubling back on the A623, we then turned onto the **B6465**, passing through the village of **Wardlow**. At a nearby crossroads, the highwayman Anthony Lingard was hanged in 1812 for the murder of a local widow. He was the last felon to hang in this county, and his execution drew an enormous crowd. So much so, that the local lay-preacher at Tideswell found himself preaching to virtually empty pews. Determined not to waste this opportunity to speak to so large a congregation, he relocated to the gibbet in order to give his sermon that day.

After Wardlow, the B6465 took us to a place for those looking for a holiday with a difference, **Cressbrook Hall**. Enjoying a beautiful and tranquil location, overlooking the limestone gorge of the River Wye, this magnificent property was built in 1835 by Thomas Johnson of Lichfield for the owner of Cressbrook Mill and today retains all its elegance and character, offering superior accommodation in three lovely en-suite guest rooms. For the self-catering enthusiast, Cressbrook Hall Cottages provide a superb base from which to explore the wonderful scenery and historic places of Derbyshire. All cottages are furnished and equipped to a very high standard ensuring maximum comfort and carry gradings of between Two and Four Keys. With 23 acres of wood and parkland surrounding the hall and cottages, there is a wealth of beautiful walks literally on your doorstep and adjoining Hall Cottage is a lovely walled garden for guest use, which leads through to a comprehensively equipped play area for the children to enjoy. For complete relaxation, visit Harriet in The Beauty Room and let yourself be pampered!

Cressbrook Hall, Cressbrook, Near Bakewell. 0298 871289

Close by you'll find **Monsal Head**, where the views are tremendous. Across the valley lies the huge **Monsal Dale Viaduct,** which was erected in the 1860s to carry the railway line from Bakewell to Buxton. It would be hard to equal the spectacular views from **Castle Cliffe Private Hotel** which stands off the B6465, proudly overlooking Monsal Dale. It would also be hard to match the very special homely atmosphere that Sheila Gilbert the resident proprietor has created in this lovely establishment. One of two houses built side by side in 1886, Castle Cliffe is now a popular touring base awarded a Two Crown Commended rating by the English Tourist Board and AA Listed.

Castle Cliffe Private Hotel, Monsal Head, Bakewell. 0629 640258

Formerly known as Headstone Head prior to the coming of the

railway, Monsal Head is popular with visitors who come to admire the viaduct and beautiful scenery. Although the railway has long since gone, the site of the track is very popular with walkers, as is Longstone Edge which stands to the rear of the hotel. Guests at Castle Cliffe are ideally situated for touring the Peak National Park and the many local places of interest, with Bakewell, Buxton and Castleton with its mines, all within easy reach. Sheila provides very comfortable accommodation in nine spacious and well-equipped guest rooms, two with en-suite shower/wc, six with private showers and all with the added bonus of spectacular views. You can relax in the comfort of the guests lounge and the cosy dining room has the added touch of freshly cut flowers on the tables, creating a lovely setting in which to savour Sheila's culinary expertise, a treat in itself. Evening meals are available by prior arrangement and the menu is changed daily, with traditional homecooked dishes given that extra something by Sheila's skilled hand.

Enjoying an enviable location on the banks of the River Wye in Monsal Dale, **Upperdale House** is the ideal base for those in search of true peace and quiet. Built from mellow Derbyshire stone, this lovely house is the home of John and June Clarke, a friendly couple who offer their many guests comfortable accommodation in an atmosphere of warm hospitality. There are four lovely guest rooms, three en-suite and one with private facilities and the house is surrounded by an acre of well stocked gardens. Despite its secluded location, Upperdale House is an excellent touring base, being within easy reach of Buxton, Bakewell, Matlock, the magnificent Monsal Head Viaduct and various other places of interest. Beautiful walks abound, beginning literally at the front door and taking you through breathtaking Derbyshire countryside, wonderful inspiration for the artistically inclined.

Upperdale House, Monsal Dale, Buxton. 0629 640536

Stone Wall Country

The road eventually led us to the picturesque **Ashford-in-the-Water.** The village developed around the ford that spanned the River Wye. Of the three bridges, **Mill Bridge** dates back to 1664, and **Sheepwash Bridge** which is some years older was the site of - well, washing the sheep! The village was once an important crossing place, and you can still see and travel on the ancient Portway which descends down to the river crossing.

Enjoying a most delightful setting beside the River Wye in the Ashford-in-the-Water, the **Riverside Country House Hotel** provides an idyllic base for that relaxing break away from it all. Awarded Four Crowns and Highly Commended by the English Tourist Board, recommended by both Johansens and Egon Ronay and awarded the AA 3 Star Red Rosette, guests staying at this magnificent Georgian mansion will find they want for nothing. The decor and furnishings really have to be seen to be believed, from the fifteen individually styled en-suite guest rooms, to the splendid guest lounge with its inglenook fireplace and fine oak panelling, all are enhanced by beautiful antique furniture and rich country house fabrics. The high point of a visit however, is dining in the elegant restaurant where an imaginative menu offers the discerning the finest cordon bleu cuisine.

Riverside Country House Hotel, Ashford-in-the-Water. 0629 814275
Fax: 0629 812873

A short run down the A6 took us into **Bakewell,** the only true town in the Peak District National Park thus attracting day trippers, walkers, campers as well as locals who come to take advantage of its amenities. The beautiful medieval five-arched bridge spanning the river is still in use today as the main crossing point for traffic. We are all familiar with the dessert that made the name of Bakewell so famous, but please remember it is referred to locally as a pudding and most definitely NOT a tart! Said to be the result of a cooking accident when the addition of strawberry jam made what was to have been a strawberry tart into the now famous Bakewell Pudding.

The cooking 'mishap' took place in the kitchens of the Rutland Arms Hotel, which was built in 1804 on the site of a coaching inn. One of the hotel's more famous guests was the novelist Jane Austen, who stayed there in 1811. The hotel featured in her book 'Pride and Prejudice', while Bakewell itself was the town of 'Lambton'. The large parish church of All Saints dates back to the twelfth century, and the graceful spire with its octagonal tower can be seen for miles around. The church contains a wonderful variety of headstones and coffin slabs, and in the churchyard, we discovered a most unusual cross. Over 1,200 years old, it stands an impressive eight feet high. On one side, it depicts the Crucifixion, while on the other are the Norse gods Odin and Loki. Behind the church is the lovely Old House Museum, which dates back to 1534. Originally the Parsonage House, this beautiful building escaped demolition and has been lovingly restored by the Bakewell Historical Society. Now established as a folk museum, it houses a fascinating collection of rural bygones.

Winner of the 1990 Rural Enterprise Award, **Lathkill Dale Craft Centre** in **Over Haddon** offers lots to see and do, with something to appeal to all ages. Housed within a beautiful array of converted farm buildings, you will find a variety of attractions including a gift shop, timber design workshop, artist's studio, stained glass design and repair shop and a book binder. All the buildings are set around a lovely central courtyard which is well stocked with beautiful and unusual plants. Another building houses The Courtyard Tearoom where you can enjoy a refreshing drink and light snack at very reasonable prices. Above the tearoom there is also a self-catering unit which can sleep 4/6 people. To find this fascinating centre, take the Over Haddon and Monyash road out of Bakewell and the craft centre is signposted from Over Haddon.

Lathkill Dale Craft Centre, Over Haddon, Bakewell, 0629 812390

The Lathkill Hotel, Over Haddon, Near Bakewell.0629 812501

AA Recommended and list in CAMRA Good Beer Guide, **The Lathkill Hotel** at Over Haddon is very much a 'hidden place' but one that is well worth seeking out. Taking the Monyash road out of Bakewell, continue to the sign for Over Haddon, go through the village passing Lathkill Craft Centre on the right and at the end of this road you will see signs for The Lathkill Hotel. With parts of the building dating back to the 17th century, The Lathkill has been an alehouse since 1820 and today is a super hotel which boasts probably the best views in Derbyshire. Popular with visitors and locals alike, a warm relaxed atmosphere combines with first class ale and excellent homecooked food. With all this plus four well-equipped en-suite guest rooms, The Lathkill makes an ideal touring base.

The Farmyard Inn, Main Street, Youlgrave. 0629 636221

Below Over Haddon lovers of traditional inns will discover a real treasure when they seek out the somewhat 'hidden' **Farmyard Inn** at Youlgrave. Taking the Youlgrave turning off the main A6, pass
541

through Alport into Youlgrave village, continue through the village and The Farmyard Inn can be found on the right. Deceptively small from the outside, it is surprisingly spacious within and careful refurbishment by the present owners Tony and Sue Howarth has created a wonderful establishment where you can call in for a pint of fine ale and excellent homecooked food in a cosy, welcoming atmosphere, enhanced by traditional oak beams and a large inglenook fireplace. The Howarths also provide first class accommodation all year round in three lovely chalets, all of which have private entrances and are separate from the inn.

Our journey from Bakewell found us back on the A6 once more, a pleasant drive running parallel to the River Wye. We then followed signs for **Haddon Hall**, which is hidden from the road by a beech hedge and trees. The Hall is thought by many to have been the first fortified house in the country. Although the house boasts turrets and battlements, they are purely for show. Since it was built it has in fact enjoyed a fairly peaceful existence and legend has it that Lady Dorothy Vernon eloped with Sir John Manners in the 16th century. A small museum by the gatehouse informs of this legend and the history of the Hall.

Below Haddon is the small village of **Rowsley** with its old toll house. From Rowsley we turned on to the B6012, passed by the pretty village of **Beeley** and came to the 'Palace of the Peak'. **Chatsworth House**, home of the Dukes of Devonshire, is without doubt one of the finest of the great houses in Britain. The origins of the house as a great showpiece must be attributable to Bess of Hardwick, whose marriage into the Cavendish family helped to secure the future of the 'Palace'.

Her husband, Sir William Cavendish, bought the estate for £600 in 1549, and it was Bess who completed the new house after his death. Over the years, the Cavendish fortune continued to pour into the house, making it an almost unparalleled showcase for art treasures. Every aspect of the fine arts is here, ranging from old masterpieces, furniture, tapestries, porcelain and some magnificent alabaster carvings.

The gardens of this stately home have some marvellous features, our personal favourite being the Emperor Fountain. Dominating the Canal Pond, it is said to reach a height of 290 feet. There is a maze and a Laburnam Tunnel, and behind the house are the famous Cascades. The overall appearance of the park as we know it today is chiefly due to the talents of 'Capability' Brown, who was first consulted in 1761. However, the name perhaps most strongly associated with Chatsworth is Joseph Paxton. His experiments in glasshouse design led him eventually to his masterpiece, the Crystal Palace, built to house the Great Exhibition of 1851.

Chatsworth House.

When you explore this great park, and especially if you climb up the sides of the valley, the massive sprawl of the House quite takes your breath away. At the southern entrance to the park there is a garden centre, and not far from the House itself, you will find a forestry and farm centre.

Situated within the Shire Horse Stud Farm just one mile from Chatsworth House you will find **Chatsworth Farm Shop**, a super place where you can browse at your leisure and purchase fresh produce direct from the estate farms. Products include the finest fresh meat, poultry and game, with home-cured bacon and homemade sausages. There is also a fine selection of cooked meats, pies and patés, all made by the chef in the farm shop kitchen, likewise freshly baked bread and mouthwatering cakes. The farm dairy produces milk and cream which is made into a traditional ice cream. There are over 60 different cheeses to choose from, all of them British and these are complemented by a fine selection of English wines. While here you can sample some of the farm shop's excellent fayre in the delightful coffee shop where teas, coffees and light lunches are available daily. It is not difficult to see why it was voted the best farm shop in the land in Henrietta Green's Food Lovers Guide to Great Britain. The Farm Shop is clearly signposted and after passing through Chatsworth Park with the house on your right, you take a left towards the village of Pilsley and the Farm Shop can be found on your left.

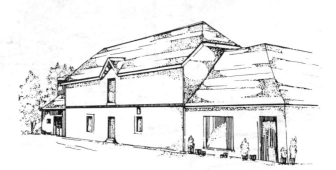

Chatsworth Farm Shop, Stud Farm, Pilsley. 0246 583392

Licensed and approved by Derbyshire Dales District Council, **Curbar Riding and Trekking Stables** is a real haven for horse lovers. Established for over 30 years, this family-run centre is situated in a most beautiful part of the Peak District National Park and rides ranging from 1-3 hours take visitors across some breathtaking moorland countryside. All ages and abilities are catered for here, with horses of every size and temperament to suit and experienced escorts accompanying each ride. You can find this 'hidden' gem by turning off the A623 to Curbar and as you travel into the village you will see Bar Road ahead of you, with the Stables situated on the right hand side.

Curbar Riding and Trekking Stables, Curbar 0433 630584

Our final call as we prepared to leave this lovely area of the country was on the way towards Yorkshire. Grindleford and the National Trusts Longshaw Estate are delightful areas to enjoy the countryside with pleasant walks and places to picnic by the Derwent. Whether it is first class ale, good homecooked food or comfortable accommodation you are looking for, you will find your every need met at **The Sir William Hotel** at **Grindleford.** Situated on the B6001, this friendly family-run hotel was built in the early 19th century and named after Sir William Chambers Bagshawe, M.D. of the Oakes-in-Norton, Sheffield.

The Sir William Hotel, Grindleford, Near Sheffield. 0433 630303

Today, the Sir William Hotel is a welcoming establishment run by Philip and Diane Cone, who in the relatively short time that they have been here have, through sheer hard work, created a lovely place to stay with a special family atmosphere. The cosy atmosphere of the bar is enhanced by a central stone fireplace and in this relaxed setting you can savour excellent homecooking from a varied menu to suit every taste. For those warmer days there is a splendid beer garden to sit out and marvel at the views across the valley. Visitors deciding to stay will find very comfortable accommodation in seven well-equipped guest rooms.

We hope that you have enjoyed this journey through the 'Heart of England' as much as we did and take the opportunity to take advantage of some of the ' Hidden Places ' we have uncovered on our travels. Should you try any of the recommendations that we have made we're sure that the establishment would be pleased to hear that you learnt of their existence from this book. Finally we'd like to thank all those who with their help and hospitality made this journey and book possible.

TOURIST INFORMATION CENTRES

ASHBOURNE, 13 Market Place 0335-43666

ASHBY-de-la-ZOUCH, North Street 0530-411767

BAKEWELL, Old Market Hall, Bridge Street 0629-813227

BIRMINGHAM, Convention & Bureau Centre, 2 City Arcade 021 643-2514

BOSTON, Blackfriars Arts Centre, Spain Lane 0205-356656

BOSWORTH BATTLEFIELD, Visitors Centre, Sutton Cheney, Nr Market Bosworth.

BRACKLEY, 2 Bridge Street 0280-700111

BROMSGROVE, Bromsgrove Museum, 26 Birmingham Road 0527-31809

BURTON UPON TRENT, Octagon Centre, New Street 0283-516609

BUXTON, The Crescent 0298-73153

CHESTERFIELD, Peacock Info Centre, Low Pavement 0246-207777

CORBY, Civic Centre, George Street 0536-407507

COVENTRY, Bayley Lane 0203-832303

DAVENTRY, Moot Hall, Market Sq 0327-300277

DERBY, Assembly Room, Market Place 0332-255802

DUDLEY, 39 Churchill Precinct 0384-250333

GRANTHAM, The Guildhall Centre, St Peter's Hill 0476-66444

GRIMSBY, National Fishing Heritage, Alexandra Dock 0472-342442

HECKINGTON, The Pearoom, Station Road, Sleaford 0529-60088

HINCKLEY, Library, Lancaster Road 0455-635106

HORNCASTLE, The Trinity Centre, Spilsby Road 0507-526636

KENILWORTH, Library, 11 Smalley Place 0926-52595

KETTERING, The Coach House, Sheep Street 0536-410266

LEAMINGTON SPA, Jephson Lodge, Jephson Gardens, The Parade 0926-311470

LEEK, Market Place 0538-381000

LEICESTER, 2-6 St Martin's Walk, St Martin's Square 0533-511300

LICHFIELD, Donegal House, Bore Street 0543-252109

LINCOLN, 9 Castle Hill 0522-529828

LOUGHBOROUGH, John Storer House, Wards End 0509-230131

LOUTH, The New Market Hall, Off Cornmarket 0507-609289

MABLETHORPE, Central Promenade 0507-472496

MARKET HARBOROUGH, Pen Lloyd Library, Adam And Eve Street 0858-462649

MATLOCK BATH, The Pavillion 0629-55082

MELTON MOWBRAY, Melton Carnegie Museum, Thorpe End 0664-69946

NEWARK, The Gilstrap Centre, Castlegate 0636-78962

NEWCASTLE UNDER LYME, Ironmarket 0782-711137

NORTHAMPTON, Visitors Centre, 10 St Giles Square 0604-604180

NOTTINGHAM, 1-4 Smithy Row 0602-47661

NOTTINGHAM (West Bridgeford) County Hall, Loughborough Road 0602-773558

NUNEATON, Library, Church Street 0203-384027

OAKHAM, Library, Catmos Street 0572-724329

OLLERTON, Sherwood Heath, Ollerton Roundabout 0623-824545

OUNDLE, 14 West Street 0832-274333

RETFORD, Amcott House Annexe, 40 Grove Street 0777-860780

RUGBY, Library, St Matthews Street 0788-535348

RUTLAND WATER, Sykes Lane, Empingham, Oakham 0780-86321

SKEGNESS, Embassy Centre, Grand Parade 0754-764821

SLEAFORD, The Mill, Money's Yard, Carre Street 0529-414294

SPALDING, Ayscoughfee Hall, Churchgate 0775-725468

STAFFORD, The Ancient High House, Greengate Street 0785-40204

STAMFORD, Stamford Arts Centre, 27 St Mary's Street 0780-55611

STOKE-ON-TRENT, Potteries Shopping Centre, Quadrant Road, Hanley 0782-284600

STRATFORD-ON-AVON, Bridgefoot 0789-293127

NORTH WEST DERBYSHIRE

TAMWORTH, Town Hall, Market Street 0827-59134

TROWELL (M1), Northbound Granada Services 0602-442411

WARWICK, The Court House, Jury Street 0926-492212

WELLINGBOROUGH, Library, Pebble Lane 0933-228101

WOODHALL SPA, The Cottage Museum, Iddesleigh Road 0526-353775

WORKSOP, Library, Memorial Avenue 0909-501148

Index

THE HIDDEN PLACES

If you would like to have any of the titles currently available in this series, please complete this coupon and send to:

M & M Publishing Ltd
Tryfan House, Warwick Drive,
Hale, Altrincham, Cheshire, WA15 9EA

	Each	Qty
Scotland	£ 5.90	......
Northumberland & Durham	£ 5.90	......
The Lake District & Cumbria	£ 5.90	......
Yorkshire and Humberside	£ 5.90	......
Lancashire & Cheshire	£ 5.90	......
North Wales	£ 5.90	......
South Wales	£ 5.90	......
The Welsh Borders	£ 5.90	......
The Cotswolds (Gloucestershire & Wiltshire)	£ 5.90	......
Thames and Chilterns	£ 5.90	......
East Anglia (Norfolk & Suffolk)	£ 5.90	......
The South East (Surrey, Sussex and Kent)	£ 5.90	......
Dorest, Hampshire and the Isle of Wight	£ 5.90	......
Somerset, Avon and Dorset	£ 5.90	......
Heart of England	£ 5.90	......
Devon and Cornwall	£ 5.90	......
Set of any Five	£20.00	
Total	£	

Price includes Postage and Packing

NAME...
ADDRESS..
....
.........................POST CODE....................................

Please make cheques payable to: M & M Publishing Ltd